Roots, Rites and Sites of Resistance

Roots, Rites and Sites of Resistance

The Banality of Good

Edited by

Leonidas K. Cheliotis
Queen Mary, University of London, UK

Selection and editorial matter © Leonidas K. Cheliotis 2010
Individual chapters © their respective authors 2010

All rights reserved. No reproduction, copy or transmission of this publication may be made without written permission.

No portion of this publication may be reproduced, copied or transmitted save with written permission or in accordance with the provisions of the Copyright, Designs and Patents Act 1988, or under the terms of any licence permitting limited copying issued by the Copyright Licensing Agency, Saffron House, 6-10 Kirby Street, London EC1N 8TS.

Any person who does any unauthorized act in relation to this publication may be liable to criminal prosecution and civil claims for damages.

The authors have asserted their rights to be identified as the authors of this work in accordance with the Copyright, Designs and Patents Act 1988.

First published 2010 by
PALGRAVE MACMILLAN

Palgrave Macmillan in the UK is an imprint of Macmillan Publishers Limited, registered in England, company number 785998, of Houndmills, Basingstoke, Hampshire RG21 6XS.

Palgrave Macmillan in the US is a division of St Martin's Press LLC, 175 Fifth Avenue, New York, NY 10010.

Palgrave Macmillan is the global academic imprint of the above companies and has companies and representatives throughout the world.

Palgrave® and Macmillan® are registered trademarks in the United States, the United Kingdom, Europe and other countries.

ISBN-13: 978–0–230–21039–4 hardback

This book is printed on paper suitable for recycling and made from fully managed and sustained forest sources. Logging, pulping and manufacturing processes are expected to conform to the environmental regulations of the country of origin.

A catalogue record for this book is available from the British Library.

Library of Congress Cataloging-in-Publication Data
Roots, rites and sites of resistance : the banality of good /
  edited by Leonidas K. Cheliotis.
    p. cm.
  ISBN 978–0–230–21039–4 (hardback)
  1. Good and evil.   2. Government, Resistance to.
  I. Cheliotis, Leonidas K., 1977–
  BJ1401.R585 2010
  170—dc22   2010004768

10 9 8 7 6 5 4 3 2 1
19 18 17 16 15 14 13 12 11 10

Printed and bound in Great Britain by
CPI Antony Rowe, Chippenham and Eastbourne

Contents

Figure vii

List of Contributors viii

Roots, Rites and Sites of Resistance: The Banality
of Good – An Introduction 1
Leonidas K. Cheliotis

1 Values, Crisis and Resistance: Prospects for Freedom
  Reconsidered 12
  Spiros Gangas

2 Narcissism, Humanism and the Revolutionary Character
  in Erich Fromm's Work 36
  Leonidas K. Cheliotis

3 Thinking after Terror: An Interreligious Challenge 59
  Richard Kearney

4 *Ecce Homo*: The Political Theology of Good and Evil 80
  John O'Neill

5 Resistance as Transformation 95
  Andrea Mubi Brighenti

6 Acting on Vulnerable Others: Ethical Agency in Media
  Discourse 108
  Lilie Chouliaraki

7 Sites of Resistance: Death Row Homepages and the Politics
  of Compassion 125
  Ezra Tessler

8 Face to Face with Abidoral Queiroz: Death Squads and
  Democracy in Northeast Brazil 151
  Nancy Scheper-Hughes

9 Resisting Submission? The Obstinacy of 'Balkanist'
  Characteristics in Greece as Dissidence Against 'the West' 178
  Sappho Xenakis

10	Legitimation and Resistance: Police Reform in the (Un)making *Justice Tankebe*	197
11	'Governmentality' and Governing Corrections: Do Senior Managers Resist? *Alison Liebling*	220

References	246
Index	274

Figure

4.1 *Ecce Homo* (or *Christ before the people*) by Albrecht Dürer (c. 1497–1500). Reprinted with permission from the University of Michigan Museum of Art.   83

List of Contributors

Andrea Mubi Brighenti is a postdoctoral research fellow at the Department of Sociology, University of Trento, Italy. He holds a PhD in Sociology of Law from the University of Milan, I. His latest work has appeared in *Current Sociology, Thesis Eleven, Law & Critique, Rassegna Italiana di Sociologia, Polis, Sociologia del Diritto, Quaderni di Sociologia* and the *Canadian Journal of Law and Society*.

Leonidas K. Cheliotis is Lecturer and Deputy Director of the Centre for Criminal Justice at the School of Law, Queen Mary, University of London. He is the editor of *The Arts of Imprisonment: Control, Resistance and Empowerment* (forthcoming in 2010) and the co-editor (with Sappho Xenakis) of *Crime and Punishment in Contemporary Greece: International Comparative Perspectives* (two volumes, forthcoming in 2010). He is currently working on a monograph provisionally entitled *Law and Order in the Margins of Europe: A Political Economy of Othering*.

Lilie Chouliaraki is Professor of Media and Communications at the London School of Economics and Political Science. Previously, she was Professor of Media and Discourse Studies at the Copenhagen Business School, where she was also Director of the CBS Media Hub and coordinator of MediaDemos (International Network on the Ethics of Mediation). She is the author of *Discourse in Late Modernity* (with Norman Fairclough) and *The Spectatorship of Suffering*, the editor of *The Soft Power of War* and the co-editor (with Mette Morsing) of *Media, Organisations, Identity*. Her next book project is entitled *The Humanitarian Imaginary* (forthcoming in 2010).

Spiros Gangas is Professor I of Sociology at Deree College in Athens, Greece. He was previously a teaching assistant at the University of Edinburgh (where he completed his PhD in Sociology with a dissertation on Simmel's epistemology) and Lecturer at the University of Wales, College of Cardiff. He has also taught at Panteion University in Athens. He has published in English on Simmel, Durkheim and Hegel, and in Greek on Vaihinger, Simmel and Durkheim.

Richard Kearney holds the Charles B. Seelig Chair of Philosophy at Boston College. He is the author of over 20 books on European philosophy and literature (including two novels and a volume of poetry) and has edited or co-edited 15 more. His most recent work in philosophy comprises a trilogy entitled 'Philosophy at the Limit'. The three volumes are *On Stories, The God who May Be* and *Strangers, Gods and Monsters*.

Alison Liebling is Professor of Criminology and Criminal Justice at the University of Cambridge and Director of the Prisons Research Centre at the Cambridge Institute of Criminology. She has published several books, including *Suicides in Prisons, Prisons and their Moral Performance: A Study of Values, Quality, and Prison Life* (with Helen Arnold) and *The Effects of Imprisonment* (with Shadd Maruna). She is co-editor of the journal *Punishment & Society*.

John O'Neill is Distinguished Research Professor of Sociology at York University, Toronto, and a Fellow of the Royal Society of Canada. He teaches in sociology, political economy, critical literary, media and psychoanalytic studies. He is the author of *Sociology as a Skin Trade, The Communicative Body, Essaying Montaigne, Plato's Cave: Television and its Discontents, Five Bodies* and *Civic Capitalism: The State of Childhood*. He is co-editor of both *The Journal of Classical Sociology* and *Philosophy of the Social Sciences*. He is currently working on Freud's five major case histories under the concept of the domestic economy of the soul.

Nancy Scheper-Hughes is The Chancellor's Professor of Anthropology at the University of California-Berkeley, where she also directs the doctoral programme in critical studies in medicine, science and the body, and heads 'Organs Watch', a medical human rights research and documentation project. She is best known for her ethnographies *Saints, Scholars, and Schizophrenics: Mental Illness in Rural Ireland* and *Death without Weeping: The Violence of Everyday Life in Brazil*. She has also published several edited volumes, including, most recently, *Commodifying Bodies* (with Loïc Wacquant) and *Violence in War and Peace* (with Philippe Bourgois). Her next book will be *A World Cut in Two: The Global Traffic in Humans for Organs*.

Justice Tankebe is a British Academy postdoctoral researcher and a Fellow of Fitzwilliam College, University of Cambridge. After being awarded the BA degree in Sociology from the University of Ghana (Legon), he completed an MPhil in Criminological Research and the PhD at the Institute of Criminology, University of Cambridge.

Ezra Tessler is a Jacob K. Javits Fellow and PhD candidate in the Department of History at Columbia University in New York. His research interests include the history of crime and punishment, international social movements and human rights. Currently he is completing a project on the history of international penal reform.

Sappho Xenakis is a Marie Curie Intra-European Fellow based at the Hellenic Foundation for European and Foreign Policy in Athens, Greece. Her project, funded by the European Commission, is a two-year study of security policy transfer from the EU, the US and Britain to Greece concerning issues of organized crime and terrorism. In addition, she is currently authoring a monograph entitled *The Politics of Organised Crime: Theory and Practice* (forthcoming in 2010) and is the co-editor (with Leonidas K. Cheliotis) of *Crime and Punishment in Contemporary Greece: International Comparative Perspectives* (two volumes, forthcoming in 2010).

Roots, Rites and Sites of Resistance: The Banality of Good – An Introduction

Leonidas K. Cheliotis

Men – men and women, that is – are prone to contenting themselves with the notion that history has always been on a steady course of progress. It is no coincidence that the Greeks coined the term *anthropos*, deriving from *ano throsko* and literally meaning 'looking upwards', to define humankind. Anthropos is said to be developing towards some preordained noble future, symbolized by the ethereal heights to which he or she gazes from below. This is presumably because, unlike other animals, anthropos has the natural capacity for self-knowledge, rational understanding and moral judgement – the capacity to 'look up' at what is in sight in the surrounding world.[1]

A careful look at the course of history, however, quickly dispels the notion. Historical change, as John Stuart Mill (1843/1891) noted well, is not necessarily tantamount to progress. And progress, such as in matters of economy, technology or health, does not necessarily affect all individuals or social groups in a uniform manner. Indeed, advancement for some may come at the expense of others. Whilst, for example, economic growth in the post-war era has most benefited the wealthiest nations, inequalities within and across states have risen dramatically (see, for example, Bata and Bergesen, 2002). The very persistence of inequality goes to show that humans have not invariably exercised their inherent capacity for pure reason, at least not as a unitary community.

The failure to exploit the capacity for reflection in order to pre-empt or redress injustice has famously been theorized by Hannah Arendt (1963) in her report *Eichmann in Jerusalem*. There she speaks of the 'banality of evil', a normalized form of wrongdoing against others perpetrated in the course of one's daily mien. Arendt conceptualizes normalization in an amoral sense, as a mind-numbing process associated with modern civilization and its overly rationalized administrative institutions (see also Bauman, 1989). An alternative, morally charged process of banalizing wrongdoing against others is described by Nancy Scheper-Hughes in her discussion of the ' "small wars and invisible genocides" conducted in the normative, ordinary social spaces of public schools, clinics, emergency rooms, hospital charity wards, nursing homes, city halls, jails, and public morgues' (Scheper-Hughes, 2002: 32). The normalization of wrongdoing, according to Scheper-Hughes, evolves from the discursive sub-humanization of victims and the various emotional and moral preconditions of wrongdoing so formed, from mere indifference towards the 'bystander effect' to fervent righteous hatred. It comes as no surprise that one's own wrongdoing may be framed in some moralistic variation of resistance, the ongoing 'war on terror' being a case in point (see further Kearney, this volume).

However, whilst the condition of a damaged ethical life has received due scholarly attention to date, only rarely is resistance to it conceived as an actual possibility with the potential of real effects on a macrosocial scale. This is not just a curious lacuna in the literature. To ignore or miss concrete possibilities or instances of resistance is to reinforce the apparent naturalness and inevitability of structures of injustice. The aim of the present volume is to help address this epistemological neglect, exploring the multiplicity of motives, presuppositions, sites, ways and consequences of acts of resistance. Why, where and how does resistance emerge? In what forms or guises does it manifest itself? When is it effective, and when is it truly progressive?

As elaborated in the chapters that follow, resistance can be recalcitrant or transformative in its aims, discursive or physical in its means, and local or generalized in its loci. If there is a single argument that can be distilled, however, it is that the emergence of progressive resistance entails what might be called 'the banality of good'. This is not to be confused with an argument in favour of what historian Jonathan Steinberg (1990) describes as habitual disobedience in the sense of thoughtless or egoistic conduct. As well as lacking moral grounding, such conduct is unimaginative and purely contingent. The banality of good consists, instead, in the incessant rational critique of so-styled 'common sense' and prevalent ethical claims with the aim to establish or preserve just social arrangements. Said differently, what makes the practice of reflexivity 'good' is its moral end-goal, and what makes it 'banal' is the unrelenting nature of its required occurrence. Yardsticks for reflexive assessment may well be sought from extant anthropological laws, such as there being material and symbolic benefits in subordinating the 'I' to the 'us', or in sacrificing individual interest to general welfare (Bourdieu, 2000/2008). Alternatively, the present may be appreciated in comparison to an imagined future which challenges it; what Jean-Paul Sartre (1958/2003) terms 'revolutionary consciousness'.

In terms of methodology, the book negates a series of demarcations. These are the demarcations between diverse disciplines, between varying theoretical realms within and across diverse disciplines, between discipline-defining and marginal theorists, between knowledge produced in the First World and elsewhere, and between theory and empirical research. Thus, a host of scientific domains that seek to theorize ethicopolitical problems and their resolution join company, from sociology, psychology and psychoanalysis to philosophy, theology and anthropology. Along the way, ideas and concepts are borrowed from realms as divergent as Aristotelian ethics, Marxist critical theory, Ricoeur's hermeneutics and religious traditions that have long existed as universal systems of civic virtue. So-called 'founding fathers' of political and social thought are examined alongside insightful theorists who have either fallen into obscurity of late (for example, Erich Fromm) or have largely escaped the attention of mainstream scholarship (for example, Canetti, Psychopedis). Partly to this end, a break is made with that epistemological orthodoxy which privileges social science produced by the First World about itself and others. Mainly through encounters between particular contributors to this book and given texts of others, a wealth of references are made to knowledge generated by the global periphery – the 'Southern' world, to borrow Raewyn Connell's (2007) felicitous term. The aim stretches beyond promoting an intellectual democracy of sorts or 'empowering' weaker states by giving voice to their critically-minded scholars and students. The substance of marginalized social science (as, indeed, the factual recognition of its relative marginalization) may broaden our understanding of local, national, regional and global arrangements (ibid.: xii). With a view to evading 'scholastic bias' or 'theoreticism' – the fetishization of concepts and their compilation, classification or elaboration (Bourdieu and Wacquant, 1992: 161) – focus is also placed on an array of concrete, empirically grounded cases, as they may help replenish our theoretical resources in the manner of a continuous dialectical becoming.

As far as structure is concerned, the book is loosely divided into two parts, one mostly theoretical and the other drawing principally on case-based data. Although self-standing and assessable in their own terms, the two parts neatly complement one another. The first part, comprising Chapters 1–5, debates the transformative operations of resistance and the values that should underpin it were a change for the better to be effected. Care is taken not to engage in authoritarianism in the sense of philosophical monism. The criteria offered for evaluating the social world and the directions proposed for altering it are not aimed to pre-determine judgement or mould imagination. After all, and as indicated by the very plurality of views expressed, escaping absolute definitions and strict prescriptions is a characteristic inherent to resistance proper (Brighenti, this volume). The point becomes all the more clear in the second and remaining part of the book. There the applicability and effectiveness of universal or universalizing moral systems are debated with reference to certain methods within given social milieux and situated ethical regimes.

In the opening chapter, entitled Values, Crisis and Resistance: Prospects for Freedom Reconsidered, Spiros Gangas traces the role of values in a range of theoretical accounts of resistance. Breaking with cultural relativism, the author's aim is to rethink coalitions between concrete universal values in the face of grave crises around the globe today (for example, poverty, environmental disasters, religious and ethnic intolerance). As a first step to this end, Herbert Marcuse, Agnes Heller and Kosmas Psychopedis are brought together in such a way as to illuminate the axiological dimensions of Marxist thought. Marcuse, for example, underlines the importance of the values inherent to value-free science, from uninhibited critical scrutiny to systematic engagement with facts, and speaks of the need to make the emerging knowledge available to the people under conditions of transparency and freedom. Heller shifts the focus to the individual. No doubt, she argues, social relations should assume an all-inclusive, universal orientation, but they should always facilitate the development and enrichment of one's own personality as well. Psychopedis, for his part, reminds us of the contingent nature of relations of domination, proposing that values become formed or activated at the very moment of crisis. The discussion then turns to Amartya Sen's libertarian approach to social justice, especially his integration of ethics into economics. Sen's is a call for upholding the institutional dimension of collective freedom without stifling individual agency. Value-hierarchies should not lead to closure, he explains, whilst agents should be given choice as to the objects of valuation.

In Narcissism, Humanism and the Revolutionary Character in Erich Fromm's Work, Leonidas K. Cheliotis gives the discussion a psychoanalytical spin. Insofar as the ultimate task of political theory is to promote progressive grassroots changes at the societal level, the author argues, it has first to clarify the need for change of the sort (for example, to reveal structural injustices) and explicate the reasons lying behind the state of affairs at issue. The dynamics of resistance cannot be actualized unless we first define the powers resistance must overcome (Butler, 1997). To this end, political theory ought to address the social processes by which common sense and prevalent ethical principles are produced and reproduced. How is it that people consent to their own subordination? And how is it that they permit or even actively participate in practices of domination over others? The analytic tools and operations favoured by Cheliotis are neither those of rational choice theory, nor of prominent scholarship on custom and habituation, for example, Pierre Bourdieu's praxeology. He rather turns for assistance to psychoanalysis and Erich Fromm. Frommian psychoanalysis traces the roots of cognitive structures in the universal narcissistic need for corporeal and existential security. It is this need that renders people prone to admire authority and submit to it, on the one hand, and to want to dominate over others, on the other hand – a two-pronged situation which Fromm terms the 'authoritarian character'. Fromm's is not a call for narrowing down our focus to the individual, or for adopting psychologism and its determinist assumptions. His intention is to put the whole of society 'on the couch' without missing or undermining the influences exerted upon the collective unconscious 'from the outside'. In the last analysis, narcissism is a catch-all semiotic metaphor Fromm employs in order to wed the innermost recesses of the ordinary self with the various layers of the outer socio-political world. But this is not all. In addition to deconstructing the narcissism of 'normal' individuals, Fromm also aspires to reconstruct it. Narcissistic cathexes, he contends, carry an inherent potential for societally progressive conduct. What is needed – and here is a further task required of critical theory – is to redirect individual narcissism towards humanism on a collective scale. For only humanism can bind individuals in harmony and love without stultifying individuality and difference.

The following two chapters throw light on the nature, scope and possibility of political theology as a means of resistance against violence. In Thinking after Terror: An Interreligious Challenge, Richard Kearney combines different religious traditions by way of responding to the phantasmagoria of terror that spread around the world in the aftermath of 9/11. Kearney distances himself from the prevalent Western view that the so-called 'War on Terror' and wars more broadly are to be understood and resolved solely by way of politics, economics and sociology. Insofar as a certain misappropriation of religion lies at the heart of aggression and violence, he argues instead, then the solution may well consist in a re-appropriation of the vision of non-violence as it is found in a range of religious 'wisdom traditions'. The solution, in other words, may entail a shift from the language of religious exclusivism, triumphalism and absolutism to that of spiritual dialogue and tolerance. Following Paul Ricoeur, Kearney concludes by outlining the steps of a 'hermeneutic of tolerance'.

In Ecce Homo: The Political Theology of Good and Evil, John O'Neill addresses Hannah Arendt's solecism on the banality of evil and the possibility of moral resistance in terms of the identity question posed in the biblical trial of Jesus. O'Neill argues that, instead of judging Eichmann as a moral 'idiot' blindly loyal to a genocidal regime, if not as an exemplary figure of modernity and its sociological 'thoughtlessness', Arendt might have posed the identity question as put to Jesus by Pontius Pilate: Who of us has the power to forgive? To put it differently, Arendt's turn to the Kantian formulation of the Categorical Imperative to capture Eichmann's stalled ethical will abstracts from the biblical narrative of 'answerability' and forgiveness. The matter, O'Neill concludes, is one of resisting ourselves as the source of reified alterity (hardness of heart, hearing, seeing) that projects itself in an 'alienology of evil'.

The programmatic logic behind all previous chapters is teased out in Andrea Mubi Brighenti's contribution, entitled Resistance as Transformation. Moving beyond the mainstream conceptualization of resistance as opposition to power, the former resembling a form of inertia and the latter an active force, Brighenti approaches resistance as a transformative endeavour. 'Resistance means transforming what is into what could be', he writes. Following Elias Canetti, the author elaborates that the political field, strictly speaking, is only one amongst numerous social locations where resistance may be practiced. But – and here Brighenti parts company with the preceding contributors – the tools of resistance are not to be found in symbolism and discourse in particular. Insofar as power imposes itself on the body, resistance in the sense of escaping the physical shackles of power and making new beginnings is first and foremost a bodily act. It is with this in mind that Brighenti also concerns himself with the tactical role played by (in)visibility in the actualization and effectiveness of resistance.

Although privileging the body as a tool of resistance, Brighenti's tactical concerns provide a bridge between the two parts of the book. To the degree that narratives may serve as means by which to make claims of justice visible and create bonds of solidarity, the *art of telling narratives* acquires primary importance (see further Solinger *et al.*, 2008). With the advent of electronic mass media, however, narrative visibility takes on what Thompson (2005) terms a 'de-spatialized' dimension. The field of vision is no longer constrained by the spatial and temporal properties of the here and now, but is rather shaped by the distinctive properties of communication media. This is why narratives and aesthetic representation more broadly carry the potential to engender a generalized sense of responsibility, for all possible cases of human suffering and injustice, beyond the micro-spaces where direct interpersonal encounters develop and particular demands for help and justice come to the fore.

Taking up this theme in Acting on Vulnerable Others: Ethical Agency in Media Discourse, Lilie Chouliaraki focuses on television spectacles of distant human suffering as means by which to mobilize critical judgement and imagination in the service of cosmopolitanism. From a rescue mission for illegal African refugees, to a famine crisis in the poor Argentinean province of Tucuman, to the 'death by stoning' sharia verdict against a Nigerian woman who gave birth to a child outside marriage, all broadcasts examined raise the issue of how to act on given instances of suffering, but each employs different aesthetic registers and proposes divergent patterns of action and ethos of viewing. Aesthetic quality, for example, spans cinematic entertainment, philanthropy and political activism; correspondingly, viewing positions span voyeurism, philanthropy and protest. Eschewing postmodernist pessimism, Chouliaraki concludes by calling for a version of mediation as moral education.

In the following chapter, Sites of Resistance: Death Row Homepages and the Politics of Compassion, Ezra Tessler also deals with the potential of the mass media to function as a tool of resistance to human suffering, only his focus is on the uses of a comparatively newer medium – the Internet – by sufferers themselves. Tessler discusses the current spread of death row homepages as an example whereby marginalized actors struggle to transgress physical borders and build communities of resistance with the general public. Prisoners employ complex, and often contradictory, narrative identities, modes of address and techniques of representation to oppose dominant attitudes towards crime and capital punishment. A critical sociology of suffering, the author concludes, should aspire to bring to the fore the progressive political value of oppositional voices, whether captive or otherwise.

To be sure, the possibilities for moral conduct are not exhausted with the prevention of further physical pain onto visible sufferers, be they proximal or distant in a geographical sense. We should raise our aspirations even higher and shift the focus of our attention from practical expressions of empathy, after an act in need of empathic response has occurred, to the prevention of such acts from occurring in the first instance – from secondary to primary prevention, so to speak (Cheliotis, 2010 forthcoming). The realization of either or both mandates, however, remains contingent upon powers of a far higher order. Not unlike the *mise en scène*, the content of mediation – which sufferings receive coverage and which messages are relayed more generally – usually entails choices and decisions by those who own or control the means of cultural production (Vetlesen, 1997: 18; see also Chouliaraki, 2006).

Are we, then, trapped in vicious circles of domination? How is it possible, for example, to democratize the conditions of access to the means of mass mediation? Insofar as official solutions prove insufficient or even contradict their stated aims, are there any alternative ways in which subordinates themselves may fight social injustice? If there are, at what personal or in-group cost, and with what degree of success? To the extent that the production and reproduction of domination presuppose collaboration on the part of street-level bureaucrats and other seneschals, when, if ever, and under what conditions do they engage in resistance? The last four chapters debate these issues by explicit or implicit reference to the logic and practices of 'modernization'. Originating from the prosperous enclaves of the West (whence its overlap with the concept of 'Westernization'), modernization is an official teleology of national and global advancement based on the intense rationalization of processes on a range of levels: from the economic and the legal to the political and the social. Thus, for instance, the poverty gap between East and West is supposed to close if the former follows the neoliberal path trodden by the latter. Similarly, managerialism is hailed as the antidote to corrupt and failing bureaucracies (for critical discussions see, Power, 1997; Rose, 1999; Ong, 2006; Wacquant, 2009).

In Face to Face with Abidoral Queiroz: Death Squads and Democracy in Northeast Brazil, Nancy Scheper-Hughes offers three crucial reminders. First, the language of resistance and its cousin terms (for example, revolution) may well be employed by the ruling class to disguise social arrangements of domination. Second, resistance proper has no foregone conclusions: just as it may fulfil its progressive aims, so too it can get trapped in cycles of reformism or simply prove utterly futile. And third, practical engagement in resistance is at times perilous, deadly even. Scheper-Hughes begins by drawing attention to the military dictatorship which ruled Brazil between 1964 and 1985, as it related to the so-called 'modernization' of national economy. Both developments were euphemistically described as 'revolutions', the latter also as a 'miracle', a kind of discourse which served to obscure the role of 'pernicious class relations', 'the macroparasitism of uncontained "market forces" that has fed and preyed on the bodies of the young, the vulnerable, and the powerless' (Scheper-Hughes, 1992: 280). With the consent of the winners of economic modernization, that is, a war was waged against loose children, rural migrants and unemployed black and brown men, all of whom were classified as pathologically dangerous by dint of their poverty and associated problems. Scheper-Hughes focuses on the dual role played by paramilitary 'death squads' during the years of the coup: to 'sweep the streets of social garbage' and suppress political dissidence. As the 'economic revolution' began to falter in the 1980s, a demand for a shift to democratic structures emerged. The military dictatorship gradually came to an end, activist groups launched conscious-raising campaigns about a host of social issues and child abuse in particular, whilst a new constitution was put in place to extend civil rights to the whole population. As is so often the case, however, neither active conscious-raising nor, indeed, 'modernization' of the law translated into practice. Public opinion polls revealed strong support for social cleansing and death squad attacks resurfaced with greater vigour. Resistance could not but acquire a local character against such a background. The protagonists in Scheper-Hughes's account are two local judges who coalesced with a small band of human rights activists, a few citizens who participated in a nationally broadcast march *contra morte*, Scheper-Hughes herself – the anthropologist-*companheira* who joined the struggle – and a musician-turned-truth-teller and 'voice of the poor' through his community radio talk show. Notwithstanding the inroads made, Scheper-Hughes avoids weaving a romantic narrative. In the manner of what Fromm terms the 'utopianism of the "awake"' (on which see Cheliotis, this volume), she demonstrates that 'happy endings are premature'.

Resisting Submission? The Obstinacy of 'Balkanist' Characteristics in Greece as Dissidence against 'the West', by Sappho Xenakis, is another case where the rewards of resistance are by no means clear or certain. The author provides an account of normative hybridity that addresses rival notions of the 'good'. Drawing inspiration from Homi Bhabha's post-colonialist framework, she describes the dialectics of transgression of 'Balkanist' and 'Western' norms within the context of contemporary Greece. Rather than accepting the common denotation of 'Balkanism' as a mere recalcitrant 'bad' and 'Westernization' as an *a priori* 'good', Xenakis invites us to consider the progressive and regressive potentials of each. She argues further that Greeks, from the general public to the elites, tend to shift from one rationale to another according to particular demands of the moment. The reflexivity presupposed in the process belies widespread concerns that normative hybridity inevitably handicaps the promise of progressive politics.

The last two chapters take the discussion to the world of criminal justice professionals. In Legitimation and Resistance: Police Reform in the (Un)Making, Justice Tankebe analyses instances of conflict and resistance within police organizations. The police, Tankebe argues, need to legitimate their authority in the eyes of the public as much as they need to legitimate authority to themselves. Organizational resistance, however, is bound to impinge on self-legitimation efforts, particularly during times of reform. Taking the example of anti-corruption reforms in the Ghanaian police, the author explores the reasons why, and the ways in which, police officers may resist, also linking resistance to legitimation enterprises. Tankebe demonstrates that the reason for police resistance to reform is more the inconsistent and discriminatory enforcement of anti-corruption measures than the substance of measures or the threats they may carry for individual interests.

Alison Liebling's contribution, 'Governmentality' and Governing Corrections: Do Senior Managers Resist?, tells a rather different story. Drawing on direct observation and interviews with senior managers at the Prison Service in England and Wales, Liebling demonstrates that, albeit still feasible, professional resistance to the ever-increasing managerialization of criminal justice is becoming all the more rare. This is partly because of a wide range of rigid organizational constraints now in place to promote compliance (for example, incessant performance testing and relentless competition) and partly because professionals tend to believe actively in the value of such constraints as tools to enforce the 're-moralization' of the prison. Managerialism, Liebling warns, is not inherently immoral, yet preoccupation with operational procedures and the management of personnel tends to overshadow ethical reflection and action on the policy-setting level. Rather than ending on a note of despair, the author suggests that raising questions about the culture and direction of criminal justice work is one way in which empirical research may help effectuate progressive change on the ground.

Much more could be said about the contributions to this collection. Before letting them speak for themselves, however, some additional notes by way of acknowledgement are due. Over half of the forthcoming chapters were presented in a preliminary form at an event organized by the editor under the title 'The Banality of Good: Roots, Rites and Sites of Resistance: An International Interdisciplinary Symposium'. The event took place on 18 April 2007 at the Institute of Criminology, University of Cambridge, with the kind permission of its

Director, Friedrich Lösel, who also delivered a warm address of welcome. Eamonn Carrabine, of the University of Essex, delivered a highly stimulating opening talk on the sociology of punishment. Panels were chaired by Carol Bohmer, Tony Bottoms and Loraine Gelsthorpe, all of whom deserve appreciation for their time and effort. Special mention needs to be made of Loraine Gelsthorpe, who generously organized a reception in the beautiful premises of Pembroke College. Whilst the book project was still at its infancy, valuable advice was given to the editor by Tina P. Gioka-Katsarou, Yvonne Jewkes and Iain Wilkinson. The project also benefited from various discussions with Sappho Xenakis. Eleni Chelioti helped diligently, and at very short notice, with the first copyedit of the manuscript. Finally, and not unlike the authors of individual chapters, Philippa Grand and Olivia Middleton at Palgrave Macmillan deserve many thanks for their patience and encouragement throughout the (lengthier than anticipated) process of preparing the manuscript for submission.

This volume is dedicated to the loving memory of Tina P. Gioka-Katsarou.

Note

1. The etymological origin of the term anthropos has been debated of late, yet the point remains. Whether anthropos actually derives from ano throsko or, as critics argue, ano throsko is the origin of anthropos according to folk etymology alone, humans have long taken comfort from the underlying belief that they are uniquely predisposed towards higher things.

1
Values, Crisis and Resistance: Prospects for Freedom Reconsidered

Spiros Gangas

This chapter addresses a theme that social sciences and philosophy have identified as central to the problem of knowledge and society, but lies underdeveloped in discourses of power and resistance. This theme reflects the hitherto camouflaged role of values in theoretical projects which developed notions of resistance. Whilst rationalist attempts to canonize solutions to social problems obscured local struggles and identities, postmodern and poststructuralist solutions to the problem of power fragmented the field of resistance's social compass embracing a form of cultural parochialism. Although insights gained by these approaches cannot be nullified, the limits to their proposals can hardly remain undisputed. What I intend to argue is that a possible channel of illuminating the discourse on resistance needs to rethink the problem of how values shape practices and theoretical models of resistance. The principal aim, therefore, is to highlight common concerns amongst theoretical schools which integrate the role of values in discourses of resistance and to rethink normative coalitions in the face of growing risks and contingencies that characterize the global situation today. In drawing affinities between diverse theoretical strands, this chapter does not gloss over deviations amongst their standpoints, which can often affect decisively the final position endorsed. The point argued is that, despite these differences, the ethical core in those theories remains fundamentally the same, and the deviations can be understood properly, if placed at the required level of abstraction.

The choice of presenting the argument in compressed form and through the voice of its various representatives serves largely pedagogic aims, keeping the discussion framed within the intellectual context of its articulation and development. However, what is offered in this essay is not limited to a mere review of particular theoretical positions. Rather, the use of these particular standpoints on values illuminates a guiding thread internal to each of these discourses, and shows that thinkers from diverse intellectual camps can, and do in fact, share a common political aim. Therefore, the original contribution to the discourse on resistance is twofold: first, establishing novel linkages between major and lesser known theses on value, and second, showing how these diverse positions entail a development within value-theory, crucial for remodelling cogent answers against relativism and against the tendency to see values as unambiguously resourceful configurations.

New issues for reflection and research on the theme of values and resistance that I will address, include the exposition from within critical Marxism of the discourse of values and its affinity to the capability approach. With respect to liberalism and Marxism, crucial mediating spaces can be brought to light, allowing us to conceive both under a unified normative theory. I choose as exemplar Amartya Sen's contribution to the theory of social justice, primarily because Sen prefers the discourse of values, thus updating the relevance of value-theory to current issues regarding political and economic unfreedom. Moreover, Sen's recognition that 'Marxian analysis has tended to have an affinity with libertarian concentration on freedom as opposed to utility' (Sen, 1999: 29) can be seen, without exaggeration, as inaugurating a new and promising research programme. To this end, and within the limits of the essay-form, I have selected theorists from the cluster of Marxian critical theory wrestling with the problem of values. Obviously, an exhaustive account is neither possible nor desirable here. Within critical theory, Herbert Marcuse (1968: 43–87), unlike Adorno and Horkheimer, makes better use of the discourse of values, whilst Agnes Heller is, to my knowledge, one of the very few Marxists to have systematically confronted the possibility of integrating values into the very premises of Marx's theory. Analogous is the attempt of a little known scholar, Kosmas Psychopedis. Co-founder of the short-lived forum of 'Open Marxism', Psychopedis shares with Heller a probing interest in drawing the value-content of Marxian categories. Drawn to the systematic character of Kantian and Hegelian conceptions of teleological explanation, Psychopedis equates teleology with value judgements residing in the exposition of categories in both transcendental and dialectical logic. With a view to sharpening the critical edge of current social theory, he confronts the Weberian legacy and locates discourses, which do not extirpate the problem of indeterminacy, but rather incorporate its agenda within a binding theory of values. Thus, he raises the idea of indeterminacy to a conceptual level that renders it compatible with freedom. This sequence of arguments drawn from a Hegelian and Marxian pool allows us to concur eventually with Sen's belief that spaces for mediation with liberalism are indeed present in reality and ought to be developed further. Sen's coupling of freedom with value forms the principal device for defending freedom without recourse to closed value-orderings. Before examining Sen's proposal, let us look briefly at the relevance of value-theory towards developing a theory of resistance.

Theory of values (axiology): pitfalls and promises

Rethinking resistance today through concepts retrieved from the heritage of axiology can be a dubious project. As modernity's fragmented identities blocked the project of reconciliation envisioned by idealist philosophy and Marxism, and as post-structuralism fractured safe value-hierarchies, such venture may ring as resurrection of past philosophical failures. As Susan Neiman (2002) has skilfully argued, the history of evil, especially since the Enlightenment, undermined the faith in the moral weight accrued to those philosophical theories that set up a utopian imagery worthy of collective pursuit.[1] To be sure, Neiman does not endorse a theory of resignation, but tries instead to rescue criticism from a moral hastiness that proclaims reality rational, whilst pushing aside its darker aspects. Once the critical function in such a defence of ethics is identified, it is possible to proceed by elucidating the appropriate social spaces that give this appeal its impetus and credibility.

This chapter argues that such 'ethical' spaces can no longer be identified either as isolated acts of concrete goodness and compassion or as Kantian ideas of reason. Notwithstanding the scepticism that legitimately follows from a systematic account of blatant violations of human rights and dignity during the twentieth century, the idea of a fragmented moral discourse that abandons binding moral identities and institutions is not itself unproblematic, both empirically and in terms of explanatory adequacy. Whilst not neglecting the historical and moral impact that the 'banality of good' thesis (Steinberg, 1990) may have in countering inhuman practices, theory can no longer place the 'good' either at the level of a 'regulative' idea of reason or at the level of everyday and offstage resistance (Scott, 1990). Both cases entail the risk of rendering the 'good' unidentifiable and hence eliminating the very moral distinctions that enable humans to clarify in concrete instances and representations what counts as desirable and worthy according to principles of justice and human dignity. Should, for example, modern institutional arrangements be seen as vehicles of ideology and alienation, as many staunch Marxists still argue,[2] then theory risks rendering unidentifiable the values of freedom, welfare, equality and justice for those agents whose daily lives crumble under the yoke of tradition, slavery, famine, civil strife, denigration of the body or unaccounted detention. At the same time, however, since modern institutions are far from being unproblematic ethical configurations, Marxian notions of resistance can still be pertinent to a normative theory of freedom.

A constructive line of response to this problem lies, perhaps, in a critical conception of resistance that rethinks the problem of binding values, their risk-laden uncoupling from our sociality, and the crises that undermine societal integration, both locally and globally. For this to stand on a safer ground than what significant explorations into post-critical resistance have to offer (Hoy, 2004),[3] a remodelling of the value-constitution of social life on premises drawn from liberalism, idealism and Marxism is required. Identifying the complex set of causes behind oppressive and inhuman practices, and developing theoretically adequate terms, in order to eschew dogmatism, constitutes an important benchmark for theories of resistance. Resisting institutional policies and practices which abstract from human dignity, must then involve a vision of the societal crises generated by those social structures tied to oppression and indignity. Yet, the very notion of a societal crisis raises the issue of a violated set of values, whilst a defence of those values is far from being a self-evident ideal. Amongst the tasks of a critical social epistemology is to expose the contradictory status of those practices tied to crises along with their theoretical backdrops. Moreover, a potential answer to the risk of dogmatism entails rethinking the openness of the invoked values (without, conceding their 'binding' ethical and normative core) as human praxis realizes them in history.

The philosophical discourse on values (axiology) has dominated late-nineteenth and early-twentieth century thought both in philosophy and sociology. Following a long gestation of ideas, axiology oscillated, eventually, between a subjectivist and an objectivist theory of values. This philosophical dilemma has been exposed in great depth in numerous critical presentations (Frondizi, 1963; Ingarden, 1970/1983; Schnädelbach, 1984; Joas, 2000) and requires no further elaboration within the limits of this chapter. As the postulate of eternal value-hierarchies (Scheler) failed to provide axiology with a foundation, it led, gradually, to disillusionment and theoretical incoherence. Adorno rightly detected, therefore, that the Weber-Scheler confrontation over values led all too quickly to a war of attrition, the chief casualty of which was the normative concept of value itself.

Rather, then, than forcing *a priori* principles on a multi-dimensional reality, or reifying the latter, a value-oriented and critical theory of resistance needs to elicit configurations of social ethics (Hegel and Sen function as exemplars here), without clouding antinomies and problems that surfaced in idealist philosophy and Marxism. This is more pressing, as the explanatory inadequacies generated by axiological dogmatism and relativism still have an impact in moral philosophy and sociology. A return to the value-discourse deserves, therefore, at least some re-examination.[4]

A dialectical conception of value and crisis

The approach to modern social theory that Hegel inaugurated, posited modern society as a totality of normative institutions and sought to ground ethics on a 'system of institutional dialectics' (Riedel, 1984: 50). This project is couched in a teleological conception of social institutions along with the logic that justifies the mediations and transitions from one institutional level to another (that is, 'civil society', 'public authority', the 'corporation', the 'state' and so on). However, this holistic interpretation of the social system as an overarching 'value'[5] can regress into structural-functionalism (Parsons), failing to account for the problem of indeterminacy during the attempt to match the logical status of social institutions with clearly identifiable social relations in history. Yet, the underlying rationale in holistic and organic approaches (from Aristotle to Kant, Hegel and Durkheim) to the social shows a remarkable persistence[6] and encourages attempts, like the one pursued here, to rethink it in terms of current debates on values.

The main thrust of the argument advanced in this chapter is inspired by Hegel's political philosophy. Obviously, I do not have the space to deal with the very challenging facets of Hegel's thought, much less to address complex issues of dialectical method in the approaches sketched. It suits better my purposes, rather, to identify theoretical projects which exhibit varying degrees of affinity to his social ethics. The discussion of Hegelian ethics within the discourse of values is not new, although most scholars prefer to avoid it. One notable exception is Harris (1987) who caps his critique of formalism and relativism with weapons drawn from Hegel's dialectical logic and addresses directly the problem of values.

Crucial to Harris's argument is the dialectical attempt to beat relativism in its own territory. Untenable forms of cultural and moral relativism regress into what Hegel termed 'bad infinity'. As Harris (1987: 10) notes, 'if all values are thus relative, no standard of value has objective validity even within a particular society; for, ... all cultures break up into subcultures, to which the same scientific considerations apply'. The infinite regress of relativism is halted when its defenders appeal to the tacit authority of cultural conventions, upon which truth is incumbent. However, since mature modernity, an overestimated consolidation of some 'pure' cultural identity is hard to defend both on logical and empirical grounds. In fact, the global interdependence of societies and cultures is likely to signify a shift towards 'common interests', insofar as disparate value-systems need to be subsumed under the umbrella of a 'meta-value'.

Although this is not the place to add another neologism, it is essential to keep in our discussion the idea of a meta-value, in order to convey better the sense that values do not necessarily operate on the same level of abstraction. Of course, what this meta-value can look like can only be surmised. Noteworthy hints as to the scope and function of this meta-value are derived from Rousseau's 'general will' and Hegel's *Sittlichkeit*. Anticipating the prime ethical consequence of Amartya Sen's project of development as freedom, Harris, for instance, posits the interdependence of cultures through relations of cooperation and mutuality as the ultimate value (or meta-value according to our use here): 'this unification can occur only through the exercise of the capacity common to all human beings to organize their lives and activities together' (Harris, 1987: 247–248).

Implicit in the invocation of an ultimate value is, according to Harris, the real possibility of planetary crises, the destructive potential of which destabilizes and even threatens common social life. Although Harris refrains from developing further the means through which dialectical logic deals with real and concrete crises, the necessity of such an engagement reveals affinities to both critical Marxism's and Sen's capability approach. By pointing to the negative possibility of crises on a planetary scale, Harris frees values from their metaphysical anchoring. The prospect of a global threat (environmental deficit, escalation of terrorism, growing ethnic and religious intolerance) bends inelastic notions of 'difference' (cultural or otherwise) and sets the context for rethinking binding universal values through concrete social conditions that are under threat and risk. Global crises upset, thus, the relativist assumption premised on cultural incommensurability. Crises bring to the fore the common historical horizon along with the possibilities and exigencies that bind cultures together. Additionally, they raise beyond the threshold of cultural convention the precariousness of those 'conditions of possibility' that render human life meaningful and worthy of development along principles of human dignity.

Let us turn now to some Marxian responses to this insight.

Strands of humanistic Marxism on values, crisis and resistance

Having theorized brilliantly the eclipse of Enlightenment values, Max Horkheimer and Theodor Adorno embraced respectfully an ethics of compassion and a dialectics of non-identity as alternative forms of resistance against the universality of instrumental reason. However, within the context of modern societal crises and the complex arrangement of causes that lead to these crises, a project of resistance grounded on mere compassion must be proclaimed as inadequate. This is not tantamount to denying the ethical significance and practical value of historical acts based on compassion. In fact, compassion brings forth crucial values tied with the ideal of freedom. As Bernstein puts it, 'compassion immediately figures the integrity of the body, its freedom from pain and suffering, as of *value*' (Bernstein, 2001: 406; emphasis added). The Nazi attempt, for example, to eradicate compassion in order for mass extermination to take place, reveals the 'sacrificial' character of 'abstract' value-hierarchies at its ideological peak. This point is crucial because it recollects the fact that theories which postulated eternal value-hierarchies, like Max Scheler's, proceeded on the nuanced premise that the *ultimate value* is no other than *human life*. Value-hierarchies need not lead to oppression as critics (for example, Foucault) of hierarchical orderings often suggest. Scheler's late philosophical anthropology recognizes *man* as the spiritual being open to the world (Scheler, 1928/1961: 39). For Scheler, human life constitutes the real *a priori*, able to realize and experience the contents associated with 'eternal' hierarchies of values in a loving world-community.

The upshot, in this digression, is that an ethics grounded on compassion runs the risk of embracing irrationalism, since it unwittingly suggests that the 'good' can be invoked only in the context of such unmediated reactions towards incidents of cruelty. In such ethical proposals of resistance, captured by Steinberg's (1990) motto of 'the banality of good', the 'good' is only abstractly attached to the universal aims of reason. Unless freedom becomes engraved in *actual* institutional arrangements that carry some binding force over arbitrary wills, it remains bound to contingency, hence essentially not yet realized. The point here is that a defence of freedom and human dignity cannot have sufficient and effective claims to adequacy unless we are able to develop a theory of society with rational, free and *actual* institutions. Failure to grasp this necessity renders freedom an arbitrary concept and abandons its internal claim to some binding and universal linkage amongst human beings and the societies they live in.[7] By contrast, amongst critical theory's tasks today we must include the attempt to locate enclaves of resistance within the institutional arrangements themselves, avoiding both the charge of reformism and the frontal assault against the 'forces of the establishment' associated with no longer extant notions of total revolution and resistance.

Critical theory: Marcuse and the determinate negation on values

Critical theory does not, however, repel the problematic of values entirely; rather, this discourse is reconstructed more productively by Herbert Marcuse. The necessity of rethinking the problem of value-constitution within projects of resistance and praxis stems, for Marcuse, from two marked inadequacies. First, from the gradual retreat of the bourgeois-liberal 'form'; where ethical justification has been replaced by cynical attempts to legitimize violence and authority. Second, it stems from a crisis in Marxian theory, which often backslides into polemical rhetoric. Reducing facts which do not corroborate Marxism, to mere ideological instances, leads many Marxist strands to suspend relevance to real and substantive political issues. Moreover, recourse to terrorism is ruled out, primarily because it undermines the very ethical core of Critical Theory, but more importantly, because it confuses the levels of abstraction targeted by acts of resistance (that is, the domain of personal and individual responsibility with the domain of a social relation at the institutional level) (Marcuse, 1977/2005: 177–179; Höffe, 1995: 311). Terrorism is, thus, rendered arbitrary and dogmatic. It defends 'value' against alienated practices and presents itself as an *immediate* corrective to a complex social reality conveniently subsumed under the spectre of total alienation. This dimension of complexity of the social has revealed – as Kant and Hegel have demonstrated – the inadequacy of such 'spontaneous' projects of resistance. Inadequacy here signifies a range of unintended and undesirable consequences catapulted by hasty projects for social reconstruction. These projects fail to notice their gradual transformation towards principles they oppose (for example, regress of revolutionary projects into terrorism, 'hasty' applications of models of democracy plunging entire societies into Hobbesian civil strife).

A more promising path may involve working from within the system. This strategy would redirect theories of resistance towards a rationale of moderation. Marcuse implies this, when he claims that 'the time of the wholesale rejection of the "liberals" has passed – or has not yet come' (Marcuse, 1972: 56). In one of his late essays titled 'A Revolution in Values', Marcuse (1973/2001) suggests that theoretical defects in the bourgeois conception of values need to be disclosed, without giving up the ethical core associated with insights gained by these values. On his view, a social theory requires as its own 'conditions of possibility' two binding value judgements. First, the judgement that human life is worth living; or rather can be and ought to be made worth living. This judgement underlies all intellectual effort; it is the *a priori* of social theory, and its rejection (which is perfectly logical) rejects theory itself. Second, social theory requires the judgement that, in a given society, specific possibilities exist for the amelioration of human life and specific means of realizing these possibilities. Critical analysis has to demonstrate the objective validity of these judgements, and the demonstration has to proceed in empirical grounds (Marcuse, 1964: 10).

I pause to note that the reservation expressed by Marcuse regarding the logical possibility of a thoroughgoing rejection of theory, refers perhaps to the risk involved when theory and its subject matter (social reality with free and living human beings) is subjected to formal rather than to dialectical logic.[8] Insisting that a value-free approach to social science (or, for that matter, natural science, too) consists of the principle form of attaining objectivity abstracts both from the richness of experience and from the very constitution of human agency through freedom. Marcuse's critique of John Dewey's theory of valuation draws these consequences and shows how value dovetails with freedom. Following Kant on the idea that 'freedom' is the prime and unconditional 'fact', verified only at the moment of its practice, Marcuse suggests that the prevailing positivism in the domain of modern science renders 'the problem of values... identical with the problem of freedom' (Marcuse, 1941: 147). Unlike Weber's pluralism of values, Marcuse's argument attempts to bridge the gap between the values that a value-free science presupposes (that is, the value of free critical scrutiny, and of the uninhibited criticism and systematic examination of facts) and the form of society, where agents could become free owners, not only of material wealth, but also of the fruits of scientific knowledge gained under conditions of transparency and freedom. However, Marcuse brackets invocations of 'a universal system of values' suggesting that, given the scale of suffering today, the truth upon which the critique of oppression is couched, is 'indeterminate' (Marcuse, 1968: 73). As long as relations of exploitation prevail, truth cannot appear in the form of an unambiguous system of values. As I argue, Marcuse's standpoint on the identity of value and freedom, is taken up today, albeit implicitly, by Sen's attempt to render freedom conditional on concrete values.

Values and abundance in the thought of Agnes Heller

Agnes Heller sought on another front to rekindle the discourse on values within a Marxian framework. Undaunted by axiology's dubious heritage, Heller struggles to isolate the principal axiological concept in Marx's critique of capitalism, in order to reconstruct a binding, yet open, value-theory. Heller believes that Marx's pivotal value-judgement is 'abundance' (*Reichtum*). She reconstructs this value-content using as aids the idea of 'normality'. The notion of normality is derived, she claims, from Marx's writings and it entails the form of social organization that enables the free development of human potentialities (Heller, 1972: 19; 1976: 4). Heller envisages a Marxian theory sensitized to the type of individualism associated with the value of the personality and argues that the true content of species-being categories includes the development and enrichment of 'personality-values'. For Heller, 'the wealth of personality depends on how universal it is (in terms of its needs, feelings, types of activity, capacities); and, finally, how free it is, that is, how fully can it realize its potentialities?' (Heller, 1972: 45). Although this is not the place to explore the 'nuts and bolts' of Heller's exposition, it is important to note that the value of the personality that she contemplates entails a person both capable and in need (see also Nussbaum, 2000).

This Marxian demand underlines also Sen's concept of 'capability'.[9] Determinate social relations aiming at the development of human potentialities express then the value of the personality. Heller's acumen that axiology's adequacy can be blighted by reactionary value-hierarchies or deterministic applications of 'freedom' in history, allows her to invoke the universal validity of values as a real possibility, when '*the determination of values is the common affair of all the people*' (Heller, 1984: 93; original emphasis). Implicitly, she develops a critical axiology couched in binding values, since what concerns humanity on a planetary scale, may be reconstructed through the forms of those societal crises which generate negative global consequences.[10] As it will be shown later, both Sen and some exponents of 'Open Marxism' structure their normative projects in similar terms. Anything less than this 'universal determination of values' renders axiological issues subject either to instrumental rationality or to irrational value-decisions.

Faced with the burdens that vulgar Marxism bequeathed on leftist projects of emancipation, Heller preserves Marxism's links to idealistic philosophy and classical sociology. Recalling Durkheim's idea of social facts and his attempt to preserve the continuity of value and reality (Durkheim, 1924/1974), Heller grasps 'values as primary social facts', sought both in the domain of indispensable regulative ideas of reason and on the level of 'systems of institutions' (Heller, 1984: 122). She follows here the Hegelian route, insofar as ethicality is part and parcel of the dialectical exposition in the logic of social institutions (family, civil society, public authority, state and so on). However, she subjects the coordination of these institutional levels to the indeterminacy that defines capitalist society. Part of Heller's strength lies in the realization that a radical philosophy of values should not straddle the divide between a genuine value-rationality and the alienation implied in instrumental rationality. Instrumental aspects are partially crucial in contributing to cherished humanistic goals as, for example, when technological coordination amongst humanity's individual components (Heller, 1984: 81) secures minimum conditions of welfare.

Heller, however, seems uncertain regarding concrete forms of resistance. She often verges on decisionism,[11] since the choice of the appropriate norm that will guide a value-discussion seems remotely detached from 'what is'. Crises leading to widespread, and often unaccounted for, violence coupled with growing feelings of social isolation, lead Heller to bypass 'spaces of utopia' within structures of bourgeois conformity. Hence, acts of resistance are portrayed either as stunted escapism from an alienated reality or as a form of nebulous resistance on the level of radical feelings (Heller, 1984: 149). It needs to be emphasized though that the project of a radical value-philosophy that she inaugurates paves the way towards the formation of an explanatory paradigm that places values in the very core of discourses of emancipation and resistance. What this value-discussion in the face of capitalist crises might look like is explored further by Kosmas Psychopedis.

'Open Marxism': Psychopedis and the transition from conditions to values

For Psychopedis, the issue of resistance against exploitative and inhuman social relations needs to address a normative theory of freedom.

Following idealist philosophy and Marx, Psychopedis (1992, 2004) associates the dialectical exposition of concepts in Hegel's logic with the value-constitution of social reality. Theory can regain coherence by rethinking the possibility of a hierarchy of values at the moment when resistance turns against injustice, exploitation and violence. This goal can be achieved through reflection on the practices, which violate the *conditions* that render social life possible. The attempt to found an interdependence of values cannot be dissociated, according to Psychopedis, from addressing the functional conditions that give these values credibility and render them actual.

Psychopedis is not alone in addressing this point. Karl Polanyi in *The Great Transformation* exposes the commodification of land, labour and money within a self-regulated market as a narrowly defined economic event that exacerbates the dissolution of the social fabric. For Polanyi, land, labour and money constitute essential prerequisites for a society's economy. As 'fictitious commodities' they conceal wider values, like nature, human activity itself and the agents' purchasing power (Polanyi, 1944: 72). Polanyi's point is that those conditions constitute both functional prerequisites *and* binding values for a social life geared to the satisfaction of collective and individual needs in conformity to human dignity. Inspired by Polanyi, but primarily from Kant and Hegel on the idea of 'condition',[12] Psychopedis elaborates a point that other eminent theorists have found worthwhile to ponder, but have left unexplored.[13] His exposition ties well with the core of Amartya Sen's project: values become formed at the moment of crisis (that is, when the 'conditions of life' become threatened and rendered precarious). By 'conditions of life' Psychopedis understands micro-relationships of friendship and love, but extends the scope of the category and makes it inclusive of the *a priori* of human life and health as well as of wider social relations of 'freedom, justice, knowledge, and aesthetic' judgement (Psychopedis, 2000: 90–91).

It is precisely on this point that a theory of resistance seems both pertinent and necessary. Its necessity stems from the asymmetrical activation between chains of destruction and chains of societal protection of those conditions that safeguard social wealth and, accordingly, the development of the individual personality. For Psychopedis (2000: 96) the 'causal chains of destruction of the conditions of life are activated directly'. For example, corporate domination renders the destruction of the Amazon basin and the Niger Delta an immediate result of narrow development projects. By contrast, *resisting* such violation of the conditions of life must involve a large-scale coordination of forces based on knowledge of facts, transparency of information and communication, prerogatives only partially realized by modern media systems. The moment of collective or institutional activation against breaches of the conditions of life (see also, Höffe, 1995: 262) generates tensions and marks the birthplace of values.

The critique of the present reality, however, does not entail an immediate transition to utopia. Psychopedis (1992: 47) prefers to talk here about 'the practical elevation within the now' as a 'process formative of values'. The murky formulation should not detract our attention from this important insight: values mediate history insofar as they are formed through crisis; it is their mediation by crisis that invests human demands with the energy that warrants exit from inhuman relations. Unlike many Marxists who interpreted the ideal's application in history in deterministic terms, Psychopedis does not recede from the problems that Weberian relativism addressed. Rather, he attempts to rework critically the idea of indeterminacy. Seen in this light, indeterminacy is theorized *simultaneously* as both freedom and exploitation. As exploitation, it is reflected in the forms of social crises which stem from a social division of labour founded on conflicting interests, injustice and deprivation; as freedom, it engages determinate values like solidarity, equality and justice. It is in this sense, as Psychopedis argues, that 'critical investigation of the question of values reveals something apparently worth questioning – values do not oppose the element of indeterminacy; on the contrary they are constituted through it' (Psychopedis, 2000: 97).

Placing this insight within the purview of Kant's critical philosophy, Psychopedis draws a Marxian theme from idealism, claiming that 'every relation of exploitation and domination... is not necessary, but exists as contingency. Underdetermined are the relations that humiliate, alienate, and exploit human life. Thus determination can only be located in the rational critical thought and free action that ends humiliation (thus negating indeterminacy)' (ibid.: 97). Two issues require special attention here: first, the idea that relations of domination are inherently unstable (an insight that political theory from Rousseau to Hegel has systematically worked out) and second, that the openness in how values are to be applied in historical reality, is couched in the dimension of freedom that characterizes agency. Psychopedis does not juxtapose alienated institutions to voluntaristic praxis. Rather, his point is that, given the indeterminacy of societies that are *not-yet* free, forms of resistance remain open. This openness involves also resistance against inhuman practices both *within* and *outside* institutions. The theoretical tension, which Psychopedis aims to curb, is embedded in the very project of resistance and carries the historical resonance of the Terror following the French Revolution (Kant, Hegel and Durkheim were deeply alarmed by Reason's hasty entry in history). How will the agents of resistance avoid falling 'into the trap of a logic of domination, but rather preserve, in the course of revolutionary transformation, critical thinking, distance, integrity, and humanity'? (Psychopedis, 2005: 71).

A discourse on power and resistance addressing historical indeterminacy has the asset of countering dogmatic social relations grounded on injustice and exploitation. Moreover, it distances values from blind praxis, when the latter abandons criticism as it defends justice and dignity. In this case, crisis yields an inversion of values and establishes negative values. In order to avoid this danger, Psychopedis brings to the fore the interdependence of values without appealing to 'stable' institutional configurations. Following Sen, he rethinks the idea of 'webs of values' (Psychopedis, 2000: 92), the intersecting points of which are formed by concrete practices. What determines though these practical outcomes is the purpose of developing 'systems of norms' regulating social life with values of justice and dignity. Embedded in this normative demand, the concept of value becomes a material force, nuanced, however, to the critical aspects of idealism that inform Kant and Hegel. Psychopedis writes that 'a *value* is the *resistance* offered to the conditions of life infringed upon by the coercive and exploitative organization of society' (2007: 109; emphasis added; see also Adorno, 1964–1965/2006: 172–174). It is, therefore, the continuity of the social that is undermined through global practices of economic extortion, political aggression and destruction of natural habitat coupled with forms of desperate counter-resistance that find refuge in terrorism and religious fundamentalism.

Resisting these manifestations of evil involves not just those everyday acts of compassion and solidarity, but rather, the opening of cooperation and coordination amongst those who bear the destructive consequences of humiliating social practices and those who, from within privileged institutions, 'can no longer tolerate injustice' (Psychopedis, 2005: 90). However, dialogue still remains problematic given the inequality of resources in the parties involved. Allowing excluded categories of people to gain greater control and freedom over their lives and their communities involves a rehabilitation of binding values and norms within the ranks of those agents and institutions, which encroach on the commons. Values, therefore, need not be set up as closed moral grids, but as relatively open (albeit binding) networks mediated by practical acts of defiance against oppression. These value-networks not only give voice to local sites of resistance, but, more crucially perhaps, help to configure wider value-claims. The voices of the oppressed may be seen as ethically relevant, not only to similarly coerced subcultures, but can also appear as coupled to the very conditions which wield power and privileges to dominant elites or collectivities.

In this way Psychopedis shields the discourse of values from pre-determined schemes and hints at the possibility of novel research programmes which cut across the 'theoretical versus empirical' division. Such a research programme forms the backdrop of Amartya Sen's endeavour to found economics on a value-ethics.

The discourse on values in the work of Amartya Sen

The paradigm of the capability approach developed by Sen has the advantage of restructuring economic categories and values from a normative perspective that emphasizes the institutional dimension of freedom. Differentiating 'values' (as 'valuational priorities') into interdependent domains of 'instrumental freedoms', allows Sen to curb the one-dimensional conception, which opposes selfish to collective interest and, moreover, to tackle intermediate institutions, characterized by mixed practices of mediation between 'oneself and all' (Sen, 1987: 20).[14] Rather than embracing an uncritical optimism regarding unmediated perceptions of collective interest Sen develops the – often denigrated by normative theories – logic of instrumental functionings. In fact, these functionings are regarded as 'complex instrumental ethics' (ibid.: 87) deeply entangled with a modern social ethics. They cover 'freedom from under-nourishment and from premature morbidity' to relations of dignity and 'creative fulfillment' (ibid.: 64).

Sen re-deploys implicitly an argument advanced by Hegel and Durkheim. For these thinkers, the ethical integration of society involves mediating 'spaces' between civil society and the state, such as corporations or public authority. Although the institution of the corporation as envisaged by both Hegel and Durkheim leads to practical difficulties, since it is premised on the contingencies generated by a free-market economy, it points to a promising path that normative theory can take: namely, to explore further the idea of intermediate institutions, in order to tackle relations between levels of values. By resorting to such a strategy, theory could, potentially, respond in more adequate ways towards societal crises. It would found resistance on a web of institutional arrangements of both functional (instrumental) and constitutive value. This web of institutional arrangements precludes the idea of closed and stable value-hierarchies.

Imparting binding force to values, however, does not imply unwarranted invocations of eternal value-hierarchies. In this respect, Sen shows a remarkable sensitivity to the problem of indeterminacy. This is achieved in various ways. For example, responding to Hayek's important objection concerning the fact that state-intervention breaches the freedom of agents in civil society, Sen dissects further the idea of action's unintended consequences. Countering an idea of human action where its consequences were not anticipated by the initial design, Sen mobilizes models from classical political economy, according to which the unintended consequences of human action are relevant only for the action that yields results *opposing* those contained in the initial design. Kant has already refuted the possibility of a complete foresight on the part of the agent regarding consequences (it would presuppose God's perspective). Sen animates Smith's metaphor of the 'invisible hand' in order to show that the 'baker's egoistic purpose' does not include amongst its aims starvation or risks in health (Sen, 1984: 92–93).

Sen's cursory reference to Marx in the same passage (ibid.: 92) reveals his scepticism regarding Marx's proclivity to burden capitalism with tensions leading ultimately to its demise. Marx cannot, however, be entirely sidestepped. A Marxian relevance regarding the intensity of social crises generated by narrow conceptions of the free-market mechanism can be reconstructed from the very premises of Sen's arguments. Sen circumvents the Marxian polemic against capitalism and recasts the concept of alienation in empirically fruitful terms (that is, as capability deprivation). He recognizes that the one-dimensional conception of human beings as workers only constitutes one of Marx's important insights and criticisms (Sen, 1995: 120). The tensions that stem from this one-dimensional idea of man force Sen to admit that the problem of inequality and of the fragility of public goods like the environment, demands a solution that 'will almost certainly call for institutions that take us beyond the capitalist market economy' (Sen, 1999: 267).

The demand for institutional reconstruction here is not tantamount to reformism; it entails, rather, a critique of those 'regulation' mechanisms which fail to achieve the results contained in their initial value-orientation. For example, the functional significance of criminal organizations like the Mafia, where violence or the threat of violence constitute necessary adjuncts to contract-enforcement (ibid.: 267–268), cannot be incorporated within a normatively coherent theory of institutions. As a social relation with a claim to adequacy, it lacks the legitimacy provided by the 'general will'. Additionally, as the conditions (freedom, human life and so on) become threatened by unaccountable forms of organizational coercion, the very functional stability and normative legitimacy required is bound to be 'contingent'. Moreover, malfunctions in democracy often emerge from an unreflective imitation of social practices, legitimized by a conventionalist interpretation of reality: 'Others do the same' emerges for Sen (ibid.: 277) as the typical invocation of an ethical retreatism, which easily recalls Arendt's thesis of the 'banality of evil'. By contrast, praxis within the framework of democracy is tied to creative value formation and enables agents to counter the moral levelling associated with an ethics based on mere inductive imitation.

Drawing on the premises of previous economic theories of 'development', Sen discloses the necessity of wider institutional arrangements couched in 'valuational priorities'. The theoretical weapons here can be gleaned amongst Aristotle, Adam Smith and Marx (Sen, 1987: 46). Viable institutions conducive to the amelioration of a person's capability include political freedoms, economic facilities, social opportunities, transparency guarantees and protective security (Sen, 1999). The entire 'capability approach' involves the very possibility of agents to *function* as *capable* of choosing objects of value (Sen, 1995: 43). These values contribute substantially to the wider scope of justice, revitalizing thus the main thrust in the natural law tradition along principles compatible with modern political institutions. Sen's defence of democracy as both constitutive and instrumental (that is, as a functional condition for survival, for example)[15] does not blind him to the fact that a formal application of democracy may tacitly invert its value contents leading to opposite values. If the elimination of poverty and its discontents is to be achieved through democracy, it must be undertaken, not only by nation-states and international organizations, but also by agents at the level of practice, which in its concrete specificity cannot be fully determined.

The presence of this regional 'specificity' forces Sen (1999: 155) to warn against a confusion of democracy with mechanical applications in history. Sen's objection to *arbitrary* attempts at 'completing' partial orderings suggests that these applications involve a coercive dimension. It is against this hastiness that a partial value-ranking ought to be defended (Sen, 1995: 134). Sen does not reify incompleteness here. On the contrary, he supersedes it as he renders claims to absolute and complete orderings of values an impractical undertaking. To expect fully developed hierarchies of values in order to start solving practical problems is a demand that neither empirical life nor theory corroborate as an adequate practical and normative standpoint. The counter-factuality of the demand for completeness in values resides in the everyday capacity of agents to reflect, evaluate, shape, control and change their surroundings in committed ways, without recourse to complete value-orderings.

Action freed from claims to absoluteness, however, does not imply decisionism. Rather, Sen takes seriously the rational recognition of agents in how they grasp the undesirable character of injustice and capability deprivation (would a rational being today recognize as desirable a premature death from undernourishment?). For Sen (2002: 622), admitting 'incompleteness does not make the use of a reasoned partial ordering "imperfect" in any sense'.[16] The unviability of artificially closed value-orderings does not cancel our ability to use freedom as a powerful tool in criticizing child labour, chattel slavery, chronic unemployment, debt bondage or servile marriage across societies. We do not need the unrestricted certitude of complete orderings of freedoms to be able to offer relevant social commentary on that subject. Sen invokes partiality here in a double way: first, by the demand that extreme poverty should be countered immediately without requiring a technical algorithm of the solution; and second, even if the technical information was available, the required 'radical changes in ownership' would entail equally radical shifts on the level of political decisions (Sen, 1987: 37). This invocation of partiality transforms the project of binding values into an open range of practice and policy-making, and frees them from some unalloyed verity implied in absolute value-orderings.

Returning to the constitutive dimension of freedom, Sen discusses the issue of capability in relation to the experiences of those agents who can achieve *less* than others and those who are *deprived* of the very possibility of achievement (Sen, 1984: 328). Epistemologically, the consequence has important ramifications. Primarily, it sets in serious doubt the very category of 'possibility' (or 'capability') that the relativist appeals to, but circumscribes in, the 'fictional' domain of an entirely self-referential culture.[17] Mobilizing arguments that form the panoply of Adam Smith's moral philosophy, Sen resorts to the prerequisite of 'necessaries' that secure not just survival, but a life of dignity. The latter is clearly an absolute rather than a relative demand (ibid.: 333). A counter-argument may, of course, suggest that such conditions of absolute deprivation are of little or no relevance to developed societies' own constitution and reproduction. Sen's response raises issues which Psychopedis addressed earlier in our exposition through the idea of a crisis, the severity of which is either practically symmetrical for all cultures involved (for example, the environmental deficit) or morally reprehensible (for example, famines) for portions of those who, directly or indirectly, are involved in its cause.

For Sen, the idea of 'symmetry' in the violation of communal goods that follows crisis, may be reconstructed via a Polanyian argument that he obliquely introduces when he identifies the incommensurability between 'existence values' and 'market values'. Theories structured around notions of 'externalities' or 'contingent valuation' face the problem of conflating two distinct, albeit related, levels of abstraction. To determine public conditions for communal life through market measurements and mechanisms renders a host of other phenomena, such as the capacity for wider social choices, recalcitrant facts, either glossed over or explained away (Sen, 2002: 531–548). Such factual dissonance betrays the narrow reach of those theories, which for the sake of parsimony adhere to the market model. It even points to an essential premise of Marxian theory: the demand for social relations that restore 'the enrichment of the powers of the species, the concrete form of which renders every individual able to "appropriate the abundance of the species"' (Heller, 1972: 19). Sen admits that this demand for 'ethics of freedom' is already contained in Marx (Sen, 1987: 48).

At this juncture, the constitutive aspect of freedom takes precedence over its instrumental aspects. The basic layer of values identified as freedom coupled with its negation in the form of 'capability deprivation', transcends narrow models of economic organization and constitutes a 'recalcitrant fact' wherever and whenever economic configurations claim completeness, whilst still embedded in policies of social exclusion and deprivation. A salient feature underlying Sen's argument subsumes this formal claim to distributive justice in rights and resources within the necessity and the moral imperative of resisting social frameworks tied to conditions of unfreedom.[18]

Concluding remarks

Value-hierarchies need not lead to closure and domination. If the argument advanced in this chapter is plausible, values can be conceptually and practically reconciled with claims to openness. Whilst many crises with devastating consequences for the moral comportment of our species emerged as a result of an uncritical belief in the efficacy of closed value-hierarchies, the flipside to that coin shows us that an amorphous concept of openness (either as anarchism, relativism or post-structuralism) may as well lead to malign forms of resistance.

Precisely because hasty resolutions of crises can often turn to negative values (post-9/11 surveillance in the US, anarcho-capitalism in Russia, civil chaos in Iraq), the centrality of indeterminacy in how the transition from crisis to values of dignity and democracy is effected, opens challenging possibilities for the power and resistance discourse.

Rethinking how Marxist thinkers (Marcuse, Heller, Psychopedis) preserved the political edge of value-discourses may enable theory to construct a viable paradigm of the power and resistance discourse. Despite a conspicuously determinist Marxist heritage, these thinkers remained committed to critical conceptions of resistance, and sought to open Marxism to insights gained by value-theory. With these issues in mind, I have argued that Sen's integration of indeterminacy as incompleteness in value-orderings is a theoretically fruitful and practically promising route for addressing the issue of poverty as deprivation from freedom. This does not mean that capability as freedom is merely a reflection of historical specificity or that it corresponds to some fixed technical optimum of welfare. If Sen can be praised for telling us something that can restore faith in the power of rationality (and humanity) during the battle against misery and unfreedom, the reason lies in the coupling of freedom to potentially quantifiable indices, without conceding theoretical sophistication.

It is perhaps worth recalling Ernst Bloch's reformulation of 'natural law' as the value-set that preserves the remembrance of human dignity. Bloch visualized it as the mobilizing force behind all attempts to counter oppression. In his own words, 'The pride of the upright carriage, natural law, whether consciously or not, is the element that *resists*, the insurgent element in all revolution' (Bloch, 1961/1987: 275; emphasis added). As argued in this chapter, the concept of revolution can no longer be endorsed along its orthodox Marxist vision. It has been laden with various ideological meanings, which obfuscate both its explanatory adequacy and, above all, damage its humanistic aims. Bloch's attempt, however, to forge a wider alliance between the Marxian project and bourgeois, idealistic or even theological thought has served as an exemplar for the thesis advanced here.

Sen's ethical project is fuelled by similar principles couched in natural law theory. Although Sen avoids using the term, it figures strongly in the way he constructs the project of a normative economics. The influence he exerted on policies for the eradication of poverty is evidenced in the UN Charter of values, set as binding and unconditional. Values of freedom, equality, solidarity, tolerance, respect for nature and shared responsibility constitute essential building blocks of human development and crucial benchmarks for human rights.[19] If the argument advanced in this essay is right, the normative claim for individual freedom as a social commitment needs to buttress webs of values under concrete and intermediate institutional arrangements, in order to counter practices that risk the very continuity of the social. Sen belongs to a strand of moral philosophy and social theory (Aristotle, A. Smith, Kant, Hegel, Marx, Durkheim) which defended freedom in both instrumental and constitutive terms. It is this latent alliance between seemingly disparate perspectives that Sen's work represents.[20] As ultimate value, freedom in the form of capability sets the criteria that render the 'pride of walking upright', which Ernst Bloch visualized as the *insurgent element of all resistance*, a realizable project, rescuing it, therefore, from mere utopian rhetoric. The dialogue highlighted in this chapter between critical Marxism and the capability approach can tilt discourses of resistance in favour of re-evaluating the role of values, as we try to fulfill Bloch's demanding task.

Notes

This chapter is dedicated to the memory of Kosmas Psychopedis (1944–2004), a true mentor in spirit and heart. Many of the issues presented here recurred in fruitful exchanges with colleagues whose critical glance contributed to the improvement of my argument. Therefore, I thank Stephanos Dimitriou, Yiannis Karagiorgos, Andreas Michalakis and Yota Spyropoulou for support and constructive criticism.

1. An appeal, for example, like Neiman's (1994, 2002: 323), to the Kantian morality of the 'as-if' is certainly laudable. However, Yovel's (1980) Hegelian reading of Kant figures as a more promising way of reconstructing Kant's ethics. Psychopedis (1980), whose thought concerns us here, has pointed to the radical and material aspects of Kant's teleology of social institutions and, more recently (2005), argued in favour of the contemporary relevance of his idea of revolution.
2. Holmwood (1999) has convincingly argued that radical theories targeting the total negation of the system tend to reproduce the conformist description of reality they wish to undermine, embracing, thus, explanatory failure.
3. Hoy (2004) draws important arguments from post-structuralists, but his attachment to their problematic interpretation of Kant's and Hegel's critical and systematic aspects inhibits him from coupling the insights gained by post-structuralism with the idealist tradition. My deployment of value-theory emerges as a complement and a partial corrective to Hoy's discourses of resistance. Similarly, Scott's fascinating study on hidden transcripts sharpens sociological attention regarding micro-sites of resistance, but risks rendering resistance a parochial enterprise since he severs, due to his allegiance to post-structuralism (Scott, 1990: x), links to wider networks of

resistance. Scott's invocation of dignity (ibid.: 113) enters the picture as an unambiguous value, but no attempt is made to pursue the path of resistance 'upwards' towards the macro-level. However, Scott's sensitivity towards the field of offstage resistance tells us something important both about the indeterminacy involved in how the oppressed will resist domination (often from within the system) (ibid.: 107) and about the political merit of local sites of resistance. The problem, however, remains: how will these local struggles be coordinated? To this, both Hoy and Scott offer little, and it is this problem that I attempt to illuminate.
4. On how the discourse on values emerges in recent moral philosophy, see Putnam (2002) and Raz (2004). A noteworthy attempt to rework the normative discourse of values, setting up our humanity as the 'value of values' is found in Korsgaard (2004: 85).
5. Nozick's (1981) admirable exposition of value as organic unity and the identification of tensions in such an inflated concept of value cannot be discussed here. However, his endorsement of value as openness on the part of creative agents in history as opposed to the reductionism of much of social science, although laudable, needs to be supplemented by a theory that accounts for the conditions of this creativity and the coordination of the pluralistic universe that he cherishes.
6. Sen (2002: 5–6) juxtaposes freedom to 'pre-selected mechanical axioms'. Freedom seen in organic terms has been a recurring theme in Hegel and Durkheim (Gangas, 2007).
7. Oddly, Steinberg bypasses the immense literature on Hegel and reads Hegel's political theory through Popperian lenses as an apology to the Prussian state or as proto-fascist (1990: 233–234). Here, the defence of freedom and dignity has reverted into dogmatism. This misguided reading has been set to rest by Hegelian studies (for example, D'Hondt, 1988; Marcuse, 1941/1977: 413). These offer ample historical and theoretical proof of Hegel's allegiance to freedom and autonomy.
8. The reference to 'applications' of formal and dialectical logic is far from being otiose. Hegel has shown how an 'apodeictic judgment', like 'the house constituted so and so is *good*, the action constituted so and so is *right*' has immense practical and ethical consequences (Hegel, 1812/1999: 661; original emphasis). A house built by building contractors who are either technically unprofessional or susceptible to bribery is likely to collapse during an earthquake (see also, Neiman, 2002: 249–250). Without being an exercise in cynical casualty logistics, the recent difference in the experience of the devastating tsunamis in Southeast Asia and in New Orleans illustrates this point.
9. Nussbaum (2000) places Marx (coupled with Aristotle) at the forefront of the capabilities approach. The chart of basic capabilities, that she draws and designates as 'universal values', corresponds roughly to Heller's ideals as well. Capability tied to freedom is prefigured in Marx (1857–1858/1993: 711–712).
10. Whilst societal crises may often involve conflicting and mutually exclusive responses amongst the agents involved, Heller regards as feasible the simultaneous achievement of different 'evaluated goals'. Anticipating Sen's logic, she writes that, 'the maintenance and development of the European culture is *conceivable* together with the development of the Third World.

A *philosophical value discussion* is therefore *possible* between the representatives of these two interpretations' (Heller, 1984: 127; original emphasis; see also Grumley, 2005: 39–43, 103).

11. Decisionist theory, too, struggles with the dilemmas of value-relativism. Carl Schmitt, for example, correctly recognizes the need for mediating values. Mediation, he tells us, implies norm-constitution. Schmitt (1967/1996: 27–28) even associates the unmediated application of values in reality with abominable consequences (that is, 'terror' and 'awesome misfortune'). However, Schmitt's denigration of modern democracy's principles of discussion places the craving for norms in the highly dubious alternative of a heroic law-giver. Schmitt's romanticism of exception has, as Agamben (2005: 31) aptly demonstrated, served as an ideology that 'normalizes' exception by invoking it as means of cynical *Realpolitik*. Sen's emphasis on the hyper-differentiation of cultural identity accomplishes the strategic aim of rendering complexity during identity-formation in history, a key factor in defending freedom. It is turned, therefore, against the version of cultural decisionist worldview and foreign policy which reduces plural identities to cultural identity, followed by Schmitt sympathizers like Samuel Huntington (Sen, 2006: 40–44). Normatively, Sen's aim is also to raise identity to its democratic dimension by showing that a common humanity need not impoverish our set of different identities, but is, rather, a condition for us being capable to fulfil the richness that these identities imply.

12. Max Scheler (1916/1973: 94–95) has also integrated the idea of 'condition' to the foundation of values.

13. Ethically distorted social practices, which impair the possibility of a democratically sustainable communal life, lead Ricoeur, for example, to envisage, 'a supranational political body' that would become 'the *condition* for the *survival* of every historical community, which... is the political problem *par excellence*' (Ricoeur, 1991: 333; emphasis added). Hans Joas also concludes his discussion of values amongst key philosophers and sociologists with the demand that the threat to the social can be averted through reflection on 'the particular *conditions* under which the values, which are *presupposed* for the *continuity* of the democratic polity, originate and can be maintained' (Joas, 2000: 186; emphasis added). Quite impressively, some exponents of logical positivism recognize the validity of values as founded on the 'conditions' for civilization in any form, irrespective of cultural relativity (Kraft, 1951/1981: 171–172). It is, therefore, this continuity that is undermined through unregulated economic processes and calls for reflecting on the possibility and necessity of raising conditions to values. For the theme of social crises through Hegel's and Marx's category of 'bad infinity', see McNally (2003).

14. British neo-Hegelianism is a putative source of Sen's ethical project. Sen cites T. H. Green, amongst others, in his attempt to ground freedom in concrete social relations (Sen, 2002: 7). Green, for example, couples the notion of 'capacity' to the entire spectrum of social relations, prefiguring Sen's emphasis on 'capability deprivation' as an index of socio-political and economic unfreedom. Green, following Hegel, regards the conditions of possibility of the self-consciousness as the gamut of social relations, which secure for the 'free' personality time: by making it available for its free development, so

that 'the series of time exists for it' (Green, 1834/1969: 199). The ethical and logical configuration revealed here is that of the 'true infinity'. As put by Marcuse: 'The infinite is the mode of existence in which all potentialities are realized and in which all being reaches its ultimate form' (Marcuse, 1941/1977: 69). But more appositely in terms of an affinity with the Marxian problematic (for example, Heller), James Seth writes that 'the true socialism is the true individualism, the discovery and the development of the person in the individual' (Seth, 1908: 277). Cogent proofs for the trail leading from Hegel to Sen are provided by Allen (2006).
15. Sen (1999: 51) refers to famines as avoidable events even in poor democracies. Psychopedis (2000: 90) goes further so as to regard democracy 'as a pre-condition for life', having in mind, for example, nuclear accidents such as Chernobyl, which would perhaps had been avoided under conditions of freedom of speech and transparency of information, both conspicuously absent in the USSR.
16. It is precisely the partiality of valuational priorities that allows us to re-integrate the concept of freedom in economics. Reflecting on Sen's argument, Putnam (2002: 60) brings back to philosophical topography the entanglement of fact and value. Ironically, this entanglement has constituted one the most substantive resources of philosophy, namely, dialectics.
17. We shouldn't overlook here Sen's critique of relativism. As discussed earlier in reference to Harris (1987), relativism's chief lacuna is its inability to account, or even conceive, internal critique; all critique of a specific culture is projected to an 'alien culture' or to 'the arrogance of cultural imperialists' (Sen, 2002: 476). By setting up critique an impossible undertaking relativists silence, rather dogmatically, dissenting voices from within a culture. Isn't possible, Sen asks, for a culture to be relativized by sceptics from the inside? There is no necessity that renders a majority rule binding when couched in conditions and procedures of oppression. Following Sen's own example, a feminist dissenter in Iran who reads Kant, Hume, Marx or Mill and opposes the theocratic regime qualifies as an internal critic, and hence, destabilizes the authority upon which the homogeneity of conventional beliefs is grounded (ibid.: 477). Nussbaum (2000: 48–49) chides relativism for being unable to grasp people as 'resourceful borrowers of ideas'.
18. A long tradition of social policy has discussed issues of poverty and deprivation in terms of violation of binding values and capacities for valued choices (Marshall, 1970: 170; Titmuss, 1974: 132–141).
19. See UNDP (2003: 28). Höffe (1995: 51–52) pursues this alliance further when he couples political justice to natural law in an attempt to overcome the reduction of ethics to either legal positivism or anarchism. Means to achieve this 'complex task of mediation' involve both normative and functional demands on the level of general societal conditions and on the level of the peculiarities of each social sphere (Höffe, 1995: 315). For a Durkheimian approach to values as human rights that points to similar coalitions in theory, see Watts-Miller (1992: 11; 1993: 97–98).
20. For a theologically informed defence of welfare on the basis of a value-discourse, see Askonas and Frowen (1997).

2
Narcissism, Humanism and the Revolutionary Character in Erich Fromm's Work

Leonidas K. Cheliotis

Scholars of Marxist persuasion argue that the ultimate task of political theory is to help create the revolutionary subject and transform society more generally. To do so, they go on to argue, political theory needs to engage with the historicity of domination, that is, to uncover and deconstruct the infra-conscious complicity between historically specified conditions of existence and the cognitive schemata of perception these conditions have produced to their own advantage (see further Bratsis, 2002). But whilst external, social realities exert immense pressures upon the apparatus of perception, so much so that they often become our 'second nature' (see, for example, Bourdieu, 1991), no historicity of domination can afford to miss the role of 'first nature' or 'prehistory': 'what must have gone on *before* the subject could establish a relationship with "external reality" – the process which... acquires the form of the I's absolute act of positing (of itself as) the object' (Žižek, 1992/2008: 57, original emphasis). Whence the necessity to shift the theoretical starting point from the ways in, and the degree to, which perception comes to adjust itself to forces external to the self, to how the content and manifestation of external forces are moulded in accordance or, at least, in dialogue with esoteric perceptive dispositions, those hidden in the region of instincts (Craib, 1990). In fact, as Slavoj Žižek argues, 'the only way to save historicity from the fall into historicism, into the notion of the linear succession of "historical epochs", is to conceive these epochs as a series of ultimately failed attempts to deal with the same "unhistorical" traumatic kernel' (Žižek, 1992/2008: 94; see also Butler, 1997).

Building on a sympathetic appraisal of Erich Fromm's writings, this chapter argues for tracing the 'unhistorical traumatic kernel' of domination within the cognitive, psychic and moral quandaries of narcissism. Against the psychoanalytical and sociological orthodoxies of his time, Fromm walks the theoretical tightrope between the instinctual and the societal within the socialized psyche, thus theorizing narcissism as a catch-all semiotic metaphor which weds the innermost recesses of the ordinary self with the various layers of the outer socio-political world, and yet does not collapse the former into the latter or *vice versa*. With the selfsame caution, Fromm's psychoanalytic imagination further allows for interpreting the self outside the mainstream, individual clinical setting, and as a broader cultural-anthropological category. Finally, whether with reference to the individual or the collective self, Fromm pays equal attention to the material efficacy of symbolic power and the symbolic efficacy of material power, as they associate with one another in the manner of a continuous dialectical becoming, also making central to such enquiry plentiful cases of explicit, physical violence.

His view of the multiple and multifarious ways in which innate narcissistic drives may correlate with mass evildoing should not be misread as a fatalistic apologia for modernity, nor as an outright condemnation of particular cohorts or individuals gone awry. Whereas, for example, Freud (1930/2002) prophesied the relapse of 'pre-Holocaust' civilization into barbarism by evoking what he saw as the ultimate impotence of any conceivable society fully and permanently to tame man's aggressive physiological and biological endowments, and whilst the mainstream Freudo-Marxists of the so-called 'Frankfurt School'[1] anchor their retrospective account of Nazism in personality traits inculcated by authoritarian right-wing families during early childhood (see Adorno *et al.*, 1950), Fromm shifts the blame to the grave politico-economic conditions which forced the overwhelming majority of Germans into authoritarian relations of dependency (see, for example, Fromm, 1941/1994: 205–238). Whatever remnants of psychologism one may manage to trace in Fromm's work, they hardly suffice to overshadow his sociological insights or to downgrade such insights to postmodernist elegies for the 'death of man'. '[T]here are probably hundreds of Hitlers amongst us who would come forth if their historical hour arrived', he argues (Fromm, 1973/1984: 574), and certainly millions who would willingly join the ranks in the face of 'psychological scarcity' (Fromm, 1949/1986), but '[f]or Fromm, man is by no means dead: he has simply not yet reached adulthood' (Ingleby, 2006: xx).[2] And, paradoxically enough, the route out of infantile attachment to the irrational authority of others and the ensuing immoralities passes through man's own need for narcissistic relatedness. To help humanity reach its potential for inner transformation and freedom, Fromm concludes, critical theory must extend beyond studying the characterological variations behind given types of conduct. It also needs to awaken and revolutionize man by revealing hidden realities and putting forth the moral philosophy of humanism, which can uniquely bind individuals in harmony and love without stultifying individuality and difference.

Some preliminary notes on Fromm's concept of man

Fromm believes that just as man is shaped by the form of social and economic organization in which he lives and works, man also affects and often even consolidates that organization in turn. The medium in which such dialectics take place, or else, the 'transmission belt between the economic structure of society and the prevailing ideas', is what Fromm terms the 'social character'. The social character is *'the essential nucleus of the character structure of most members of a group which has developed as the result of the basic experiences and mode of life common to that group'* (Fromm, 1941/1994: 276; original emphasis). As such, the content of the social character always pertains to the range of needs deeply rooted in the nature of man. For ideas to become powerful ideological forces, then, they have to respond directly to specific human needs prominent in a given social character; if not, they remain at best a stock of conscious convictions. Ultimately, the function of the social character is to maintain and enhance civil order by '[shaping] the energies of the members of society in such a way that their behaviour is not a matter of conscious decision as to whether or not to follow the social pattern, but one of *wanting to act as they have to act* and at the same time finding gratification in acting according to the requirements of the culture' (Fromm, 1955/2006: 77; original emphasis).

In elaborating on the issue of needs, Fromm poses a socio-biological question: 'What kind of ties to the world, persons, and things, must – and can – man develop in order to survive, given his specific equipment and the nature of the world around him?' The answer is twofold. First, man 'has to provide for his material needs (food, shelter, etc.) and for the survival of the group in terms of procreation and protection of the young'. This Fromm terms 'the process of assimilation'. But, again, man 'could not remain sane even if he took care of all his material needs, unless he were able to establish some form of relatedness to others that allows him to feel "at home" and saves him from the experience of complete affective isolation and separateness' (Fromm and Maccoby, 1970: 14). Elsewhere Fromm also refers to happiness, rootedness and transcendence as indispensable to successful human life (see, for example, Fromm, 1962/2006: 64). These man achieves in the 'process of socialization' (Fromm and Maccoby, 1970: 14).[3]

The primordial need to have one's own needs satisfied derives from *narcissism*, an overarching state common to all humans, albeit variable in its particular objects or, indeed, morality. From the standpoint of self-preservation, 'one's own life is more important than that of another' (Fromm, 1995: 87), whereas, from the standpoint of self-experience, '[one's] sense of identity exists in terms of...being identified with [a] group. He as a separate individual must be able to feel "I"' (ibid.: 85). Which of the two narcissistic needs will acquire primacy in the sense of greater urgency, and under which affective guises; who or what poses threats to corporeal survival and/or the identity; what comprises identity and which group appears preferable to the individual; the degree to which objective judgement is distorted and whether narcissism takes on a creative and benign or a destructive and malignant form – these are all matters dependent upon the social character predominant at a given historical moment.

It is through this open-ended lens that Fromm proceeds to dismiss the 'naïve optimism of the eighteenth century', as this is reflected in Marx's 'romantic idealization of the working class'. 'The famous statement at the end of the Communist manifesto that the workers "have nothing to lose but their chains", contains a profound psychological error', Fromm explains. 'With their chains they have also to lose all those irrational needs and satisfactions which were originated whilst they were wearing the chains' (Fromm, 1955/2006: 256–257). The aim here is to draw attention to the prior macro-social awakening of those irrational forces in man which, on the one hand, make him afraid of freedom, and, on the other hand, produce his lust for power and destructiveness, albeit by subjugation under higher external powers, be it the state of a leader, natural law, the past or God. This development Fromm describes under the rubric of 'authoritarian character', the person who 'admires authority and tends to submit to it, but at the same time...wants to be an authority himself and have others submit to him' (Fromm, 1941/1994: 162).

It follows that, if the theoretical vision of a better society is ever to be effectuated, if the biblical urge to 'love thy neighbour as thyself' is ever to find its concrete expression in universal reality, then political and economic reforms should be accompanied by a new *moral* orientation. The former cannot but be utterly futile in the absence of the latter. And this moral orientation, according to Fromm, is none other than an unyielding commitment to humanism. Conceived *in abstracto*, his ideal man is the 'revolutionary character', the committed humanist who 'is capable of saying "No". Or, to put it differently, the revolutionary character is a person capable of disobedience. He is someone for whom disobedience can be a virtue' (Fromm, 1955/1992: 161).

In what follows, I explicate Fromm's conceptualization of narcissism, of the authoritarian and revolutionary characters, and of the ways in which they may all relate to one another.

The paradox of narcissism

In conceptualizing narcissism, Fromm takes the lead from Freud and the distinction between 'primary' and 'secondary narcissism' in particular. Primary narcissism, on the one hand, is that condition whereby the libido of the newborn infant is wholly directed to the self, and does not extend to objects in the outside world (Freud, 1914/1986). Every infant, in other words, is born into a state of narcissism, in the belief that the whole world revolves around it, indeed, that the world *is* it. All people, it follows, are bound to harbour in a secret corner of their psyche some narcissistic delusions of grandeur, delusions which may be reduced to the socially accepted minimum, yet never fully disappear. Narcissistic delusions may nurse exaggeratedly favourable evaluations of the self (or parts of it, for that matter), coupled with extreme anxieties of being found weak and worthless. Such states Freud describes in pathological terms, as manifestations of 'secondary narcissism'.

Although a devoted advocate of the Freudian '*dynamic* concept of human behaviour; that is, the assumption that highly charged forces motivate behaviour, and that behaviour can be understood and predicted only by understanding these forces' (Fromm, 1964: 65, original emphasis), Fromm ultimately finds that 'Freud's concept of narcissism [is] quite restricted, for it [relies far too heavily] on libido theory and because it [is] applied mainly to the problems of the mentally sick' (Fromm, 1995: 87). Fromm's self-imposed task is, instead, to deconstruct *and* reconstruct the narcissism of 'normal' individuals, particularly the dynamic *social* processes by which the narcissistic character becomes typical of many 'normal' people in their symbiotic relatedness.

Before continuing, it is necessary to point out the basic constitutive elements of the intense narcissism experienced by normal individuals, particularly in light of the arguments which will follow. Narcissists, according to Fromm, have the tendency to transform into psychic facts not just positive forms of self-regard (for example, intelligence, physical prowess), but also 'qualities about which normally a person would not be proud, such as [the] capacity to be afraid and thus to foretell danger' (Fromm, 1964: 71). In response to perceived ego threats, narcissists end up turning others into what is often referred to in psychoanalytical jargon as idealized or archaic 'self-objects'. Narcissists, that is, deny others their unique individuality, fuse them into their own extended self-conception and employ them as mere mirrors of their own exhibitionistic being – mirrors that serve but constantly to protect, maintain, or enhance the narcissists' self-esteem (see further Kohut, 1986). The most dangerous result of intense narcissistic attachment is the distortion of rational judgement. It is not simply that the object of narcissism is thought to be valuable because 'it is me or mine', nor just that the 'extraneous ("not me") world is inferior, dangerous, immoral'; that the person is convinced that there is no bias in the judgement 'leads to a severe distortion of his capacity to think and to judge, since this capacity is blunted again and again when he deals with himself and what is his' (Fromm, 1964: 73–74).

Of self-defensive necessity, narcissists treat any type of criticism as unfair, hostile and worthy of furious reaction. Here we find what is sometimes paraded as a psychological truism: that narcissists are not incapable of loving others, yet they are incapable of loving another as another person. But is not this the very proof that '[t]he narcissist cannot love' himself, either? That 'at most he desires himself'? That 'he is egotistic, "selfish", "full of himself"' (Fromm, 1995: 87)? Indeed, Fromm takes the argument to the end. As a result of unproductiveness, he argues, '[t]he selfish person does not love himself too much, but too little; in fact, he hates himself'. Much as he may appear to care for himself, he tries in vain to 'cover up and compensate for his failure to care for his real self' (Fromm, 1949/1986: 131). This is by no means to say that narcissism should be equated with selfishness or egotism. To be sure, there is some resemblance between the concepts in that they both imply an inability to love oneself and others, as well as a desire to satisfy exclusively the ever-greedy self. But, says Fromm, whilst the narcissist 'cannot know himself, for he is in his own way, because he is so full of himself that neither he himself, nor the world, nor God can become the object of his knowing' (ibid.), the selfish or egotistical person does not necessarily over-evaluate his own subjective processes, nor does he always lack awareness of the world outside (Fromm, 1964).

To complicate things further, personal narcissism is often transformed into group or social narcissism. The functions, biological as well as sociological, of the transformation are discussed further below. At any rate, group narcissism is not as recognizable as its individual counterpart, not to group insiders at least. For *'within* the favoured group...everybody's personal narcissism is flattered and the fact that millions of people agree with the statements makes them appear as reasonable' (Fromm, 1964: 79; original emphasis). Fromm clarifies that the pathological qualities of narcissism are not reduced as such. That which appears as reasonable, he tells us, 'is that about which there is agreement, if not amongst all, at least amongst a substantial number of people; "reasonable", for most people, has nothing to do with reason, but with consensus' (ibid.).

Ironically, not only is there still a theoretical possibility of wedding so intense a solipsistic state of narcissism with love for neighbours and strangers, but the possibility in question even appears to be exemplifying the biblical 'difference-blind' concept of equality in an ideal-typical manner. Implied is, alas, Søren Kierkegaard's claim that only death can truly erase all distinctions between the self and others – that the ideal (and, perhaps, the one and only) neighbour cannot but be the dead neighbour (Kierkegaard, 1994). What are we, then, to make of the fact that deadly confrontations most usually occur between neighbouring communities or groups (Blok, 2001)? Should we surmise a macabre expression of political correctness, a perversely literal application of Kierkegaard's philosophical insight? I think not.

Bloody wars have often been fought between neighbours and former allies under such banners as equality and justice, yet, from a psychoanalytic perspective, banners do not always signify the primordial motivating force behind the decision to join the ranks or the act of killing on the battlefield. We might argue, instead, with Freud, that the loss of cultural differences in close circles, and of the attendant power differentials – in short, 'the narcissism of minor differences' –, represents itself a threat as grave as to trigger irreparably explosive situations. Not the grand 'metanarrative' schema of Kierkegaardian equality, but its secular alternative that is the psychic lure of inequality is what drives the narcissist to kill his neighbour. 'It is always possible to bind quite large numbers of people together in love, provided that others are left out as targets for aggression' (Freud, 1930/2002: 50; see also Blok, 2001).

Generally speaking, malignant group narcissism finds symbolic satisfaction in the commonly shared ideology of superiority of one's group, and of the inferiority of all others. '"We" are admirable; "they" are despicable. "We" are good; "they" are evil' (Fromm, 1964: 82). Notwithstanding that words themselves *are* deeds in that they bear the traces of the socio-spatial dichotomies they help moralize and perpetuate (see, for example, Bourdieu, 1991), the satisfaction of the narcissistic images of a group also pleads for some degree of confirmation in concrete reality. The validity of stereotypes only appears retroactively, 'when those upon [and, in this case, also those from] whom they have been wished seem to acquiesce in them' (Herzfeld, 1992: 131). Let us give the floor to Fromm again.

> As long as the whites in Alabama or in South Africa [had] the power to demonstrate their superiority over the Negroes through social, economic, and political acts of discrimination, their narcissistic beliefs [had] some element of reality, and thus [bolstered] up the entire narcissistic thought-system. The same held true for the Nazis; there the physical destruction of all Jews had to serve as the proof of the superiority of the Aryans (for a sadist the fact that he can kill a man proves that the killer is superior). If, however, the narcissistically inflated group does not have available a minority which is sufficiently helpless to lend itself as an object for narcissistic satisfaction, the group's narcissism will easily lead to the wish for military conquests; this was the path of pan-Germanism and pan-Slavism before 1914. In both cases the respective nations were endowed with the role of being the "chosen nation", superior to all others, and hence justified in attacking those who did not accept their superiority.
> (Fromm, 1964: 86)

Indeed, at least on the impalpable level of talionic emotions, the justification for waging ever-new wars is what we may now describe as a widespread sense of wounded narcissism. That the narcissistic person reacts with intense fury to criticism, and that 'only the destruction of the critic – or oneself – can save one from the threat to one's narcissistic security' (ibid.: 75), also applies to the narcissistic group. Disparagement of the symbols of group narcissism, from the flag and a territory to one's own God, emperor or leader, to what Douglas (1970/2007) names 'natural symbols' (for example, race, blood and kinship), has often led to mass feelings of vengeance, which, in its turn, instigated further conflicts. 'The wounded narcissism can be healed only if the offender is crushed and thus the insult to one's narcissism is undone. Revenge, individual and national, is often based on wounded narcissism and on the need to "cure" the wound by the annihilation of the offender' (Fromm, 1964: 86–87).

For fear that moral guagmires may slip into the equation and offend the ever-fragile ego of the group, a rabbit-in-the-hat-trick is performed. On the one hand, the real, grave consequences of vengeful attitudes remain in obscurity for good. On the other hand, vengeful attitudes are clothed in the disguise of moral paternalism, in pharisaic gestures of openheartedness and democratic republicanism that allow for satisfying mass illusions of infallible nobility as well. The murderous war in Iraq, now construed apocalyptically as a patriotic crusade against the evil scourge of terrorism, now packaged as a humanitarian intervention by the enlightened West, and the sea of so-dubbed therapeutic programmes for the millions of incapacitated prisoners on both shores of the Atlantic, constitute just two of numerous ready cases in point where universalistic standards are applied in a one-eyed fashion, where '[a]ny criticism of one's own doctrine is a vicious and unbearable attack; criticism of the others' position is a well-meant attempt to help them to return to [or get to know] the truth' (ibid.: 82; see also Cheliotis, 2008).

That the lowest of the low may refuse to turn the other cheek often only serves to reinforce the very stereotypes it is meant to renounce (see, for example, Scott, 1990; Wacquant, 2009). Overt struggles waged by the oppressed materially and ideologically against their oppressor may increase the loyalty even of those not wholly identified with the narcissistic group, as in the case of defamatory propaganda against 'the Germans' as a whole and the 'Hun' symbol of the First World War (Fromm, 1941/1994). To invert the point, but to make the same observation, it may be in the narcissistic interests of the target to exhibit what Derrida terms 'autoimmunitary perversion', that is, 'to immunise itself against its "own" immunity', and to 'expose its vulnerability, to give the greatest possible coverage to the aggression against which it wishes to protect itself' (Derrida, in Borradori, 2003: 94, 108–109). To seal the deal, as the list of atrocities committed grows in response, so does the need to apply them ever more resolutely to prevent the victims from making their voices not just heard but also listened to as such (Bauman, 2003: 86).

Even if awareness ever allowed for any degree of guilt over one's own role in the creation of the problem in the first instance (call it terrorism, street crime, prostitution or what have you), or in the disproportionately harmful and, at any rate, inhumane treatment of 'wrongdoers', that guilt now quickly boils over, as if it has always been directed against false foes. The repression of guilt and the consequent consent to the continuation and increase of exclusionary behaviours are to be explained by reference not just to the high 'exit costs' (for example, potential material losses and the alleged riskiness of philanthropic alternatives), or to the sequential nature of the behaviour in place, whereby the decision to dissent equals to confessing to one's own errors up to that point (see further Milgram, 1974/2004). No doubt these are losses a narcissistic group feels too uncomfortable to stomach. But, when an ideology or what social psychologists term 'cover story' is present to justify a goal and the use of otherwise unacceptable means to bring that goal to completion, there is no need to assess alternatives, nor any past errors to be recognized, only guilty enemies to be corrected, if not exterminated.

Throughout history, for instance, religious discourse has often served to support the power of cosmic rulers by preaching that obedience is a virtue and disobedience a vice. Christian teaching, writes Fromm, 'has interpreted Adam's disobedience as a deed which corrupted him and his seed so fundamentally that only the special acts of God's grace could save man from this corruption'. As a consequence, secular authority was resisted only by those 'who took seriously the biblical teachings of humility, brotherliness, and justice', only to risk being labelled and punished themselves as rebels and sinners against God. In a similar vein, the Protestantism of Luther claimed that 'nothing can be more poisonous, hurtful or devilish than a rebel' (Fromm, 1981: 46).

Still, one might wonder, do we really need to stretch the analysis so much? Is it not the case that, prior to its apparent emotive functions, narcissistic pathos assumes a vital biological role? If the individual did not attribute to himself an importance far greater than what he holds in storage for anybody else, 'from where would he take the energy and interest to defend himself against others, to work for his subsistence, to fight for his survival, to press his claims against those of others?' (Fromm, 1964: 72). The aim of what Fromm terms 'reactive violence', for instance, is preventative, and more often than not consists in biological 'preservation, not destruction. It is not entirely the outcome of irrational passions, but to some extent of rational calculation; hence it also implies a certain proportionality between ends and means' (ibid.: 25). True as all this may be, antagonism to whatever lies outside the realm of the self also stands, paradoxically, in stark opposition to the very principle of survival. '[F]or the individual can survive only if he organises himself in groups; hardly anyone would be able to protect himself all alone against the dangers of nature, nor would he be able to do many kinds of work which can only be done in groups' (ibid.: 73). Survival, in this case, is inseparably tied to the vigour of the favoured group, be it the clan, an organization, the nation, a religion or even the state itself. So much so – and here is a further paradox – that 'its members consider its importance as great or greater than that of their own lives, and, furthermore, that they believe in the righteousness, or even superiority, of their group as compared with others' (ibid.: 78).

To those who may object that the paradoxical nature of narcissism now appears even more complex, I would readily respond that they are absolutely right. In and of itself, the transmutation of reality into illusions that fit and boost the self-idolatry of the group and of the people that comprise it, cannot always safeguard against the corporeal, biological threats of narcissism. Nor, surely, can it guarantee complete emotive satisfaction of a sort. It is merely cold comfort, if any, to the thousands of American and British troops facing death on the battlefields of Iraq (and to their families and friends) that supernumerary locals are under the same threat. For the experience of loss and death, whether in its own right or, even more so, when caused by allegedly inferior enemies in the heat of warfare, is what man fears the most. It is the quintessential expression of irreversible impoverishment, the shameful sense of absolute weakness, vulnerability, helplessness and impotence. It is the epitome of universal equality before the laws of nature. This being the case, how are we to account for the continuing proliferation of surpassingly costly wars under such narcissistic banners as national and individual security, territorial sovereignty and humanism? Which are the forces that impel people willingly, and actively, to consent in their masses to their own subordination, sacrifice even? What hegemony has this power? Or, to phrase the question differently, under what conditions can corporeal and emotional loss be of narcissistic value?

To answer these questions would require that we turn back to historicity, that is, enrich our perspective of subordinates and their very own psychic motives to obey displeasing commands with an intricate account of the ways in, and the broader cultural climate within, which such commands are communicated effectively by superiors. Space does not allow such an account here, only to mention that, for Fromm, particularly susceptible to authoritarianism are the lower middle classes. Classes, that is, with little, if any, foreseeable hope of upward socioeconomic mobility (Fromm, 1964) – or of socioeconomic stability and security, we may add. The 'psychological scarcity' so created, whether in physiological or ontological terms, compels man to hate, to envy or to submit (Fromm, 1949/1986). The authoritarian character, then, is not to be confused with the rational actor of neoclassical economic theory. Whilst in rational activity 'the *result* corresponds to the *motivation* of an activity – one acts in order to attain a certain result', the strivings of the authoritarian character stem from 'a compulsion which has essentially a negative character: to escape an unbearable situation', and is so strong that the person is 'unable to choose a line of action that could be a solution in any other but a fictitious sense' (Fromm, 1941/1994: 153; original emphasis). No wonder states lacking either the means or the will to provide adequately for the majority of the populace, or for large segments of it, often tend to pre-empt the spread of dissatisfaction and necessitate infantile attachment to their rule by cultivating a malignant type of narcissistic pride on a mass scale. Targeting weak or comparatively weaker out-groups serves to reaffirm power relations based on fear of force and to divert negative attention away from leaders and their role in generating or not resolving insecurities on the socioeconomic front, at the same time as providing the public with a concrete outlet onto which to transfer their anxieties, angers and complexes (Fromm, 1964; see further Cheliotis, 2008).

Apparently, it does not take much more than a gifted demagogic orator (or, at the very least, an extraordinarily arrogant man of action in a position of great power) and a millenarian rhetoric that, whilst promulgating the urgent need for reactionary or revengeful violence, subtly serves to plant the seeds of 'compensatory' destructiveness as well. This, explains Fromm, is the violence 'of those to whom life has denied the capacity for any positive expression of their specifically human powers. They need to destroy precisely because they are human, since being human means transcending thing-ness' (Fromm, 1964: 31). The sadistic pleasure one finds in exerting complete mastery over another animate creature, often comes along with compensatory violence, whether this be committed individually or via identifying oneself with a powerful person or group. 'By this symbolic participation in another person's life [what Fromm, building on Freud's work, calls "transference" (see Fromm, 1962/2006: 40–41)], man has the illusion of acting, when in reality he only submits to, and becomes a part of, those who act' (Fromm, 1964: 31). Sadism, in other words, is the flipside of masochism in the authoritarian character.[4]

The unavoidable question is whether we can break the cycle of malignant narcissism. For one, Fromm argues, narcissistic cathexes are not innately destructive. It is therefore possible to divert them away from war and class struggle, away even from a shaky Hobbesian truce, and into a common normative commitment to human solidarity.

Life is elsewhere – but where?[5]

Not dissimilar to the concept of the authoritarian character, the concept of the 'revolutionary character' is both political and psychological. That is to say, it, too, combines a political category, humanism, with a psychological one, the character structure, the latter constituting the basis for the former. Implicit here, as earlier, is the distinction between behaviour and character in the Freudian, dynamic sense. That a person utters revolutionary phrases and partakes in a revolution – that he *acts* as a revolutionary – does not alone suffice to prove the revolutionary character of the person in question. For character to be classified as revolutionary, behaviour must emanate from particular, indeed, higher motives.

As such, Fromm expounds, the revolutionary character should not be mistaken for the '"rebel without cause", who disobeys because he has no commitment to life except the one to say "no"' (Fromm, 1981: 46). Not that pursuing any given cause suffices to turn the 'rebel' into the revolutionary character. The rebel only resents authority for not being appreciated and accepted in its circles. He wants to overthrow authority for no other reason than to acquire and exercise power himself. When the aim is finally attained, he may well befriend the very authority he was bitterly fighting just before. To Fromm, 'twentieth-century political life is a cemetery containing the moral graves of people who started out as alleged revolutionaries and who turned out to be nothing but opportunistic rebels' (Fromm, 1955/1992: 151). Such is also the case in our times. To take just one example, whilst allegedly seeking to effectuate grassroots reforms and combat corruption in states and societies throughout the world, neoliberal elites tend to thirst for archaic, absolutist power and guard it closely by privileging those who fit in (see, for example, Xenakis, under review; and this volume).

The revolutionary character is not a fanatic, either. Clinically speaking, the fanatic is an exceedingly narcissistic person, completely unrelated to the world outside. To shield himself against manifest psychosis, the fanatic has chosen and idolized a cause, political, religious or whatnot. '[B]y complete submission to his idol, he receives a passionate sense of life, a meaning of life; for in his submission he identifies himself with the idol, which he has inflated and made into an absolute'. Extremely cold and passionate at one and the same time, the fanatic resembles 'burning ice', he is close to what the prophets called an 'idol worshiper' (Fromm, 1955/1992: 152). Even those rare instances in which the fanatic actively disobeys irrational authority, are to be understood as expressions of submissiveness: whether as provocative acts 'intended to force the irrational authority to uphold and strengthen its control', or as attempts at 'turning away from one irrational authority in order to submit to another, more powerful one' (Funk, 1982: 94). Similar arguments may be raised with respect to the person prone to adopt majoritarian attitudes in the name of majoritarianism alone (Fromm,

1955/1992: 159) or, conversely, to engage in the status-seeking, 'fashionable' type of minoritarian resistance. All in all, the rebel and the fanatic represent the dominating and submissive facets of the authoritarian character, respectively.

But if the revolutionary character is not all this, then what is she? Or, to put the question otherwise, which are the prerequisites of revolutionary action? To start with, the revolutionary character is fearless of power. The demanding nature of the struggle for what Bauman, echoing Fromm, terms 'human survival', cannot prod her to forsake natural survival altogether, that is, 'to *reject* a life that is not up to our love's standards and therefore unworthy of living' (Bauman, 2003: 80; original emphasis). In breaking with resignation, but also with passivity and weightless, bourgeois reformism, the revolutionary character has the courage to 'err' and to 'sin', to be alone, to suffer the consequences of disobedience. Unsuccumbed to the prospect of falling in the course, she fights to the end (Fromm, 1981). Apparently, the concern here differs from James Scott's (1990) 'hidden transcripts of resistance', the various day-to-day techniques by which subordinates manage to insinuate their resistance, in disguised forms, into the public domain (see also Cheliotis, 2006), hence courage remains crucial to Fromm's account.

Albeit a necessary ingredient of disobedience, however, courage is hardly enough. The very need for courageous conduct presupposes sufficient knowledge of the social functions of power, whilst the actualization of courage requires satisfactory apprehension of where power lies, the variable forms it takes (visible or invisible), the mechanisms it employs (for example, sanctions and rewards) and a realistic appraisal of the effectiveness thereof. The revolutionary character is not a 'dreamer'; that she holds a deep and genuine conviction does not blind her to the fact that 'power can kill you, compel you, and even pervert you' (Fromm, 1955/1992: 160). All things considered, the most fundamental trait of the revolutionary character is that she is *free*, *independent* and *authentic*, in the sense of being able to think, feel and decide for herself. Although not a cynic, the revolutionary character thinks and feels in a 'critical mood'. In her life, the practice of reflexivity amounts to an unrelenting occurrence – a banality, as it were. She is always alert to the possibility that fictions are made a hegemonic substitute for reality in the form of tradition, superstition, clichés or so-styled 'common sense', and that, in any case, deviation from the norms entails given perils (Fromm, 1955/1992). In this latter respect, the revolutionary character is aware that, just as the strength of power and the ineluctability of submission are liable to overestimation, due, for example, to such overt exhibitions of pure force as staged military reviews, highly publicized nuclear weapons tests and the brutal suppression of dissidence (Wrong, 1979/1988), so they may be inordinately undermined by foolhardy comrades and manipulative political opportunists.

It is not only courage that depends upon freedom of reason. The reverse is equally true. To evade the bonds of power, man needs to be willing to deal with the narcissistic dangers and burdens inherent to freedom of reason. Neutralization techniques do not behove. For example, one needs to accept any hitherto sublimated guilt for submission and even evildoing, the disconcerting prospect that enemies may be discovered amongst friends and allies, the endless nature of the newly started struggle, the label of cowardice for giving up, and the sheer chance of eventual failure and frustration (see, for example, Fromm, 1981). The process of trying to resist power resembles the mythical encounter between Hercules and the beast Hydra: when one head is cut off, multiple heads grow in its place. We might say that the revolutionary character merges two variants of courage, the capacity to overcome fear of almighty power in practical terms with the ability to over-rule the psychological fear of positive freedom construed as the accomplishment of uniqueness and individuality. In a continuously dialectical fashion, the former requires the latter inasmuch as it helps sustain it. This is why, in the final analysis, the revolutionary character may only superficially direct disobedience against irrational authorities as such. 'Disobedience is not primarily an attitude directed *against* something, but *for* something: for man's capacity to see, to say what he sees, and to refuse to say what he does not see' (ibid.: 48; original emphasis).

Whilst often struggling on her own, and whilst freedom, independence and authenticity are the realization of individuality, as opposed simply to emancipation from external coercion, the revolutionary character does not live in isolation. '[T]he growth of personality occurs in the process of being related to, and interested in, others and the world' (Fromm, 1955/1992: 157). The revolutionary character is not identified merely with the culture in which she happens to be born and raised, 'which is nothing but an accident of time and geography' (ibid.: 158). Thanks to her capacity to judge the accidental on the criteria of 'that which is not accidental (reason), in the norms which exist in and for the human race' (ibid.), she is identified with humanity as a whole. This relatedness is entirely different from 'dependence', 'heteronomous obedience' or '*ipso facto* submission' to an alternative 'irrational authority' (Fromm, 1981: 19, 20). 'The question is not really one of disobedience or obedience, but one of disobedience or obedience to what and to whom' (Fromm, 1955/1992: 162). Obedience, if the term is to be used at all here, becomes 'autonomous', an act of affirmation rather than submission (Fromm, 1981: 19, 20). Fromm also imputes positive value to the replacement of irrational authority with its rational equivalent, whereby 'the authority, whether it is held by a teacher or a captain of a ship giving orders in an emergency, acts in the name of reason which, being universal, I can accept without submitting' (ibid.: 21). Eventually, however, Fromm divorces rational thinking, self-liberation and revolutionary action from all claims deriving from an authority other than the endogenous authority of the self itself (see further Funk, 1982: 95–101).

A profusion of questions now need to be addressed. Is it not utopian to long for the day when humans will think and behave rationally, if their very nature is laden with narcissistic irrationality? Realistically speaking, how much rationality, if any, can they exercise? And is it at all possible to combine, by way of rationality, *de facto* desires with higher goods? Why would the exhorting and only promissory vision of all-inclusive equality under humanism prove more appealing than the comfortable orthodoxies of actualized distinctiveness? Lastly, is not to prescribe any higher good, humanism not excluded, an authoritarian act in its own right? Is not Fromm the humanist putting himself forward as a 'rational authority', a Platonic guardian of sorts?

On the abstract level of historical progression, Fromm argues for what he terms 'benign narcissism'. In the benign form, the object of narcissistic attachment is focused on achievement or, more precisely, on the effort so made by private individuals or groups. The finite end of *having*, in other words, matters less than the infinite struggle for *being* (Fromm, 1976/1997). Such 'being mode' is not to be confused with the lifework of Hannah Arendt's *animal laborens*, the armies of Eichmanns and Oppenheimers who view their work uncritically, as a mere end in itself. Nor is the 'being mode' akin to the lifework of the Arendtian alternative, the *homo faber* who judges material labour and practice only once the process is complete (see further Arendt, 1958/1998). As Richard Sennett would argue, the 'being mode' is to be found at the meeting point between *animal laborens* and *homo faber*, there where 'thinking and feeling are contained within the process of making' (Sennett, 2008: 7).

As concerns private individuals, the mode of being requires that 'the biologically necessary degree of narcissism [be] reduced to the degree of narcissism that is compatible with social co-operation' (Fromm, 1964: 73). There is nothing wrong with nurturing narcissistic pride, say in one's work as a carpenter or as a scientist, as long as the object of attachment entails personal industry and connection to external reality. Exclusive interest in one's own work and achievements is constantly balanced by one's interest in the process and material of work itself. 'One who has learned to achieve cannot help acknowledging that others have achieved similar things in similar ways – even if his narcissism may persuade him that his own achievement is greater than that of others' (ibid.: 77). The dynamics of benign narcissism are, therefore, self-checking. An analogous case may be argued with regard to social or group narcissism. Here, too, one may hope, or, at the very least, hypothesize, that the collectivity may help individuals maintain a narcissistic equilibrium and direct their passion towards the actualization of progressive ideals and aims. For instance, '[i]f the object of group narcissism is an achievement... [t]he very need to achieve something creative makes it necessary to leave the closed circle of group solipsism and to be interested in the object it wants to achieve' (ibid.: 78).

Mindful of the Freudian maxim that attempting to impose quantitative controls upon the 'narcissistic core' is utterly futile, Fromm soon takes two crucial detours. For one, he decides to posit benign narcissism as subject solely to a prior qualitative change in the object of attachment. 'Even without reducing narcissistic energy in each person, the *object* could be changed', he writes (ibid.: 90; original emphasis). For such qualitative change remains contingent upon the existence of progressive authority structures, however, Fromm no longer situates the object of benign narcissism within the narrow ethical spheres of private individuals, the family, particular cohorts of the general population or localist political systems, nor within the glamour of their respective achievements. Man, Fromm now suggests, needs to free himself from 'the ties of blood and soil, from his mother and his father, from special loyalties to state, class, race, party, or religion' (Fromm, 1955/1992: 165). For, '[i]f the individual could experience himself primarily as a citizen of the world, and if he could feel pride in mankind and in its achievements, his narcissism would turn towards the human race as an object, rather than to its conflicting components' (Fromm, 1964: 90). What is more, pride in the achievements of mankind would not exhaust itself to nostalgic retrospection; '[c]ommon tasks for all mankind are at hand: the joint fight against disease, against hunger, for the dissemination of knowledge and art through our means of communication amongst all peoples of the world' (ibid.: 91).

Albeit (or, perhaps, because) himself a declared atheist since the age of twenty-six, Fromm wishes for a theanthropic form of religious awakening from 'narcissistic madness'. Despite a few linguistic lapses verging on the self-contradictory as much as on the absolutism of ideal-typical oneirism, he is deeply aware that, in reality, '[o]ne can only examine what the *optimal* [as opposed to maximal] possibilities are to avoid the catastrophe' (ibid.: 90; emphasis added).

> The Old Testament says: 'Love thy neighbour as thyself'. Here the demand is to overcome one's narcissism at least to the point where one's neighbour becomes as important as oneself. But the Old Testament goes much further than this in demanding love for the 'stranger'. (You know the soul of the stranger, for strangers have you been in the land of Egypt). The stranger is precisely the person who is not part of my clan, my family, my nation; he is not part of the group to which I am narcissistically attached. He is nothing other than human. One discovers the human being in the stranger, as Hermann Cohen has pointed out. In the love for the stranger narcissistic love has vanished. For it means loving another human being in his suchness and his difference from me, and not because he is like me. When the New Testament says 'love thine enemy', it expresses the same idea in a more pointed form. If the stranger has become fully human to you, there is also no longer an enemy, because *you* have become truly human. To love the stranger and the enemy is possible only if narcissism has been overcome, if 'I am thou'.
>
> (ibid.: 89; original emphasis)

The crucial point here is that, if equality is a necessary prerequisite of solidarity, equality itself requires difference, not uniformity. Unless, then, one remains stubbornly attached to a relativism that leaves one vulnerable to abuses of power, Fromm's version of humanism may be said to offer criteria that are broad enough to guide our assessment of social developments without being pre-formative. In all, Fromm manages to navigate between the Scylla of 'moralism as egoistic universalism', whereby the formal recognition of humanity to all is not accompanied by reminders of the repressed economic and social conditions of access to the universal or by some form of political action aimed at universalizing these conditions in practice (Bourdieu, 2000/2008: 65), and the Charybdis of authoritarianism in the sense of philosophical monism (Pietikainen, 2004).

Some additional comments by way of clarification and qualification need to be made on the concept of difference. Just as killing one's neighbour in the Kierkegaardian essentialist sense is more often than not the veil of totalitarian designs (for example, ethnic cleansing), so too is the sustenance of difference in the mere form of the Aristotelian *zēn*, nowadays referred to rather fashionably as multiculturalist tolerance. Jacques Derrida puts the point thus:

> [T]olerance is first of all a form of charity.... Tolerance is always on the side of the 'reason of the strongest', where 'might is right'; it is a supplementary mark of sovereignty, the good face of sovereignty, which says to the other from its elevated position, I am letting you be, you are not insufferable, I am leaving you a place in my home, but do not forget that his is my home... In France, the phrase 'threshold of tolerance' was used to describe the limit beyond which it is no longer decent to ask a national community to welcome any more foreigners, immigrant workers, and the like. François Mitterrand once used this unfortunate expression as a self-justifying word of caution: beyond a certain number of foreigners or immigrants who do not share our nationality, our language, our culture, and our customs, a quasi-organic and unpreventable – in short, a natural – phenomenon of rejection can be expected.
> (Derrida, quoted in Borradori, 2003: 127–128)

The Derridaean reverse of tolerance is pure hospitality, a notion reminiscent of Aristotle's *eu zēn* and closest to Fromm's idea of difference. 'Hospitality *itself* opens or is in advance open to someone who is neither expected nor invited, to whomever arrives as an absolutely foreign *visitor*, as a new *arrival*, nonidentifiable and unforeseeable, in short, wholly other. I would call this a hospitality of *visitation* rather than *invitation*' (ibid.: 128–129; original emphasis). Fromm also divorces difference from the conditionalities inherent to relations of superiority or inferiority. As a matter of fact, he views the accentuation of difference, that is, the cultivation of the positive sides of individual peculiarities, as the foundation of a richer and broader human culture (Wilde, 2004).

This analytical leap allows Fromm to level one final criticism against the Freudian conceptualization of secondary narcissism, particularly against the 'almost mechanical alternative between ego-love and object-love'. According to Freud, 'the more love I turn towards the outside world, the less love is left for myself, and *vice versa*'. Fromm's philosophical counterargument is this: '[i]f it is a virtue to love my neighbour as a human being, it must be a virtue – and not a vice – to love myself, since I am a human being, too. There is no concept of man in which I am not included' (Fromm, 1956/2000: 54). What, on the level of practice, dispels the utilitarian dilemma of narcissistic love is that the human objects of our attitudes are, in and of themselves, unique and unduplicable.

Granted, no more than a handful of persons can become the object of our *manifest* love at any given time (or throughout life, for that matter). But this is not to be confused with what Derrida and Kierkegaard describe as the original sin of love, whereby 'I always betray the Other because *toute autre est un autre* [every other is absolutely other], because I have to make a *choice* to *select* who my neighbour is from the mass of the Thirds'. Nor should we conclude, as Žižek does, that '[j]ustice and love are structurally incompatible' and that 'the universal proposition "I love you all" acquires the level of actual existence only if "there is at least one whom I hate"' (Žižek, 2005: 182–183; original emphasis). Fromm's concept of love for man as such is hardly a matter of numbers. Or, if it is, then it can only concern the infinite, all that is alive, mankind as a whole. 'If I love my brother, I love all my brothers; if I love my child, I love all my children; no, beyond that, I love all children, all that are in need of my help' (Fromm, 1956/2000: 49). Even in erotic love for a single person of highly individual qualities, Fromm goes on to argue, others are excluded solely in the sense of erotic fusion, of full commitment in all aspects of life. What is commonly referred to as erotic love, in other words, transgresses the narrow confines of symbiotic attachment and qualifies as true love inasmuch as 'I love from the essence of my being – and experience the other person in the essence of his or her being. In essence, all human beings are identical. We are all part of One; we are One. This being so, it should not make any difference whom we love' (ibid.: 52).

Towards a conclusion?

Fromm believes that, just as human history began with an act of disobedience – Eve's decision to eat the fruit against the wish of God –, so too it may end with an act of blind obedience: 'the obedience of the men who push the button to the men who give the orders, and the obedience to ideas which make it possible to think in terms of such madness' (Fromm, 1955/1992: 162). Such being the case, disobedience is more than an entitlement; it is a duty. Fromm is well aware that wishful theorizing does not suffice to give rise to the cognitive, psychological and moral bases of the socialist humanist world order he envisions. Whether or not malignant narcissism is 'so deeply ingrained in man that he will never overcome his "narcissistic core", as Freud thought' and whether or not there is 'any hope that narcissistic madness will not lead to the destruction of man before he has had a chance to become fully human' are pragmatic questions in need of answers as heads-on and concrete as possible (Fromm, 1964: 90).

How, then, to effectuate the idea of a universal human? Lilie Chouliaraki (2006) explains *ex negativo* that the highly sensationalized discourse of a universal humanity falls short. By virtue of its exclusive reliance on sensationalism, such discourse does very little to raise, let alone answer, the questions of why and what to do to eradicate destructive phenomena. It rather reinforces narcissistic sensibilities and practices, either by presuming that we – perpetrators, bystanders or unaware others – already possess a kind-heartedness in wait only for specific directions, or by framing victims as human only insofar as their stories reflect our own emotional world. Speaking *ex positivo*, the capacities of narcissists to become 'public figures' and connect to others depend on those technologies of the self that tap into their reflexivity in the sense of contemplation (Chouliaraki, 2006: 211). For television mediation to perform this pedagogical function, for instance, it must '[combine] the emphasis on emotion – which facilitates the spectators' capacity to "connect" – with an element of impersonality, which interrupts rather than reproduces their narcissism' (ibid.: 212; see also Chouliaraki, this volume). Impersonality entails the use of deliberative genres of the media in ways that foreground the distinction between the spectacle and authentic reality, and between the act of watching and the appreciation of the need to undertake ethical action.

In various writings, Fromm takes up the challenge by offering a number of suggestions, some more utopian in their applicability and effectiveness than others. In *The Heart of Man*, Fromm argues that supranational organizations should establish symbols, holidays and festivals that would help change the object of narcissism to the image of human race and its achievements. 'Not the national holiday, but the "day of man" would become the highest holiday of the year' (Fromm, 1964: 91). Concurrently, the focus of our educational effort should be to cultivate 'critical thought, objectivity, acceptance of reality, and a concept of truth which is subject to no fiat and is valid for every conceivable group' (ibid.: 92). The teaching of philosophy and anthropology, for example, would 'enable man to experience in himself all of humanity...the fact that he is a sinner and a saint, a child and an adult, a sane and an insane person, a man of the past and one of the future – that he carries within himself that which mankind has been and that which it will be' (ibid.: 93). History and geography textbooks, too, should be rewritten in ways that counter the distorted glorification of national accounts.

For these things to happen, however, all nations must first reduce their own political and economic sovereignty in favour of the sovereignty of mankind. 'A strengthened United Nations and the reasonable and peaceful solution of group conflicts are the obvious conditions for the possibility that humanity and its common achievements shall become the object of group narcissism' (ibid.: 91–92). In *To Have or to Be?*, Fromm sets out in detail a series of further measures: from prohibiting all brainwashing methods in industrial and political advertising to creating the conditions for participatory democracy, to separating scientific research from application in industry and defence, to replacing bureaucratic management with humanistic management, to liberating women from patriarchal domination, to introducing a guaranteed yearly income that would ensure real freedom and independence (see further Fromm, 1976/1997: 141–164).

Every now and then, true to his dictum that 'ideas do have an effect on man if the idea is lived by the one who teaches it; if it is personified by the teacher' (Fromm, 1981: 42), Fromm himself left his private practice as a psychoanalyst to campaign actively against the Vietnam War, the Cold War, nuclear and biological armament, hunger and sickness in the Third World and much more. For 'man can be human only in a climate in which he can expect that he and his children will live to see the next year, and many more years to come' (Fromm, 1964: 94; see further Wilde, 2004: 135–136). Despite hardly ever seeing mankind reach any closer to its great potential for productivity, Fromm's sense of hope remained unscathed throughout. As he wrote in *The Revolution of Hope* – his pugnacious response to America's dehumanized situation in 1968 –, 'to hope means to be ready at every moment for that which is not yet born, and yet not become desperate if there is no birth in our lifetime' (Fromm, 1968: 9). Fromm's utopianism was, and is, the utopianism of the 'awake', of hard-headed realists who shed all illusions and fully appreciate the difficulties (Fromm, 1976/1997: 141).

Notes

A preliminary draft of this chapter was presented at *Roots, Rites and Sites of Resistance: An International Interdisciplinary Symposium*, Institute of Criminology, University of Cambridge, 18 April 2007. Thanks are due to Tony Bottoms, Andrea Brighenti, Spiros Gangas, Jerry Gerza and John O'Neill for their constructively critical responses on the day. Later drafts benefited from the comments of Loraine Gelsthorpe, Eric Heinze, Peter Krepski, Alison Liebling, Shadd Maruna and Sappho Xenakis. Tina P. Gioka-Katsarou endorsed and encouraged my idea of grappling with Frommian thought. Needless to say, the responsibility for any shortcomings rests fully with me.

1. 'Frankfurt School' is the name commonly used to refer to the Institute for Social Research, which was founded in 1923 and constituted the major centre for critical theory during the 1930s. In the face of the dangerous political climate in antebellum Germany, the School moved first to Geneva and then to New York. Fromm was made the tenured director of the School's Social Psychology Section in 1930 and he left in 1939 (see further McLaughlin, 1999).
2. Fromm uses the male pronoun to refer to either males or females. This, according to some of his critics, does not acquit Fromm of the charge of Freudian androcentric bias (on which, see, amongst others, Ingleby, 2006: xlvii–xlviii; Brookfield, 2005: 150–151), quite the contrary. Whilst such a discussion stretches beyond the scope of this chapter, it is worth noting that, for Fromm, the archetypical act of emancipatory disobedience, indeed, the act which forced humans on the road to history, is one committed by a woman: Eve (Fromm, 1955/1992: 161). Outside quotations, I have chosen to use the male and female pronouns interchangeably throughout the chapter.
3. Here Fromm draws inspiration from Marx's distinction between the 'constant drives' and the 'relative drives' or 'desires'. Indeed, in his later work, Fromm proceeds to admit that, whilst not developed in a systematic fashion, Marx's contribution to psychology deserves greater recognition (see, for example, Fromm, 1962/2006, 1970).
4. Notwithstanding some obvious similarities, Fromm's concept of the authoritarian character should not be mistaken for its infamous cousin that is the 'authoritarian personality', put forward ten years later by Adorno and a research team he led at the Frankfurt School (see Adorno *et al.*, 1950; also Cheliotis, 2008).
5. The first part of the title I have borrowed from Milan Kundera's homonymous novel. Kundera himself borrowed the title from Rimbaud, Breton and the decked walls of the Sorbonne in May 1968.

3
Thinking after Terror: An Interreligious Challenge

Richard Kearney

One of the images broadcast on the Internet in the aftermath of 9/11 was that of a face peering through the fumes and ashes, rising like sacrificial smoke from the twin towers. This, we were ominously informed, was the visage of Bin Laden: the enemy who was there and not there. The face of an unspeakable, inexplicable, unlocateable terror which was now suddenly, mysteriously, crossing our radar screens. Here was the epitome of all those impure substances that infiltrate our being: nicotine, drugs, alcohol, the AIDS virus; or more ominously still, the anthrax powder filtering through buildings and letter boxes. Like planes slicing through air-conditioned offices of a New York high rise. Like terrorists impersonating law-abiding neighbours next door. This horror of horrors was threatening to invade the very borders of the nation, the frontiers of the state, the precincts of our cities, the walls of our homes, the skin of our bodies – spiralling into the core of our being. This was one particular phantasmagoria of terror in the wake of 9/11.

The philosopher Spinoza offered this counsel in the face of enigma: 'Do not complain, do not rejoice, try to understand'. But how are we to understand Bin Laden and Al Qaeda? How do we even begin to attempt to get into the minds of those who slaughtered so many innocents on that fateful morning in Manhattan? It is hard to proffer some response without sounding homiletic, naïve or downright insensitive. But one thing that must surely be clear at this stage is that the inflated apocalyptic language used by both sides in this aggression has not helped. In fact, I will argue that it has led to a double impoverishment of our politics and our spirituality. Let me begin with a brief account of the apocalyptic demonizing of the enemy which occurred in the wake of 9/11 before endeavouring to sketch some tentative responses from the perspective of religion.

In the aftermath of terror

The initial response of President Bush was to carve the world into good and evil. In the days immediately following the terror, he declared a 'crusade' against the evil scourge of terrorism. He cited his Second World War predecessor, President Roosevelt, invoking the 'warm courage of unity' that possesses a nation at war. And reaching further back into the missionary history of American warfare, Bush quoted the famous Wild West phrase that the outlaw (Bin Laden) should be brought in 'dead or alive'. Manifest Destiny was back with a vengeance. There was much use of religious idioms of apocalypse and purification. Terms like 'sacrifice' and 'purge' were frequently heard and the military campaign launched against the enemy was initially called 'Campaign Infinite Justice' (later altered, because offensive to Muslims, to 'Enduring Freedom'). War had been declared and everyone, as Bush made plain, had to 'take sides': for the 'civilized' or the 'barbarians'; for the innocent or the damned; for the courageous or the 'cowards'.

Most mainstream media responded in kind. Images of apocalypse were commonplace. One commentator spoke of the attackers as many-headed beasts whose tentacles were threatening to violate every secure space in the Nation. Another invoked the image of a fearsome incubus invading the free world. Idioms of virus, poison, pollution, disease and contamination were variously deployed to express the sense of an omnipresent menace – especially when the terror *from* the air was accompanied by terror *in* the air: the fear of anthrax, smallpox and other agents of bio-chemical destruction. Fear filtered through the land. Yet the flip side of this was a phenomenal upsurge of patriotic fervour evidenced in the proliferation of star-spangled banners and typified in the 24 September cover headline of *Time* magazine – 'One Nation, Indivisible'. This sentiment was emotively evoked in an anonymous street poem, entitled 'We Are One', written over a picture of the US Flag and posted in a store window situated beside Ground Zero in New York. It read: 'We stand behind our Country/We stand behind our Faith/And Pray that in our Future/Our Flag will stand and Wave'.

President Bush reinforced this notion of a single Nation united in war against barbarism when he delivered a broadcast address on 8 November, wrapping up with this rousing military summons: 'We wage a war to save Civilization itself.... We have our marching orders. Fellow Americans, Let's Roll!' As the philosopher, Paul Virilio, remarked in *Ground Zero:* 'On September 11, 2001, the Manhattan skyline became the front of a new war' (Virilio, 2002: 182).

Al Qaeda deployed even more emphatically apocalyptic terms. The issue was not in doubt – *apocalyptic war*. In messages broadcast on Al-Jazeera satellite television, Bin Laden summoned all Muslims to embrace the ultimate battle between good and evil, demonizing America as the Great Satan and Israel as the Little Satan. He called on the Islamic faithful throughout the world to join a Jihad or holy war (the traditional Islamic counter-term to 'crusade') and denounced the American campaign against the Taliban as a 'terrorist Christian crusade'. Bin Laden went on to castigate the Pakistan government for 'standing beneath the Christian banner', provoking wide-scale riots in that country and prompting thousands of Pakistani tribesmen to cross over the border to join the Taliban. Al Qaeda insisted that any Muslim who supported the US-led military alliance in any way was 'an apostate of Islam'. And one found many propaganda statements replete with references to the US and its allies as monsters, dragons and other demonic beasts who needed to be purged from the earth through acts of sacrificial violence, so that the world may be made 'holy' again.

In both these rhetorics – though I am not proposing a moral equivalency here – we witnessed a disturbing tendency to endorse the dualist thesis that divides the world schismatically into West and East. This echoed the 'Clash of Civilizations' scenario, famously outlined by Samuel Huntington in the summer 1993 issue of *Foreign Affairs*, and subsequently republished as a best-selling book in 1996. Here one found a vivid schema of the West-versus-Islam dichotomy, making for what Edward Said (2001) has called a 'cartoonlike world where Popeye and Bluto bash each other mercilessly, with one always more virtuous pugilist getting the upper hand over his adversary'. Such caricature totally ignored the plurality, complexity and interdependence of each civilization.[1] A crude mythico-religious terminology of *pure versus impure* took precedence over a more reasoned discourse about justice and injustice. It must be said, of course, that, despite the dualist metaphors, some members of US government went to considerable lengths – after Bush's 'Crusade' gaffe – to make clear that this was *not* a war against Islam. So doing they were concurring with the wise counsel of intellectuals like Alan Wolfe (2001) that '[t]he more we think that what is at stake is a clash of civilizations, the more like our enemy we become'.

To the extent that such rhetorics promulgate the notion of religious war, it has to be admitted that this is religious war with a *difference*. That is to say, it is a postmodern religious war. First, as even Secretary Rumsfeld himself admitted, this would not be just a conventional war fought with tanks and bombs, but a cyber-war fought with computers and information flows. In short, it would be a credit war: a war of credit cards, credit transfers and, above all, credibility in the sense of belief and persuasion. A war of psycho-propaganda (Psy-Ops). 'The uniforms of this conflict will be bankers' pinstripes and programmers' grunge just as assuredly as desert camouflage', said Rumsfeld. 'Even the vocabulary of this war will be different. When we "invade the enemy's territory", we may well be invading his cyberspace. There may not be as many beachheads stormed as opportunities denied'. (There are echoes here, curiously, of Jean Baudrillard's thesis that contemporary war is TV war).

But if the battle was shifting from hardware to soft-war, as it increasingly virtualized and immaterialized the weapons of engagement, it was also shifting from a battle conducted exclusively on foreign territory – like all of American's interstate wars since 1812 – to one also fought *within* US national territory. With the alarming introduction of so-called 'weaponized' anthrax, an almost invisible toxin of corrosion and death, the Pentagon was compelled to 'shuffle its command' (as a front page headline in the *Boston Globe* put it on 27 October). The military spotlight was now on 'home soil'. This division of the battle into 'overseas' and 'domestic' had radical repercussions. Once again, Secretary Rumsfeld had to change gear, appointing a pair of military commanders with additional responsibilities for defending US territory and considering the option of a permanent 'homeland' defence command. Up to this point, the US military's defence focus was on guarding the borders and protecting the country from *external* threats. But this response to the unprecedented threat of bio-terrorism sparked a nervous debate in Washington over the extent to which the active-duty military should be involved in domestic 'civil defence'.

With the arrival of the anthrax scare, another front opened up. War against terror was now being fought, as mentioned above, both inside and outside the national borders. And, in the process, borderlines themselves became blurred and undecidable. The Minotaur, the horror, evil itself, was now within 'US' – inhaled like imperceptible spores of anthrax into the body politic – as well as 'somewhere out there', in THEM. Moreover, the difficulty of tracking down the culprits in their cellars or caves – due to the continuing elusiveness of the enemy – was further exacerbating the sense of uncanny anxiety. Al Qaeda was proving to be as invasive as anthrax itself. In significant part, this was a war of disturbingly protean substances: a deadly game of smoke and mirrors. Nightly TV images showed grey fumes still smouldering from the subterranean bowels of Ground Zero or rising up from the bombarded front-lines of the Taliban. While the mirrors became the Bush–Bin Laden game of satellite images and counter-images, bouncing back and forth across the global air-waves. The war of terror had indeed entered the digital realms of cyberspace. In a curious echo of the choral ode of *Antigone* on uncanniness, the postmodern warrior had found himself trapped in a labyrinthine web: 'with no way out (*aporos*) he comes to nothing' (Greisch, 2002).

A major documentary on George W. Bush's apocalyptic mentality entitled 'The Jesus Factor', broadcast on 'Frontline' in April 2004, confirmed that the President's evangelical relationship with Jesus was no longer just a matter of personal salvation, but a global battle between good and evil. And there was no doubt whatsoever in the President's mind as to which side the Messiah was on. His disciples in the Pentagon plainly agreed, as evidenced in Lieutenant General William G. Boykin's much-publicized declaration of theological superiority *vis-à-vis* the rival God of the Muslim enemy: 'I knew that my God was bigger than his.... My God was a real God, and his was an idol'.[2] The rest was silence... until the bombs dropped.

But the sacrificial-demonic scenario did not end with the invasion of Iraq. The heinous abuse of enemy prisoners, in Iraq military camps and the Guantanamo Bay penitentiary, was also symptomatic of the apocalyptic vision. Many of those tortured belonged to the telling category of 'unlawful combatants', deprived of the legal status of either 'political prisoner' or 'common criminal'. And in the case of Guantanamo, there was the additional factor that, in being 'de-territorialized' – that is, transplanted thousands of miles from the local battlefields of the Middle-East to an army camp in the Caribbean –, they could be not only deprogrammed, but dehumanized. These prisoners were no longer recognized citizens of a recognized state, nation or community. They were placeless nobodies entitled to no legal or constitutional protection. Indeed the Red Cross reported that 70–90 per cent of those held appeared to have committed no crime other than being in the wrong place at the wrong time when the 'sweep of suspects' occurred. The main reason for their being held was not, so it seemed, punishment for crimes but for 'interrogation' purposes.

Writing of such abuse, Susan Sontag offered this observation:

> The notion that apologies or professions of 'disgust' by the president and the secretary of defence are a sufficient response is an insult to one's historical and moral sense. The torture of prisoners is not an aberration. It is a direct consequence of the with-us-or-against-us doctrine of world struggle with which the Bush administration has

sought to change, change radically, the international stance of the US and to recast many domestic institutions and prerogatives. The Bush administration has committed the country to a pseudo-religious doctrine of war, endless war – for 'the war on terror' is nothing less than that. Endless war is taken to justify endless incarcerations. Those held in the extralegal American penal empire are 'detainees'; 'prisoners', a newly obsolete word, might suggest that they have the rights accorded by international law and the laws of all civilized countries. This endless 'global war on terrorism' – into which both the quite justified invasion of Afghanistan and the unwinnable folly in Iraq have been folded by Pentagon decree – inevitably leads to the demonizing and dehumanizing of anyone declared by the Bush administration to be a possible terrorist: a definition that is not up for debate and is, in fact, usually made in secret.

(Sontag, 2004)

Sontag goes on to conclude that if 'interrogation' is the main point of detaining prisoners indefinitely, 'then physical coercion, humiliation, and torture become inevitable' (ibid.).

The us-versus-them strategy is not, of course, new. Rene Girard traces the origins of apocalyptic scapegoating of adversaries back to the origins of all sacrificial religions, where the need to separate 'pure' from 'impure' is paramount. Many communities in crisis and conflict reach for some kind of binding consensus by choosing to direct their violent aggression towards an 'outsider'. The ritual humiliation and immolation of this threatening alien then provides the divided community with a renewed sense of unity and mission: a miraculous (if perverse) catharsis. Julia Kristeva adds a psychoanalytic perspective on this process in her study of sacrificial fear and abjection in *Powers of Horror*. And many modern thinkers as different as Carl Schmitt, Jacques Derrida and Slavoj Žižek, have recognized the deeply political implications of the Same–Other polarization in the waging of both psychological and physical warfare.

Commenting on Schmitt's famous 'friend/enemy' model, Žižek applies this scenario to the current compulsion to put a face on terror, to translate its invisible and ineffable dimension into some kind of visage:

> The lesson to be learnt here... is that the divide friend/enemy is never just the representation of a factual difference: the enemy is by definition, always – up to a point, at least – *invisible*... he cannot be directly

recognized – this is the big problem and task of the political struggle in providing/constructing a recognizable *image* of the enemy.

(Žižek, 2002: 109–110)

Žižek goes on to argue that 'enemy recognition' is invariably a performative procedure which, like Kant's notion of the transcendental power of imagination (*Einbildungskraft*), 'schematizes' our experience of the Other (alien, stranger, monster, adversary, demon), thereby furnishing it with 'concrete tangible features which make it an appropriate target of hatred and struggle' (ibid.: 110). Žižek addresses the emergence of Bin Laden as follows:

> After 1990, and the collapse of the Communist states which provided the figure of the Cold War enemy, the Western power of imagination entered a decade of confusion and inefficiency, looking for suitable 'schematizations' for the figure of the Enemy, sliding from narco-cartel bosses to a succession of warlords of so-called 'rogue states' (Saddam, Noriega, Aidid, Milosovic...), without stabilizing itself in one central image; only with September 11 did this imagination regain its power by constructing the image of Osama Bin Laden, the Islamic fundamentalist *par excellence*, and Al-Qaeda, his 'invisible' network. What this means, furthermore, is that our pluralistic and tolerant liberal democracies remain deeply 'Schmittian': they continue to rely on the political *Einbildungskraft* to provide them with the appropriate figure which reveals the invisible Enemy. Far from suspending the 'binary' logic Friend/Enemy, the fact that this Enemy is defined as the fundamentalist opponent of pluralistic tolerance simply adds a reflexive twist to it. Of course, the price of this 'renormalisation' is that the figure of the Enemy undergoes a fundamental change: it is no longer the Evil Empire, that is, another territorial entity (a state or group of states), but an illegal, secret – almost virtual – worldwide network in which lawlessness (criminality) coincides with 'fundamentalist' ethicoreligious fanaticism – and since this entity has no positive legal status, this new configuration entails the end of the international law which – at least from the onset of modernity – regulated relations between states.

(ibid.: 111)

The anthrax scare dramatized by the media in the wake of 9/11 and the convenient morphing of Bin Laden (disappeared in his cave) into

Saddam Hussein (caught in his cave), were further instances of how the invisible/visible dialectic unfolds. Unimaginable terror calls out for images in order to keep the game of hide-and-seek going indefinitely. Now you see it, now you don't. Now here, now gone. *Fort/Da*: one of the oldest games in the world that never seems to lose its fascination for the human mind. Bush played right into Bin Laden's court as the latter began to assume quasi-mystical proportions – going up in the holy/unholy smoke, rising from the towering inferno of New York. And his magical morphings, reincarnations and sightings did not end there. As the philosopher Jean Baudrillard dramatically put it in his commentary on 9/11, *The Spirit of Terrorism*: 'A (key) aspect of the terrorists' victory is that all other forms of violence and the destabilization of order work in its favour. Internet terrorism, biological terrorism, the terrorism of anthrax and rumour – all are ascribed to Bin Laden. He might even claim natural catastrophes as his own. All the forms of disorganization and perverse circulation operate to his advantage' (Baudrillard, 2002: 33).

In citing the examples above, however, one can never repeat enough how the slaughter of 9/11 – not to mention subsequent heinous acts of beheading hostages and systematic suicide bombing – is irrefutable evidence of just how far the 'terrorists' themselves are prepared to go in the game of apocalyptic demonization. The larger point is that, whichever side of the US/THEM polarity one chooses to explore, the fact remains that such Armageddon scenarios signal an impoverishment of both our politics and our theology. In the remaining part of this chapter, I want to look at some ways in which we might begin to respond to this double impoverishment by exploring new resources within our spiritual cultures.

The power of wisdom traditions

How do we overcome the terror of 9/11? How do we mourn the loss? How do we work through the trauma? How do we even begin to imagine pardoning Bin Laden? How do we transform hate into love? War into peace? Before I try to respond to these questions, let me first acknowledge the huge difficulties involved.

Christopher Hitchens, writing on the first anniversary of the atrocities, offers this powerful defence of war as the only appropriate remedy:

> [I]t is impossible to compromise with proponents of sacrificial killing of civilians, with the disseminators of anti-Semitic filth, with the

violators of women and the cheerful murderers of children. It is equally impossible to compromise with stone-faced propagandists for Bronze Age morality: morons and philistines who hate Darwin and Einstein and who managed, during their brief rule of Afghanistan, to erase music and art while cultivating their skills at germ warfare.

(cited by Dooley, 2003: 335)

This is strong, if emotive, stuff. An even more vehement justification of this line of thinking is offered by the philosopher Mark Dooley, who pushes Hitchens's logic to an all-out apologia for violence as the most fitting response to terror. The good-versus-evil scenario could hardly find a more articulate advocate:

When faced with the likes of Al Qaeda, our response should not be to look for sophistication and theory in order to 'understand' what it is we are dealing with. Rather, a better response may, in fact, be the one that Bush propounded. ... In this case, it really is a good old-fashioned fight between good and evil, which is why Bush was quite justified in using the rhetoric of the 'evil scourge of terrorism' to describe Bin Laden's hideous activities.

(Ibid.)

Dooley concludes: 'Neither neutrality nor pacificism are luxuries we can afford in our dealings with this particular monster, given its odious ambition to destroy everything, even our children' (ibid.: 335–357).

Persuasively put. But if that is the only adequate response to terror and 'evil' (I have no quarrel with this designation to describe 9/11), then it is hard to convince our 'enemy' – in this case, Al Qaeda and its associated terrorist movements – that there is another way of responding to what *they* consider to be the 'terror' and 'evil' inflicted on them by us. One does not, of course, have to fall into moral relativism or equivalency here. One does not have to endorse Bin Laden's lurid apocalypticism to try to persuade him and his many supporters that there is another way, besides bombs and blood, to work through anger and aggression. However much we are appalled by Al Qaeda's logic of demonization – and the atrocious acts which follow from it –, surely one of the *worst* ways to respond is by demonizing the demonizers in turn! That is very understandable in the immediacy of the moment, after one's loved ones are butchered, violated, tortured, murdered. But is it the wisest mode of reaction in the long term, or the most *effective*? There is a long history of wisdom traditions in the world which suggests otherwise. And it is to some examples of this history that I now turn by way of offering an alternative to the Bush–Bin Laden logics (for they are specific in each case) of moral fundamentalism.

The common phrase 'Wisdom Traditions' applies to most of the world's great religions. It refers to the widely held view that certain profound spiritual teachings and practices can guide us to tolerance, that is, to a more peaceful, compassionate and just life beyond the violence and rivalry of power politics. The pioneering Benedictine monk, Bede Griffiths, writes about this parallelism (but not syncretism) of wisdom traditions in his Christian commentary on the Bhagavad Gita entitled *River of Compassion*. Referring specifically to the 'holy history of India', where he spent most of his life as spiritual director of an Ashram, Griffiths comments:

> It is really remarkable how one can see this new understanding, this conception of a personal God, coming to light a little before the time of Christ. I think that it is a movement that took place in many parts of the world, not simply in Israel. There was an advance both in Buddhism with its idea of the *bodhisattva* and in Hinduism with the idea of a personal God as the embodiment of love and compassion, these developments taking place at about the same time. We realise that God is revealing himself in many ways, not only to Israel but to India, to China, and to (so-called) primitive people also.
>
> (Griffiths, 1995: 117)

In more practical terms, this spiritual wisdom translates into a certain 'middle way' of prudent judgement, discriminating discernment and right action. When it comes to the primary qualities that lead to wisdom, Griffiths points out, these are largely universal and can be found alike in Christianity, Judaism, Islam, Buddhism, Hinduism and so on. In the Vedantic tradition, as presented in Chapter 13 of the Gita, these include the virtues of non-fearful non-violence (*ahimsa*) issuing in the ultimate good of forgiving toleration (*kshanti*), so central to the life of the wise person (*sannyasi*).

Griffiths explains:

> Harmlessness (*ahimsa*) is the virtue which Gandhi made the basis of his life and philosophy, but it is fundamental also for a *sannyasi*. It is said that a *sannyasi* is not afraid of anyone and no one is afraid of him. It is not simply negative in the sense of 'not killing', but it is a whole attitude of mind involving freedom from aggression. Then there is *Kshanti* – 'forgiveness', 'forbearance', or 'tolerance'. This is

central to St. Paul's list of virtues in the letter to the Colossians, with which this whole passage can be compared.

(Col. 3.1, 13)

It is also at the very heart of Gandhi's teaching on non-violent resistance (*satyagraha*). 'Nonviolence is the greatest force at the disposal of mankind', wrote Gandhi. 'It is mightier than the mightiest weapon of destruction devised by the ingenuity of man' (Tolstoy, 1984: 116).

One finds similar wisdom teachings on non-violence in the Buddhist tradition. The Mahayana school, for example, recommends 'four boundless attitudes' – namely, unconditional love (*maitri*), compassion (*karu*), sympathy (*mudit*) and equanimity (*upek*) – as the most effective response to violence. It identifies the construction of a demonic enemy as a projection of our minds resulting from non-virtuous *karma*. The Buddhist scholar, John Makransky, explains the cycle of vengeance, aggression and scapegoating in the following contemporary language:

> For example, in a moment of intense anger at someone, very quickly a narrow, inaccurate image of self and other is projected (e.g., oneself as simply the righteous wronged one, the other as simply a demonic being). That projection is accompanied by a painful mental feeling. From that projection and feeling, the emotive energy of rage takes shape in the wish to hurt the other by word or physical action. That invention, and any actions following from it, are an example of non-virtuous karma. Karma is activity of mind and body reacting to one's own thought-made projections of self and other, unaware that the projections have been mistaken for the actualities. As we react in that way, it is taught, we make new karma, i.e., further imprint the habit of experiencing the world through our own projections and reacting to them unawares.
>
> (Makransky, 2003: 337)

By a practice of skilful means (*upaya-kaushalya*), the Buddhist seeks to overcome the limits of the friend or enemy distinction, eventually embracing a position of 'no enemies'. The process goes something like this. Diagnosis:

> In the moment we falsely apprehend 'enemy' (not as a thought construct projected upon another person, but as an object inherently deserving of hatred), we feel hatred, act from hatred, and the conditioned arising of suffering goes on. Until we discern the emptiness of

our moment by moment construction of reality, we reify our representations of it, cling to them unawares, grasp to some, hate others, and suffer.

(Ibid.: 348)

Prognosis:

Compassion for all beings caught in the subtle confusion that reifies and clings to representations, who suffer for it in all realms of rebirth, is called 'universal compassion' (*maha-karuna*). Transcendental wisdom (*prajna-paramita*), by seeing through that confusion into its empty, thought-constructed nature, realizes freedom from it, eliciting even more intense compassion for all who are caught in it. Thus, transcendental wisdom and compassion, mutually empowering, are cultivated in synergy on the Bahisattva path to full enlightenment.

(Ibid.: 348)

And this is not some naïve piety. It actually *works*. The most useful and practical way of protecting oneself and one's loved ones from violence is, the Buddhist saint Shantideva taught, 'to practice exchanging self for other, the great mystery' (cited by Makransky, 2004).

The teachings of peace-activists like Tich Nhat Hahn (Vietnam), Aung San Suu Kyi (Burma) and the Dalai Lama (Tibet) epitomize this practice of non-violence. What each of these figures shows is that Buddhist wisdom is not just an attitude of non-violence professed by 'beautiful souls', but also a matter of *efficacity*. These are not aloof spiritual mandarins, but politically effective activists. Just like Gandhi in the Hindu tradition of non-violence, or people like Martin Luther King and Terence McSwiney in the Christian tradition – peace-makers who offered their own lives so that their world might be radically transformed. And it was. Gandhi liberated India; McSwiney and fellow martyrs led the way for Irish emancipation; Martin Luther King brought about Civil Rights for Blacks; and spiritual founders like Jesus, the Buddha and Socrates changed the entire nature of their world by choosing to suffer violence rather than inflict it on others.

These are powerful testimonies – and there are many others – to the fact that peace is more powerful and more efficacious than the most heavily equipped armies. Right is greater than might. It is not really surprising to find such suggestive intersections between the different wisdom traditions, given the insights of so many of the great spiritual mystics that God is ultimately one even as the ways to God are many. The earliest Vedic scripture, *Rigveda*, suggests as much when it states that 'to what is One, sages give many names' (1.164.46). And one finds similar convictions being expressed within the Christian tradition as when, for example, Saint Martin observes that 'all mystics speak the same language since they all come from the same country' (Underhill, 1974: 80; see also Myladil, 2000; Saux, 1998; Clooney, 2000). Such a belief is deeply resistant to the triumphalist dogma of fundamentalism, which claims that only one's own particular religion is legitimate.

In the biblical tradition, this wisdom revelation is powerfully manifest in the three books of Solomon the wise ruler, namely, Proverbs, Ecclesiastes and the Song of Songs. What is striking about these books is how they manage to convey the heritage of wisdom through particular narratives and metaphors. This mode of wisdom is deeply figurative, communicating in multi-layered 'figures of speech'. Indeed, the third and final book of Solomon's wisdom, the Song of Songs, is so richly symbolic in meaning as a marriage-drama of bride and bridegroom, that it has provoked the hermeneutic imagination of many great thinkers. These include early Church Fathers like Origen, Gregory of Nyssa and Maximus the Confessor, medieval commentators in both the Christian and Jewish traditions, celebrated mystics like Bernard of Clairvaux, Theresa of Lisieux and John of the Cross, and, more recently, such contemporary philosophers as Paul Ricoeur, Andre LaCoque and Julia Kristeva. The polysemantic resources of the Canticles are hermeneutically inexhaustible.

This is a wisdom that does not translate easily into *theoria*, the abstract propositions of purely scientific and mathematical knowledge. It calls rather for a special exercise of practical wisdom, what Aristotle called *phronesis*, capable of articulating a more provisional, tentative, approximate mode of understanding, open to multiple interpretations and applications (which does not mean limitless relativism). Above all, this mode of phronetic understanding is capable of negotiating a medial position between the claims of universality and particularity, thereby conjoining the all-inclusive claims of timeless *sophia* with the more specific claims of temporal faith traditions – Biblical, Buddhist, Hindu and so on; and each of these wisdom traditions, in turn, possesses its own special historicity of production, transmission, translation and reception. Whether the nuptial poetics of the Song of Songs are really about the relation between Israel and Yahweh, the Soul and Christ, the Church and the Father, or simply a love-sick fiancée and her long-awaited lover, is a matter of interpretation.

Because these, and several other meanings, are not just allowed, but actually solicited by the pluralist potencies of this wisdom text, we find here a powerful example of hermeneutic tolerance. As the Talmudic rabbis liked to remind us, each line of this wisdom story calls for at least ten different readings! Moreover, the fact that the books of Solomonic wisdom are committed to a particular blending of the moral and the aesthetic, again confirms their proximity to the Greek notion of *phronesis*, which comprises these same dual functions. The advantage of this double duty of ethics-poetics is that religious wisdom is not allowed to become either too moralistic (ethics without poetics) or too arbitrary (poetics without ethics). The proper balance between these two wisdom functions promises, I would suggest, a reliable recipe of toleration, religious or otherwise (see also Chouliaraki, this volume).

However, the poetics of the Song of Solomon also call for an ethic of generosity to the extent that it portrays a deity who is vulnerable, that is, dependent on humanity for love. This theo-erotic drama between human and divine lovers reveals a God who needs humans, who calls out to his finite lovers to be made flesh, incarnate, embodied. Far from the power politics of omnipotence, the Solomonic bringer of wisdom is, to use Joyce's expression, a 'bringer of plurabilities', a harbinger of infinite reference, allusion and association. This is the God who *may be in the flesh of history* only if we say yes to the call of love and justice. A God of little things, of the least of these, of mustard seeds and yearnings and longings of the heart. A God desperate to desire and be desired, to love and be loved, to transfigure and be transfigured, to say and be said in many different ways to many different people. A God of infinite tolerance far removed from the totalizing metaphysics of omnipotence and omniscience. A God, in short, of radical non-violence (see further Dillard, 1999).

The biblical art of polysemy was not confined to rabbinical and talmudic traditions. Within Christian traditions, too, we find a radical commitment to the Middle Way – what elsewhere I call 'diacritical interpretation', that is, discernment of signs between opposite extremes (Kearney, 2003). Jesus did indeed claim, true to his monotheistic heritage, that he was the 'way, the truth and the life'. But he never claimed to be the *only* way, the *only* truth and the *only* life. Indeed, had Jesus done so, he would, arguably, have disqualified himself from his avowed role as Lord of all-embracing love. One only has to recall such narrative scenes as the exchange with the Samaritan woman at the well, or the healing of the sick on the Sabbath, or the writing in the sand during the trial of the woman taken in adultery, to appreciate what an extraordinary master of hermeneutic tolerance – and ethical toleration – Jesus was. We sometimes forget that Jesus took great care never to *write anything*, except those discreet words in the sand that resisted murder. And when some of his words were eventually committed to writing, the Spirit that likes to blow where it will made sure there were a healthy plurality of scribes and witnesses (four at the very least) to translate it. Jesus's word was revealed by love rather than dogma – as is dramatically illustrated in his sharing of bread with the disciples at Emmaus *before* 'their eyes were opened and they recognized him'. Only after love do they receive *retrospectively* the wisdom he revealed to them 'when he opened the Scriptures' to them on the road from Jerusalem (Luke 24). In other words, the wisdom attested to by Christ, as by the Jewish prophets before him, was one of embodied action which subsequently called out for an endless hermeneutics of attentive interpretation and translation.

The followers, Peter and Paul, also testified to the tolerant wisdom of the Middle Way in the famous compromise of the Jerusalem Conference. This was a crucial meeting of opposed minds, a negotiated settlement between those who wanted to keep Christianity as a local movement within Judaism (James and Peter) and those who wanted to break all such historical ties and open up a purely spiritual universalism (Paul and the Gentiles). The conference was a historic *combinatio oppositorum* which set the tone for an open and flexible legacy within Judeo-Christian monotheism – a way of acknowledging that, if God is indeed One, there are many different paths leading to this Oneness. In his recent book, *Saint Paul: The Foundation of Universalism*, Alain Badiou sums up the importance of the Jerusalem accord:

> By allowing Paul's (universalist) action to develop at the same time as that of Judeo-Christians of strict observance, the Jerusalem conference ultimately prevents Christianity from becoming a Jewish sect, another precarious scission (in the wake of many others). But in curbing the zeal of those Gentile-Christians hostile to Judaism, and perhaps that of Paul himself, it prevented Christianity from being merely a new illuminism, one just as precarious because devoid of all basis in historical Judaism. The Jerusalem conference is genuinely foundational, because it endows Christianity with a twofold principle of opening and historicity. It thereby holds tight to the thread of the event (Christ's incarnation and resurrection) as initiation of a truth procedure. That the event is new should never let us forget that it is such only with respect to a determinate situation, wherein it mobilizes the elements of its site.
>
> (Badiou 2003: 25)

If something analogous to this hermeneutic tolerance were to be applied to the opposition between Palestinians and Israelis in today's Jerusalem, or Catholics and Protestants in Belfast, or Christians and Muslims in Bosnia, might it not be possible to imagine such intractable hostilities coming to an end? For the Jerusalem formula allows one to remain faithful to one's particular identity while expressing equal fidelity to a common vision of love and justice. This is something which should not be so inconceivable for Muslims, Christians and Jews since, as noted, all claim allegiance to the same monotheistic deity. (Even Bush and Bin Laden, let us not forget, invoke a common Abrahamic heritage.) We have discussed this in relation to Jewish and Christian sources; but we have said little or nothing yet on Islamic sources. It is surely timely, then, at this point in our review of possible religious responses to 9/11, to recall just how central to the Koran are the notions of non-aggression, charity and hospitality to strangers. One need only cite here the importance of the notion of *Ihsan* – referring to exalted spiritual actions of profound beauty, love, growth and human connection, and praised in the Koran prayer 'Allah loves those who do Ihsan' – to realize the deep resources for non-violent resistance within the Islamic tradition. A brief look at the life of Khan Abdul Ghaffar Khan, whom Gandhi praised as his teacher in non-violence, offers a powerful testimony to the power of this deeply cherished Muslim principle. The promotion of the practice of *Ihsan* is crucial for the reformist movement of Salafi Islam even as it is all too often ignored and betrayed by many in the Jihadi movement (from which Bin Laden hails) whose absolutism and exclusivism denounce all reformist tendencies as idolatry.

To assist in the task of tolerance between adversaries, another crucial function of phronetic wisdom might be called into play here, that of exchanging readings with other traditions (Ricoeur, 1996: 3–14). The more Muslims, Jews and Christians (to speak only of the biblical heritage) can learn to re-tell and re-narrate their own versions of sacred history and exchange them with their rival opponents, the more likely they are to discover that each has a history of suffering and persecution, of bondage and exodus, of death and rebirth, and that, in many instances, they actually share the same founding Abrahamic narratives of commemoration. Thomas Mann made a powerful point about this exchange of wisdom memories in his rewriting of the Exodus stories in *Joseph and his Brothers*, a novel written in the middle of the Second War World. His aim was to remind his fellow Germans that the Nazi hatred of Jews was a total betrayal of the narrative wisdom traditions commonly shared by Christianity and Judaism. And this argument has been reiterated in different ways since by other advocates of narrative tolerance such as Hannah Arendt, Franz Rosensweig and Paul Ricoeur.

What is true of interreligious dialogue between the Abrahamic faiths – so travestied in the apocalyptic distortions of Bush and Bin Laden – is, equally, perhaps even more, the case when we come to interreligious exchanges with non-biblical traditions. I strongly believe that the voice of the 'stranger' adds hugely to the reading of one's own wisdom tradition. It is often 'by indirection that we find direction out'. In other words, it is frequently by means of hermeneutic detours through foreign and unfamiliar perspectives that the wisdom of one's own particular heritage is most powerfully revealed to us. I think of Bede Griffiths' reading of the Bhagavad Gita, the Dalai Lama's reading of the Gospels, Chiraqi's translation of Saint John's Gospel, Tich Nhat Hahn's reading of the Bible, Thomas Merton's reading of Taoist and Buddhist scriptures and so on. So often it is the voice that comes from the wilderness, from the outside, from a land and language alien to our own, which reveals us to ourselves – sometimes as the thinnest and smallest of voices. If only we have ears to hear its wisdom. Is that not why, in the Song of Songs, the Shulamite woman desires Solomon and Solomon desires her? And is it not why, in the Gospels, the Samaritan woman listens to Jesus and Jesus listens to her?

For a hermeneutic of tolerance

Let me conclude with some remarks on the hermeneutic of tolerance sketched out by my friend and mentor, Paul Ricoeur. Such a hermeneutic would provide, first, a basis for an *ethic of narrative hospitality* which involves 'taking responsibility in imagination and in sympathy for the story of the other, through the life narratives which concern the other' (Ricoeur, 7). In the cross-over of testimonies and memories between people of different religious traditions we might witness a salutary transference and translation permitting us to welcome the story of the other, the stranger, the victim, the forgotten one. Second, such hermeneutic tolerance solicits an *ethic of narrative flexibility*. Religions constantly face the challenge of resisting the reification of a founding religious event (Creation, Incarnation, Revelation, Enlightenment, Theophany, Manifestation, Sermon, Martyrdom) into a fixed dogma. The best way of doing this would be to show how each event may be told in different ways by different generations and by different narrators.

Not that everything thereby becomes relative and arbitrary. On the contrary, acts of foundational religious suffering, for example, call out for compassion and justice, and the best way of achieving this is often to invite empathy with strangers and adversaries by allowing for a plurality of narrative perspectives. The resulting overlap may thus lead to what Gadamer calls a 'fusion of horizons', where diverse horizons of consciousness and conscience may at last find some common ground (Gadamer, 1975): a reciprocal transfer between opposite minds. 'The identity of a group, culture, people, or nation, is not that of an immutable substance', writes Ricoeur, 'nor that of a fixed structure, but that, rather, of a recounted story'. A hermeneutic exchange of stories effectively resists arrogant conceptions of religious cultural identity, which prevent us from perceiving the radical implications of the principle of narrativity, namely, 'the possibilities of revising every story which has been handed down and of carving out a place for several stories directed towards the same past' (Ricoeur, 1996: 7). This mode of attentiveness to stories other than our own might be said to consort well with the virtue of detachment (the stage in yoga called *pratyahara*) vis-à-vis one's own obsessive attachment to what is 'mine' and 'ours'. It is such a practice that Christian and Muslim fundamentalists who propagate the language of apocalyptic absolutism – before and after 9/11 – could heed instead.

This leads us to a third tolerance principle, that of *narrative plurality*. Pluralism here does not mean lack of respect for the singularity and uniqueness of a particular religious event. It might even be said to increase our sense of awareness of such singularity, especially if it is foreign to us in time, space or cultural provenance. '*Recounting differently* is not inimical to a certain historical reverence to the extent that the inexhaustible richness of the event is honored by the diversity of stories which are made of it, and by the competition to which that diversity gives rise' (ibid.: 8).[3] Multiple perspectives need not betray the concrete specificity of a confessional event; on the contrary, they may eloquently testify to its exfoliating richness and inexhaustible suggestiveness. And this faithful testimony may, in fact, be deepened as we extend the circle of reference to include further perspectives from other religious confessions. Ricoeur adds this critical point:

> The ability to recount the founding events of our (religious) history in different ways is reinforced by the exchange of cultural memories. This ability to exchange has as a touchstone the will to share symbolically and respectfully in the commemoration of the founding events of other cultures, as well as those of their ethnic minorities and their minority religious denominations.
>
> (Ibid.: 9)

This point applies as much to events of pain and trauma as to events of grace and epiphany. And 9/11 may well serve, in time, as another such watershed 'foundational' event. The jury is still out.

A fourth feature of hermeneutic tolerance is the *transfiguring of the past*. This involves a creative retrieval of the betrayed promises of history, so that we may respond to our 'debt to the dead' and endeavour to give them a voice. The goal of tolerant testimonies is, therefore, to try to give a future to the past by remembering it in a more attentive way, both ethically and poetically. A crucial aspect of reinterpreting traditions is the task of discerning past promises which have *not yet* been honoured. For 'the past is not only what is bygone – that which has taken place and can no longer be changed –, it also lives in the memory thanks to arrows of futurity which have not been fired or whose trajectory has been interrupted' (ibid.: 8; see also Ricoeur, 2004a: 5–11, 12–17; 2004b). In other words, the unfulfilled future of the past may well signal the richest dimension of a religious tradition, for example, Islamic, Christian, Jewish. And the emancipation of 'this unfulfilled future of the past is the major benefit that we can expect from the crossing of memories and the exchange of narratives' (Ricoeur, 1996: 8; see also Gross and Muck, 2002; Tyagananda, 2000).

It is especially the founding events of a religious community – traumatic or revelatory – which require to be reread in this critical manner in order to unlock the potencies and expectancies which the subsequent unfolding of history may have forgotten or betrayed. Fundamentalism, of whatever confession, is another term for such betrayal. This is why hermeneutic tolerance involves a special acoustic, a particular practice of auditory imagination attuned to certain seminal moments of suffering or hope, and to the various complex testimonial and textual responses to those events, which are all too often occluded by Official History. 'The past is a cemetery of promises which have not been kept', notes Ricoeur. And attentive modes of remembrance may provide ways of 'bringing them back to life like the dry bones in the valley described in the prophecy of Ezekiel' (Ricoeur, 1996: 9).

A fifth and final moment in the hermeneutics of tolerance is *pardon*. Here, surely, we touch on what must be the most difficult aspect of our response to 9/11. If empathy and hospitality towards others are crucial steps in an ethic of non-violence, there is something *more* – something which entails moving beyond narrative imagination to forgiveness. In short, the exchange of memories of suffering demands more than sympathy and duty (though these are essential for any kind of justice). And this something 'extra' involves pardon in so far as pardon means 'shattering the debt'. Here the order of justice and reciprocity can be supplemented, but not replaced, by that of the more explicitly religious order of 'charity and gift'. Such spiritual forgiveness demands huge patience, an enduring practice of 'working-through', mourning and letting go. But it is not a forgetful forgiveness. Amnesty can never be based on amnesia. It remembers our debt to the dead while at the same time introducing something other, something difficult almost to the point of impossibility, but something all the more important for that.

One thinks of Brandt kneeling at Warsaw, Havel's apology to the Sudeten Germans, Hume's dialogue with the IRA, Sadat's visit to Jerusalem, Hillesum's refusal to hate her hateful persecutors. Or of certain extraordinary survivors of 9/11 who, having witnessed what they did or lost loved ones, still refused to cry vengeance. Such exceptional moments signal a point where an ethics of justice is touched by a poetics of pardon. And such a poetics, I would argue, is usually of a spiritual or religious nature. But I repeat: the one does not and cannot replace the other; *both* justice and pardon are crucially important in our response to suffering. One cannot replace the other. They are both called for. For, as Ricoeur reminds us, if at moments charity does indeed exceed justice, 'we must guard against substituting it for justice'. Charity remains a surplus; and it is this very 'surplus of compassion and tenderness (which) is capable of giving the exchange of memories its profound motivation, its daring and its momentum' (Ricoeur, 1996: 11; see also Kearney, 2003). The surplus, evidenced in pardon, is endless in its demands and inexhaustible in its resources. It is what makes the impossibility of forgiving possible. Though no less difficult for that. That is why, as Julia Kristeva observes, 'to forgive is as infinite as it is repetitive.'[4]

In the difficult act of pardon, religious tolerance must always remain attentive to the demands of moral and political justice. In response to 9/11, as to other terrible atrocities, the bottom line is this: pardon cannot forget protest any more than love can forget action.

Notes

Abridged version of the homonymous article published in the *Journal of the Interdisciplinary Crossroads* (Vol. 2, No. 1, April 2005).

1. Samuel Huntington later published a full-length book on the subject entitled *The Clash of Civilizations and the Remaking of the World Order* (2001), where he expanded on his prediction that twenty-first-century global conflict would not be waged between nation-states but between general 'civilizations' defined by shared cultures, values and religions, and transgressing the boundaries of sovereign nations. Of the eight major civilizations, Huntington predicts

that the most violent clash will occur between the Christian West and the Muslim nations of the East stretching from Africa and the Middle East as far as Indonesia. While I do not deny that this scenario may indeed be the preferred view of Bin Laden and certain generals in the Pentagon, I would support Said's argument that we should do everything to combat such monolithic models of schismatic thinking to the extent that they deny the complex realities of difference, diversity and dissent within every civilization, no matter how hegemonic or totalizing it may presume to be.
2. For further commentary on the apocalyptic character of the Bush–Bin Laden war, see Lifton (2003), Falk (2003), Rockmore and Margolis (2004), Chomsky (2003) and Derrida (2004).
3. This principle of radical hermeneutic plurality calls for an equally radical pluralist politics. I would suggest a political theorist like Chantale Mouffe who offers some interesting possibilities here when she talks about moving beyond an 'antagonistic' politics of us-versus-them to a more democratic 'agonistic' politics which fosters a robust and creative conflict of interpretations. She argues that, when the political channels are not available through which conflicts can take an 'agonistic' form, they degenerate into the 'antagonistic' model of absolutist polarization between good and evil, the opponent being perceived as an 'enemy' or 'demon' to be destroyed. The mistakenness of apocalyptic politics is evident here. But there is a more subtle error committed by certain strands of liberal rationalism and individualism when they ignore the crucial motivational role played by communal affects, passions and identifications in our contemporary world. Mouffe concludes that the goal of genuine democracy is not to move from a bipolar to a unipolar system of politics but to foster the emergence of a multipolar world with a balance among several regional poles allowing for a plurality of powers. By converting *antagonism* into *agonism* we allow dissent to express itself within a common symbolic space rather than resorting to violence. Adversaries thus become legitimate opponents rather than illegitimate enemies. This, she suggests is the only way to avoid the hegemony of one single hyperpower or the collapse into violent chaos (see further Mouffe, 2005).
4. Cited by Kelly Oliver (2003: 280). Oliver offers a very useful critical overview of some of the most recent discussions of forgiveness in contemporary psychoanalysis and deconstruction, with particularly instructive attention to the work of Derrida, Arendt and Kristeva. She proposes this response:

> The notion of the unconscious gives us an ethics of responsibility without sovereignty. We are responsible for what we cannot and do not control, our unconscious fears and desires and their affective representations. In addition, we are responsible for the effects of those fears, desires, and affects on others. This impossible responsibility entails the imperative to question ourselves and constantly engage in self-critical hermeneutics, which also gives meaning to our lives. Responsible ethics and politics requires that we account for the unconscious. Without doing so we risk self-righteously adhering to deadly principles in the name of freedom and justice. (ibid.: 289)

4
Ecce Homo: The Political Theology of Good and Evil

John O'Neill

Our public life owes much to our expectation that we will prefer good to evil in our everyday exchanges with one another. Admittedly, this expectation is as much disturbed by exceptional acts of goodness as of evil. In either case, we are forced to examine our commonplace assumptions invested in the injunction to do more good than harm towards others whose vulnerability we share. This is that law of the Gospel:

> Whatever you require that others should do to you, that do ye to them. And that law of all men, *quod tibi fieri non vis, alteri ne feceris*.... Do not that to another, which thou wouldst not have done to thyself.
>
> (Leviathan, Ch. XIV: 85; Ch. XV: 103)

I am aware, of course, that the global scale of the two-sided misadventures in contemporary political life threatens to overwhelm any notion of sympathy – if not the very idea of suffering altogether. It may also overwhelm our very own capacity for thinking at all upon events that reach us only as the dark side of entertainment, news and weather. At the very heart of things lies the problem of the conjunction of good and evil that is the scandal in our theology, politics and ethics. Our responses to it range unevenly from hope and resistance to despair and defeatism, depending on where we locate exemplary cases of the pursuit of goodness or of incorrigible evil. Here we propose to explore Hannah Arendt's notorious solecism on 'the banality of evil' appended to her *Eichmann in Jerusalem* (1963).

> Out of the unwillingness or inability to choose one's examples and one's company, and out of the unwillingness or inability to relate to

others through judgment, arise the real *skandala*, the real stumbling blocks which human powers cannot remove because they were not caused by human and humanly understandable motives. Therein lies the horror and, at the same time, the banality of evil.

(Arendt, 1982: 113)

Arendt's extended *Report on the Banality of Evil* (1963) is resolutely antisociological. It is not directed to a study of the 'Eichmann effect' as the work of everyone and no one. Rather, it asks, 'Who was he to judge?' It is essential to her case against Eichmann that she dismisses any naturalization of the history and causes of evil. This would exempt us from individual responsibility, allowing us to wash our hands of events that exceed one's moral imagination. Instead, her report on the Jerusalem trial seizes upon Eichmann's bad faith and his clownish, idiotic surrender of our commonplace capacity for thoughtful conduct. Eichmann is charged with acting upon the poor man's reduction of Kant's Categorical Imperative to not daring to *think otherwise than others*, but rather to adopt their faceless choices as if they were his own 'semblance' (Arendt, 1977: 38). Her final verdict is that the 'inability to think' is the bedrock of the collective evil that swamped Eichmann and his times in the triumph of evil over Reason.

The banality of evil makes its appearance in many forms, but always fueled by the delirium of blind loyalty that substitutes for thinking. In this sense, and in this sense only, Arendt saw Eichmann as Everyman pointing to the need to understand what we mean when we say in our commonsense language, that we are capable of thinking.

(Bergen, 1998: 34–35)

I propose to treat Arendt's reflections on the 'banality' of evil and the very possibility of moral resistance in terms of the identity (or 'who') question as it is posed in the context of the biblical trial of Jesus (*Ecce Homo*) at Jerusalem (John 18:27–19:22; see also Figure 4.1). Here it is Pontius Pilate who sought to judge otherwise than the parties to the murder of an innocent man (*homo sacer*). Although the harshness of Arendt's judgement of Eichmann as a moral 'idiot' blindly loyal to a genocidal regime – if not as an exemplary figure of modernity's sociological 'thoughtlessness' (Arendt, 1958) – is only the preface to her exposition of a Kantian concept of self-knowledge and answerability (Arendt, 1977), both her moves are excessive expressions of critical irony. In the first place, Arendt's turn to the Kantian reformulation of the Golden

Rule (Luke, 6:31) as the Categorical Imperative to capture Eichmann's stalled ethical will ignores the biblical narrative of 'answerability' located in the Godhead's own change of heart (*metanoia/conversio*) from acting as the Lord of Violence to becoming the Lord of Love. I would argue, rather, that Kant's Categorical Imperative must be read in terms of the political theology of The Sermon on the Mount. The latter underwrites resistance to ourselves as the source of a reified alterity (hardness of heart/hearing/seeing) that projects itself in an alienology of evil. It is important to recall that Arendt's identity-question – *Who* did Eichmann even imagine he was he to judge? – was first put to Jesus by Pontius Pilate: 'Who of us has the power to forgive?' Here Pilate asks, how are the two kingdoms of power and love to be ordered? This question is put to one who preached the 'scandal' of our loving one another on the model of forgiveness prefigured in the biblical narrative of God's relation with Israel and Israel's relations with the Gentiles. To be fair, in *The Human Condition* Arendt (1958: 212–223) had earlier turned to the Gospel texts on forgiveness and promise in a last effort to reverse the unhappy split between freedom and sovereignty that has disappointed both right and left parties in the history of political modernity (O'Neill, 1972a: 20–37; O'Neill, 1972b: 57–67). But, as we shall see, she grounds the ultimate source of forgiveness – at dispute between Pontius Pilate, the Sanhedrin and Jesus – in the *human* capacity for forgiveness as enabling God's very own forgiveness. Yet, at the same time, Arendt excludes the labouring majority of mankind from the revisionary human speech acts of promise and forgiveness which renew history and politics on the ground that the banality (*banausia*) of their work condemns them to the repetition and homogenization that constitute mass society and totalitarian politics (Featherstone, 2008).

Ecce Homo: Behold the man!

> 'Who are we?' as opposed to 'what are we?', that is the revelation
> whose inherent tension enlivens Arendt's philosophical work.
> (Kristeva, 2001: 172)

We must now turn to the more specific, if not scandalous, Biblical formulations of the Golden Rule or Commandments that forbid killing and prescribe love and forgiveness rather than the tit-for-tat (*lex talionis*) in our intemperate relations with one another. These prescriptions are, of course, embedded in the political theology of Israel (Baudler, 1992) and the narrative transition from the Law's law to

Figure 4.1 Ecce Homo (or *Christ before the people*) by Albrecht Dürer (c. 1497–1500). Reprinted with permission from the University of Michigan Museum of Art.

Love's law achieved through God's own change of mind or heart (*metanoia/conversio*) revealed in the teachings of Jesus. The Law's law is its sovereign power over bare life exercised in death and exile (Agamben, 1998). This is the model of kingdom that Pontius Pilate represents; the power to take or to release a life, as he reminds Jesus and the crowd who press for his execution:

> Pilate, therefore went forth
> again, and saith unto them, Be-
> hold, I bring him forth to you,

that ye may know that I find no fault in him.

Then came Jesus forth, wearing the crown of thorns and the purple robe. And Pilate saith unto them, Behold the man!

When the chief priests, therefore, and officers saw him, they cried out, saying, Crucify him, crucify him! Pilate saith unto them, Take ye him, and crucify him; for I find no fault in him.

The Jews answered him, We have a law, and by our law he ought to die, because he made himself the Son of God.

When Pilate, therefore, heard that saying, he was the more afraid;

And went again into the judgment hall, and saith unto Jesus, From where art thou? But Jesus gave him no answer.

Then saith Pilate unto him, Speakest thou not unto me? Knowest thou not that I have power to crucify thee, and have power to release thee?

Jesus answered, Thou couldest have no power at all against me, except it were given thee from above; therefore, he that delivered me unto thee hath the greater sin.

> And from then on Pilate
> sought to release him; but the
> Jews cried out, saying, If thou let
> this man go, thou art not Caesar's
> friend; whosoever maketh him-
> self a king speaketh against Caesar.
>
> (John 19:4–12)

Thus what the Passion narrative (Marin, 1980) preserves is the *collective* rather than individual pragmatics of confession, avowal and disavowal. The irony in Pilate's question is twofold. Is this the man (*this wretch*) whom you think threatens my kingdom with his talk of salvation when all that can save him from common crucifixion is the law's pleasure? And do you refuse him that forgiveness? The confrontation of the two kingdoms of life and death is inscribed in the figure of the Man of Sorrows, the King of the Jews, presented to the Roman governor Pilate. What unfolds in the gospel trial narrative is a catastrophe foretold and yet to be taken up as the gift of life that ransoms death from the dereliction of the Cross, to which the Roman centurion is witness: 'Truly, this was the Son of God ... a righteous man' (Mark, 15:39, Luke, 23:47).

When Arendt shifts her own foundation myth of political action (promise and forgiveness) from Greece back to Rome and Jerusalem, she reverses the ground of what I shall call the *theological novelty* in the Old and New Testament narratives of *promise and forgiveness*. Although she notes that Jesus's teaching on forgiveness has its precedent in the Roman Law's provision for sparing the life of a prisoner (*parcere subjectis*), she reduces it to a political demand on the part of a small dissident community within Israel. At the same time, however, she argues that the religious context of the doctrine of forgiveness should not prevent its appropriation in a 'strictly secular sense', that is, provided that it be understood to have reversed the biblical priority of divine and human forgiveness:

> It is decisive in our context that Jesus maintains against the 'scribes and pharisees', first, that it is not true that only God has the power to forgive, and second, that this power does not derive from God – as though God, not men, would forgive through the medium of human beings – but on the contrary must be mobilized by men toward each

other before they can hope to be forgiven by God also. Jesus' formulation is even more radical. Man in the gospel is not supposed to forgive because God forgives and he must do 'likewise', but 'if ye from your hearts forgive', God shall do 'likewise'. The reason for the insistence on a duty to forgive is clearly "for they know not what they do" and it does not apply to the extremity of crime and willed evil, for then it would not have been necessary to teach: 'And if he trespass against thee seven times a day, and seven times in a day turn again to thee, saying, I repent; thou shalt forgive him'. Crime and willed evil are rare, even rarer perhaps than good deeds; according to Jesus, they will be taken care of by God in the Last Judgment, which plays no role whatsoever in life on earth, and the Last Judgment is not characterized by forgiveness but by just retribution (*apodounai*).

(Arendt, 1958: 215–216)

Thus, Arendt insists upon Jehovah's creation-power of beginning the made-world (*factum*) shifting to the birth (*genitum*) of one who is a beginner himself – [*Initium*] *ergo ut esset, creatus est homo, ante quem nullus fuit*/'that there be a beginning, man was created before whom there was nobody'(*De Civitate Dei*, Xll: 20). But because she separates work from speech, consigning labour to banausic repetition whilst assigning innovation to speech, Arendt abandons any notion of an emancipatory political voice of labour and social justice.

What in each of these instances saves man – man *qua animal laborans, qua homo faber, qua* thinker – is something altogether different; it comes from the outside – not, to be sure, outside of man, but outside of each of the respective activities. From the viewpoint of the *animal laborans*, it is like a miracle that it is also a being which knows of and inhabits a world; *from the viewpoint of* homo faber, *it is like a miracle, like the revelation of divinity, that meaning should have a place in this world.*

Thus, to reverse our secular historical and political evils, Arendt turns to a 'miraculous' trinitarian formula of the faculties of speech, forgiving and promising:

The case of action and action's predicaments is altogether different. Here, the remedy against the irreversibility and unpredictability of the process started by acting does not arise out of another and possibly higher faculty, but is one of the potentialities of action itself. The possible redemption from the predicament of irreversibility – of being unable to undo what one has done though one did not, and could not, have known what he was doing – is the faculty of forgiving. The remedy for unpredictability, for the chaotic uncertainty of the future, is contained in the faculty to make and keep promises. The two faculties belong together in so far as one of them, forgiving, serves to undo the deeds of the past, whose 'sins' hang like Damocles' sword over every new generation; and the other, binding oneself through promises, serves to set up in the ocean of uncertainty, which the future is by definition, islands of security without which not even continuity, let alone durability of any kind, would be possible in the relationships between men.

(Arendt, 1958: 212–213; my emphasis)

Here, surely, Arendt's quest for an *ethics of natality* has embraced its own extraordinary sacrificial logic. In effect, her counter-intuitive notion of the 'banality' of evil only arises from her figure of speechless labour outside or beyond the domain in which we forge our humanity, our deeds and misdeeds (Morris, 1990). The separation of work and speech excludes a large part of humanity from the politics and poetics of suffering and resistance that are more enduring than its ideological misadventures. Above all, Arendt's insistence upon the speechlessness of labour cuts off the critique of the sacrificial logic underlying religion, politics and society that runs from the Bible, through the Gospels to Hobbes (1651/1946), Kant (1951), Marx (1844), Rawls (1972) and Ricoeur (1995), which we must now explore.

Otherwise than the law

To elaborate the anti-sacrificial logic that is the underlying norm of civic charity and social justice, I shall argue that it is the God of violence who 'repents' (*metanoia/conversio*) His first history to become the God of Love. The moment God withdraws the monotheistic privilege of the chosen people, He has cancelled the law of genocide as its sanction. In effect, the God of Love suspends the patriarchal family in favour of a non-sacrificial fraternity. We may then envisage an ethical covenant in which the Law of Love proscribes the exclusion of the least one amongst us. By commuting the violence of ethnic, class and gender difference into the violence of unjustifiable difference, we inaugurate a double covenant of social justice and personal inviolability for which we assume civic responsibility (O'Neill, 1994, 2004).

Consider the parable of the labourers in the vineyard (Matthew 20: 1–16) who were paid the same wage at the end of the day, despite being hired for a longer or shorter period, but who complained of the 'injustice' in the master's policy. How are 'we' to hear this story? We might take the viewpoint of any of the individual labourers whose ordinary sense of justice (equal pay for equal work) is violated by the master. In turn, the master might well consider his dealings with the labourers to be given solely by his right of ownership. His rejection of the labourers' inegalitarianism would then be a Derridaean exercise of the autonomy of the gift (Derrida, 1991; O'Neill, 1999). Rather, what the master challenges is the labourers' weak capacity for fraternity. What they are ready to risk in the name of justice is demanding that the master treat them equally but as exploited day labour! Here, then, is the old sacrificial logic of collectively (mis)recognized violence. But the master's act exemplifies God's mercy and grace in forgiving difference. What 'we' (moderns) do is to subsume the Two Kingdoms in the Categorical Imperative, suppressing Love's lexical ordering (firstness/secondness) of them in favour of a Benthamite minimax rule of majority happiness that accepts the daily misery of a disadvantaged remainder. But it is the incalculability of the turn (*metanoia/conversio*) from the law of everyday difference and inequality towards love's indifference to our capital accounting that funds Christian fellowship.

Metanoia/Conversio (a change of heart) is not achieved in a single moment of epiphany. The old law of violence is not simply melted down by the new law of Love. It requires a double reorientation (a) with respect to one's knowledge of the everyday world, and (b) with respect to one's ethical orientation to events in (a) so that in the process our grasp of the law is deepened yet turned towards love whose behaviour is otherwise than the law. Christian love is enabled by the prior gift of God's grace towards us which universalizes individual worth, even though we cannot consciously draw upon its credit without turning the contingency of love into a ritual account. Our hearts are opened up (*metanoia/conversio*) by the narrative of God's incarnation and assumption of human suffering. The incarnate God of the New Testament no longer inflicts violence upon us because He is not the 'wholly other' whom our sacrifices never appease – anymore than Matthew, the former tax collector, is the same man who relativizes the two kingdoms of God and Caesar. By the same token (Incarnation), we cannot spin-off the forgiveness of sins into a 'celestial economy' (Caputo, 1997: 223) to float charity upon a Derridaean 'aneconomy' of the gift – or a 'religion without religion'. By substituting for the God-term the polarity of an absolute alterity with whom we experience only 'a fraternity existing in extreme separation' (Levinas, 1989: 84), these gestures still strain towards autonomy apart from reciprocity.

I am not arguing that there is no God of Love in the Old Testament, nor that the God of Neighbourly Love dwells only in the New Testament. It is the lexical order of the two love-imperatives that is the question:

> Thou shalt love the Lord thy God
> With all thy heart and with all thy soul,
> And with all thy mind;
> And thy neighbor as thyself.
>
> (Luke, 10:27)

The message is the same in Mark (12:29–31). In each case, Jesus is questioned about the law. The Sadducees ask, Will the Levirate rule in the Kingdom of Heaven? The answer is that there is no family in the after-life. In the same text, the Pharisees ask Jesus, Which is the first commandment? They are told that there are two commandments of equal weight. In Luke, it is a lawyer who asks, What must be done to get eternal life? When told, the lawyer puts the supplementary question: *And who is my neighbour?* (Luke, 10:29).

The answer is that the love we owe to God and to our neighbour cannot be particular; it is no longer tribal, nor familial; not sexual nor even meritocratic. It is beyond calculation even of sin:

> Ye hath heard that it hath been said,
> An eye for eye, and a tooth for a tooth;
> But I say unto you that ye shall not resist evil,
> But whoever shall smite thee on thy right cheek,
> Turn to him the other also.
>
> (Matthew, 5:38–39)

The divine economy of love and forgiveness

To render what is outrageous in Matthew's economy of forgiveness, I propose to schematize the relation between the Two Kingdoms of religion and politics in the Judaeo-Christian narrative as follows:

1) *Love thy neighbour* (as thyself) but not as
   (a) God exclusively loved Israel, nor
   (b) under God's threat of exclusion and punishment (*lex talionis*);

2) Love thy neighbor *as God loves us*, that is, by giving His Son
   (a) to change our heart (*metanoia/conversio*), as He did Himself;
   (b) to suspend the law of difference and violence, and
   (c) to subordinate tribalism, familism, racism and sexism to fellowship; therefore

3) *Love thine enemies*, that is, with the same love you have for your neighbors as fellow beings in accordance with 2 (a, b, c).

The lexical order (Rawls, 1972: 42–43) of the Two Commandments – Love thy God and Love thy Neighbour (enemies) – cannot depend upon a first-order *self-love* as the guarantee of ethical autonomy. The love of fellowship must be modelled upon God's renewed love (*metanoia/conversio*) and not by the universalization of our *self-love* (as in Kant's translation of the Golden Rule into the Categorical Imperative). Thus, the order of the First and Second Commandments must be:

> God's love
> Neighborly love
> Love for God who loves us (through His incarnate Son)
> Self-love.
>
> (Nygren, 1969: 219; modified)

I have underscored (i) and (iv) as versions of God and Self that cannot drive the commandment to love thy neighbour as thyself until (iii) *God's incarnate love for us* provides the model for neighbourly love (ii) and fellowship.

A Kantian, I believe, would argue that the change of heart (*metanoia/conversio*) that I have moved from the exclusionary Hebrew God (i) to the inclusive Christ/God (iii) can occur on the level of (iv) self-love grounded in the autonomy of rational will to secure (ii) fellowship and freedom (Adams, 1996). However, I am arguing that Christian love transcends family and thereby the 'murder in the family' that may be traced to God's first violent affection for Israel and its colonization of the land of Canaan (Cross, 1973; Assman, 1996; Dozeman, 1996). To achieve this, God redeemed the Covenant through the death of His Son so that all of humanity is called into brother/sisterhood, displacing tribalism and familism, friendship/enmity as determinants of neighbourliness and self-love. In the redeemed economy of love (*Agape*), however, the specifically ethical principle of fellowship is funded by the 'forgift' (*par-don*) of God's mercy (*grace*) which is the model for what I shall call the *declaration of forgiveness* in the Lord's Prayer.

PATER NOSTER
Our father, who art in heaven,
T(i)   Hallowed be thy name.
T(ii) Thy kingdom come.
       Thy will be done in earth, as it is in heaven.
W(a)   Give us this day our daily bread.
W(b)   And forgive us our debts, as we forgive our debtors.
W(c)   And lead us not into temptation, but deliver us from evil.
T(iii) For thine is the kingdom, and the power, and the glory, forever, Amen.
                    (Matthew, 6:9–13 emphasis added to show
                     embedding of Thou/We petitions)

The *Pater Noster* may be read to show a further deficiency in the Derrida/Caputo (1997: 226–229) attribution of an 'aneconomy' of prayer in Matthew. Consider the doubling of the 'Thou-petitions' (T) and 'We-petitions' (W), as they are called (Jeremiàs, 1967: 98–103; Vögtle, 1978). I shall call the T-petitions (i–iii) *Promise-Petitions* and the W-petitions (a–c) I shall call *Forgiveness Petitions*. Once again, there is a lexical order ruling the two petition-clusters so that they are not to be read so as to *polarize* into the power of the Kingdom of Heaven and the passivity of the community on earth. Nor are Promise-petitions to be read only *eschatologically*, that is, without any transformation by the Forgiveness-petitions. Thus W(a) 'Give us this day our daily bread' invokes the 'hallowing of life' depicted in Christian commensalism. The latter also practices at table the fraternal suspension of difference through the efficacy achieved in W(b) 'And forgive us our debts, as we forgive our debtors', which expresses our resolve to forgive others the harms we do ourselves. However, the principle of Forgiveness

(Pardon, Atonement) in W(b) cannot, *pace* Derrida/Caputo, come in *equal* amounts from us and from God – anymore than, *pace* Arendt, can it be a lazy reliance upon God's munificence. That is why in the total economy of the Lord's Prayer, the We-petitions are lexically ordered to follow the Thou-petitions through which we seek to resist evil.

Civic theology

The Kingdom of Heaven is not a 'kingdom' at all. For the same reason, it does not have a celestial economy providing for its members to live like improvident birds or the bare-naked lilies of the fields. Love's indifference does not ask us to close our eyes to social difference nor does it hypnotize us into believing the poor are the other side of heaven. The two kingdoms cross over in this world, that is, in the mundane practices of fellowship mediated by the civic state (O'Neill, 2004), which clothes bare need in the goods of welfare administered in our name, but not as an individual gift (Titmuss, 1970; Ignatieff, 1990). Today, the two kingdoms overlap through tax transfers that transform another's needs into civic rights to our duties of support and care. What is difficult is to weigh the practices of equality which cancel exclusion with the practice of respect for what in each of us is a remainder of character and circumstance that tests our fellow love. In effect, Christian love operates through a 'veil of ignorance', setting aside social inequality in favour of moral equality. Christian love preaches equality in the midst of inequality because of its indifference to difference, or its embrace of Rawls's blind choice of justice principles that favour the 'least advantaged' amongst us, the poor who may thereby hope in citizenship (Rawls, 1972).

Ethical reason without enabling civic institutions grounded in a *non-sacrificial logic* is soon starved of any goodness in this world. Whilst Kant's rejection of 'particular duties' cuts us off from natural determinism, it does so at the price of lifting our anchor in the life-world. It also risks putting us beyond the absolutely non-sacrificial blessing of the life-world loved *unknowingly* in-the-name-of-God:

> For I was hungry, and ye gave me food;
> I was thirsty, and ye gave me drink;
> I was a stranger, and ye took me in;
>
> Naked, and ye clothed me;
> I was sick, and ye visited me;
> I was in prison, and ye came unto me.

> Then shall the righteous answer him,
> saying, Lord, when saw with me thee hungry,
> and fed thee; or thirsty, and gave thee drink?
>
> When saw we thee a stranger,
> and took thee in, naked,
> and clothed thee?
>
> Or when saw we thee sick,
> or in prison, and came unto thee?
>
> And the King shall answer and say unto them.
> Verily I say unto you, Inasmuch as ye have
> done it unto one of the least of these my brethren,
> ye have done it unto me.
>
> (Matthew, 25:35–40)

Christ's reference to what we may call an *ethical unconscious* is puzzling because it appears to divorce moral achievement from ethical insight. But I think what is involved is the reminder that the ethical subject cannot stand apart from the everyday involvements, interests and preoccupations occasioned by the needs one encounters anywhere, anytime, and to which one responds without elaborate reflection upon self-or-other-regarding principles (O'Neill, 1975). This is a matter of a *Divine surd* in moral habit rather than those random acts of love or beauty called for on bumper stickers. The love we owe to one another is the expression of our moral capacity for civic love which we cannot neglect without injury to our own personality. What is revolutionary in the *gift* of civic love is its prescription for the integration of the whole individual into a whole society – working against its own practices of exclusion and exploitation on the basis of religion, race, class, gender and disability (Marshall, 1950). What remains difficult is to discover those social policies and charitable practices which exemplify that kingdom of ends in which none of us is fated to be sacrificed to power and efficiency or to cruelty and greed.

In my view, Arendt overburdens the innovations of promise and forgiveness as singular acts that lift us out of the repetitive, dead-end temporality of work and mass society which she holds to be the root of the politics of evil. If we are to conceive history and politics as *otherwise than they have been*, we must regard ourselves as those others upon whom the violence of history continues to fall. Thus it is the *mutual vulnerability of anyone of us as another* that is invoked in the Golden Rule (Ricoeur,

1991, 1992, 1995, 2004). This is the gospel story we are to *re-member*; it is the lesson of radical compassion (*Agnus Dei*) that is the gift in-and-of the biblical narrative itself as a civic theology whose ethical norm is the practice of public generosity. Here, perhaps, we are beyond Arendt's question 'Who am I?' We set aside heroic deeds for prosaic acts of kindness whose promise and forgiveness respond to our vulnerability and to our recognition of one another's (mis)deeds as one's own possibility. Here, too, once we concede that established religions must resist their own temptation to power, we may still hope to find civic poets and compassionate communities which struggle to bring Love's word to justice, resisting our own evils.

5
Resistance as Transformation

Andrea Mubi Brighenti

> Those who do not resign themselves, are the spice of earth, the colour of life,
> they condemn themselves to unhappiness, but they are our happiness.
>
> – Elias Canetti, Aufzeichnungen

By and large, academic and non-academic discourses make two important assumptions about the nature of resistance. The first is that resistance is an act *against* something: against command, against exploitation, against imperialism, against power and so on. The second assumption, which is related to the former yet not equivalent to it, is that resistance operates *from below*, or is bottom-up rather than top-down. Even when it is accepted that the subject of resistance may be a person in a high place (see, for example, LaNuez and Jermier, 1994), resistance is seen as operating against the formal scheme of the organization or institution in question. What follows these two assumptions is the canonical opposition of domination and resistance. Resistance is thus viewed as counter-action, that is, as a type of action which reacts, in various guises, against a dominant arrangement or system. In most cases, this view is a prelude to an account of resistance as a political category. An additional coloration, which characterizes the critical take on power, is that the system of domination against which reaction takes place, is basically unequal, unjust and oppressive. Besides the mere domination-versus-resistance dichotomy, it is also often argued that resistance, not unlike domination, operates along a continuum of intensity, ranging from mere coping to task avoidance to pilfering and sabotage to active struggle.

There are many differences as to how resistance-in-action is described, but not as many as to how resistance is accounted for. The two main traditions in conceptualizing resistance are the objectivist and the subjectivist. The orthodox Marxist tradition, for instance, heralded the former conception. For pre-Gramscian Marxist authors, resistance was a substantive, material action undertaken against, or interfering with, the dominant capitalist socio-economic system. By contrast, phenomenologist and culturalist studies have privileged the subjectivist view that resistance is primarily a matter of symbolic challenge, rather than necessarily having a strictly material basis. In this latter view, the subjective meaning conveyed through action is what really constitutes resistance.

This chapter argues that the dichotomy between the objectivist and subjectivist approaches is somewhat misplaced.[1] Instead, resistance is taken to be a descriptive concept for a practice, or a series of practices, which may be described by social actors in various ways – often, in ways that are themselves open to contradictory interpretations –, and which may even pass unnoticed. The conception of resistance proposed here is distinctive, if not idiosyncratic. Resistance will consequently appear to be a much more disseminated activity, yet at the same time one that is much more circumscribed in its actualizations than is usually conveyed. Individual scholars and scholarly traditions may well stand opposed to such interpretation, particularly since it leads to a restrictive definition of resistance, indeed, to a re-tailoring of its conceptual shape, which is sometimes narrower, sometimes broader. Yet I take it as a sign of the importance of the concept of resistance that there is no general agreement on how resistance exactly manifests itself, at least insofar as theorists may feel the need to resist the definitions of one another.

In what follows, I try to embed resistance within a network of sociological concepts. The main focus is on an 'overlooked classic' of sociology, Elias Canetti.[2] The chapter is exploratory rather than systematic, its main aim being a comparison between Canetti's and Foucault's conceptualizations of power and resistance. Canetti's (1960/1978) take on power, I argue, offers one of the best props both to emancipate resistance from strictly political terrains and to advance a general conception of resistance as transformation.[3] Following Canetti, I suggest that resistance is neither a discourse nor a political symbol, but rather something one does with one's own body, albeit in a non-oppositional manner. My stance in this chapter is minoritarian in Deleuze and Guattari's (1975) sense of the word. This means that I am not interested in developing a comprehensive theory of resistance or in conducting an articulated critique of existing theories thereof. Whereas the analytic is the founder of systems and the critic is the detractor, the master of suspicion, the minoritarian, neither affirmative nor refutative, indicates a way to thought that operates 'by subtraction'. In other words, as the minoritarian stance suggests, I merely wish to show an 'otherwise' of power and resistance.

Resistance and the subject

Because agents do not only have their own motivations, but also their own theories of action, social scientists are always faced with the problem of how to position themselves *vis-à-vis* their research objects. Generally speaking, in order to define an action as resistant, one needs to know the subjective attitude of the actor. In many cases, however, such attitudes are unobservable or inaccessible. Consequently, speaking of resistance may well be tantamount to attributing to a certain action meanings that the actor herself might not have meant to convey. And yet, might it be the case that we are confronted with a genuine act of resistance?

Campbell and Heyman (2007) have recently put forward the term 'slantwise' to describe actions that fall somewhere along the continuum between submission and resistance. 'Slantwise', Campbell and Heyman argue, is not an emic term, but an etic one. It is not a category employed by actors themselves, nor even a category that we might expect actors to recognize. It is, instead, a category that reveals the opaque space of motivations that guide action, without forcing the language of naturalization or resistance upon them. Campbell and Heyman thus also manage to avoid that form of romanticization which turns actors into symbolic heroes only insofar as they mirror the researcher's own values.

However, the concept of 'slantwise' is limited, perhaps even self-defeating, in that it keeps the power–resistance continuum intact, whilst distorting the role of motivational factors. The guiding presumption is that resistance is grounded upon unidentifiable motives, and, as such, must recede into 'slantwise' action, always operating under conditions of ignorance. To put the point differently, 'true' resistance can only be detected there where actors have consciously meant to act thus. Here, however, the work of Albert Camus (1961) is a powerful reminder that those who set themselves the task of resisting oppression, may well end up being the worst oppressors themselves. For Camus, *l'homme revolté*, the true rebel, must first revolt against the discourse of resistance and its claim to truth. Resistance is not a discourse, but an action whereby one transforms oneself and the world at one and the same time.

Moreover, one should not ignore that resistance exists and situates itself in relation to power. To clarify the relationship between the two, it is helpful briefly to remind ourselves of one of the most controversial claims made by Claude Lévi-Strauss that is his hypothesis regarding the inevitability of ethnocentrism. Lévi-Strauss (1952) observed that the essence of ethnocentrism is not simply that the actions of others are judged according to one's own code of values, but also, and most crucially, that each human group has a strong, almost undefeatable, sense of its own intrinsic goodness and rightness. Resistance is an inevitable residuum of ethnocentrism; it is what remains outside the constitution of a group as the 'majority of itself'.

Resistance, I will argue further, is not a mere anti-majoritarian endeavour, confined to the level of aggregates. It is much more widespread and diffused in social action, at the level of everyday existence, single human acts even.

Resistance and struggle

A large body of literature on resistance deals with political resistance, or with resistance as a political category. For instance, James Scott (1985, 1990), frames resistance as a form of relationship which occurs between the dominant and the subordinate classes. As we shall see later, a Canetti-inspired view of resistance enables us to broaden the enquiry, as it suggests that, whether overt or covert, political resistance is only a subset of the more inclusive phenomenon of resistance in the human domain. In this section, I review some important interpretations of resistance as a form of socio-political struggle with a view to arguing that resistance should not be confused with, or reduced to, mere struggle between political antagonists.

A useful starting point is Gramsci's (1975) concept of hegemony, whereby domination is based on a widely accepted framework of consent in which even conflict and dissent can be accommodated. At the micro level, people pursue individual lives in specific local contexts which appear meaningful as such. But the texture of each of these apparently 'independent' local lives makes a substantial, if unconscious, contribution to the constitution and continuation of the larger hegemonic pattern. *Contra* Gramsci, Scott (1985, 1990) argues that the absence of direct confrontation does not mean necessarily that hegemony goes unchallenged. Resistance, Scott claims, is mainly to be found in the everyday constellation of the 'weapons of the weak', that is, such tactical, offstage behaviours as dissimulation, false compliance, pilfering, feigned ignorance, foot dragging, slander, arson and sabotage (see also de Certeau, 1984). The idea that hegemony is not omnipotent and can be eroded from beneath by multifaceted forms of political resistance does not, however, really contradict what Gramsci maintained. For one, Gramsci recognized that each class and social group defines and expresses its own ideology. Also, he was well aware of the politics of visibility inherent to ideological confrontations, as his analysis of the mass media, *inter alia*, shows. But, if hegemony is made up only or mostly of appearances, as Scott contends, one must still explain how and why these thin appearances are so pervasive and preserved most of the time; this was Gramsci's core concern.

Following from Gramsci, critical theorists have committed themselves to the development of counter-hegemony, that is, conscious and explicit political opposition, capable of facing domination not only in the hidden domain, but also, and especially, in the public one. Contemporary counter-hegemony theorists have, in fact, extended the analysis of the dominant–dominated relationship from the national to the global scale. In the analytics proposed by Santos (1995), for instance, globalization is a composite plural phenomenon – to the point that Santos (2006) prefers to speak of 'globalizations', in the plural –, comprising at least four different patterns: two hegemonic forms, which he calls globalized localisms and localized globalisms, and two counter-hegemonic forms, insurgent cosmopolitanism and the common heritage of humankind. Whereas the former two give shape to the neoliberal hegemonic mechanism through the double move of universalization of local phenomena and their subsequent imperialist-like localization, the latter are substantiated in organized resistance against injustice produced or amplified by the two hegemonic forms. Resistance may be as global as hegemony: it can act on the same scale and through the same types of coalitions used by the dominant. Santos contends that the classes and social groups which suffer the consequences of hegemonic globalization progressively join each other in social movements that carry forward transnational struggles against exclusion and subordinate inclusion, against political oppression and ecological destruction.

However, contemporary critical thinkers tend to conceive of resistance as an *incomplete stage* in the revolutionary project. For instance, Hardt and Negri (2003) understand resistance as one of the three elements of 'counterpower', along with insurrection and constituent power. In their conception, counterpower is ultimately indistinguishable from power itself, as the two are perfectly symmetrical to one another. Thus, implicitly – and, probably, unwittingly –, Hardt and

Negri present resistance as the negative term in the dialectic struggle for power: what resistance can do, as an organic part of the power chain, is at best oppose the stream of global power, in order to prepare the terrain for action by the multitude. In this account, which is not dissimilar to that by Santos, the importance of resistance is limited to the fact that it constitutes the inception of counterpower. In and of itself, it remains merely reactive and, therefore, insufficient. All else being equal, reformists seem to converge on a similar conception of resistance. In his discussion of environmental restoration, for example, Light (2003) speaks of an ideal of 'reengagement', thus implying that resistance falls short of positive action, which is the type of action involved in active engagement with environmental issues. Another critique of resistance is that provided by Knights and Vurdubakis (1994). Following late Foucault, they argue that power is nearly omnipresent in social life, but this does not pre-empt the possibility of resistance. On the other hand, much like all human action, 'acts of resistance are also exercises of power' (Knights and Vurdubakis, 1994: 191).

My contention here is, first, that resistance is irreducible to power, and, second, that, if resistance accomplishes anything at all, it is that is brings the *otherwise* of power to the fore. As Foucault himself argues, power is different both from a function of consent and a function of violence; whereas the former acts upon actions, the latter acts upon bodies and things. The existence of power requires an acting subject who remains 'other' and who positions him or herself in various ways in a predetermined 'field of responses'. The subject is subject to power yet never wholly subsumed by it. Consequently, power is a type of relationship which is neither 'victory' nor 'struggle'. Power and struggle, Foucault says, constitute a 'permanent limit' for each other and a 'point of possible reversal' of one another: 'It would not be possible for power relations to exist without points of insubordination which, by definition, are means of escape' (Foucault, 1982: 225). However, by contending that power relations necessarily imply means of escape, Foucault remains ambivalent as to whether such means of escape belong to the field of power, struggle or some third field.

Later on, I shall try to show how Canetti may help us solve this difficulty by imagining resistance as a third pole in the equation of power and struggle. As a preliminary to such consideration, I only wish to point out that Simmel, too, provides elements with which to move beyond a conception of resistance as oppositional. Indeed, Simmel (1908: §II: 69–70/1950: 137) distinguishes between two types of personality: 'strong individuality' (*starke Individualität*), which he associates with opposition (*Widerstand*), and 'decided individuality' (*entschiedene Individualität*), which we may associate with a resistant attitude, although he himself does not use the word explicitly. 'Strong individuality', Simmel argues, is of a *quantitative* nature, as it finds its realization in contrasts and one-to-many relationships. On the other hand, 'decided individuality' is *qualitative* in nature, shuns situations where it may be confronted with majorities and prefers one-to-one relationships. As such, decided individuality implies a *transformative* drive, which is the necessary pathway of any movement towards achieving liberation from a given power relationship, the path of the 'means of escape'.

In/visibility of resistance

As noted earlier, Scott urges us to study the ways in which, despite appearances to the contrary, social groups resist subordination in the domain of the everyday. If we accept this account, we must also acknowledge that resistance is meaningfully intertwined with visibility. Visibility can be imagined as a field that contributes to defining and shaping the relations amongst sites, subjects and their actions (Brighenti, 2007). It is an effect of the relative positionings of actors and actions, and, in its turn, produces effects that shape these relationships. There is no linear correlation between visibility and resistance, however. Resistance may be helped by invisibility, which furnishes a place to hide from domination, but it may also be harmed by the same invisibility, which makes it impossible to find supporters and allies and to gain recognition.

In this context, de Certeau's (1984) distinction between strategy and tactic is helpful. Strategy is the dominant model in the political, economic and scientific realms. It is essentially a territorial form exercised upon proprietary bounded *loci*, and articulated into discourses. Outsiders are subordinates or adversaries. By contrast, tactic is deterritorialized, because those who practise it have no territory of their own and have to act on a territory that belongs to others. It is not articulated into discourses, but into practical ways of operating, and it does not recognize outsiders (this would be impossible, because it has no bounded territory that enables identification of people as insiders or outsiders), but only allies. Whereas strategy is self-centred, territorial and spatially bounded, tactic is fragmentary, deterritorialized and temporally linked. Tactic has no cumulative character, it cannot capitalize on victories, nor achieve any overall coherence; it can only combine heterogeneous elements and constantly try to turn events into opportunities.

Resistance has a tactical nature. Its social locations do not correspond to any institutionalized field of knowledge, but rather to the realms of the informal, the implicit and even the trivial. Resistance entails the acknowledgement that one cannot win in the enemy's field, but this acknowledgement is also accompanied by the constant attempt to *create new fields*. Though Scott observes that open resistance is rare in comparison to its hidden counterpart, the need to make resistance visible may as well be crucial at times. The *Journal of Prisoners on Prisons Anthology*, edited by Bob Gaucher (2002), reminds us that writing is a practice of resistance for invisible subjects forced into an invisible place. Writing provides a way out of jail, albeit a non-physical one: most of all, it provides access to social visibility and recognition.

If we move from the jail to the factory – following a trajectory that makes a great deal of sense from a Foucauldian perspective – we observe that worker resistance revolves around creating and performing a regime of informal work organization whose visibility features are always shifting. Hodson (1995) has advanced four basic agendas of worker resistance: first, at the interpersonal level, resistance focuses on deflecting abuse; second, at the technical level, resistance aims at regulating the amount of work; third, at the bureaucratic level, resistance attempts to defend worker autonomy; and fourth, at the participatory level, resistance represents a way to expand worker control over production. The complex configuration of visibility thresholds influences the effectiveness of these patterns of resistance, as they require distinctive combinations of invisible and visible action, such as, with respect to the former, duplicity towards the employer's forces, and, with respect to the latter, the need to gain social support from other workers.

Even a specific case such as sabotage (Sprouse, 1992), which fits into Hodson's technical level only imperfectly, reveals the distinctive nature of visibility: sabotage must produce visible effects, obstructing the normal working rhythm, but the intentionality of this obstruction – or, at the very least, the name of the agent – must remain covert. When we move further back to the political field of contemporary social movements, we see that insurgent cosmopolitanism (Santos, 2006), or resistance against neo-liberalism, is concerned with reclaiming the visibility of public issues, such as those concerning the social and environmental effects of economic globalization, which otherwise would recede into invisibility and fall outside the domain of public deliberation. Visibility of resistance, however, is a matter not confined within the official political realm. Consider the case of discourse. Bourdieu and Wacquant (1999) have polemically described as 'imperialist reason' the diffusion of Anglo-American lexis and lemmas at the academic as well as the wider societal level. Cultural imperialism, they argue, obfuscates the socio-historically contingent nature of particular constructs, rather presenting them as genuinely universal. Thanks to their imperceptibility (indeed, invisibility), the emerging worldviews are difficult to resist. Bourdieu and Wacquant call for a strategy of visibility, whereby the perils of imperialist reason are denounced.

Resistance and subtraction

Thus far, we have seen how power may be confronted in a way that is different from struggle. We have also suggested focusing neither on the sphere of intentions, nor on that of free will, but rather on the body. Although a systematic comparison stretches beyond the scope of this chapter, it is worth noting that both Foucault and Canetti locate the basic ground of power in the body. The 'avoidance of the concrete', in which most theories of power or society indulge, is described by Canetti as one of the most 'sinister phenomena in intellectual history' (Canetti, 1979: §2). For his part, Foucault devoted a large part of his research programme to shifting attention away from theories of sovereignty, in order to narrate genealogically the concrete body, and in particular the bodies of the ill, the inmate and the foolish. Both authors arrive at what we may call an anti-symbolic conception of power. For Canetti, postures and gestures do not symbolize power; power is rather the ability to adopt postures and make gestures. For Foucault, the symbols of sovereignty hide the diagram of the government.

Despite their shared attention to the body and their anti-symbolic view of power, Canetti and Foucault propose different conceptions of resistance. This is basically due to the fact that, whereas Foucault advances an essentially discontinuist thesis on power (indeed, his whole Nietzsche-inspired genealogical methodology is discontinuist; see Foucault, 1971), Canetti elaborates a deeply continuist thesis (and it is, perhaps, no accident that Canetti had serious reservations about Nietzsche). When Foucault (1975, 1976, 1977–1978/2004) describes the transition from sovereign power to disciplinary and governmental power, he speaks of it in terms of 'replacement', 'substitution' and 'profound transformation'. This profound transformation consists in a passage from repressive to productive power, from a power that imposes to a power that disposes, from the power to take life or to let live to the power to foster life or disallow it from dying. Yet death occupies a distinctive place in Foucault's work, because power needs to keep its subjects alive; death is a limit to power. This is why power no longer kills, but fosters and administers life and the body. But Foucault also claims that power needs to preserve subjectivity. Subjects are always required to position themselves in the field of power: even when they are recalcitrant, they are always inside the field of power.

According to Canetti, by contrast, every type of power is essentially an extension or amplification of the primal act of seizing. Canetti (1960/1978: §5) finds that even the most sophisticated forms of power are extensions of the clutch of the hand. Canetti also introduces a distinction between violence (*Gewalt*) and power (*Macht*). By connecting the word *Macht* to the Gothic root *magan*, meaning 'being able to', rather than to the German verb *machen*, meaning 'to do', he suggests that power is not directly an action, but rather a capacity or possibility to act. Thus, the 'extension' that characterizes power in comparison to violence seems to correspond to the difference between the actual and the virtual as described by Deleuze. The ultimate stage of seizing is killing, and power is always intimately bound up with death (ibid.: §6). But whilst, strictly speaking, the dead are outside the relation of power, Canetti draws attention, not simply to the duality of life and death, but, more subtly, to the moment of survival. Survival confronts an individual with a crowd – better yet, a number of crowds – the crowds of the living and the dead.

So long as it is framed as 'replacement', Foucault's discontinuist thesis on disciplinary power fails to explain why the nineteenth and twentieth centuries have been, in absolute terms, the bloodiest in the history of humankind. From a strictly disciplinary perspective, that is, it is difficult to explain the persistence of the power of death. Foucault himself never studied war, totalitarianism, crowds and genocide, not in great depth at least. It was not until the late 1970s, in his writings on the bio-political government of the population, that Foucault addressed such issues as mass murder, whilst also acknowledging – implicitly – that the power to seize hold on life has not been superseded, and is not simply a residual 'counterpart' of disciplinary power (see Foucault, 1977–1978/2004). Canettian analysis is useful at this juncture, as it allows us to reinterpret Foucault's 'productive', 'disciplinary' power as a form of clenching the body. Disciplinary institutional enclosure is effective if and only if it ultimately manages to gain a grip on bodies. That bodies may be directed at a distance – for example, by classifying crimes and criminals according to an ideal of 'optimal specification' – is still a 'territorial' type of constraint in the most profound sense of the word, for it is based on the amplification of the original power to command. Likewise, that power is virtual *and* actual may be explained through Canetti's distinction between *Gewalt* and *Macht*.

Another important difference between Foucault and Canetti is with respect to the locus of resistance. Foucault's view conveys the rather pessimistic idea that there is no 'outside' to power; struggle, recalcitrance and, possibly, resistance, are constituent parts of power. At the same time, however, this view also contains some optimism, because it admits that resistance, albeit within power, is in principle always possible. By contrast, Canetti believes that *there is an outside* of power. Resistance is precisely this movement *towards* the outside. The challenge advanced by Canetti is the idea that there can be human relations outside power. Resistance implies the search for a way out, it is a movement of liberation from the grasp of the hand in all its different versions. Resistance is a type of flight, the flight from command.

Canetti has developed one of the most original accounts of commands (see Elbaz, 2003; Brighenti, 2006), one which highlights the distinctively 'dissymmetric' relationship between command and flight. On the one hand, the oldest command is a death sentence, which compels the victim to flee (Canetti, 1960/1978: §8, 304); on the other, flight is also the origin of subtraction from the order of command, and, as such, it marks the inception of all resistance. One could say that resistance is the anti-command. This is not to say that resistance is the same as disobedience. However noble and necessary it may be under oppressive regimes, not all disobedience is resistant. Bakhtin's (1981) conceptualization of laughter helps illustrate the distinction. In the satirical and masquerading mood of the carnival, in its grotesque realism focused on the body and its functions, laughter enacts a specific type of flight from the established social order. Laughter transforms the social frame of power, not by opposing or attacking the King, but rather by multiplying the number of kings. Laughter introduces a dethroning centrifugal element which enables a type of resistance to authority through the infinite pluralization of the centres of authority. It is clear that carnivalesque laughter is a flight which cannot be interpreted as resistance.

But how is it that resistance may be creative, as opposed to merely oppositional?

Resistance: Transformation...

Resistance is not resistance to change, but rather, as Deleuze (1987) suggested, resistance to *the present*. Deleuze and Canetti agree that, contrary to what is widely believed, resistance is on the side of change. Resistance is the 'no' to power, the latter being a 'no' to life. The present that is resisted is the present of power, and power is always grounded 'in the present' and death simultaneously. It is from this point of view that Canetti criticized history for breeding an in-built cult of power. History records only the present, the effectuated. Resistance is, instead, an anti-reductionist experience, for it looks into the ineffectuated in search of ways to create newness out of experience, often out of bitter experience. Resistance is whatever distances itself from the 'seduction' and the 'false greatness' of death. Whereas the critical perspective conceives resistance as a struggle and as a moment of power conflict – eventually, conflict in the political domain, such as revolution – Canetti suggests a perspective that conceives resistance, not as revolution but – if I may say – as 'diavolution' (Brighenti, 2008).

Indeed, if in revolution the point is being an avant-garde, in diavolution the point is being the avant-garde *of oneself*. This concept is similar to Deleuze's *devenir-minoritaire*. The movement of subtraction from power so fundamental in Canetti's view of resistance is termed *ligne de fuite* by Deleuze, who regards it as the starting point of becoming. When questioning what constitutes an act of creation, Deleuze discovers a fundamental similarity between the work of art and the act of resistance. There is not much to say about creation in itself, he writes, because it is *through* creation that one has something to say to others; and he goes on to claim that creation is a necessity, and not at all a pastime for the creator. Therefore, creation highlights two basic aspects of humanity: address to others, and the sense of necessity. This is what happens with resistance as well: humanity and art (the necessity of creation and the necessity to address others) are both 'revealed' in the act of resistance. To say that resistance reveals humanity and art is to recognize that resistance is not something that occurs *ad interim*, for lack of better solutions. Resistance *is* the best solution of each given moment – that is, contingently – insofar as it subtracts each moment from power's clutch of the present.

Resisting means transforming what is into what could be. It is a movement from being, not towards power, but towards 'potency'. Canetti's concept of transformation, or metamorphosis (Canetti, 1973/1960: §9), which Arnason (1996: 109) deems to be 'tantalizingly underdeveloped but central to his whole intellectual project', addresses precisely the issue of potency. In this chapter I have suggested that resistance and transformation can both be better understood if their closeness is thematized. For Canetti, transformation refers to something different from the transformative power of man over nature: it is, in the first place, the transformation of the human being itself, which signifies her or his openness to becoming. The 'talent for transformation' is possessed by everyone, although it can – and, indeed, does – become easily atrophied. Atrophy of the talent for transformation is due to the fact that power constantly imposes new prohibitions on metamorphoses. Caste systems and slavery are the starkest examples of such prohibitions discussed by Canetti. By contrast, the crowd retains the capacity to be a transformative moment because it represents the unstable state of undifferentiated differences, the unrestrained thriving of differences. However, the twentieth century is replete with crowds subjugated by power. This may be the reason why, ultimately, Canetti (1979: §15) assigned to the writer (*Dichter*: *lato sensu* the artist, the thinker) and his or her 'irrational claim to bear responsibilities', the task of being the 'keeper of transformations' (*Hüter der Verwandlungen*). This task Canetti divides into two essential parts: on the one hand, rescuing all stories of the world from oblivion or falsification; on the other hand, retaining the capacity of transformation in the sense of respecting and preserving difference.

Notes

1. Steven Lukes's (2005) 'radical view' of power similarly moves in the direction of overcoming dichotomic conceptions, pointing out the existence of a 'third dimension' of power, referred to as the 'dimension of consent'.
2. The contention that Canetti ranks as a sociological classic has been advanced by various contemporary social theorists, in particular Arnason (1996), Elbaz (2003) and Rutigliano (2007), who have also recounted the difficulties that Canetti's work has found in gaining acceptance within the sociological community. Arguably, Canetti has long been ignored by sociologists because he ignored them. Canetti instead referred to anthropologists and ethnologists, but mainly as sources of information and repertoires of cases. As a scholar, Canetti was deterritorialized from the institutional academic world as asystematic and thoroughly trans-disciplinary in his explorations. Ishaghpour (1990: 14) sums up Canetti's situation thus: he 'was not the representative of any country, of any school, of any movement, of any single genre of writing'. Here, being aware of the limitations inherent to such an operation, I will confine myself to considering only Canetti's essays, leaving aside his novels, plays, aphorisms and autobiography, an accurate interpretation of which would require more extensive studies.
3. As a consequence of such shift, scholars in the political sciences may perceive the treatment of the power – resistance couple carried on here somewhat vague, insofar as it is aimed at addressing phenomena that fall outside their usual domain of enquiry. In the social sciences, resistance has been studied mainly by political scientists, political sociologists and scholars of social movements, who deal with class conflict and social movements as political phenomena (see further Tilly, 2004).

6
Acting on Vulnerable Others: Ethical Agency in Media Discourse
Lilie Chouliaraki

One valuable insight in Hannah Arendt's definition of evil as banal lies in its articulation of action with judgement: without the capacity to reflect, action is dangerous – not simply amoral, devoid of ethical content, but an inherently immoral intervention on the world.[1] Drawing on Eichmann as a radical example of immoral action, Arendt favours a view of agency that thematizes the importance of reflexive engagement with the consequences of local practice as a pre-condition for public ethics. In this chapter, I draw on Arendt's definition of agency in the context of an increasingly mediatized public realm, in order to investigate the extent to which the media, in confronting us with a number of moral dilemmas about our world, may also provide us with the resources of judgement that enable us to act reflexively on this world. To this end, I investigate the extent to which the television spectacles of human poverty and suffering, parading everyday on our screens, may offer us the resources to recognize these spectacles as causes worthy of our attention, emotion and even action – a concern with cosmopolitan forms of agency.[2]

Insofar as we live in a world divided in zones of prosperity and poverty, safety and danger, peace and war, this concern with the potential of the media to enable judgement and action towards vulnerable others renders Arendt's definition of agency instrumental in the agenda of critical media analysis. In this light, far from implying that spectatorship without action bears resemblance to Eichmann's evil, the Arendtian conception of spectatorial agency as potentially cosmopolitan highlights a crucial ethical relationship under conditions of global mediation. This is the relationship between, on the one hand, the role of mediation in mobilizing imagination in the service of action and, on the other, the social and moral implications of such action for distant others, whose lives we can make a difference in – not a banality of evil, therefore, but perhaps a banality of good. Indeed, Arendt's approach to human agency, as the disposition to act in ways that are informed by an awareness of the consequences of action, has inspired recent normative accounts of the mediatized public realm (Peters, 1999; Chouliaraki, 2006; Silverstone, 2006). Such accounts recognize that, despite the pervasively sensational character of mediated suffering in our culture, the possibility for cosmopolitan agency stems precisely from the properties of imagination and judgement that are inherent in the media stories about vulnerable others.

Yet, there is serious scepticism regarding the capacity of the media to inform moral dispositions to action, a scepticism best exemplified in post-modern social and cultural theory, where Baudrillard stands out as a prototypical figure.[3] The post-modern argument is grounded on a conviction that the market-driven images and superficial messages of the media enchant audiences through the seductive power of the spectacle without seeking to communicate a moral cause or enable action on vulnerable others. Rather than imagination and judgement, mediated suffering numbs cosmopolitan sensibilities and incites immoral voyeurism, an unarticulated but intense pleasure at the spectacle of distant misfortune. This controversy around the role of the media in providing resources for the formation of moral agency inevitably raises questions about the textual quality of mediation and the moral power of representation: Which dispositions to thinking and feeling do news stories of suffering cultivate *vis-à-vis* faraway others? Can the spectacles of suffering, most common on our home screens, lead to forms of public action towards these distant others?[4] Despite ongoing debates on the role of the media in cultivating or numbing new cosmopolitan dispositions, the crucial connection between media representation and moral agency remains under-theorized.

Representation and suffering

In order to theorize this connection, I first address the inability of the post-modern approach to conceptualize spectatorial agency as reflexive engagement with mediated suffering (in the section 'Post-modern pessimism: the deletion of agency'). In the light of such critique, I suggest that we move towards an analytical approach to media representations, which investigates the ways in which such representations may offer a broad spectrum of options for us to engage with distant suffering. This approach, inspired by an Aristotelian phronetic view of the study of ethics as contextual practice rather than as abstract normative discourse, goes beyond the pessimistic view of mediation as leading to voyeurism and draws attention to the various proposals of action towards suffering that may be embedded in media stories.[5] Such proposals to action capitalize on a repertoire of civil dispositions that are historically available in our collective imaginary as resources for the public representation of suffering, such as indignant denunciation towards the perpetrators of suffering, charitable tender-heartedness towards its victims or fear and shock at the sight of human misfortune (section: 'An analytics of mediation').[6]

To be sure, these forms of agency are not enough in themselves to constitute the spectator as a public actor. For this to happen, broader frames of interpretation and links to action must also be in place in the contexts of media reception. Rather, media texts are 'performative': they enact paradigmatic forms of agency towards suffering, which may or may not be followed up by media publics. What this performative role of the texts points to, however, is that the media do not simply address a pre-existing audience that waits to engage in social action, but they have the power to constitute this audience as a body of action in the process of narrating and visualizing distant events. To this end, I discuss three examples of news on suffering in terms of (i) their *aesthetic quality*, that is, their combination of talk with image and their narrative properties (section: 'Aesthetic quality') and (ii) their *moral agency*, that is, the proposals they make for engagement with distant suffering (section: 'Moral agency').

In the light of this discussion, I conclude that the analytical approach to mediation enables us to grasp the interplay between media texts and moral agency in terms of a double economy of freedom and constraint. Mediation is here considered to be a resource for the symbolic definition of suffering that, following Arendt, taps onto the spectator's capacity for judgement and enables us to respond to the spectacle of suffering at our own free will, but always within the premises of action already defined in the contexts of historical and political power relationships of viewing (section: 'The conditional freedom of moral agency').

Post-modern pessimism: The deletion of agency

Confronted with the question of how human suffering in the media may affect the spectators' moral sensibilities and dispositions to action, post-modern theories are pessimistic: the image of suffering fails to re-present human pain; it aestheticizes human pain. This negative role of media texts on our experience of distant suffering is best captured in Baudrillard's work on *simulation*. Simulation is mediation without a referent. Let us think of the 11 September attack on the World Trade Centre. Its television image, Baudrillard claims, refers less to an actual plane crash and more to pervasive cultural icons that we all know about through other mediations:

> In this Manhattan disaster movie, the two 20th-century elements of mass fascination are intertwined to the greatest degree: the white magic of cinema and the black magic of terror. The white light of the image and the black light of violence. (2001)

Simulation, Baudrillard tells us, is not a representation of something other than itself, that is, the plane, but a representation of already existing spectacles of mass fascination that refer to themselves as the 'real'. In this self-referential definition, simulation cancels any claim to reality, the violence of terror, except for the reality of the spectacle itself: the terror attacks become *this Manhattan disaster movie*. Suffering, here, only exists as a story on our screens, echoing other stories of suffering that we have already encountered as spectacles before. What is it, then, that turns the reality of other people's human pain into cinematic experience for us?

For Baudrillard, it is technology. It is, specifically, the capacity of the camera both to represent by analogy, in perfect image copies, and to dissociate the image from a reference source, through montage or digital processing, that turns mediation into simulation. These possibilities of manipulation turn the television image into a floating element in a network of relations which continually re-combine and circulate it (Mcquire, 1999: 92–104; 132–150); more than that, Baudrillard claims, which strive to perfect it. Indeed, for him, this capacity of the medium to depict and manipulate external reality creates not a quasi-real, a faded representation of the real, but a 'hyperreal', an accentuated or perfected sense of the real that blurs the distinction between image and reality; what takes the place of reality is 'the implosion of the medium and the real in a sort of nebulous hyperreality where even the definition and distinct action of the medium are no longer distinguishable' (Baudrillard, 1983: 44).

Our age, then, marks an end-point to traditional aesthetics, where images promised a better vision for human life. The present is the age of post-aesthetics, where images are just surfaces for the play of a sensuous hype, a frenzied reception of visual stimuli (Baudrillard, 1988: 43–44; for a discussion, see Delanty, 2000: 8–31). As a consequence, Baudrillard says, spectators today are not required to call on their capacities to interpret meaning, to imagine or to judge. We are voyeurs. We only watch, surrendering to the seductive attraction of television where everything is displayable and on constant display (Baudrillard, 1988: 33). Because of this total visibility, no space is left for strong emotions such as surprise, challenge, shock, or for any sort of connectivity with other people; our home turns 'into a kind of archaic, closed-off cell, into a vestige of human relations whose survival is highly questionable' (ibid.: 17–18).

It is evident, then, that the post-aesthetics account cannot open the possibility of moral agency to develop through television, because it misleadingly simplifies the role of representation in mediation. In conceptualizing media representations only as image and surface, the post-aesthetics thesis ultimately underestimates television's capacity for a more complex production of meaning. Specifically, the thesis ignores the role of language to generate various narrative forms and to combine with images in multiple ways that complicate television's proposals to ethical action beyond the hyperreality effect. As a consequence, the thesis cannot tell us much about how the capacity for judgement on the part of the spectator may indeed emerge as a consequence of the textual properties of mediation; it also fails to show us how such textual properties may be giving rise to forms of moral agency that go beyond the spectators' seduction by frenzied visual stimuli, possibly even enabling us to reflect on how to make a difference in the lives of distant others.[7]

An analytics of mediation

In my view, this pessimism is the consequence of an important epistemological mistake in the post-aesthetic account.[8] The thesis takes up a historically specific description of contemporary culture, that media technologies privilege a visual aesthetics at the expense of ethical content, and use it as a model to tell us how mediation creates the world in meaning. Indeed, Baudrillard's *simulacrum* is a category of description that tells us about the conditions of mediation today and simultaneously a category of analysis that explains how meaning-making takes place on the television screen.

My own position is that, although technology has indeed intensified the role of visuality in our culture, we should provisionally bracket out the pessimistic narrative on hyperreality as a model for mediated meaning-making and seek to develop an analytical language about how television produces the scene of distant suffering as an aesthetic and ethical reality for the spectator. Drawing on Aristotle's advice that our enquiries into public life should be driven by the practical consideration of how to live ethically together with other people, I wish to approach media texts as particular manifestations of moral value that open up concrete and local possibilities of action to spectators – what I have elsewhere called an 'analytics of mediation'.[9] This engagement with moral values, which Aristotle calls 'phronesis' (prudence), grasps the question of ethics from the pragmatic perspective of praxis. This is the perspective that takes each particular case to be a unique enactment of moral principle that, even though it transcends the case, cannot exist outside the enactment of cases.

This phronetic approach suggests that studying how media stories present distant suffering to us can tell us something important about how mediation makes our encounter with distant others ethically acceptable and practically relevant. In this light, we may consider the spectacles of suffering on television as forms of public spectacle that expose audiences to stories of human tragedy and suffering and, through the visual and verbal staging of such stories, they contribute to cultivating audiences' dispositions towards human affairs. This view of mediation, therefore, strongly relies on what I have earlier referred to as the performative capacity of representation: its capacity not only to re-present the world to its audiences, but also to propose to them how to think and feel about or act on the world.

Two analytical implications follow from this phronetic perspective on mediation. First, the *aesthetic quality* of representation, that is, the ways in which verbal and visual texts combine to tell the story of suffering, is inextricably linked to the moral stance towards suffering that the media propose to us (Sontag, 2003). The second implication of the phronetic approach to mediation is that, as a consequence, the exercise of power in the media cannot be narrowly understood in terms of the voyeurism of seduction. It should be understood more broadly in terms of the options of *moral agency* the media make available, that is, the subtle proposals for engagement with distant suffering, which news stories introduce in the contexts of our everyday life.

In order to address the question of how the aesthetic quality of the news impacts on forms of moral agency, I now focus specifically on a sample of news stories that incorporate a demand for action *vis-à-vis* the suffering they present. These include prime-time news on a rescue mission for illegal African refugees who were caught in a storm in the Mediterranean sea on their way to Southern Europe; a famine crisis in the poor Argentinean province of Tucuman leading young children to emaciation; and the 'death by stoning' sharia verdict against the Nigerian Amina Lawal, a woman who gave birth to a child outside marriage.[10] Let us first look at the aesthetic quality of these stories before turning to a discussion on the forms of moral agency each one makes available to audiences.

Aesthetic quality

By aesthetic quality, I refer to the ways in which talk and image are combined on screen so as to represent distant suffering as an immediate reality for the spectator (Chouliaraki, 2006: 70–96). Let us see how these variations are played out in the three news examples.

- Cinematic entertainment: rescue mission of African refugees

This piece of news is presented through footage with voice-over. The event takes place in the open sea and is filmed mostly by camera situated at the upper deck of a Maltese coast-guard vessel. The coast-guard has approached the refugees' wooden boat and tied it to itself by ropes, so as to enable the transportation of the passengers on board. Scenes of the evacuation of a mass of people from the wooden vessel are followed by the arrival of a rescue helicopter under stormy weather and the story ends with the arrival of the refugees on safe ground in Valetta.

The position of the camera, on-board the coast-guard boat but from a distance and above the scene of action, provides the spectator with the point of view of an uninvolved onlooker, whereas the voice-over describes the development of action on the visual plane. More than simply describing what we see, the voice-over further provides extra-visual information on the dangers involved in the rescue action; for example, images of groups of refugees jumping on board the coast-guard boat are verbally illustrated as 'they rush to get on board the coast guard, running the danger to find themselves in the sea or to get crashed between the two vessels'. In this way, verbal commentary capitalizes on the drama of visual imagery. Danger reaches a peak with the arrival of a rescue helicopter, under worsening weather conditions. This frame, especially the imagery of a rescuer hovering over the grey sea holding onto a rope, adds to the scene of action the visual quality of a Hollywood adventure. The story has a happy ending, yet the final visual frame of this news brings us back to the initial pictures of the vessel sinking in mid-sea. Illegal refugees, we are told, may 'be obliged to return to their country. Perhaps in order to begin yet again the dangerous journey towards a better life'. There is a fictional element here, too, casting the news as a never-ending story and the protagonists as victims of fate trapped in a time loop.

The aesthetic quality of this piece of news is that of cinematic entertainment, inviting the spectator to relate to it as a thrilling adventure, rather than to reflect on the event's circumstances, both local (Could this have been avoided? How often do such events occur?) and general (What are the causes? What is being done?). Far from opening up a space for thinking about the conditions of the refugees' misfortune, the sense of emergency in this piece of news begins and ends with the viewing experience of the rescue mission – an experience that, much along the lines of Baudrillard's seduction of the spectacle, may thrill the viewing publics but renders the demand for reflexive action irrelevant.

- Philanthropy: Argentinean famine news

The news is introduced in studio by the anchor: 'Argentina suffers the worst economic crisis in its history. In the past few days, ten children died of hunger in the province of Tucuman in North Argentina'. The sentimental potential of children dying, evident in this opening line, becomes the main theme of the reportage, which centres around a press conference with Hilda Duhalde talking about the government's self-help programmes for the poor. The press conference sequence is preceded by a briskly edited flow of children close-ups and of emaciated children lying in hospital beds, followed by shots of what are reported to be famine-stricken city streets, where adults search in rubbish bins. The news concludes at a custom's office, where US medical aid to Argentina was checked and found to be out of date.

The spectators' point of view here is that of omnipresence. We are everywhere where suffering occurs and where attempts to alleviate it take place. At the same time, the children's close-ups on screen renders this sequence iconic: this hectic proliferation of images no longer refers exclusively to specific children from Argentina, but comes to represent the concept of 'starvation' itself, so familiar to us through the abundance of 'icons of starvation' in humanitarian campaigns for African children. Throughout, verbal references to *tragedy, terror, despair* and *death* further capitalize on the images of children and, later on, on their emaciated legs, arms and bellies, or the sound of their cry, sustaining the emotional appeal of this suffering. The screen bar, *dying of hunger*, combined with the direct address to the spectator, *does not leave* you *space for complacence*, are strategic in providing a desirable meaning horizon for the interpretation of such images: 'feel for them'.

The aesthetic quality of this piece is that of philanthropy, an aesthetic characterized by the priority of feelings over facts (Boltanski, 1999: 96–99). Spectators do not need to be convinced by way of proof or argument; it is enough that we feel moved and compelled by the spectacle of suffering. This pure sentimentalism of philanthropy, however, leaves minimal space for the exercise of spectatorial judgement over the key questions of 'why' and 'what to do', cutting off any considerations for action in this news story and ultimately reducing its moral appeal to the momentary consumption of emotion.

- Political activism: death by stoning verdict in Nigeria

This news story consists of footage with voice-over. We are transported from the Nigerian courtroom scene, where the convict Amina Lawal holds her baby in her lap, to city streets, where we witness a violent mobbing scene against an African woman. We then move on to an Amnesty International event in a European capital, which carries the news value of the story, before we return to the streets of Nigeria and the repetition of the mobbing scene. The story hangs together through the use of visual contrasts. The key one is the juxtaposition between the scene of mother-with-baby in courtroom and the mobbing scene in the street. Each of the two images, separately, works iconically: the mother-baby imagery evokes the Western humanity of the 'madonna', whereas the mobbing scene signals the 'savage mind', an alien cultural disposition beyond (Western) rationality and civility. *No to death by stoning*, the screen bar asserts.

This news story, then, works as an ideological statement insofar as it castigates the injustice of the Islamic sharia court and makes a concrete demand on the spectator to act on this injustice by signing the Amnesty International petition. Indeed, instrumental to the practical orientation to action of this piece is the visual presence of Amnesty International, which explicitly invites *everybody* to save Amina Lawal's life and to protest *against practices of stoning, humiliation, mutilation*. The aesthetic quality of the Nigerian convict news is that of the political activism of pamphleteering: the public denunciation of the sharia verdict in the name of human rights. This is an aesthetic that, rather than appealing exclusively to emotions, rests on the presupposed and, therefore, all the more powerful rationality of humanism and universal rights: how can Amina, the young mother of a baby, be condemned to death by stoning simply because she gave birth to this baby?

We have now followed specific variations in the aesthetic quality of three pieces of news on suffering. The African refugees rescue news is that of an adventure spectacle, whereas the famine in Argentina news draws on a philanthropy aesthetic that seeks to touch on the spectators' hearts. Finally, the Nigerian convict news takes us towards the demand for justice and calls spectators to practically oppose the death verdict of the sharia.

Moral agency

It is the spectator as an *actor* that occupies the viewing position in all three news examples, though the form of agency that each news story proposes is substantially different across examples – it is discursive, in the rescue mission and the starvation crisis pieces, and it is practical, in the Amnesty International petition. Let me now discuss in more detail the three positions proposed in these news examples: the spectator as *voyeur*, the spectator as *philanthropist* and the spectator as *protester*.

The spectator voyeur

The spectacular aesthetic of the rescue mission news qualifies the witness position as a *voyeur* position. This is the position of a witness freed from the moral obligation to act and, therefore, able to sit back and enjoy the high adrenaline spectacle unfolding on screen – a position, let us recall, well described by Baudrillard. In which manner can the voyeur act? The voyeur can contemplate in awe. The news footage captures a single moment of danger that could have led to great loss of life. Indeed, it is one thing to imagine what it is like for hundreds of refugees to cross the rough sea in a fragile boat and quite another to witness their struggle in close proximity. This is perhaps good enough. It already fulfils a minimum moralizing function: the rare encounter of safe spectators with the concrete reality of misfortune, even if this misfortune cannot become an object of our own action.

However, there is a significant moral deficit in the voyeur position: its cinematic emphasis on immediacy and adrenaline offers no horizon of historicity in which the massive displacement of refugees today can be understood as a pressing political and humanitarian issue. The news offers, in other words, no resources for judgement over the conditions of the suffering and over a possible horizon of political action on it. A brief comparison to the national Danish television (DR) news report on a similar incident less than a year later, in June 2003, illustrates the point. The news was about a wooden vessel with illegal refugees, which capsized close to the Tunisian shore on its way to southern Italy. The news presentation provided figures for the number of illegal refugees entering Europe per year, 1.5 million, and politicized the issue by connecting it to the EU Summit on the pending European immigration legislation, which, ironically, was taking place that same day of the incident.

The point of the comparison is to draw attention to a news story, which, brief as it is, provides a useful interpretative horizon for the event it reports. In this story, the incident did not 'just happen'. It was situated in a political context, bringing to the fore the controversy surrounding European immigration policies and the problem of refugees' security. Although not an alternative to practical action, this story nevertheless appeals to the spectators' faculty of judgement: it thereby transforms our disposition to this suffering by enabling us to critically reflect on the tragic implications of trans-national mobility for populations inhabiting the zone of danger.

The spectator philanthropist

In famine in Argentina, we are interpellated by a politics of gaze: the children's eye contact with the camera. The moral position we are offered is that of the philanthropist who cares for and, potentially, acts on vulnerable others. Yet, there is no practical connectivity between the individual spectator and the victims of the famine. In which way, then, can the spectator as philanthropist act? The philanthropist can feel. He or she can feel tender-heartedness for the Argentinean sufferer and for the nation's own efforts to comfort the sufferers; he or she can also feel anger towards the United States for sending medical aid *beyond its expiry date*. The spectator's inability to act practically on the suffering is thus displaced on that agent who has the power to act promptly from afar, the state. What we have here is a relationship of philanthropy between states: states are humanized and treated as collective persons, having and provoking emotions. Argentina *cries* and *seeks solutions* whereas the US aid action provokes *anger*.

How far can the philanthropic aesthetic take us, however, when moral action applies in inter-state relations rather than between individuals? Philanthropy is about pictures that move us, not arguments that persuade us. It may succeed in striking a chord, but it says nothing about the causes of, or solutions to, the starvation crisis. Indeed, the news tells us nothing about what led Argentina to this crisis, nor does it explain how the situation might be alleviated through political or humanitarian measures.[11] In its preference for easy sensationalism and drama in the television market of human misfortune, then, philanthropy is achieved at a cost: the Argentinean crisis, chronic, complex and global, is represented as sudden, simple and local.

A brief comparison with a BBC World news piece on child kidnapping in Uganda, in July 2003, illustrates this point. This piece of news combined dramatic on-location footage and interviews with local people, social workers and experts, who not only explained to the public the causes of the problem, but moreover described the international efforts for humanitarian aid and stability in the region. Though no immediate action was obviously required by individual viewers, this piece of news facilitated a process of judgement on the local and global context of these events, thus contributing to shaping an informed public opinion on the Ugandan suffering.

The spectator protester

In the Nigerian sharia news, it is precisely the formation of public opinion that takes over. The aesthetic quality of this story is pamphleteering, a quality that sets up an antagonism between the Islamic sharia and Western humanism. The moral position that this aesthetic offers is that of the cosmopolitan citizen, who empathizes with Amina Lawal and who publicly denounces her death verdict. In which way can the citizen protester act? Empathy with the sufferer takes, in this news story, a form that neither the spectacular aesthetic of the rescue mission nor the philanthropic sentiment towards starving children have been able to achieve. This is the swing from observing and feeling to doing.

Instrumental here is the presence of Amnesty International, a global institution with the moral authority to expose the violation of human rights and to legitimize international action against a perpetrator. In this capacity, Amnesty International provides the resources for judgement that enable spectators to decide where they stand with respect to this moral–political dilemma and whether they would like to sign the petition and form part of a broad network of civil action. In this respect, the Nigerian news represents an important moment in the mediation of suffering, as it demonstrates that media representations can both articulate the demand for public action and invite the spectator as a citizen to participate in it.

The conditional freedom of moral agency

The temptation may be strong to question the call for action in the news as failing to make a real difference in the sufferers' lives. But if we hastily reject the news' proposals for action, discontinuous as these may be, we end up with no other alternative than the pessimism on the role of the media in public life that Baudrillard endorses.[12] It is precisely the inability of Baudrillard's accounts to address the content of mediation as the practical enactment of ethical discourse that leads them to pessimistic diagnoses of media power as one-sidedly leading to voyeurism and passive consumerism.

The repertoire of news proposals we have just seen suggests, instead, that the analytical approach to mediation throws into relief the set of capabilities for judgement and action that television both 'imagines' on behalf of the spectator and enables the spectator to enact as a 'free' subject. The value of this approach to mediation lies in its power to conceptualize moral agency in Arendtian terms as potential for judgement – a potential that cannot be determined theoretically, but needs to be investigated empirically in the ways in which media representations use the *aesthetic quality* of action to expose audiences to specific forms of *moral agency*.

Concerning *aesthetic quality*, we saw that there is a hierarchy of action in the construal of the spectacle of suffering ranging from an aesthetics of adventure, where the spectator is a voyeur of a mass of unfortunates mid-sea, to an aesthetics of political protest, where the spectator is a citizen actively engaging with Amina Lawal, a sufferer with a name, a face and a history – the aesthetics of philanthropy exhausting its humanism in the spectator's consumption of a heart-breaking spectacle. Tellingly, it is only the aesthetics of protest that combines emotions for the sufferer with concrete justifications as to why we need to act on this suffering and how to do so, issuing forth a demand for reflexivity on the conditions of her misfortune.

Concerning *moral agency*, we saw that Baudrillard's voyeur is only one of the options available in the news. The option of social solidarity in the sharia verdict news makes an explicit appeal to the spectators' faculty of judgement and links this to the demand for action in the name of human rights. In so doing, this news grants audiences with a form of moral agency that cannot be conceptualized within the premises of the pessimistic thesis – at least not without being quickly rejected as yet another form of spectatorial narcissism.[13] Yet, recognizing this positive potential of mediation is necessary if we wish to develop caring relationships with distant others and promote options for action that may change the conditions of their suffering.

Instrumental in this view of power is that individual viewers are already conceptualized as actors, because it is only upon their relative capacity for action – their agency – that the power of mediation can come to bear its effects. In this manner, the power of mediation does not take place by force of explicit instruction over what is right or wrong, but rather by force of exemplary stories as to what matters in a particular situation and how to act appropriately in it. This is power exercised as performative action, action that intends to influence, guide or inspire the action of individuals – what Foucault has eloquently described as a power over the *conduct of conduct*.[14]

In this view of mediation, the relationship between media representation and moral agency is best formulated as a relationship of *conditional freedom*. I use the term conditional freedom to refer to the function of the television text to regulate, but by no means determine, the spectator's capacities for judgement by opening up multiple ethical positions for them to engage with. This multiple economy of representation is not resolutely negative, but rather inherently ambivalent, positive as well as negative. It is positive, because we can only relate to others on the condition that we are already constituted as free subjects that draw selectively upon an existing repertoire of identity resources. And it is negative, because the hierarchical variation in the resources for moral agency across news stories is tightly linked to a political economy of global broadcasting that ultimately reproduces an exclusively Western sensibility towards 'our' own suffering at the expense of sufferings of the distant other.

It is this ambivalence in television's economy of representation that makes the relationship between media representation and moral agency a political relationship, *par excellence* – one that we need to critically analyse in order to understand how informed action on distant suffering may become possible in the age of global mediation.

Conclusion

In this chapter, I draw on an Arendtian definition of moral agency as the articulation of action with judgement about the causes and implications of action, in order to investigate the extent to which the media, in confronting us with a number of moral dilemmas about our world, may also provide us with the resources that enable us to act reflexively on this world. Drawing on Aristotelian insights on an analytical rather than theoretical approach to the question of ethical action, I discuss a number of news broadcasts on distant suffering as examples that illustrate the practical enactment of ethical discourse in the media. Whereas all broadcasts beg the question of how to act on specific instances of suffering, each represents suffering in different aesthetic modes and proposes different patterns of engagement to viewing publics. This approach escapes the pessimism of post-modern theory and advocates the critical analysis of mediation as a symbolic technology of power, which endows spectators with conditional freedom, that is, the capacity to exercise judgement and engage in action as we will, yet under the constraints of a global hierarchy of place and human life, as this is reflected in the practices of television broadcasting.

Notes

1. For similar discussions on the concept of judgement in Arendt's work, see Benhabib (1988), Villa (1999) and Silverstone (2006).
2. I draw on a sociological definition of cosmopolitanism broadly understood as 'an orientation, a willingness to relate with the Other' (Hannerz 1996: 103). For a discussion of the term 'cosmopolitan outlook', see Beck (2006) and Beck and Sznaider (2006). Regarding a media-induced 'banal' cosmopolitanism, see Urry (2000).
3. I take Baudrillard (1983, 1988, 1994) to be a prototypical figure of this strand of post-structuralist theory, but figures like Maffesoli (1993, 1996) and Virilio (1991, 1994) also belong here. From a sociological perspective, the works of 'network society' theorists, such as Castells (1996, 1997), Lash (1990, 2001) and Lash *et al.* (1994) constitute an affirmative version of the post-modern account on the aestheticization of the social (Delanty, 2000: 142; for a similar categorization, see also McQuire, 1999; Armitage, 2000).
4. The claim that media texts make available proposals for identification and action to spectators is shared by a number of critical hermeneutic approaches that, breaking with the a-historical and static interpretations of 'spectatorship theory', ask the question of how media texts may participate in turning a group of spectators into a media public – a collectivity with a will to act (Alexander and Jakobs, 1998: 28–32; Corner, 1999: 6–8; Dayan, 2001: 743–765; Seaton, 2005: 102–132; Silverstone, 2006: 43–55). It is this line of enquiry that this chapter follows.
5. Not all news stories on suffering incorporate the demand for action in their narratives. Much of distant suffering, in fact, either gets reported as a brief fact or remains below the threshold of mediated visibility (Cohen, 2001; Silverstone, 2006). I have elsewhere drawn a distinction between news on suffering without pity, a class of news that contains no emotional or practical appeal (Chouliaraki, 2006: 97–115), and news on suffering with pity, a class of news that incorporates an emotional or practical appeal in its stories of distant suffering (ibid.: 118–125), this latter being the focus of this chapter.
6. Boltanski (1999: 57–131), in a historical overview of the forms of the public representation of suffering (what he calls 'topics of suffering'), distinguishes between the topic of denunciation, the topic of sentiment and the aesthetic topic. Boltanski's three topics have informed the description of the aesthetic quality of news in this piece of analysis. These topics can be traced back to

classical Hellenism and, later on, to the emergence of the modern public sphere in Europe and its Enlightenment ideal of universal moralism (Arendt, 1973/1990: 70; Peters, 1999: 33–62). Today, appropriated and reconfigured by modern technologies of mediation such as television, they still perform the crucial political function of presenting human misfortune in public with a view to arousing the emotion of the spectators as well as inviting their impartial deliberation on how-to-act upon the misfortune.
7. For an illustration of this point, see Alain Minc's criticism of Baudrillard's 'The Mind of Terrorism' article on the 11 September terrorist attacks: 'The collapse of the Twin Towers could only signal, in his [Baudrillard's] eyes, the definite triumph of the virtual, the moment when he deafeningly snatches up the real'. From this perspective, Minc attacks Baudrillard for his incapacity 'to recognize that there exists a hierarchy of values and that referring to morality is not incident' (Minc, in *Le Monde*, 6 November 2001).
8. Baudrillard's pessimism reflects a more general pessimism about the role of technology in social life, which haunts the sociological imagination of the twentieth century (Delanty, 2000: 130–135). In the shadow of Adorno's critique of technology, Baudrillard came to view the electronic image as an impoverished aesthetic and to understand the power of mediation as a totalitarian force that suppresses public sensibilities and social solidarities. The connection between this view and the pessimism on the role of mediation as an ethical force today is rather straightforward. Technology transforms the nature of media representation in ways that thoroughly fictionalize or manipulate suffering, thus cancelling or minimizing the demand for public action on the condition of suffering.
9. I have elsewhere developed a post-structuralist appropriation of Aristotelian analytics in critical media studies (Chouliaraki, 2006); see also Flyvbjerg (2001), for the epistemic value of Aristotelian analytics broadly in social scientific research, and Ross (1995: 31–49), for Aristotle's inductive methods and analytics.
10. The news pieces in this article come from Greek national television (NET); Danish national television (DR) and BBC World. The main pieces come from NET (prime-time news on 23 July 2002, for the African rescue news, and 8 November 2002, for the economic crisis in Argentina and the death-by-stoning verdict in Nigeria). I selected them, because each piece gradually propels my argument that there is an internal hierarchy of proposals for action in the news and helps me illustrate the discursive features of such proposals in each news story. The key aesthetic features and moral agency options of these examples, however, are partially shared by the DR (20 June 2003) and BBC World (12 June 2003) examples and can be said to belong to a broad repertoire of options for the public staging of suffering, available in contemporary Western media.
11. Such causes are both internal to Argentina (political, institutional and economic) and external to it (regulations imposed on Argentina's economy by the International Monetary Fund and its dominant partner, USA). For the internal chronic government trouble in Argentina, and the incapacity of the state to manage the crisis, see *The Economist*, 1 February 2003; *BBC News* website Country Profile: Argentina, 19 July 2002. For an overview on Argentina's international debt see *The Economist*, 25 January 2003 and *Global Exchange*

Website (five case studies on the IFM and World Democracy; and IMF/WB Fact Sheets).

12. To be sure, there are good reasons for pessimism. Hierarchies of news reporting, whereby some sufferings are presented as of no concern to spectators whereas others are presented as relevant to all, do exist in the media and reproduce more vital hierarchies of geographical place and human life across the globe. My argument is that, unless we turn to an analytical language that shows us just how these hierarchies are created in media representations, we will not be able to challenge these hierarchies and change the symbolic conditions for action towards distant others.
13. For similar perspectives, see Barnett (2003: 81–107), Thompson (1997: 10–49) and Hall (1997: 208–236).
14. Foucault (1982) talks about *'conduire la conduite'* to define power exercised as the ability to act on the field of possible actions of others (see also Foucault 1991/1978: 87–104). In this conception of power, not necessarily antagonistic to a view of power as domination, the subject of power is a 'subject' in two senses of the word: as endowed with the capacity or possibility for action and as subjected to power relations (see further Patton, 1998: 67–69).

7
Sites of Resistance: Death Row Homepages and the Politics of Compassion

Ezra Tessler

Contemporary forms of state-sanctioned violence present a stark challenge to understanding the place of empathy and moral solidarity in modern society (Ginzburg, 1994; Sznaider, 1998; Moyn, 2006). A vast body of ethnographic research on social suffering points to the consequences of cultural practices that place certain people outside the realm of human category (Scheper-Hughes, 1997; Glover, 1999; Das and Kleinman, 2001). All too often, these practices prove central to garnering public consent for state-sanctioned policies of violence. To combat these effects, sociologists like Iain Wilkinson highlight the potential for the mass media to engender amongst members of the public a greater imagination of the suffering of others (Wilkinson, 2005: 15). Wilkinson's point is that people's mediated experiences of suffering play a central role in what he calls 'the politics of compassion' (ibid.: 6, 92). Wilkinson calls for a critical sociology of suffering to attend to the diverse ways in which people 'encounter and give voice to their suffering' (ibid.: 166). With this goal in mind, I examine a current form of state-sanctioned violence, the death penalty in the United States, and a unique form of resistance to it, the death row homepage, in order to reflect upon the contemporary politics of compassion. I suggest that the death row homepage, as a personal act of resistance aimed at inciting, through empathy and solidarity, broader forms of public resistance, may herald new moral possibilities unleashed in the mediated structures of contemporary society.

Facing the death penalty

Around 3400 men and women currently await execution on death row in the United States. Over 120 countries around the world have abolished the death penalty either in law or practice, yet the United States remains the last Western democracy to retain it (Hood, 2001: 334). Nonetheless, the anti-death penalty movement, fuelled in part by international outrage at US policy, has gained momentum in recent years. Amongst these abolitionist efforts, a key debate has surfaced about strategically useful ways to campaign against capital punishment (Bedau, 1982; Radelet, 1989; Paternoster, 1991; Streib, 1993; Coyne and Entzeroth, 1994; Haines, 1996). Joining the debate is Austin Sarat's *When the State Kills* (2001), which focuses on the cultural practices that shape public attitudes to crime and punishment and infuse the death penalty with its moral force and popular legitimacy (Sarat, 2001: 15). Hoping to erode public support, Sarat stresses the importance of studying oppositional voices in the sphere of penal politics. With the dramatic growth of new media, exploring diverse voices on the Internet may indeed contribute to a critical sociology of suffering and succeed in unsettling the dominant ways of thinking about the death penalty in the United States.

Death row homepages represent the newest generation in a long-established genre of prisoner autobiography-as-public-appeal (Summers, 2004: 1–3). First appearing in the late 1990s, there are now between 400 and 500 death row homepages on the Internet.[1] Most sites are simple one-page texts consisting of a photograph and personal statement, though these personal statements can range from short paragraphs to lengthier tracts that include life histories and case explanations. A small minority of sites provide additional material, either on the main site or on derivative sites linked to the main homepage. This material often includes poetry, essays and other writings. Despite this variety, death row homepages represent a uniquely large and coherent group of oppositional texts.

A homepage is defined as a website containing material archived specifically about the author (Graham, 1999: 69). Because death row prisoners do not have direct access to the Internet, their sites are administered by individuals on the outside and groups posting material provided by prisoners.[2] Although death row homepages are composite texts, for which their administrators have a substantial degree of editorial control, the administrators' influence is largely limited to decisions about layout (for details, see www.ccadp.org). Regardless, prisoners are the principal authorial source of their material and can view and edit their sites from printed versions.[3] The death row homepage should, therefore, be understood as a highly edited and managed form of autobiographical text (Hines, 2000: 26; for elaboration see Turkle, 1995).

How, then, do death row prisoners use the material they post on their sites to challenge the death penalty and appeal to the public? Stanley Cohen's *States of Denial* (2001) provides a helpful guide for studying death row homepages as public appeals. Cohen's study of famine-relief campaigns examines their use of images and words to contest the cultural practices that enable the public to permit the suffering of others (ibid.: 215–217). For Cohen, the goal is to understand how these campaigns hope to touch their viewers (ibid.: xiii). Similar to these famine-relief campaigns, death row prisoners hope to use their homepages to convince the public of the validity and urgency of their individual cases and to motivate involvement in the anti-death penalty cause. In doing so, they comment directly on the death penalty as an institution and on the broader social conditions that support it, suggesting specific steps that their viewers can take to help them in their fight against perceived injustice.

Following Cohen's example, how do death row prisoners frame their efforts and how do they seek to shape specific responses from their viewers? How do prisoners' representation of themselves and modes of address attempt to oppose certain ways of seeing, feeling and acting about capital punishment in order to recruit the public's help? Finally, what do these efforts and the relationships they hope to foster show about the opportunities for recognition, empathy and solidarity in contemporary society?

Punishment and sensibilities

In *Punishment and Modern Society* (1990), David Garland argues that punishment forms a set of signifying practices that prescribe specific notions about moral boundaries and social relations. In its institutions, rituals and self-representations, punishment 'dramatizes and authoritatively enacts some of the most basic moral-political categories... which help shape our symbolic universe' (Garland, 1990: 195). Garland suggests analyzing the ways that punishment's messages are deployed and negotiated, as well as their effects on the relations between the public and the offender. In order to understand death row homepages as sites of resistance, it is necessary first to examine the cultural practices that inform the contemporary death penalty, the narratives enacted through its rituals and representations in society, and the relations these formulate between the public and the punished.

The study of the trends in death penalty practices over the last three centuries is a major theme in both social theory and historical sociology (Foucault, 1977; Bowers, 1984; Spierenberg, 1984; Masur, 1989; Linebaugh, 1992; Gatrell, 1994; Meranze, 1996). These accounts describe the 'pre-modern' execution as a public spectacle, enlisting the public, inscribing the sovereign's power onto the offender's body and enacting brutal force for all to see (Foucault, 1977: 50). The pain of the condemned displayed the power of the authority: suffering was intended to bring salvation, reconstitution of the moral order and a strong warning to any potential wrongdoer (Kaufman-Osborn, 2002: 479–480). Nonetheless, because punishment took place in public, participants could contest its meanings and disrupt its scripted rituals (Foucault, 1977: 60).

In the nineteenth century, the death penalty, like punishment more broadly, moved behind prison walls, where its procedures could be tightly controlled. Whilst accounts vary as to the exact causal factors involved in this transition, numerous scholars focus on the 'sensibilities' and cultural norms that girded the changing penal forms (Vaughan, 2000: 73–75).[4] Connected to broader social, economic and geopolitical structures, sensibilities represent the socio-cultural and psychic constitutions of a society (Tonry, 2004: 420). In *The Civilizing Process* (1978), Norbert Elias tracks the changes in European sensibilities since the Middle Ages, showing the development of modern sensibilities marked by the suspicion of public arenas and the increasing sensitivity to seemingly senseless cruelty (Vaughan, 2000: 77). 'As with other signs of brutishness, the sight of violence, pain, and physical suffering became highly disturbing and distasteful to modern sensibilities' (Garland, 1990: 223). In David Rothman's words, the spectacle of suffering 'seemed at once disorderly and dangerous, garish and cruel' (Rothman, 1990: xxiv). In line with Elias's claims, the nineteenth and twentieth centuries saw the increasing occlusion of the mechanisms of death.

From hanging to firing squad, electrocution, gas chamber and, finally, lethal injection, the US death penalty has aimed progressively at masking physical pain and concealing its own violence. In its current routine, 'officials perform mechanistically before a small, silent gathering of authorized witnesses' (Johnson, 1990: 5). The machinery of death proceeds 'quietly, invisibly, bureaucratically' (Sarat, 2001: 55). In place of sovereignty, calculated science presides, and the instant of death becomes a virtual non-event (Kaufman-Osborn, 2002: 213). As an execution without an executioner, the death penalty displaces the direct responsibility of the public in the act of killing and denies the ambiguities wrought by human suffering (Abernethy, 1996: 423; Sarat, 2001: 194). In its current state, the rituals of capital punishment ensure that people 'are shielded from the full meaning and moral consequences' of state-sanctioned murder (Sarat, 2001: 277).

Although most western countries abolished capital punishment in the second half of the twentieth century, the continued use of the death penalty in a majority of US states represents a stark contrast (Garland, 2002: 472). Garland's *The Culture of Control* (2001) provides insight into the relationship between late twentieth-century American sensibilities and contemporary penal politics that have led to the continued popularity of the death penalty in the United States. He argues that the massive economic, social and demographic changes of the second half of the twentieth century have led to increasing public fear over crime and a sense that the state is unable to deal with crime effectively (Garland, 2001: 73). Within the increasingly emotionalized discourse on crime and punishment, tough-on-crime measures like the death penalty represent the 'abandonment of reasoned, instrumental action', a form of state-sanctioned 'acting out' (ibid.: 110).[5]

The dominant cultural practices that inform this development 'recruit punitive subjects and construct privileged viewing positions through which individuals are addressed as vengeful victim-citizens' (Valier, 2004a: 4). Depicting good people versus bad people, the result is a broad 'set of powerful, affectively provocative narratives about those who do violence, and about those harmed by violence, which demand punitive vengeance' (Lynch, 2000: 227). No longer the aberrant folk devil, the criminal now pervades political, judicial and popular narratives as an ever-lurking presence (Valier, 2004a: 114–115).[6] These reductionist narratives of crime and punishment enable capital punishment to proceed with moral clarity as the death row prisoner is liquidated of his or her human worth and feeling (Lynch, 2000: 227).

Ultimately, the narratives that swirl in and around the death penalty enable certain modes of ethical relations between the public and the condemned, denying moral ambiguity and diverting the public's responsibility in the act of state killing. Reinforcing strict moral dichotomies between the offender and victim, and between legitimate violence and murder, the death penalty enacts a heated, emotional call to retribution in the cold, calculated ritual of justice. Within this context, death row can be seen as one more step in the smooth procedural march towards abstract justice. Central to this process is the question of whose suffering can and cannot be seen and heard. Similar to Giorgio Agamben's description of concentration camps, death row becomes a place 'outside of life and death' (Agamben, 1999: 70): a spectral place where prisoners wait invisibly until they reappear in the announcement of their execution on the nightly news (Lynch, 2000: 280). Yet these punitive practices are ripe with ambiguities and spaces for critique (Valier, 2004a: 6).[7] In a world increasingly dominated by new forms of media, it is important to examine the specific mediated spaces and sites of oppositional narratives.

Botching death, raising voices

The debate regarding the Internet's social and political implications focuses on its potential to transcend traditional boundaries of space and time (Jones, 1999: 6). In this sense, the Internet is a crucial component of the globalizing developments that shrink spatial and temporal barriers and link distant localities (Giddens, 1990: 64). By constructing a viewing community in which images and texts flow beyond traditional borders, the Internet allows individuals and groups – albeit largely confined to privileged socio-demographic enclaves – to reach out and link up through the use of textual and graphical material (Jones, 1999: 22). What, then, are the implications of death row prisoners' entrance into cyberspace where, with the help of site administrators, they speak beyond the prison walls and appeal to the public for help?

The goal of providing a forum for prisoners' voices reflects a growing number of abolitionist efforts to present alternative ways of thinking about the death penalty. The 'botched execution' provides an apt analogy for these efforts (Haines, 1992). In a botched execution, the executioner, victim, witness or death process fails to conform directly to the official script (Smith, 1996: 241). One such form of botched execution is when the body of the condemned responds unexpectedly by prolonging the execution or reacting gruesomely, reinserting the sentient body into the process of death (Haines, 1992: 126). The 1999 execution of 'Tiny' Lee Allen Davis in Florida presents a vivid example: when Davis was electrocuted, he released a series of screams and blood streamed down his face and onto his chest (Garland, 2002: 466). Photos of his bloodied body were leaked to the public and an outcry led Florida to retire the electric chair as a method of death.

The botched execution, therefore, destabilizes the pretence of humane murder and hints at the hidden violence involved in state killing (Haines, 1992: 126–127). In so doing, it injects a level of moral ambiguity into the relationship between the public and the condemned. Evi Girling's examination of Benetton's campaign 'We, on death row', illustrates another anti-death penalty effort to reinsert the prisoner's presence in the process of death and open it up for the viewing public's interpretation (Girling, 2004: 281). Girling argues that the advertising campaign, which featured death row prisoner portraits on posters and billboards, provided 'a window into another world of narrative possibilities' (ibid.: 284).

The hope of botching the death penalty is central to understanding death row homepages, as many death row homepage site administrators confirm using the Internet to give prisoners a 'voice' (Berkowitz, 2002: A1). For example, Tracy Lamourie, the director of Canadian Coalition Against the Death Penalty, a key organization administering death row homepages, explains that prisoners 'have been sentenced to death, not to silence' (Word, 2002: H12). Her statement repeats those made by others who administer death row homepage sites, supporting prisoners' right to express their experiences on death row, plead their cases and seek aid (Berkowitz, 2002: A1).

Framing the death penalty

Considering the public forum provided by the Internet, one can easily imagine why death row prisoners post their homepages. Often convicted of heinous crimes, they are fighting desperately for their lives. In the politicized debate over capital punishment, it may be tempting to see their efforts as either deceptive public relations stunts or the last stand of heroic victims. But prisoners' homepages reflect a much more complicated reality and their subject matter and their goals demand a more nuanced approach. No doubt, death row prisoners use their homepages for a host of reasons, including therapeutic or creative ends. But an unmistakeable and overriding feature of all death row homepages is that they are oppositional texts – they seek to evoke empathy for their individual cases and resistance to capital punishment more generally. It is in this light that the literature on 'framing' offers useful guidance for analysis. This body of scholarship suggests examining the ways in which people 'participate in public deliberation strategically' in order to make sense of the world to themselves and others (Pan and Kosicki, 2001: 39).

Building on Erving Goffman's early formulation, social movement scholars suggest that people use frames as interpretive devices to 'locate, perceive, identify, and label' the raw data of experience (Goffman, 1974: 21; Snow *et al.*, 1986: 464). By framing their cause in certain ways, individuals and groups within social movements seek to shape public discourse (Hertog and McLeod, 2001: 146). Their goal is 'to promote a particular problem definition, causal interpretation, moral evaluation, and... treatment recommendation' (Entman, 1993: 52). Thus, they assign meaning to 'relevant events and conditions in ways that are intended to mobilize potential adherents and constituents, to garner bystander support, and to demobilize antagonists' (Snow and Benford, 1988: 198). A core part of this process involves diagnosing a problem, offering a prognosis or solution to it, and providing a motivational vocabulary or rationale for engaging in ameliorative steps (Benford and Snow, 2000: 616–617). Individuals and organizations within social movements frame events and circumstances not only to mobilize consensus from their intended audience, but also to stimulate action (Klandermans, 1988: 175–178).

As autobiographical texts, death row homepages provide the opportunity for prisoners to reframe the death penalty. How a person decides to present him or herself autobiographically is intimately tied to questions of intended audience, for which the self is meant to be highly persuasive. Webpages highlight this dimension of autobiography as a form of personal advertisement for the viewer-as-consumer. The death row homepage represents a medium within which the self is enacted as a strategic resource in the act of speaking from death row (Hines, 2000: 139). In giving prisoners the space to present themselves and the medium through which to voice their experiences, death row homepages address the distant, emotionalized relation of condemnation between the public and the capital offender.

Like all forms of address, the very act of presenting oneself in an autobiographical context shapes the relationship between the author and the reader: in this sense, it prescribes certain ontological and ethical relations (Shotter, 1989: 147). In being addressed, a reader is instructed how to 'be', particularly with regard to the author. In other words, the language, content, voice and mode of address within an autobiography call forth certain types of 'you' (ibid.: 144–145). Autobiographical narratives provide the medium through which the author constructs a self and shapes the reader's own status *vis-à-vis* the author. The goal, then, is not just to explore how death row prisoners make sense of their world: the goal is also to understand how they make sense of it to others.

Moving images[8]

As described above, the contemporary form of the death penalty denies the offender's humanity as well as the public's responsibility in the act of state killing. But as Claire Valier suggests, there is the possibility that images could move people 'elsewhere and otherwise than towards vengeance' (Valier, 2004b: 252). Hoping to evoke empathy and compel their viewers to act, death row prisoners post photographs to frame capital punishment in minutely personal terms as well as in relation to larger questions of justice in society. Towards this end, they provide warm and friendly portraits of themselves, their families and their friends. They challenge the binaries between criminal and victim, appeal to broader beliefs and values about family and community, and cast themselves as legitimate sources of moral authority. Confronting the viewer with his or her role in state killing, they request an ethical audit in which the viewer takes responsibility for the prisoner's fleeting mortality. With these images, death row prisoners hope to make the idea of state-sanctioned murder seem unfathomable.

Greeting injustice

Although scholars often overlook the ways that visual language participates in the framing process (Gandy, 2001: 371), images have the capacity to convey messages that might 'meet with greater resistance if put in words' (Messaris and Abraham, 2001: 221).[9] In *Camera Lucida*, Roland Barthes explains that photographic images hold a sensuous, pre-semantic power to affect the viewer (Barthes, 2000: 79). Barthes uses the term *punctum*, or wound, to refer to those elements within an image that are particularly moving. Through this wound, the world behind and within the photograph stirs the viewer and incites feeling (ibid.: 3; Valier and Lippens, 2004: 320). The image's poignant details catch the viewer's eye, gaining emotional and cognitive traction in his or her mind. Describing his own reactions to a photograph's *punctum*, Barthes explains, 'I see, I feel, hence I notice, I observe, and I think' (Barthes, 2000: 21).

Upon visiting a death row prisoner's homepage, the viewer first meets the prisoner's face. Placed at the top of the homepage, the majority of prisoners' photographs are simple, upper-body portraits. A minority of sites also feature images of the prisoners with their families and friends. Piven and Cloward use the term 'injustice framework' to describe the means by which individuals and organizations diagnose a situation as problematic and define their cause (Piven and Cloward, 1977: 12; Snow et al., 1986: 466). Towards this end, death row prisoners use their photographic portraits as tangible and immediate evidence, introducing themselves and challenging the abstract notion of justice that supports contemporary capital punishment. Against the anonymity of death row, the prisoner becomes an individual. In the search of his eyes, the twist of his smile, the set of his jaw, in all of these details the prisoner becomes a flesh-and-blood person. No longer can he be a faceless killer, for now he is endowed with a discrete physical presence and personality.

Thus, whilst the death penalty shuts the public out, the prisoner's photograph welcomes the viewer in. This invitation can be seen in the typical homepage photographs of Florida death row prisoner Terence Valentine (http://ccadp.org/terencevalentine.htm) and Texas death row prisoner Miguel Martinez (http://ccadp.org/miguelmartinez.htm). With his upturned eyebrows and half-smile, Valentine reaches out with the warm embrace of an elder loved one. In a similar vein, Martinez's pleasant grin and beaming eyes welcome the viewer into a friendly interaction that is open and compassionate. Like all photographs on death row homepages, these images ground the issue of the death penalty in immediate and personal terms. Meanwhile, they contrast the abstract or vengeful state with the warm and inviting traits of a familiar face. These photographs provide the foundation from which prisoners launch their injustice framework.

Innocence and dissonance

Hoping to make the idea of the death penalty seem misplaced and reprehensible, death row prisoners use their photographs to cast themselves in ways that are radically incongruous with the stereotype of a murderous convict. This dimension is particularly explicit in the photographs that present prisoners with their family members and friends. In these images, prisoners exploit the tender innocence of universally recognizable, familiar relationships of love and trust. The common image of a caring, sensitive man can be seen in the homepages of California death row prisoner Chay'im Ben-Sholom (http://ccadp.org/chayimmarshall.htm) and Connecticut death row prisoner Daniel Webb (http://ccadp.org/danielwebbphotos.htm). In Ben-Sholem's photograph, he lovingly grasps an older woman's hand and protectively embraces her frail frame. In Webb's image, his beaming smile expresses a father's pride as he displays his two daughters to the viewer. As with all prisoner homepages, particularly those showing family members, they seek to emote simple moral tenderness.

These photographs reorient the moral compass of capital punishment in order to establish prisoners as legitimate sources of moral authority. They further contest the death penalty's claim to justice – and seek to establish their own – by recruiting the moral capital provided by friendship and familial piety. In doing so, they seek to pry open what one scholar of social movements calls 'the span of sympathy' (Coser, 1969). Turning the dominant binary between killer and victim on its head, the prisoner challenges the viewer to choose sides in a debate that pits love and hope against the stark threat of death.

By displaying the lateral consequences of the death penalty, prisoners attempt to make capital punishment seem all the more immoral given its destructive effects on the innocent and unassuming bonds of family and community. Thus, they provide photographs that frame their cases for potential supporters in terms of values and beliefs that are both basic and familiar: their fate is tied to family and friendship, love and devotion, commitment and community. Snow *et al.* describe these attempts to amplify certain beliefs and values as a central step in the process of 'frame extension' (Snow *et al.*, 1986: 469–472). As they explain, the goals of certain actors or organizations within social movements often 'appear to have little if any bearing on the life situations and interests' of the public' (ibid.: 472). Faced with this challenge, activists extend the boundaries of their immediate cause to include themes that are relevant and personally important to potential adherents. Death row homepage photographs emphasize specific values that are 'worthy of protection and promotion' – like the familial bond – and amplify beliefs about death row prisoners, like their tender and loving qualities" (ibid.). In seeking to promote these values and beliefs in visceral and immediate ways, prisoners use their photographs to cast their appeals in terms of protecting the basic building blocks of a just society.

Towards responsibility

Death row prisoners challenge the death penalty by presenting the visual evidence of their individual lives and linking their personal fate to the promotion of broad and inclusive values and beliefs. At the same time, however, they seek to recast the social actors involved in state-sanctioned murder. Throughout their images, the prisoner's gaze addresses the individual viewer's role in state killing. They posit the death penalty not as a relationship between the prisoner and the state, or between the offender and the victim, but as an immediate relationship between the individual prisoner and the individual viewer. As Susan Sontag writes, photography is an elegiac art: it captures a passing moment and invites the viewer to participate in the fleeting mortality of the photograph's subject (Sontag, 1979: 15). This transience is explicit in death row photographs. The death row prisoner portrait seeks to move the viewer exactly because this person awaits death: the threat of execution pervades the relationship between the prisoner and the viewer, and the prisoner casts the viewer as a witness to his impending death. It is in this moment of vulnerability that the prisoner asks the viewer to step in and act.

The death row prisoner's photographs directly challenge the viewer's ontological and ethical status. Jean-Paul Sartre's *Being and Nothingness* (1968) points to the ways in which the other's gaze constitutes the self. Sartre describes a scenario in which an individual who is spying through a keyhole suddenly realizes that he or she is being watched. In the other person's stare, the individual is exposed, suddenly becoming conscious of his or her actions as they appear to someone else (ibid.: 260). Evoking a strong sense of shame, this gaze marks a shift in one's relationship to the other: the individual must account for his or her self in relation to another individual (Butler, 2004: 138). In a similar way, prisoners look out at the viewer, requesting that the viewer justify his or her status *vis-à-vis* the prisoner. This goal is made all but explicit in now-deceased death row prisoner James Allridge's photograph (http://www.deathrow.at/allridge/).[10] In this image, Allridge stares out at the viewer with an intent curiosity, his outstretched hand greeting the viewer directly. As with all prisoner portraits, he strives to force the viewer to clarify his or her complicity in his suffering. This accusation not only seeks to touch the viewer but also make explicit his or her status as a participant.

The prisoner portrait, whilst hoping to garner emotive traction in the powerful act of accusation, builds on the desperation and vulnerability captured in the photograph's voyeuristic dimension. The prisoner is not only trapped in an uneven gaze – he looks but cannot see (Barthes, 2000: 111) – but also by the physical barriers between the prisoner and the viewer. Whilst prisoners reach out in the hope of forming a deeply intimate connection through the flesh of the face, this relationship is foiled by the prison plexi-glass and redoubled with the camera's own lens, now the computer screen.

With their photographs, prisoners seek to evoke empathy and 'the affliction that one experiences for the pains and sufferings' of familiar others (Valier, 2004c: 8). Levinas argues that the face of the other calls out with a noiseless scream of vulnerability (Butler, 2004: 137). According to Levinas, the face captures a mortality that seems both frightening and pleading to the viewer (Levinas, 1986: 23–24). The encounter with the face is fraught with anxiety and tension, for 'the face is, from the start, the demand of the one who needs you, who is counting on you' (Levinas, 1988: 169). Death row homepages draw on this power to frame an intimate bond with their viewers, challenge their complacency and evoke a sense of responsibility. And yet, these images seek to draw their viewers in to read further.

Texts and the appeal

In addition to their photographs, death row prisoners post writing on their homepages to contest the stereotypes of capital offenders and reconstitute the ethical relations between themselves and the viewing public. Framing their cases as specific examples of injustice, prisoners present themselves simultaneously as victims and survivors, seeking to evoke pity and empathy whilst also trying to inspire action. With this dual identity, prisoners claim to speak with a privileged voice of truth, reason and justice against the forces of death. As the common man turned messianic defender of the public good, prisoners construct a public community of mutual interests. They cement this community in a personal relationship with the reader, establishing this closeness in the very act of sharing their experiences on their homepages. By positioning themselves as intimate friends, public protectors, agents of truth and compassion – in trying to seal their fate to that of the reader and the public good more broadly – prisoners hope to connect with the reader so that in reading the homepage, he or she feels already personally responsible and inspired.

Becoming victims, becoming survivors[11]

The most immediate and pervasive point that death row homepages make is that prisoners are helpless victims of injustice. Though a substantial minority of prisoners claim they are innocent of the crime for which they were convicted (around 25 per cent of all websites), almost all of the remaining prisoners evade the direct question of their guilt. These prisoners claim that they were convicted unfairly, either due to faulty evidence, improper legal defence or other legal mistakes. Nonetheless, in seeking to evoke empathy and shock from their readers, all prisoners argue that their experiences on death row, regardless of guilt or innocence, reflect the punishment's cruelty and injustice.

A characteristic attempt to present death row as a place of unjust suffering is Texas death row prisoner Richard Cartwright's site. Cartwright gives an account of the daily pains that he suffers. He describes his struggles with guards and details the violence, humiliation, loneliness and sense of futility that he experiences. His account, like many others, draws a frequent parallel to the 'Nazi concentration camp', as if to gain momentum from the moral capital embodied in the consummate image of evil and victimization (http://ccadp.org/uncensoredcartwright.htm). Comparing prisoners to Holocaust victims, Cartwright explains that death row prisoners 'sit passively by as we wait our turn to be slaughtered' (ibid.). Like all homepages, Cartwright's attempts to assault the palatable 'humane' countenance of the modern death penalty that enables public complacence.

Death row prisoners describe the effects of this victimhood, confronting the reader in minutely palpable terms with their overwhelming physical and mental suffering. William Leonard's homepage provides a typical example in which prisoners divulge the personal grief and loneliness wrought by the realities of death row and deploy them as tangible indicators of unjust suffering: 'I'm on Nevada's death row – a forgotten being, a discarded human.... I'm oppressed, ostracized and seemingly unsalvageable. Human interaction is a rarity in my world. I have never felt so alone, adrift, absolutely cut-off [sic] from everything and everyone' (http://ccadp.org/williamleonard.htm). With this depiction, Leonard points to the immediate and personal effects of an unjust punishment. As in all homepages, Leonard battles the stereotypical images of the capital offender as cold and unfeeling and blurs the rigid boundaries between victim and offender. As victims of injustice, they reach out in misery, seeking empathy and action from their readers.

At the same time, death row prisoners paradoxically present themselves as strong and forceful survivors. A characteristic claim to strength and hope appears in Texas death row prisoner John Huggins's statement: 'This one thing I've learned from coming to the Row, you can take everything from a man, but you can't kill his soul' (http://www.lampofhope.org/fl059121poems.html). This move serves a distinct goal in framing their case and the death penalty more broadly. According to Cohen, making the sufferer appear vulnerable is an important means to gain empathy, but too much vulnerability may leave the viewer feeling overwhelmed with hopelessness (Snow *et al.*, 1986: 470–471; Cohen, 2001: 183). Thus, flanking a lonesome, lingering helplessness, prisoners depict themselves as unyielding agents of hope, pointing to the opportunity to turn a sealed fate into an open future. It is in the shadow of this tension that they appeal to the reader for help.

The dual identity of helpless, suffering victim and active, hopeful survivor plays out in all aspects of prisoner homepages as they try to inspire action. Cohen explains that a central component of affecting involvement from distant strangers is what he calls an 'empowerment chain' (Klandermans, 1984: 585; Cohen, 2001: 219). By showing the reader that urgent help is needed but that there is hope – and specific steps can be taken – prisoners try to empower action. Throughout prisoner homepages, this empowerment chain is set in motion by a plea. A typical example is William Clark's plea:

> The first thing you can do is pray.... Secondly, you can help by becoming an 'ACTIVIST' for my unconditional release. Third, you can help by sending donations to help me pay for a competent, caring, experienced appellate attorney. Finally, you can help by being a friend, by writing me to help add a sense of enjoyment and normalcy to an otherwise demeaning, dehumanizing, frustrating situation. (http://ccadp.org/williamclark.htm)

Whether it means bringing a new friend into their forlorn world by writing them a letter, assisting them financially, getting involved with their defence or working against the death penalty, prisoners tell their readers how they can make a difference.

A privileged stance, a realized self

Death row prisoners also use their status as victims and survivors to sanction their claims to truth. Echoing standpoint theorists' arguments that the experience of oppression provides marginalized groups with privileged epistemological insight (Harding, 1990: 95), prisoners describe how their time on death row has given them particularly valuable and unique knowledge. This claim can be seen in the homepage of Florida death row prisoner Anthony Mungin: 'We, the men on death row, are the true experts on capital punishment' (http://ccadp.org/anthonymungin.htm). Donald Palmer presents himself, on his webpage, also as a particularly unbiased voice because of his status on Ohio's death row: 'Being a death row prisoner has given me a unique advantage over most people... Suffering and being hated by the majority of society has freed me' (http://ccadp.org/donaldpalmer.htm). This 'realized self' – a self that has experienced suffering and therefore has achieved a privileged authority to speak the truth and a commitment to a higher calling – is equally as prevalent in the accounts of prisoners who claim innocence as it is in the minority of prisoners who admit their guilt.

The small minority of prisoners who admit their guilt present themselves as speaking from privileged vantage points by constructing narratives that reflect what Maruna calls 'condemnation' and 'redemption' scripts. Following these scripts, prisoners who admit their guilt distance the new self from a past criminal self that they describe as the result of factors beyond their control (Maruna, 2001: 12–13). The attempt to displace guilt by portraying themselves as victims of addiction, abuse or a poor and violent environment, can be seen in the homepage of Texas death row prisoner Oswaldo Soriano:

> My problems began at the early age of 10 when my father abused me.... I had my first experience with youth gangs, and drugs use, after running away from home. By the age of 11, I'd developed a behavior that caused me to end up in state school, where youth gangs, child abuse, and drug use was the everyday activity.... I was released back into the same environment which was the cause of my problems to start with. The old behavior returned. (http://www.deathrow-usa.us/oswaldo_soriano.htm)

Alongside these condemnation scripts, prisoners deploy redemption scripts that posit the emancipation of a 'true' self from the fetters of their past and the suffering of their present (Maruna, 2001: 85). Thus, Efrain Perez, a prisoner on Texas' death row, contrasts his old criminal self with his new self, explaining: 'I changed, improved, got smart, and found a new way of thinking on my own' (http://ccadp.org/efrainperez.htm). In Perez's homepage, as in other accounts, the only trace of the guilty self is the wisdom he has gained through self-education, giving him privileged insight to impart to the world.

Truth, reason, justice and the public good

Speaking with a privileged claim to wisdom earned by suffering on death row, prisoners also present their homepages as an act of reaching out and promoting a message of truth. They become near-prophets pursuing a transcendent goal with pragmatic consequences for the fate of the reader. This messianic public service message is repeated in California death row prisoner Andre Burton's site: 'Don't you realize this reality? We are the human family, which is created with a life and divine spirit but have become like unto bones amongst each other? I am trying to do my part by writing this message to you. It is important that you understand' (http://ccadp.org/andreburton.html). Like most prisoners, Burton's account beseeches the reader, attempting to unite a moral community built around the tenets of humanity and faith initiated by his act of speaking the truth.

In seeking to construct this community with their readers, death row prisoners become crucibles of reason, protecting the public against the evils of an irrational, corrupt and biased justice system. Amplifying these values and linking them to the public good plays a central role in prisoners' attempt to recast the death penalty. Richard Rossi, a prisoner on Arizona's death row, reiterates this claim to represent reason and sense in his poem entitled 'Man's Humanity': 'When people cry for executions/then cheer and shout/have we not lost sight of what/humanity is about/Do we solve our problems by/Killing some more/when killing is what we/say we abhor/can we justify our pain and/Does it feel more real/by sacrificing a poor few/just to prove our zeal' (http://ccadp.org/rossipage8.htm). With this poem, Rossi brings an abstract question of humanity into practical relief, speaking as a defender of sense and reason.

This claim to embody truth and reason in the fight for justice becomes most explicit in prisoners' assertions of innocence. Referring to dishonest and predatory prosecutors, inept and inexperienced public defence lawyers and corrupt police investigations, prisoners attempt to evoke outrage at the details of injustice. This accusation can be seen in Ben-Yisrayl's indictment: 'I now stand in the process of appeals to the Indiana Supreme Kourt where the rulings they're making on all death penalty cases aren't based upon law, but upon arbitrary rules and raw ignorant emotions' (http://ccadp.org/obadyahben-yisrayl.htm). Although Ben-Yisrayl makes no explicit mention of racism in his homepage – homepages rarely, if ever, do – his thinly veiled reference to the Klu Klux Klan adds a dimension of insidious hatred to the accusation of arbitrary ignorance. Against these forces, Ben-Yisrayl and other death row prisoners hope to claim their status as a moral crusader armed with the tenets of justice.

Garnering the forces of truth, reason and justice, prisoners seek to represent the voice of the public good and community action. This organizing tactic can be seen in the remarks of Keith Henness, a prisoner on Ohio's death row: 'It is time we make our elected officials earn their positions by doing things that raise our quality of life – not simply for feeding some primal urge to see blood.... Now is the time!' (http://www.geocities.com/wkhenness/). In this passage, Henness joins the ranks of the public masses and exclaims their common grief. With his rallying cry, Henness presents himself as a voice of civic service hoping to inspire solidarity. This statement and others are grounded in prisoners' depiction of themselves as the everyday citizen and common man facing the machinery of an unwieldy bureaucracy. For example, Martin Draughon, a prisoner on Ohio's death row, describes himself as merely a 'statistic' in 'some upper-class bureaucrat's speech' (http://www.fdp.dk/martin/index.htm). Throughout their homepages prisoners rail against the malicious forces of 'money, influence, power' (http://ccadp.org/daleflanagan.htm) in order to build a community of shared interests that requires unified action.

Within these arguments, there is an implicit claim: *This could happen to you!* In fact, prisoners often appeal directly to their reader to imagine being in the prisoner's shoes, seeking to instil a sense of dread in the reader such that the prisoner's fate becomes equally a matter of the reader's self-defence. Cohen describes this attempt at inducing the reader to identify with the victim as 'cognitive perspective taking' (Cohen, 2001: 219). In this vein, Dale Flanagan demands of the reader: 'Imagine being locked in your bathroom all that time, wondering if there will be a knock on the door from someone who leads you away to your death' (http://ccadp.org/daleflanagan.htm). These words reiterate a forceful dimension throughout all prisoners' attempts to stoke their readers' imagination and forge an imminent cause for solidarity.

In tying their fate to that of the reader, death row prisoners try to seal a community of mutual interests whose membership establishes important personal, political and ethical commitments. As they emphasize in their sites, prisoners intend for this community to be an alternative public and personal space based on the principles of reason and accountability and the virtues of tolerance and open-mindedness. These values pervade prisoners' self-descriptions as they not only define the terms on which they hope to build a connection with their readers but also the goals they hope to inspire people to pursue.[12] A characteristic self-description can be seen in the homepage of Pedro Rodriguez, a prisoner on Nevada's death row: 'I am very open-minded, and honest. I am also a great listener' (http://ccadp.org/pedrorodriguez.htm). Likewise, Jimmy Kirksley, a prisoner on Nevada's death row, asserts: 'I am a good listener and I don't judge nobody. Only God can judge people' (http://ccadp.org/jimmykirksey.htm). Death row homepages repeatedly refer to these traits, hinting at the concept of rationality – thinking that submits to criticism and systematic examination (Habermas, 1981: 20) – they hope to inspire. These prisoners dare their readers to get to know them through engagement in a personalized communicative space that nurtures honesty, tolerance and reason.

The personal bond

Meanwhile, prisoners seek to cement this public community in a close personal relationship with the reader formed in the communicative medium of the webpage. Speaking in profoundly intimate and personal voices, prisoners use the epistolary form to address the individual reader directly, often using cordial and affable greetings. For example, Billy Kuenzel, a prisoner on Alabama's death row, greets viewers with a friendly 'Hi, I'm Billy' (http://www.geocities.com/athens/atlantis/5450/). Similar to a personal advertisement, the prisoner homepage attempts to draw the reader into the prisoner's inner world, sharing his history, case, family, friends and innermost thoughts. The pervasive effort that prisoners make to welcome the reader can be seen in the homepage of Miguel Angel, a prisoner on Texas' death row. He ends his homepage with the following statement: 'I invite you to be informed and get involved. For what you have done and/or you will do, thank you from the bottom of my heart' (http://www.geocities.com/miguelangelmtz/). With this invitation, Angel posits himself as an active host who draws the reader into an intimate relation where information and feelings are shared.

The close personal bond that prisoners' hope to seal with their readers is described as a relationship of mutual trust and responsibility initiated by the act of sharing their lives and reaching out to their readers. They also point to the responsibility that their readers must accept in witnessing the prisoners' vulnerability. Anthony Ehler, a prisoner on Illinois' death row, presents a poem entitled 'Naked and Fearless' on his homepage that expresses the emotional investment he makes in his reader through his homepage: 'I stand before you/This is me in all my glory/Nothing to cover, nothing to hide/This is who I am/This is all I am and nothing more/There are no pretences [sic], no innuendoes/I have no secrets from you/Take me as I am' (http://ccadp.org/anthonyehlers.htm). Ehler confronts the reader directly, demanding that he or she respond. In the very act of reading, the reader is posited as a witness. As in all death row homepages, Ehler intends to change the reader's status from passive bystander – someone who receives his or her information from a secondary source – to an immediate witness and close personal participant.

By stepping forward, making themselves vulnerable, taking the responsibility to forge a personal and public relationship of mutual interest with the reader, prisoners situate the reader as already responsible for the prisoner's fate. The homepage of Richard Vasquez, a prisoner on Texas' death row, reflects one of the ways in which prisoners draw the reader into a relationship of bonded responsibility. He concludes his page by stating: 'I have only presented the truth.... And I ask for very little in return, my friend. I would like the opportunity to first ask all of you not to take your lives for granted. I have learned how precious a gift life is. And second, I would like a second chance. A chance to prove my innocence' (http://www.cyberspace-inmates.com/vasqezr.htm). In Vasquez's site and in others, the prisoner positions the visitor so that in the very act of reading the homepage he or she has already joined a personal relationship and a larger shared community. In the structured exchange between prisoner and reader, the prisoner has already made his personal and public contribution. Cemented in this personal relationship, the reader must hold up his or her end of the bargain, positioned as the responsibility to act in support of the prisoner's fate.

Ultimately, through images and words, the death row homepage appeals to its viewer to take responsibility for the prisoner's fate. Hoping to challenge the reader to ask *Can I let this person die?*, the death row homepage tries to form an intimate, personalized bond with the reader and condition a response such that state-sanctioned murder seems incomprehensible. Equating indifference with abandonment, abandonment with murder, the death row prisoner strives to ensure the viewer's response: *I must save this person*.

Conclusion

In the final chapter of *Contingency, Irony, and Solidarity* (1998), Richard Rorty claims that the examples of human solidarity during the Holocaust in places like Italy and Denmark – where Jews were relatively assimilated – suggest specific social conditions more conducive to fostering empathy than others (Rorty, 1989: 189). He explains: 'our sense of solidarity is strongest when those with whom solidarity is expressed are thought of as "one of us", where "us" means something smaller and more local than the human race' (ibid.: 191; compare Cheliotis, this volume). Acknowledging the critical relationship between distance and imagination (Ginzburg, 1994: 109–114), Rorty emphasizes the role that narratives play in fomenting solidarity, chiefly those localized, parochial narratives that depict 'particular varieties of pain and humiliation' (ibid.: 192). With this understanding, he touts the 'thick description of the private and idiosyncratic' to inspire the imagination and arouse empathy for the suffering of others (ibid.: 94).

The death penalty homepage attempts to garner the potential for individual narratives of suffering to foster empathy and solidarity. As the death row prisoner's personal act of resistance against his fate, the death row homepage attacks the broader narratives that legitimize capital punishment. Framing themselves as victims and survivors, prisoners seek to establish the authority of their voice and cement a community of shared interests. They hope to use the Internet to form an intimate relationship with their viewers that has at its core urgent questions of justice, responsibility and the public good. At once helpless, hopeful, emotional and logical, they speak as individuals suffering pain and injustice. Prisoners structure an encounter with their viewer: in reaching out, they situate the individual viewer such that in the very act of reading he or she is already made to feel responsible and compelled to act. Through this personal act of resistance, the death row homepage strives to incite broader public forms of resistance to state-sanctioned murder.

Whether it is the novel or the newspaper, people 'have always exploited "new media" ' to instruct others in sympathetic feeling (Moyn, 2006: 401). But certain media or 'mobilization contexts' may be more successful than others in achieving this goal (McAdams, 1988: 137). Against the vast body of literature that depicts the dehumanizing effects of rationalization, some theorists of the Internet see the normative possibilities unleashed in the structural developments of modernity (Sznaider, 1998: 136). With the 'the societal turn away from groups and toward networked individualism', people are 'connected to each other as individuals rather than as members of households, communities, kinship groups, workgroups and organizations' (Wellman and Hogan, 2004: 11). This person-to-person connectivity suggests a growing tide of individualized telling and witnessing of experience.

Indeed, the Internet provides increasing opportunities for one-on-one encounters with which to foster the emotive power of the parochial, personal narrative celebrated by Rorty. The death row homepage seeks to animate this structured encounter for the prisoner's benefit in the highly crafted autobiography-as-personal-advertisement. But as Oscar Gandy argues, the individualized context in which new media content is consumed may reflect a 'bowling-alone' society in which, despite the expanding variety of frames, people are exposed to fewer frames in common (2001: 366–368). In other words, death row homepages may articulate marginal voices, but they may only speak to people who already oppose the death penalty. And yet, numerous comments on discussion boards hosted by death row homepage administrators suggest otherwise: whilst it is impossible for us to know the truth of their claims, they declare themselves to be former death penalty supporters recently converted by prisoners' homepages.[13] Despite the danger that this cacophony of voices contributes to a fractured public sphere or to 'compassion fatigue' (Wilkinson, 2005: 137), the proliferation of individually structured encounters provides the platform for localized narratives to break through and speak to the imagination via personal homepages. Ultimately, the expanding market for the citizen-as-producer-and-consumer of personal narratives, as seen in the death row homepage, reflects new opportunities for fostering moral solidarity in contemporary society.[14]

Unsurprisingly, death row homepages also point to new opportunities for mobilizing resistance *vis-à-vis* the state. Several state legislatures in recent years have tried to block death penalty homepages by refusing to let prisoners provide material. Site administrators, along with the American Civil Liberties Union, have challenged these efforts in court and have won, arguing that such curtailments infringe on First Amendment rights (Bowman, 2002). Numerous site administrators – and many of the people who comment on their discussion boards – live outside the United States. Protected now by the courts, death row homepages use the Internet to challenge state-sanctioned killing outside the scope of US sovereignty.[15] It remains to be seen whether these opportunities have tangible effects. But a recent Supreme Court decision citing foreign and international law to interpret the US Constitution (Segal, 2006: 1421–1425) suggests that new global realities are shifting the contours of justice in the nation state. The death row homepage is evidence of this growing global dimension to resistance in contemporary society.

Death row homepages illustrate that the certain ways of speaking and thinking about crime and punishment in society may dominate public debate, but they are not the only narratives being told. Nonetheless, there is an obvious danger in idealizing death row homepages and other forms of resistance. Doing so turns a blind eye to the ways that dominant narratives and the corresponding institutionalized inequalities inhibit democratic goals and the diverse voices that might foster them. It also overlooks the ways that certain forms of resistance, like the death row homepage, often reproduce the same binaries they seek to dismantle. For example, despite invoking a radically inclusive community, death row prisoners frequently fail to mention the victims of the crimes for which they were convicted. If they seek to open the span of sympathy, they often do so at the exclusion of other voices. Support for the death penalty no doubt stems from very real and legitimate concerns over justice: to ignore these concerns in the realm of public debate and policy is to cut short the search for meaningful solutions to injustices of all kinds in a democratic society.

Whilst there may be growing opportunities for personal and public acts of resistance to incite empathy, like the death row homepage, to speak of the 'the banality of good' threatens to overlook the important normative dimensions of the solidarities they seek to foster. It is important, therefore, to acknowledge the limitations of the central descriptive component of this brief study, which does not examine the effectiveness of death row homepages in achieving their goals of getting readers to help them.[16] The next step to understanding the contemporary politics of compassion requires studying how people respond to the mediated spectacle of suffering, and how social contexts bear on these responses (Wilkinson, 2005: 167). More work should be done on the ways new media affect their viewers' perception of distant suffering and how this corresponds to real-world action (Gandy, 2001: 374). Nonetheless, the immediate goal is to contribute to a critical sociology of suffering, highlighting marginalized voices by clarifying how they speak out as personal and public forms of resistance. And the aspiration, as Judith Butler explains, is to promote a public forum 'in which oppositional voices are not feared, degraded or dismissed, but valued for the instigation to a sensate democracy they occasionally perform' (Butler, 2004: 15).

Websites cited

http://ccadp.org/andreburton.html
http://ccadp.org/anthonyehlers.htm
http://ccadp.org/anthonymungin.htm
http://ccadp.org/chayimmarshall.htm
http://ccadp.org/daleflanagan.htm
http://ccadp.org/danielwebbphotos.htm
http://ccadp.org/derricksmith.htm
http://ccadp.org/donaldpalmer.htm
http://ccadp.org/efrainperez.htm
http://ccadp.org/jimmykirksey.htm
http://ccadp.org/miguelmartinez.htm
http://ccadp.org/obadyahben-yisrayl.htm
http://ccadp.org/pedrorodriguez.htm
http://ccadp.org/rossipage8.htm
http://ccadp.org/terencevalentine.htm
http://ccadp.org/uncensoredcartwright.htm
http://ccadp.org/williamleonard.htm
http://www.ccadp.org
http://www.cyberspace-inmates.com
http://www.cyberspace-inmates.com/vasqezr.htm
http://www.deathrow.at/allridge/

http://www.deathrow-usa.com
http://www.deathrow-usa.us/oswaldo_soriano.htm
http://www.fdp.dk/martin/index.htm
http://www.geocities.com/athens/atlantis/5450/
http://www.geocities.com/markaduke/writings/Whoami.html
http://www.geocities.com/miguelangelmtz/
http://www.geocities.com/wkhenness/
http://www.lampofhope.org
http://www.lampofhope.org/fl059121.html
http://www.lampofhope.org/fl059121poems.html
http://www.lampofhope.org/webpage.htm

Notes

I wish to thank Leonidas K. Cheliotis, Shadd Maruna, Alison Liebling, Ben Crewe, Jana McLean and Lorenzo Bernasconi for their comments on earlier drafts of this project.

1. I provide this estimate after an exhaustive search that was able to find over 400 homepages, acknowledging the challenges in locating dispersed sites, the limitations of Internet search engines and the quick pace of change on the Internet. I exclude from the category of death row homepages sites devoted solely to pen pal requests or outside campaign pages. Pen pal request pages, though often mistakenly described as homepages, consist of concise one-to-five sentence-long appeals for personal correspondence delineating the qualities required of the pen pal. Campaign pages, alternatively, are sites set up by outside individuals or groups for prisoners, and do not contain material written and provided by prisoners themselves. Though there are substantial numbers of pen pal requests and campaign sites set up for all prisoner categories, few, if any, actual homepages exist for non-death row prisoners. It is often difficult to distinguish between these types of webpages. Yet the category of webpage described here as death row prisoner homepage tries to include only those sites that involve prisoners' substantial attempts at self-representation and therefore consist of material largely provided by the prisoners themselves. It should also be understood that the fast pace of change on the Internet makes the content on these sites subject to change frequently. Indeed, it is not rare for homepages to be out of date or even expired. Thus, the references provided herein reflect the content and Internet addresses of homepages at the time of writing, but not necessarily at the time of publication. As will be noted, in examining around 400 death row prisoner homepages, I have tried to glean the central themes that appear in the typical homepage. Nonetheless, the goal is to ground a broad content analysis in close reading, and whilst I make no claim that each example perfectly represents the group, together they elucidate critical dimensions of all prisoners' homepages. Though the subset of homepages I reference here reflects the disproportionately high number of men of Afro-American and Latin-American descent on death row (Dieter, 1998), it does not take

into consideration the homepages of women on death row. The number of women's homepages roughly matches the 1 per cent of women on death row (Streib, 2008). Women's sites reflect important gender differences and I proceed with the acknowledgement that I examine the homepages of male prisoners only.
2. These groups include Canadian Coalition Against the Death Penalty (www.ccadp.org), Lamp of Hope (www.lampofhope.org), Cyberspace-Inmates (www.cyberspace-inmates.com), Death-Row USA (www.deathrow-usa.com) and others.
3. Families and friends no doubt provide certain material and help edit and administer prisoners' sites. However, CCADP and other organizations suggest that prisoners play a principle role in providing and editing the material on their homepages.
4. Linebaugh (1992) points to the limitations of accounts that emphasize 'sensibilities'. For an expansive analysis of the varying approaches to the historical changes in penal forms, see Garland (1990); for a review of accounts that privilege structural factors, see Weiss (1987).
5. As Garland (2001), Feeley and Simon (1992) and others explain, emotionalized and retributive policies coincide and intercede with bureaucratic, rehabilitative penal forms in the contemporary penal field.
6. There is a vast body of literature devoted to the mainstream media that situates crime and punishment – captured in the perennial emblem of murder victim and capital offender – as a schematic tale of good versus evil (Haney and Manzolati, 1992; Sparks, 1992; Cavender and Bond-Maupic, 1993; Chermack, 1994; Anderson, 1995; Surette, 1996; Beckett, 1997; Tunnell, 1998; Beckett and Sasson, 2000).
7. As abolitionists have long argued, polling suggests that, despite the high level of support for the death penalty amongst Americans as a whole, opinions vary widely amongst different demographic groups (Jackson, 1996: 47–49). Polling shows that the level of support has shifted in recent years, and that it changes dramatically when polling subjects are offered a choice between the death penalty and life in prison without parole (New Jersey Death Penalty Study Commission, 2007: 35). Indeed, recent developments in evidentiary technology and news reports about wrongful convictions suggest that the dominant narrative landscape surrounding crime and punishment may not be as conclusive as some scholars suggest.
8. This phrase is taken from Valier and Lippens (2004).
9. For a discussion on the ways that images, as opposed to verbal language, seem to reflect reality in more immediate ways, see Messaris and Abraham (2001: 220).
10. James Allridge's homepage has been altered substantially since his execution in 2004. The materials posted on the site now are his supporters' contributions and not his own.
11. Phoenix (2000) clarifies the concept of a dual victim-survivor identity.
12. The community that prisoners invoke is radically inclusive. Whilst very few homepages mention the victims of the crimes for which they were convicted, prisoners who admit their crimes, emphasize that they have sought to make amends to the victims of their crimes. Gene Hawthorn, a prisoner on Texas' death row, explains: 'I have ... attempted to contact all those who

were hurt by the ripple effect of my past actions. To the ones with whom contact was successful, I acknowledged their loss and pain [and] apologized for causing same' (http://www.lampofhope.org/webpage.htm). Prisoners who maintain their innocence often claim that the victims have been desecrated by convicting innocents, setting off a chain of victimization. Throughout these specific websites there is an attempt to include all victims, from original murder victims to victims on death row, as seen in Derrick Smith's statement that 'a victim is a victim and all merit compassion and consideration' (http://ccadp.org/derricksmith.htm). Not only does this statement unsettle the status of victim as inherently vengeful, but it also promotes a democratic space for the voice of all victims to be heard.

13. For example, see the discussion board hosted by Canadian Coalition Against the Death Penalty (http://ccadp.proboards40.com/index.cgi#general). As one might expect, these discussion boards feature sympathetic comments, as well as dismissive and combative responses.

14. Nonetheless, one need only think of the proliferation of sites like YouTube and MySpace for the ambivalent effects of the technologies of the self described by Foucault.

15. This context differs sharply with that of the written accounts of nineteenth-century condemned men, who 'were granted... permission to speak and to write' in exchange for confessions that 'substantiated and made real the justice of the state' (Fabian, 2000: 51).

16. For a discussion of the factors involved in whether or not a frame attracts and mobilizes constituents – what scholars call frame 'resonance' – see Babb, 1996. To explore this side of death row homepages, one would need to investigate who visits prisoner homepages, how those visitors are affected and how they respond. Exploring how death row homepages affect different viewers in different ways is difficult, but such a study could explore the pro-death and anti-death penalty web discussion boards, blogs and other forums for debate in which people discuss not only what they think about prisoners having websites, but also how they respond to the websites themselves. These questions would help understand the role this specific form of oppositional text plays in building local and international communities of opposition to the death penalty.

8
Face to Face with Abidoral Queiroz: Death Squads and Democracy in Northeast Brazil

Nancy Scheper-Hughes

Between 1964 and 1985, Brazil was a military police state run by senior army generals. The 1964 coup, initially euphemistically described as a 'revolution', ushered into power (with support from the CIA) a repressive military dictatorship that justified itself as stabilizing a volatile and inflationary economy and a politically volatile population of rural workers who were organizing in the backlands of Northeast Brazil under the *Ligas Camponese* (Peasant Leagues), whilst rural migrants to Brazil's cities settled their land problems by 'invading' hillsides and other under-utilized public land creating new shantytowns.

Under the tight-fisted hand of the 5th Army, Brazil's industrial economy flourished, ushering in the so-called 'Economic Miracle' that turned the country into an economic powerhouse, the world's 8th largest economy. Not all sectors of Brazilian society benefited from the military years. Millions of rural workers, urban migrants, factory workers, domestic workers, as well as artists, intellectuals and political dissidents, suffered from economic exclusions and political oppression. As for sugar plantation workers and rural migrants from the impoverished Northeast, the only economic miracle for them was that some managed to stay alive at all during the penitential military years.

During the late 1970s, the harshest period of the dictatorship, those suspected of subversive activities such as participation in outlawed social movements were illegally detained, 'disappeared', tortured, some to their death, forcing thousands of Brazilians into exile (Archdiocese of Sao Paulo, 1985; Amnesty International, 1990). Although never approaching the horrendous situation in Argentina during the so-called 'Dirty War' (1976–1982), when the army there turned its force against ordinary citizens (Suarez-Orozco, 1987), the military years in Brazil were ruthless enough, the aberrations of a large and nervous state gone haywire. The operations of paramilitary 'death squads' and the mere *rumours* of these were sufficient to frighten political dissidents into exile and the undifferentiated poor into silence.

The complicity of more affluent Brazilians with the succession of military generals derived from a belief that their country could only 'develop' under authoritarian rule (Alves, 1985). It was only when the 'economic miracle' began to falter in the early 1980s that a demand for a gradual return to democratic structures emerged. But even here the military dictatorship left its mark in overseeing and managing the democratic transition that began in 1982 and culminated in the 1989 presidential elections that brought into power a mass media-created populist named Fernando Collor de Melo, a corrupt politician from the old *latifundist* class who was rather quickly impeached and removed from office.

Nonetheless, during the shaky transitional years, Brazil produced a new constitution (1988) that is one of the most enlightened, progressive and admired documents of its kind. The special attention given to the social rights of women, children, prisoners, peasants, urban workers, squatters and shantytown dwellers and to cultural and sexual minorities was a source of inspiration to other transitional democracies, including the authors of South Africa's new constitution. The newfound 'rights' of children and youth included: the right to use public spaces; free expression; freedom of religion; ability to practice sports and engage in leisure activities; participation in family, community and political life; access to refuge and assistance; and freedom from violence. These same principles were adopted one year later at the UN Convention on the Rights of the Child. Once again, Brazil served as a model of radical consciousness with respect to recognizing the special needs and rights of unprotected children.

New laws were a fine beginning, but in a struggling democracy in which structural inequalities remained fierce, where authority was centralized within a weak federal state and where 'childhood' was revered for one class and despised for another (see Calligaris, 1991 on the 'two childhoods' of Brazil), new social and political institutions were needed to see that these rights were implemented and protected. Social movements, such as the National Movement of Street Boys and Girls (MNMMR) founded by activists and street educators fought to organize and empower Brazil's street youth.[1] Their achievements were impressive: exposing police brutality, establishing street schools and alternative employment, fostering HIV/AIDS education and prevention, and advancing model legislation. One result was the 1990 Child and Adolescent Statute, which created Children's Rights Councils and Child Rights' Advocates in each of Brazil's 5000 municipalities. These councils, made up of representatives from grassroots organizations, churches, commercial institutions and local government, were meant to prevent the more egregious abuses against Brazil's millions of semi-autonomous 'street children'[2] and minority (that is, mostly Afro-Brazilian) youth who, during the military years, were routinely rounded up and thrown into state reform schools that were worse than prisons.

The paradox: during this phase of active consciousness-raising (*conscientizacao*) and 'democratization', death squad attacks on vulnerable populations did not cease. They resurfaced with even greater vigour (Almeida and Wagner , 1991; Alvim, 1991; Amnesty International, 1992). By the mid 1990s, it was clear that the targets of the new 'death squad' executions were not only politically-engaged 'trouble-makers', radical environmentalists and members of militant groups, but ordinary people, most of them young, poor, semi-illiterate and 'marginal' (a term that is synonymous in Brazil with deviant and criminal). These attacks occurred in the absence of national (or even significant international) public outrage. To the contrary, public opinion polls in Brazil showed strong popular support for social cleansing (*limpeza*) campaigns. In short, the demilitarization of Brazil's government was not accompanied by a demilitarization of everyday life.

The racialization of criminal discourse

Why would ordinary people accept violent attacks on street kids and marginal youth as the legitimate business of the police? How does one explain this extraordinary consensus? As described in *Death without Weeping* (Scheper-Hughes, 1992), the everyday experience of violence leads poor people to accept their own deaths and those of their children as predictable, natural, *cruel but usual* events. The history of authoritarian rule – whether by local landowners, political 'bosses' or military police – extinguished any incipient culture of protest. A deep lack of trust in the legal and judicial systems, which were largely untouched by the democratic transition, contributes to a cynical attitude towards the possibilities of real political change, as the recent scandals within President Lula's Workers' Party have reinforced.

The entrenched racism of Brazilian society, a social fact that has been successfully deflected by the Brazilian national sociology of 'racial democracy', at best the fleeting 'sexual democracy' of the hammock and the canvas cot in the maid's bedroom (see Freire, 1986) is manifest in the colour of death squad victims. The crimes of the poor – of the *favela*, the housing project and the shantytown – are viewed as race crimes, as naturally produced. Poor black youth are freely referred to as 'bandits', because crime is 'in their blood', because they are *'bichos da Africa'*, wild African beasts. Unacknowledged class and race hatreds feed the popular support of violent and illegal actions against the poor. The subtext of references to 'street kids' is colour-coded in 'race blind' Brazil, where most street children are black.

Meanwhile, despite democratization, Brazil lacks a viable political culture of civil rights (Zaluar, 1994). The language of human rights entered Brazil in the 1980s in part through radicalized Catholic clergy who had come into contact with Amnesty International, Americas Watch and other international 'rights' organizations. In Brazil, however, claims made in terms of human rights were easily subverted by manipulating people's fears of escalating violence blamed on human rights 'protectionism' towards common criminals. The problem is that, whilst it has many surreal qualities, violence talk is not just the product of social and moral panics. The democratic transition in Brazil (as elsewhere in the world) was, in fact, accompanied by a violence transition, a real spike in crime due to the simultaneous entry into the country of Colombian Cartels, international crime networks and cocaine trafficking.[3] The drug trade brought modern, upscale fire-arms into the Brazilian 'ghetto' and into the hands of *favela* youth who were readily recruited as drug couriers (Zaluar, 1995; Zaluar and Ribeiro, 1995; Pinheiro, 1996).

As Teresa Caldeira (2000) has argued, to a great many affluent Brazilians, the mere proximity of rural migrants, unemployed black and brown men, and loose children is seen as an affront to 'decent' people. In response to the threat of 'engulfment' by the 'masses' of undifferentiated poor, once public spaces – the *rua* and the *praça* – were redefined as the *private* domain of middle class and propertied people. The segregation impulse is expressed in modern urban planning. The 'utopian' model city in Brazil today is not Brasilia, the failed experiment that looked to the vast Brazilian interior, but the internationally celebrated city of Curitiba, a minutely planned, ecologically correct, public transportation-minded community, supported by a peripheral working-class community of artisans, shopkeepers and mechanics. The only thing 'wrong' with the picture is the absence within this utopian bubble of rural migrants and the urban poor.

Marginal people (the poor and property-less classes) are not seen by a great many Brazilians as rights-bearing individuals but rather as *bandidos*, 'public enemies', and rubbish people (*'lixo'*), those who often are better-off dead. Thus, the introduction of human and civil rights embodied in the 1988 constitution, promising civil liberties to the homeless, street children, vagrants, the unemployed and prisoners, was counter-intuitive to a great many people in Brazil. Every gain in civil rights law and in innovative public policies and programmes was fought tooth and nail by those seeking to restrict the extension of civil rights to 'populations' thought of as having no right to rights at all. Empowering marginals (read 'criminals') was perceived as an attack on the freedom of respectable people who began to fortify themselves inside buildings and on 'gated streets' protected by mechanical security devices and by gun-toting armed guards (Caldeira, 2000). A strong popular backlash against the dangerous classes of sub-citizens fuelled 'street cleaning' campaigns, the Brazilian version of 'ethnic cleansing' (with the support of police, political leaders, commercial firms and armed response groups) in the *favelas, morros* and public housing projects of Brazil's own inner cities.

Throughout the 1990s, police and vigilante attacks on street children and marginal youth in Sao Paulo, Rio de Janeiro, Salvador and Recife (see Louzeiro, 1990; Dimenstein, 1991; MNMMR, 1991, 1992; Piccolino, 1992; Penglase, 1993; Milton *et al.*, 1994; Vermelho and Melo 1996) produced youth mortality statistics that rivalled South Africa's during the armed struggle against apartheid (see Scheper-Hughes, 1996). Democratic Brazil had the demographic profile of a nation at war, which, in a sense, it was.

The transformation in political culture is captured in the very different feel and content of two acclaimed Brazilian films, one produced in 1981 at the close of the military years and the other in 2003, both treating the lives of marginalized youth in Brazil. Hector Babenco's *Pixote: A Lei do Mais Fraco* (*Pixote: the Law of the Weakest*) is a film of social critique and political protest, a devastating exposé of the detention of street kids in brutal reform schools run by the military police. At the time, *Pixote* struck the conscience of the nation and inspired social protest. By the late 1980s, however, and well into the democratic transition, some 700,000 youths were still being housed in state correctional institutions in Brazil (Swift, 1991). And, in 1990, Pixote himself, the street kid turned national symbol, was shot dead in the city streets that remained his only home.

In 2003, an equally gripping Brazilian film, Fernando Merirelles's *Cidade de Deus* (*City of God*) presented a very different view of dangerous and endangered street kids growing up in the peripheral housing projects of Rio de Janeiro: a portrait of savage, fratricidal violence amongst competing gangs (never mind that a few of the kids are loveable and righteous). Rather than focus on the structural violence of race and class and the institutionalized violence of Brazil's police and state prisons, this film focuses on the inter-generational cycles of violence and the anarchy of the *favela* itself. It is a portrait compatible with Oscar Lewis's (1961) 'culture of poverty' thesis and with a neo-liberal ethos that attributes 'equal agency' to all, including those with their backs up against a wall of social and economic exclusion. The film glorifies the solitary heroes who manage to escape their homes.

Social cleansing in Timbaúba

I first became aware of the violence practiced with impunity against young residents of the Alto do Cruzeiro, Timbaúba, in the late 1980s. Timbaúba ('Bom Jesus da Mata' of my 1993 ethnography, *Death without Weeping*) is a sprawling market town on the border of Pernambuco and Paraiba in Northeast Brazil, a persistent pocket of the third world in Brazil, and the site of my long-term anthropological and political engagements that now span four decades. At the end of 1987, half a dozen young black men, all in trouble for minor infractions, were seized from their homes by masked men 'in uniform'. Two showed up dead several days later, their mutilated bodies dumped unceremoniously between rows of sugarcane. Police arrived with graphic photos for family members. 'How do you expect me to recognize my man in this picture?', Elena screamed hysterically. 'Ah, but this is the fate of the poor', she said bitterly some days later: 'They don't even own their own bodies.' Finally, 'they' came late one night for the 19-year-old son of 'Black' Irene, the boy everyone in the *favela* knew affectionately as Black De, 'Nego De'. A death squad with ties to local police was suspected, but on this topic my shantytown friends were silent, speaking, when they did at all, in a rapid and complicated form of sign language. No one else wanted to be marked.

Even more troubling, however, was the public silence that accompanied these disappearances and deaths. The extrajudicial killing of shantytown men and street children in Timbaúba was not thought worthy of a column in the progressive 'opposition' newspaper of the community. 'Why should we criticize the "execution" of *malandros* (good-for-nothings) and scoundrels?', asked a frequent contributor to the newspaper. 'How can one verify a *bona fide* "disappeared" street kid from the multitude of runaways, or those who were murdered by death squads from those who died in street fights?', the 'Children's Judge' responded to my first tentative enquiries about the fate of several disappeared street kids. As for the older young men of the shantytown, those like Nego De, 'executed' through some form of rough or vigilante justice, they were written off by 'decent' citizens as *malandros* (knaves) looking for trouble. 'The police have to be free to go about their business', said Mariazinha, the old woman who lives in a small room behind the Church and who takes care of the altar flowers. 'They know what they're doing. It's best to keep your mouth shut', she advised, zipping her lips shut to show me. And many in the shantytown sided with the actions of police and the death squads, commenting when one or another young thief disappeared or was murdered: 'Good, one less'. It often escaped the tacit supporters of the Brazilian version of social and ethnic cleansing that their own sons had suffered from police brutalities in prison and that the democratic reforms were meant to protect *their* social and economic class in particular.

Meanwhile, rumours surfaced about the disappearance of some street children, several of whom lived in the open-air market place taking shelter at night in between the stalls and under canvas awnings, foraging bits of fruit and starch from the crates and baskets. It was rumoured that their bodies were wanted for spare parts to feed a growing international market in transplant organs. Roaming vans driven by medical agents for Japanese and North American medical centres were cited. On the Alto do Cruzeiro, where so many people are illiterate and where rumour is often the main source of information, everyday life has an almost *literary* quality so that fact and fiction, event and metaphor, are often merged. Whilst the educated classes scoffed at the organ-stealing rumours, young people in the shantytown continued to disappear and then, some time later, to reappear dead, and their bodies stripped of vital organs (see further Scheper-Hughes, 2004).

Given the undeclared war against the shantytown, and the terror which prevented poor people from acknowledging even to themselves what was going on, the insecurity, the terror of it all, was expressed in bizarre and surreal ways. When the life-sized body of the Christ disappeared from the huge cross that gives the shantytown of O Cruzeiro (Crucifix Hill) its name, the more devout and simple, like Dona Amor, wondered whether Jesus, too, had not been kidnapped. The old woman wiped a stray tear from her wrinkled cheek and confided in a hoarse whisper: 'They've taken Him, and we don't know where they have hid Him'. 'But who would do such a thing?', I asked. 'The Big Shots'. 'But why?' '*Política*'. Amor was referring to the politics and pathologies of power, to all the inchoate forces that accounted for the misery of their lives. '*Politica*' – power – explained everything, including the size of one's coffin and the depth of one's grave.

The sad collusions of poor people with the authors of their own 'extra-judicial' executions are a common phenomenon in situations of political terror and instability. Perhaps the phenomenon is similar to the Stockholm Syndrome, whereby victims identify with their kidnappers or prison guards in a desperate bid for security and survival. The reluctance to speak out was reinforced by invoking the '*lei de silencio*' – the law of silence and of '*deixa pra la*', leaving bad enough alone, as it were.

The complicity of Timbaúba's middle classes with the death squads is more consistent and 'logical', if none the less devastating. The campaign of social hygiene intended to sweep the streets of its social garbage was a residue of the military years and a result of the 'shock' of democratization. For 20 years, the military state had kept the social classes segregated and the 'hordes' of 'dangerous' street youths contained to the *favelas* or in detention. When the old military policing structures loosened following the new dispensation, the shantytowns ruptured and poor people, especially unemployed young men and street children, descended from the hillsides and climbed up from the river banks and seemed at once to be everywhere, flooding downtown streets and public *praças* once the normal preserve of *gente fina* (the cultivated people). The presence of the poor and working classes flaunting their misery and their 'criminalized' needs 'in broad daylight' and 'in public' (of all places!) was seen as a direct assault on the social order.

Unwanted and perceived as human waste, shantytown youths and street children evoked contradictory emotions of fear, aversion, pity and anger. Their new visibility betrayed the illusion of Brazilian 'modernity' and made life feel very insecure for those with 'decent' homes, cars and other enviable material possessions. Excluded and reviled, the loose and abandoned street kids of Timbaúba were easily recruited to work for local small-time 'mafia' (as they are locally called), especially as drug messengers (*avioes*).

To repeat: death squads and vigilante justice are nothing new in Northeast Brazil (see further Scheper-Hughes, 1993; Huggins, 1997). During the colonial period up through the 'post-colonial' years of the Republic, hired guns worked for sugar plantation and sugar mill owners to keep first their slaves and after abolition their debt-slaves cutting and milling sugarcane at the same levels of human misery. Then, during the military years, death squads returned in the employ of the state to deal with political dissidents. In the democratic 1990s, vigilantes and *justiceiros* arose within a policing vacuum, an excessively weak state, and in the wake of a new trans-national, trans-regional traffic in arms, drugs and children for commercialized international adoption.

Dangerous and endangered youth

During fieldwork in 1992, 2001, 2004 and 2005, I turned my gaze from infant mortality to youth mortality, first following the 'disappearances' and unexplained deaths of street children, and later following the summary executions of other young 'marginals' in Timbaúba. In 1992 (accompanied by Dan Hoffman) I followed a large and loosely defined cohort of 'street kids' who identified 22 of their *companheiros* (peers and buddies) who had been killed by hired guns (*pisoleiros*), by police (and thus classified as 'legitimate homicides') or by other former street children. Some had simply vanished (see Scheper-Hughes and Hoffman, 1998).

Meanwhile, despite new laws that prohibit the incarceration of children and older youths in jails, we found several minors detained in Timbaúba's local jail alongside adult offenders. A former judge explained that they were being held there 'for their own safety' in the absence of alternative shelters or other forms of protective custody. The youths, he explained, had been rejected by their families, were despised by local merchants who described the younger ones as pests and flies and the older ones as criminals and bandits, whether or not they had actually committed a crime. Some of the bright-eyed kids we met in jail in 1992 were indeed already 'marked for extermination'.

In one cell were 'Caju' and 'Junior', two 15-year-olds whom I remembered as cute *molekes* (street urchins) who attached themselves to my field household in the mid-1980s. Since then, 'Caju' had been elected by his peers to attend the first National Convention of Street Children held in Brasilia and his photo had appeared in a national magazine story about that historic event when street children from all over Brazil converged in the capital city to voice their grievances and to demand their human rights. Now, a few years later, 'Caju' was imprisoned for the usual behaviours born of street life. But the 'final solution' that awaited Caju, was, as the Judge suggested, even worse. When I next returned, in 2001, 'Caju' was dead, the victim of summary execution, and he himself had become the member of an incipient death squad, recruited whilst he was still in jail. Indeed, as the guard at the local jail reflected: 'The life of a young marginal here is short. It's like this: for a street kid to reach 30 years of age, it's a miracle'.

More than five thousand children were murdered in Brazil between 1988 and 1990, according to a Federal police report (cited in the *Journal de Comercio*, June 19, 1991). During the same period the Legal Medical Institute (the police mortuary and forensic lab) in Recife, the state capital of Pernambuco, received the bodies of approximately 15 children a month. Black and brown (mixed race) bodies outnumbered white bodies 12 to one, and boys outnumbered girls at a ratio of seven to one. In 80 per cent of the cases the bodies had been damaged or mutilated (Filho *et al.*, 1991: 42). These routine extra-judicial executions represent an unofficial death penalty, one carried out with chilling cruelty and without any chance of self-defence. Official statistics identified the state of Pernambuco as the 'champion' of violence in Brazil, and Timbaúba, with a population of 57,000 as the crime capital of the state between 1995 and 2000, with an estimated homicide rate of more than 30 per 100,000.

The state of political anarchy peaked in 2000, when an unexpected turn of events led to an aggressive pursuit and arrest of 14 local men associated with a single death squad (*group de extermino*) that had been terrorizing the city and its surrounding rural areas. A small band of local activists, some of them constitutionally empowered as human rights and child rights advocates, joined forces with a fearless and head-strong woman judge, indifferent to death threats, and a brilliant, tough-minded and independent *Promotor* (Public Prosecutor) in a battle to wrest the *municipio* from its murderous vigilantes.

These activists were armed with little more than the new Constitution and their passion for 'human rights', a term of very recent currency in this community, where Marxist and neo-Marxist analysis, sometimes in the language of progressive education (as in Freire's radical pedagogy), sometimes in the language of liberation theology, was for generations the only idiom of resistance against class and race oppression. It was something quite new and unprecedented in the interior of Northeast Brazil. Facing a complicit and brutal police force, and with a general populace that was either actively supporting the activities of the death squad or terrorized into silent complicity, the initial success of their struggle is a tale worth telling, although its aftermaths indicate that happy endings are usually premature.

Face to face with Abidoral and his 'Guardian Angels'

In the spring of 2001, I received a startling fax from Dr Marisa Borges, a newly appointed judge, and Dr Humberto da Silva Graça, a newly appointed public prosecutor in Timbaúba. The fax included a 12-page report of the investigations by the prosecutor and the legal case against a man named Abidoral Gonçalves Queiroz and his band of accomplices, who had been – depending on one's class position and politics – 'protecting' or 'terrorizing' this economically strapped interior town for the latter half of the 1990s. Abidoral's 'public security' operation, the 'Guardian Angels', was in the words of the prosecutor's brief , 'a hyperactive death squad of hired killers – a *groupo de extermino*' charged with the executions of more than a hundred people, most of them former street kids and young men, poor, uneducated, unemployed and black. Prominent figures in Timbaúba society – well-known businessmen and local politicians – applauded the work of the death squad, also known as 'Police 2', and were themselves active in the extra-judicial 'courts' that were deciding who in Timbaúba should be the next to die. Not one of these prominent citizens were detained or brought to trial as their fingerprints were not found on the smoking guns, even if they had paid for the deaths, which could be purchased for as little as R$500 (US$217).

When a 'job' was decided upon, normally in the hillside slums of Timbaúba, the vigilantes, dressed in black and armed with guns and automatic weapons, walked together in formation to their appointed destination. Doors and windows were quickly shut and soon thereafter shots were heard. Everyone knew the assigned script: 'I didn't see! I didn't hear! I don't know anything!' Depending on the gravity of the accusation, the 'accused' victim might receive a warning, or might simply be 'rubbed out' without knowing what they were accused of. Abidoral's gang was also involved in the traffic and distribution of drugs and fire-arms (rifles, 12-caliber guns and pistols) throughout the Brazilian Northeast. The public prosecutor spoke of a 'peaceful coexistence' between the parallel traffic in murder, arms and drugs. Minors who delivered the drugs were protected by Abidoral as long as they obeyed orders.

Abidoral himself came from a line of notorious outlaws. His father, Antonio Gonçalves, was a notorious cattle rustler and a paid gun to shoot animals or people on demand. By adolescence, Abidoral had already developed a reputation as a hooligan, marijuana and alcohol abuser, a virgin spoiler and a petty thief. He broke benches in public plazas, harassed young girls and was a public nuisance, despite the fact that, like his father before him, Antonio junior was 'claimed' by an influential politician who tried to keep him out of prison, if not out of trouble.

During the 1970s, Abidoral was arrested for the rape and murder of a domestic known as 'Tonha'. Tonha's body was placed on the Timbaúba train track that cut across the city. Abidoral and his accomplice were tried and briefly imprisoned, but there is no record of his case in the local justice department. In addition to his natal home in Timbaúba, Abidoral acquired an impressive three-storey house in Sapucaia, a scrubby new 'settlement' on the outskirts of town, and a country house near the sugar mill of Curanji. He also owned a garage in the small town of Ferreiros used to store illegal weapons. And very much like the notorious outlaw of the backlands, Lampião, Abidoral collected a weekly tribute from the majority of businessmen in Timbaúba, a tax to terrorize and to eliminate 'problematic' individuals. The list of Abidoral's victims included dozens of former Timbaúba street children. Abidoral's gang used intimidation, kidnappings, beatings, torture and public execution. They staged train and car accidents, and drownings, and they hid the cadavers in clandestine graves in sugar plantations and in forest undergrowth. Over the years, a few members of the band were arrested and tried, but acquittals were always easily arranged by intimidating or bribing the jury members.

During the 1990s, Timbaúba, a place where more than 80 per cent of the population lives in deep poverty, became a primary transit point for the new regional traffic in drugs, arms and stolen merchandise (motorcycles, cars and trucks). At the same time, local brokers involved in black markets for babies preyed on young, poor and disabled shantytown mothers to supply international adoption networks (see further Scheper-Hughes, 1990). The town's outlaw status had become so legendary that young boys took to wearing baseball caps with '#1 Mafia' sewn across the front. 'What does "Mafia" mean?', I asked a cute little street urchin who could not have been more than five years old. 'I don't know – beautiful, right?', he replied.

It was in the midst of this transition that Timbaúba fell into the hands of Abidoral Queiroz, a man who promised to deliver what the police were seen as no longer capable of providing: security and protection. Abidoral and his men gave protection to local businesses, settled bad debts, carried out vendettas, protected stolen cargo and ran drug and arms trafficking markets throughout the region. They could be 'gentlemanly', almost courtly, as when they provided around-the-clock surveillance of a small cornmeal factory owned by the neurotic aunt of a town council member. And they could be ruthless as when they accepted commissions to kidnap, torture and humiliate young women caught in extramarital relations. But most of Abidoral's death squad activities fell under condoned neighbourhood surveillance, protection and 'street-cleaning', ridding the *municipio* of vagrants, drifters, chicken thieves, trouble makers, sexual deviants and, eventually, just plain poor people. Only disobedient drug runners in the employ of the extermination group were killed. Otherwise, local drug traffickers were safe. The small business community of Timbaúba was grateful for the activities of the 'Guardian Angels', which they saw as a gift to their social class.

As the band grew stronger, other groups and institutions fell under its control, from the mayor's office to the town council to the police to some members of the Catholic clergy. Those citizens who refused to pay for Abidoral's protection were added to the hit list. Between 1995 and 2000, the squad killed most of Timbaúba's older male street children. However, not only street children, but also those who dared to defend or shelter them or to report their deaths, were executed as a warning. When there was no concerted effort to stop them, Abidoral and his men became bolder. They began to conduct their activities in public, flamboyantly and in the company of high-profile citizens, members of the commercial and landed classes. Eventually, the mayor and members of the town council capitulated to the extermination squad. No one dared to raise a voice in protest when Abidoral's gunmen showed up at the town hall to collect their tribute from the city council or when Abidoral was seen in public bars and restaurants hobnobbing with the mayor. Indeed, by the late 1990s, no one in Timbaúba knew exactly where the local government began and where the *'grupos de exterminio'* ended. Things veered so out of control that, at the 7 September national-holiday parade in 2000, Abidoral and a dozen of his men wearing matching jackets decorated with the insignia 'Security: Guardian Angels' led the marchers, with the mayor and town council members in tow. They usurped the role normally filled by civil police. Thus, they brazenly announced in public their semi-official role as a paramilitary unit. In short, the death squad became an official organ of the city.

Before Abidoral's reign of terror was interrupted, somewhere between 100 and 200 people had been murdered, execution style. In a small town like Timbaúba, the death toll was like an *intifada*, but the 'state of emergency' that existed in this backwater place would never be covered by the national, let alone international, media. Similar events were occurring elsewhere in Brazil, especially in urban slums where 'gangs' and drug lords also ruled the roost and exacted tribute and decided who should die. But *favelas* are not administrative units or *municipios*, and the idea that an old plantation town, known regionally for its small sugar plantations, its failing shoe factories and its hand-woven and work-a-day hammocks, could simply collapse and fall under the sway and thrall of a socio-pathological death squad, is, I believe, a unique instance.

Towards the end, Abidoral's band became involved in providing protection to highway robbers. Guardian Angels, dressed in black with insignia armbands, were observed providing an armed entourage to truckloads of stolen and contraband merchandise. From the folk heroes of small businessmen the squad began to be perceived as dangerous robber barons. The band had begun to exceed the outer limits of acceptability and to spoil their 'usefulness' to the landowning agricultural and commercial classes. Emboldened, the Guardian Angels began to demonstrate their fascist tendencies beyond the *favela*, in their loathing 'deviant' white working-class and middle-class people, in addition to the more socially acceptable 'targets' of hatred: poor blacks, the illiterate, vagrants and poor sick people. Sexual transgressors and sexual outlaws (public homosexuals, *travesti* [cross-dressers], cross-racial and cross-class lovers) fell under their purview, under an alien code of puritanical morality that was not embraced by most Brazilians, even in this corner of rural Northeast Brazil. Had Abidoral and his gang kept their activities contained to the *favelas*, shantytowns and rural 'villas of misery' around Timbaúba, they might still be in control today.

Anthropology and human rights

The fax I spoke of earlier caused considerable consternation in the Scheper-Hughes household. It included a request for me to return to Timbaúba to put my anthropological skills to work in supporting the human rights vanguard in its efforts to recapture the *municipio* from vigilantes. As Judge Borges explained the mission: 'We are trying to restore "the rule of law" and to extend basic rights to all the people of Timbaúba, including the shantytowns and peripheral rural districts'. The choice of words – rule of law, basic rights and so on – was jarring. It sounded odd, almost like promotional materials from Amnesty International or the Open Society Institute. Then came the question, 'Will you join us in the struggle?'

Specifically, Judge Borges and Dr Graça wanted my help in identifying the many still unknown and unidentified victims and survivors of the death squad. The relatives of victims and survivors were afraid to come forward and testify. They did not trust the police or the courts. Thus, only a fraction of the executions had come to the attention of the public prosecutor and the judge. Some of the victims' bodies were buried in unmarked graves owned by small, Protestant churches. Some of the deaths were registered and shelved at the privately owned municipal registry office. I was asked to identify the hidden victims of the death squads by using the same skills I had employed in uncovering infant and child mortalities.

I hesitated. Was this an appropriate role? At what point does one leave anthropology behind and join a frankly political struggle? Or was this a false dichotomy, as Pierre Bourdieu argued when he called for a scholarship *with* (rather than opposed to) commitment?[4] In the end, I really did not have a choice. I was already implicated in the arrests. Dr Graça, the prosecutor, explained that my writings on 'everyday violence' and on violence against young black men and street children of the Alto do Cruzeiro were noted in the proceedings against Abidoral and his band. Although I was unable to interest a Brazilian publisher in a Portuguese edition of my book, a Spanish translation of *Death without Weeping* (1997) had reached members of the local intelligentsia and emerging human rights 'communities' in rural Pernambuco. Meanwhile, local activists in Timbaúba had a high school teacher produce a rough translation of Chapter 6, 'Bodies, Death and Silence', which was copied and distributed to the judge, prosecutor and local police force of Timbaúba.[5]

Thus, nearly a decade after its publication in English, some members of the local community had access to my rudimentary analysis of what was (at the time of my writing) a small and incipient death squad, restricted largely to poor and shantytown neighbourhoods where the executions were protected by a culture of terror and a political culture of impunity. Brazil's democratic transition was incomplete, I argued, and the failure of the 'Economic Miracle' to 'trickle down' to the vast majority left the community vulnerable to urban violence, drugs and crime. It was little wonder that social banditry and vigilante justice (see Scheper-Hughes, 1995; Hobsbawm, 2000) gave people a false sense of security, of 'order and progress', the elusive promise of Brazilian modernity. At the time I could see 'no exit' from the vicious cycles of poverty, hunger, crime and vigilante violence.

I had not anticipated the openings initiated by the new constitution and its 'bourgeois' vision of 'human rights' and the institutions it allowed to flourish, including the watchdog roles created to protect the rights of children and other vulnerable people. In Timbaúba, those elected or appointed to fill the roles of child rights counsellors and human rights advocates were largely working-class or 'popular' intellectuals lacking professional credentials, material resources or symbolic capital. Nonetheless, these rights workers mobilized around the constitution to begin to rescue the endangered population of street children and unemployed young men of the shantytowns, the main targets of Abidoral's 'hygienic exterminations'.

The formation of these organic intellectuals was slow and anything but steady, interrupted by police and government crack-downs during the military and even the post-military years. Nonetheless, they gained force and courage, working through networks of trust that were often betrayed by pernicious class interests. Those involved included radical lawyers, Catholic nuns, Marxist intellectuals, ordinary working-class and middle-class individuals who could no longer 'stand' the egregious violations of justice and human rights. One is a local pharmacist in her early seventies. Another was a *farinha* (manioc flour) salesman before he became a poor people's lawyer. Yet another was the son of a failed shoe factory owner. One is a woman who grew up with local street kids and who talks rough and wears low-cut dresses. Another is a German nun who works closely with a local black educator and rights activist. The activists are black, white, and in-between. It is politics, not race, which runs in their veins. They are married, single, celibate...and in-between. They are devout Catholics, sceptical agnostics and quiet atheists. They have met over the years in small rooms sharing dog-eared paperbacks and pamphlets. They read and passionately debate Marx, Gramsci, Leonardo Boff, the Scriptures, Paulo Freire, Celso Furtdao and Cristovan Buarque. They are critical thinkers and astute strategists who use the techniques of the *bricoleur*, taking advantage of every possibility, every theoretical or practical opening at hand. They make political alliances and just as quickly break them. They do not have reliable access to e-mail or the Internet. They campaigned and voted for Lula and had their hopes dashed when Lula cut deals and made coalitions with the forces of the old regime. Whilst not cynical, they never expect to succeed and when they do, they are quick to disparage their victories, mindful that optimism must be tempered by the expectancy of reversals and betrayals.

Amongst their initial successes was a programme that took them to the streets to identify and gather up Timbaúba's most threatened street children into a 'safe house' run in large part by the older children themselves, and following the philosophy of empowerment espoused by the MNMMR and the new child and adolescent statutes. They worked diligently to expose a corrupt judge and prosecutor who were linked to commercial international child trafficking adoption networks that preyed upon the poorest and weakest women of the community.

On my return to Timbaúba in the summer of 2001, accompanied by my husband, Michael, a clinical social worker with many years of experience working in the field of violence against children, I took up residence in the community centre run by Irma Sofia and her circle of local human rights and children's activists. As usual, the residents of Timbaúba had very mixed views about the activists' efforts. Many in the larger community had grown accustomed to the protection that the Guardian Angels seemed to provide in the absence of a 'strong' or 'efficient' police force, and they referred to the death squad terrorists as *justiceiros*, representatives of popular justice. For those residing on the two hillside slums of Alto do Cruzeiro and Independencia, the hardest hit by Abidoral and his men, the near nightly executions had turned them into shut-ins, living under self-imposed curfews. Many recalled with horror a night in 1999, when six people were murdered on the Rua do Cruzeiro, the principal street of the Alto. 'During the revolution', Irene said, using the local idiom to describe the terror as a war or revolution against the poor, 'we all went underground. The streets were deserted; we kept our doors locked and our wooden shutters closed tight. We would slide in and out our back doors to go to work or to the fields, or to the market. You never knew when the "exterminators" might appear or why someone had been "fingered"'.

Biu, my 56-year-old friend and key informant of many years, was amongst the last in Timbaúba to lose a family member to Abidoral's extermination group. Biu explained how her 24-year-old son had met his untimely end walking home along the main road leading up to the top of Alto do Cruzeiro. Neighbours heard the shots and screams, but they were too frightened to leave their homes. The next morning it was left to Gilvan's older sister, Pelzinha, to discover what was left of his body, sprawled over a mound of uncollected garbage. A crowd of greasy winged vultures had discovered Gilvan first and Pelzinha could barely recognize her brother. Well-seasoned by a lifetime of traumatic events, Biu was stoic, elliptical and ambivalent about the murder of her son. She began with a disclaimer: 'Gilvan was no angel. My family had turned against him, saying he was no good, a brawler, a drinker and a thief who was always getting into trouble. In one fight he even lost an eye. But when they say to me that Gilvan really had to be killed, I feel dead inside. He was still my son! But I can't tell anyone, except you, how much I miss that boy. My own niece said, "Be grateful, Tia, for the little bit of tranquillity that Gilvan's death has brought into your life". What does *she* understand?'

The banalization of violent death

In addition to collecting testimonies from old shantytown friends who had resisted going to the police or the court with their stories, I returned to my old 'stomping ground', the civil registry office located in the municipal courthouse of Timbaúba. There, Michael and I reviewed all the duly and officially registered deaths from 1995 to 2000, the height of Abidoral's reign of terror. Officially recorded homicides represented, of course, only the tip of the iceberg, as most extrajudicial killings were disguised as accidents, suicides and train- and car-related deaths. Many homicides were not registered at all and the bodies hidden in small, 'clandestine' graves in the rural surrounds. In all, our search through death records led to the identification of an additional 31 homicides that appeared to be linked *specifically* to Abidoral's 'exterminations'.

In most cases, the police were not even alerted. The relative of the deceased would arrive at the registry office and report the name, age and cause of death to Amintina, the discreet record keeper. With no questions asked, the death certificates would be signed and stamped with the municipal seal and the information was shelved. The only reason for reporting the deaths was so that the deceased could be buried in a free plot at the municipal graveyard. No one wanted any trouble with the law – which at that time happened to be the death squad itself.

Initially, I pretended to be looking for infant and child mortalities according to my familiar role in the civil registry office. After a few weeks, however, I had to explain to the proprietor of the records what we were looking for, and, although she expressed no emotion, she began to facilitate my search in subtle ways. She would say, 'Here, look at this', shoving a book towards me with a particular page open. A total of 93 homicides recorded via hand-written entries in the monthly ledgers of the Timbaúba civil registry between 1995 and 2000, roughly 19 per year. Few of these murders were investigated, which is hardly surprising considering both the 'social invisibility' of the victim population, on the one hand, and the likely involvement of civil and military police linked to Abidoral's extermination squad, on the other. The majority of recorded homicides were of young men between the ages of 15 and 30. The youngest homicide victim was a boy of 12 years and the oldest a man of 41. The average death squad victim, a subset of all homicides in Timbaúba, was a 26-year-old black (*negro*) or mulatto (*moreno*) male, unemployed, or casually employed, and residing in one of the 'informal' settlements on the hillsides and peripheries of Timbaúba. In the early 1990s, most homicides were of street kids and vagrants; towards the end of the decade, the homicides included those who had gotten tangled up in petty crimes, sexual and/or personal vendettas and drug deals gone wrong. We presented our report on 'likely' death squad victims to Dr Graça and the Ministry of the Public in Timbaúba to be used in continuing investigations and arrests. But our work was not finished.

Camanhada contra morte – the march against death squads

Our status as outsiders and our highly visible and matter-of-fact involvement in the ongoing criminal investigations was seized upon by the human rights vanguard of Timbaúba as a useful tool towards building a broader-based anti-death squad coalition. Our conspicuous note-taking on violent deaths, our open conversations in public spaces, and our visits to the homes of death squad victims and survivors flew in the face of the normal regime that Dr Graça described as 'the law of silence, the law of 'let it be' and the 'law of forgetting' adhered to by most members of the community. The time seemed ripe, the activists felt, for a public denunciation of the death squad. A meeting, called by the rights activists, brought together a larger group of political leaders, teachers and officials from the local Ministries of Education, Justice and Public Security, who planned a public demonstration, a *camanhada*, or march, against death squad violence, and to declare a truce and a time of peace.

The unique event was held on 19 July 2001, marking one year following the arrest of Abidoral and several of his accomplices. Whilst most residents were still too fearful of, or complicit with, the death squads (some of whom were still at large) to join the march, the municipal secretary of education declared the day a public school holiday and she herself fearlessly led the town's grade-school children and adult school youths in the march down the main streets of Timbaúba. She was joined by a few brave citizens including José Carlos Araujo, a bold radio journalist well known in the region for his popular free-wheeling daily talk-show on 'community radio' (poor people's public radio), and his wife, Maria do Carmel. Although the day was miserably 'cold' and rainy, hundreds of local residents came out of their homes to watch the unheard-of event from the sidewalk, registering their amazement and their excitement that it could be happening in Timbaúba. A small rented sound truck accompanied the procession with Marcelo, the poor peoples' lawyer, doing his best to animate the event and to call others from the sidelines to join the march against death. His broadly accented Nordestino voice, announcing an 'end to the reign of terror' and declaring a 'cease-fire in the war against the poor' in Timbaúba, made him particularly vulnerable. But none were more vulnerable than the front lines of the demonstration, which were reserved for the surviving cadre of local street children, who were dressed in white, each carrying a wooden cross bearing the name of a sibling or a friend who had been executed by Abidoral's gang. Following immediately behind them were about two dozen women, the mothers, older sisters, aunts and wives of the men and boys who had been murdered, making public for the first time what had happened to them. My closest friends on the Alto do Cruzeiro were among them. Irene was laughing and shaking her head in disbelief that she could be brave enough as to protest 'in front of the world' the execution-murders of her husband and two young adult sons. Biu was a more reluctant protester and she shyly hid herself in the midst of the 'mothers', refusing at first to carry the cross with the name of her murdered son, Gilvam. Thus, we took turns carrying the sign for her and to honour her executed son.

Suddenly, two heavily armed police jeeps appeared at the front of the march as though intending to interrupt it. Stifled cries of warning split the protestors down the centre, with the front lines of street children and human rights workers taking one street and the teachers and public-school children taking another. There was a moment of panic. Would the newly installed and human rights-trained police force show their true colours and turn on the demonstrators and open fire? But instead, and to our relief, amazement and delight, the police were going to accompany and protect the marchers. Moreover, inside the cab of one of the jeeps was the shackled figure of Abidoral Gonçalves Queiroz himself, who the police put on view before the marchers, forcing the leader of the death squad, his head initially bowed, to snap to attention and witness the spectacle of raised crosses bearing the names of the victims that he and his gang had brutally and wantonly murdered. Later, we learned that Judge Borges had arranged this dramatic 'confrontation' as a display of the power of the law and a visible sign that the new police force were representing all the people of Timbaúba, even street kids and 'marginals' from the *favelas* and peripheral, informal settlement of Timbaúba.

The march terminated in front of the City Hall and spontaneous, if somewhat nervous, speeches were made by the new mayor, 'Galvaozinho', who had replaced the corrupt former mayor and his henchmen, who were allies of Abidoral and his gang. The current mayor and his staff were presented with a large brass plaque memorializing the end of the most recent reign of death squad terror in Timbaúba. The organizers of the march requested that the plaque be placed on the wall of a small public square facing the Town Hall, which they hoped could be renamed the Praça de Paz. The plaque read: 'With the Gratitude of the People of Timbaúba for All Those who Fought Against Violence and for Human Rights. Commemorating One Year of Peace, July 19, 2001'.

What made this march a politically significant event? It was unique enough that Brazilian national radio and TV (Rede Globo) sent reporters to film the demonstration and to interview some of the participants as well as spectators. That evening people gathered in front of their TV sets and on the Alto in groups at the few homes with operable television sets, to observe the interviews with local residents, including residents of the Alto do Cruzeiro, along with the wrenching profile of an emotionally overwrought middle-class woman, the adoptive mother of a teenage girl who had been kidnapped and tortured by Abidoral's gang. As Holston (2000) has noted, citizenship includes the right to be visible and to be heard, the freedom to participate openly in politics and social movements in the public sphere. The claiming of these rights by 'disgraced' and stigmatized populations residing in peripheral neighbourhoods is new, and Holston's term 'insurgent' citizenship captures the 'revolutionary' feeling of those participating for the first time in public protest. Amongst other things, citizenship is about the right of *public* self-representation, self-expression, the right to be seen, to be visible, which entails the notion of 'public-ness' and the acknowledgement of being seen. The television coverage represented a 'coming out' (to the public) and 'the public eye', underscoring the importance of seeing and being seen in the affirmation of the citizen-subject. For the mothers and wives of the death squad victims, the *camanhada* was their 'coming-out' party. It made them feel strong and courageous, which, of course, they were.

A death foretold

And so, for the first time, I returned from the field with a relatively happy ending to a sad saga. I knew, of course, that violent deaths would not cease in Timbaúba, but at least for a time they would not be organized by roving bands of professional paramilitary death squads. Although I checked in with my friends from time to time, my subsequent field trips to Brazil took me elsewhere and were concerned with human trafficking for organs.

Whilst in Recife in February 2004 giving testimony at a Parliamentary Investigation of a gang of human traffickers that had infiltrated the slums and recruited desperately poor men to serve as paid kidney donors in Durban, South Africa, a contingent of human rights workers from Timbaúba arrived at the open session to relay discouraging stories of Abidoral and his henchmen re-arming themselves in jail and communicating with local bandits via cell phones, which are sometimes allowed to prisoners as a constitutional right. They also intimated that new death squads were forming, that Dr Graça had been re-assigned and Judge Marisa Borges, without Graça's moderating presence, was becoming something of a liability, a 'cowgirl judge', brave but belligerent and less than a well-informed and dependable resource for the community. Some in the loosely formed group of human rights activists were receiving anonymous death threats and feeling betrayed, subject to local 'double agents', powerful citizens (especially in the local business community, the 'commercial class', as they put it) who were playing dirty, appearing to support the rule of law and the rights of the poor, whilst actively supporting hired guns and arms traffickers from behind the scenes. A huge cache of arms including illegal and restricted automatic weapons had been discovered in the warehouse of a local shopkeeper, an affable fellow who sold children's toys, party favours and cheap sports equipment. Additional stockpiles of illegal weapons and bullets were found in the garages of his friends and neighbours. The ring leader was arrested, tried and convicted, but would his conviction and his prison sentence 'stick'? My friends doubted it. 'He has friends all the way up', said Marcelo. Even more personally tragic was their report of the death of my age-mate and friend, Biu, mother of 15 children, only six of whom survived, hunger and diarrhoea taking some of the little ones and bullets taking a few of the older ones, including her 'baby', Gilvam. Is there a term for poetic injustice? If so, it applies to Biu's death from uterine cancer and multiple, drug-resistant tuberculosis.

Despite such discouraging reports, I still wanted to sing the praises of this small band of rugged, rag-tag 'rights workers' who demonstrated that, despite well-reasoned anthropological critiques of the limits and deficiencies of constitutional and/or universal declarations of civil and human rights (such as the UN Proclamation on the Rights of the Child), these discourses can empower and enable (as Margaret Mead famously put it) thoughtful and committed citizens trying to transform the world in which they live.

Then, a few months after my meeting with the Timbaúba contingent in Recife, word reached me of a death that could have been foretold. Timbaúba's loose canon, the popular (indeed populist) working-class hero and community radio talk host, José Carlos Araújo, was shot in the chest, belly and mouth by two young gunmen on motorbikes who ambushed Araújo on 24 April 2004 (during Holy Week) outside his home in Timbaúba and in view of his wife, Maria do Carmel, and his three children. The 37-year-old folk musician – he and his wife and children performed *forro* music for dance parties throughout the region – turned truth teller and 'voice of the poor' had made enemies in Timbaúba after denouncing the continued existence of death squads run by criminal gangs and, even worse, revealing the involvement of well-known local figures and businessmen in wanton murders in the region. The local police later captured one of the suspected assassins, 19-year-old Elton Jonas Gonçalves, who confessed to killing Araújo because the journalist had accused him on the air of being a bandit.

On my return in July 2005, I resumed my meetings with the dispirited activists of Timbaúba. Marcelo brought me to the home of Maria do Carmel and her grieving family. There, I had to confront the role of the rights activists – and our march against silence – in further inciting Maria's husband to name and disclaim Timbaúba's deadly killers. She gave me copies of his taped radio programmes leading up to his death. In one of these, in a fit of fury, José Carlos screamed:

People from Alto do Cruzeiro are calling us and giving us details about the murder of a young man from the Alto. I'll pass this information along to the police, to the sheriff and his team. People are outraged! The boy was shot and killed last Saturday, about 7:30 a.m. in public in the open market! No kidding!... [The informants] are not yet ready to reveal the name of the assassin, but this guy knew what he was doing. The police patrol begins at 8 a.m., and he did his business at 7:30 a.m.! In other words, he is very smart. He uses his intelligence to do evil, to commit crimes. He could use his same skills for good deeds... but evil begets evil, and the police won't be demoralized forever. The [common] people will put pressure on the police, and they won't eat dust forever. They will eventually blow up, they will lose their patience and use the power they have, within the law, to catch him. ... I don't give a damn about bandits or bums. They should all go to hell to smoke Satan's pipe. If the police don't arrest him, even better. I hope they send him off [kill him]! If he had respected fathers and good citizens, I would shut up. But this guy does evil in his own community, he kills a father from his own neighbourhood. To reign in a community of poor people is not bravery, it's cowardly!

Some days later in a conversation with Timbaúba's chief of police the following dangerous conversation took place on the air:

> Chief of Police: 'I want to give a personal message to Antonio de Joana, from the Alto do Indpendencia. Dr. Guilherme [a local businessman] and I were up there on the Alto after a meeting last Friday looking for him until 3:45 a.m. Then we spent all of Saturday looking for him. If it weren't for the "warning" sounds a young man, we would have arrested him. But don't worry, we'll catch you next time'.
>
> José Carlos: 'So, now he's the one, the latest cause of all evil, is that it?'
>
> Police Chief: 'Yes, he's been trying to get everyone from Alto de Independencia in trouble, but he should know that [we] are on his tracks and will find him sooner or later. That's also true for "Pio" and "Jonas". We know that Jonas is bringing in people [reinforcements] from Recife, but it doesn't matter: Antonio de Joana, Pio, and Jonas will fall any day now'.
>
> José Carlos: '... So beware Pio, Jonas, and Antonio de Joana, you are all in trouble. I always say that bandits and outlaws don't have much time to live, you either end up in jail or in hell! Any day now! Today's show is over, I'll be back tomorrow to talk more about violence'.

In one of his final programmes before the voice of the people was silenced forever, José Carlos, seems to be prepared for his end and bidding farewell to the people of Timbaúba and the surrounding areas:

> My friends, I do my duty with a clear conscience.... But now it's time to return to reality, to the world of God, a world where I will never be betrayed.... At the end of my programme I always say that life is very good, but it also has difficult times. The way out of hard times is never to bow your head – quite the opposite – it is time to rise up and keep going. Victory cannot be bought or stolen. The sorrow and tears of being vanquished are more valuable than the shame of not participating in this journey and this struggle. And it is constantly fighting for victory where you will find me later, anywhere, anytime, at any corner, and you will say, 'José Carlos, you were right'.... From the bottom of my heart I wish that God will be your main guide and give you reason to live through difficult times.

Epilogue – face to face with Abidoral Queiroz

I returned to Brazil in the summer of 2007 to work with a cohort of young men from the slums of Recife who were recruited as kidney sellers to supply the needs of Israeli transplant tourists in South Africa. I spent a great deal of time in the military prison cell of one of the Israeli brokers, Gadalya Tauber, and used my new contacts with military prison guards to contact the Superintendent of Hannibal Bruno, Brazil's largest state penitentiary, where Abidoral, the putative head of Timbaúba's death squad, was serving a 30-year sentence.

'No, of course, the prisoner does not want to speak with a stranger', said the superintendent after several attempts to reach him by phone. With the clang-clang of banging cells and yelling men – 4000 prisoners under one roof – any phone conversation was nearly impossible. 'But I'm not a stranger', I yelled over the background din. 'Tell Abidoral that I am the *Americana* Nanci who lived for a long time on the Alto do Cruzeiro and who used to travel by bicycle and *burro* through the main street of Timbaúba, when he was a kid. He knows who I am'. 'OK, OK', said the superintendent. 'I can convince him to show you his face, but I can't force him to talk to you. Abidoral is very popular here, he is a "message boy" for us [implying a step-and-fetch-it], very pliant, very likable'.

So, this is what I wanted: to gaze at the face of the terrorist. I had in mind so many Brazilian television and film images of commando leaders, and I imagined Abidoral as a tall, dark, brooding young man, full of energy, native intelligence and rage, spewing rap and hip-hop couplets praising freedom, money, death and power. But the tiny little man who was brought in front of me, literally pulled by his ears by a prison warden, or so it seemed, was just a Nordestino peasant, and he refused the meeting in a high-pitched nasal Nordestino whine. 'I don't have to talk to the United Nations.... I have my rights'. In Abidoral's four-square field-worker hands was a black felt bowler-hat which he kept turning around, rubbing the brim nervously. He was dressed in a cheap, wrinkled white shirt and thick black pants, and, on his feet – the tiniest feet I have ever seen – were a pair of rubber-tire soled sandals. Abidoral, I found, could be mollified by using the patronizing intimate 'you', the privilege of the noble patron to his poor client – Tu, Tu, Tu... Abidoral.

Of course, he was innocent (he said). How could he possibly be the head of an illegal death squad when he was a paid civil servant, employed by the previous mayor, Gilson Queroiz? The accusations and arrests were all 'politics', the handiwork of the enemies of *prefeito* Gilson who wanted to take control of the city. 'Besides Mayor Gilson, who else paid you?', I asked. 'Was it "Totinho" [a wealthy businessman, now dead, believed to have financed the death squad]?' Abidoral's eyes rolled to the back of his head. 'If I was the chief of the *bandidos,* tell me, have the deaths ended in Timbauba?' 'No', I replied. 'They say that your son has taken over for you'. 'What business is it of yours? The only ones who are erased, are worthless dope fiends, drug addicts, thieves. The trouble is if you kill one or two, they blame every murder on you! I don't have to talk to you. Who sent you? The priest? The nuns? Give me your cell phone number – I will call you tomorrow. [Abidoral had my number already, that I could see.] Excuse me, Dona Nanci, but I am taking my leave now'.

And so am I. As the ballad of 'Frankie and Jonnie' ends, so does this mordant tale about banditry and death squads in democratic Brazil. A story that has no (certain or stable) moral, and a story that has no end – at least not in the sight of this chastened anthropologist-*companheira.*

Notes

Abridged and amended version of 'Death Squads and Democracy in Northeast Brazil', in Jean and John Comaroff (eds) *Law and Disorder in the Postcolony,* pp. 150–187 (Chicago: Chicago University Press, 2006). This chapter was made possible through collaborative work with the human rights activists of Timbaúba, Brazil: Irma Sofia Christa Maria Salanga; Tania, Rute Borba, Marcelo (Joao Marcelo Gomes Ferreira), Gildete, Celma Vasconcelos and all the members of the Conselho de Direitos Humanos. Dr Marisa Borges and Dr Humberto da Silva Graça were inspirational in their moral courage and deep integrity. The members of the Union of the People of Alto de Cruzeiro and the Clube das Maes (Mothers Club) of Alto do Cruzeiro continue to struggle and to affirm their right to live choking on their swallowed grief following the hundreds of 'small wars and invisible genocides' that have turned their infants into 'angel babies' and their sons into the living targets of race and class hatred in democratic Brazil.

1. MNMMR/IBASE/NEV (1991) and Alvim (1991) provide a rich chronology on the major events, including the work of human rights oriented street educators and activists – denouncements, demonstrations, studies – that influenced the government to define measures to combat the violence against children.
2. 'Street children' is a global nongovernmental organization folk classification. Brazilian human rights activists include under the designation both children who live in the streets (*meninos da rua*) and children who may have a home but spend most of their day in the streets (*meninos na rua*).
3. Edmundo Campos Coelho argues in his essay '*A criminalidade Urbana Violenta*' that, until the 1960s, bank assaults were virtually unknown in urban Brazil,

as were kidnappings for ransom. Drug dealings existed but lacked the well-structured network and entrepreneurial organization that emerged later in the 1990s. In Rio de Janeiro and São Paulo crime was basically an individual activity. Whilst a few decades ago homicides were predominantly 'crimes of passion', today homicides are an organized activity occurring within the conflict between drug-dealing gangs, clandestine 'death squads' and police (p. 145). 'Extermination squads' which had first targeted adults accused of being local criminals, later pointed their revolvers at the heads of kids and adolescents. (This footnote thanks to Benedito dos Santos, 2003.)

4. 'To do so, writers, artists and especially researchers (who, by trade, are already more inclined and more able than any other occupation to overcome national borders), must breach the *sacred boundary*, inscribed in their minds, more or less deeply depending on their national tradition, between *scholarship* and *commitment*, in order to break out of the academic microcosm and to enter resolutely into sustained exchange with the outside world (that is, especially with unions, grass-root organizations and issue-oriented activist groups), instead of being content with waging the "political" battles at once intimate and ultimate, and always a bit unreal, of the scholastic universe. Today's researchers must innovate an improbable but indispensible combination: *scholarship with commitment*, that is, a collective politics of intervention in the political field that follows, as much as possible, the rules that govern the scientific field' (Pierre Bourieu in his public lecture on 'Scholarship with Commitment', presented at the University of Chicago, 2001).

5. The police, both civil and military, had frequently been involved in earlier death squad activities, and the mere idea of the local police in Timbaúba, reformed or not, knowing and reading what I had to say about their predecessors filled me with foreboding.

9
Resisting Submission? The Obstinacy of 'Balkanist' Characteristics in Greece as Dissidence Against 'the West'

Sappho Xenakis

The theoretical prism of normative hybridity

One of the challenges that were set to the contributors of this volume was to explore the distinctions between banal and reflective, superficial and effective and recalcitrant and progressive resistance to power. Each of these distinctions is difficult to prove. The first, because it requires an insight and certainty about the internal decision-making of the 'actor' in question that may well be impossible (see, for example, discussion in Murdoch, 2003; 2006); and the latter two, because their very definition may be regarded, self-evidently, as culturally and politically determined (see discussion in Jusdanis, 1991). In contemporary Greece – as with other postcolonial societies that continue to experience direct and transposed Western guidance in their strategies of governance (see Gourgouris, 1996) – the conundrum of assessing resistance appears to be even more pronounced in light of the omnipresent clash between 'Western' and 'traditional' norms governing social values. Citizens of such societies confront, at a 'banal', everyday level, the imperative of negotiating two competing sets of social expectations of 'correct' behaviour, as much as understandings of the core values that constitute the overarching 'good' towards which such behaviour is directed.

This chapter aims to provide an account of normative hybridity that enunciates rival notions of the 'good', as evidenced in the case of contemporary Greece. Taking inspiration from Bhabha's conception of 'cultural hybridity' (Bhabha, 1994), the term 'normative hybridity' is used here to invoke the dialectics of transgression of external and local norms (expectations of behaviour and the values that underpin them). This, then, is posited as a process that has the power to disrupt and dislocate efforts to holistically import external norms via challenges inherent in the necessary tasks of their translation to, and negotiation within, the local arena. With this account of normative hybridity, the chapter contests the common stereotypical portrayal of 'Balkanist' characteristics in and of Greece as simple, shallow, recalcitrant 'bads', whether real or imaginary. Whilst not seeking to deny the existence of negative dimensions of either 'Balkanist' or 'Western' norms (space prohibiting their equal elaboration here), it is argued that the existence and significance of a rationale of the 'good' inherent to Balkanist characteristics, whose perpetuation challenges and repositions the effective domestic extension of the 'Western good', requires due recognition. This, in turn, necessitates a controversial acknowledgment of the existence of difference underpinning the 'Balkanist' label, and points to the merit of going beyond a critical deconstruction of the term (contra Lambropoulos, 2004). Furthermore, seeking to refute the accusation that the stubborn continuation of 'Balkanist' habits is responsible for holding back the healthy advancement of Greek society and state, the chapter posits that 'Balkanist' resistance has functioned as a vital motor of constructive change, propelling an emancipatory logic that has served to moderate the impact of 'Western' norms upon the country.

In a very practical sense, 'Balkanist' and 'Western' conceptions of the 'good' are not incommensurate value systems in the Greek space. This is evidenced not least by the way in which so many individuals appear rehearsed in switching between them. The two conceptions are applied reflexively, according to a particularist logic determined by the political and social parameters of the situation and its actors. That is to say, the plurality of moral creeds leads to a situation in which the 'good' thing to do is selectively chosen on a case-by-case basis, rather than being decided in accordance with a single, invariant set of moral principles (on particularist ethics, see Dancy, 2004). References here to 'Western' and 'Balkanist' characteristics are not meant to imply that each and every act of resistance or conformity is executed in conscious or declared pursuit of, or opposition to, either overarching paradigm by the actor. Likewise, the terms 'Western' and 'Balkanist' are employed as shorthand for the innumerable everyday designations of such acts with terms that are commonly understood to encompass them. Indeed, it is to some extent the 'banality' – here in a simplified Arendtian sense, denoting an unreflective, habitual nature – of the inspiration underpinning the acts that underlines the suitability of their characterization as illustrative of a 'banality of good'.

That 'Balkanist' habits in Greece could constitute a *progressive* form of dissidence against 'the West' might seem implausible to many, and no doubt offensive in equal measure. To the extent that Balkanist characteristics are associated with incivility, laziness, deception and self-indulgent familism (the privileging of family obligations over those to non-family members and institutions), the undesirability of their continued existence within Greek society and, indeed, their tenacity in the face of efforts to quash them, appears self-evident; the notion that they might embody a rival logic of the 'good' to that favoured in the West – fairness-and-equality – could easily be considered perverse.[1] Furthermore, a reasonable scepticism is to be expected regarding the intentionality of Balkanist miscreants in their resistance: Do they truly want to resist anything, or are they just seeking to play the system to their advantage? Does what they (might) want matter in determining whether their acts are to qualify as (progressive) 'resistance'? Perhaps most challenging of all, does the nature of such resistance condemn it to succeed only in reproducing the marginalization of Greeks (its fate, as suggested by Herzfeld, 2004)?

This is not a chapter in support of pure moral relativism: all moral codes are not equal; the radical exclusionary creeds of some are profoundly anti-humanist. The legitimacy of recognizing in both 'Western' and 'Balkanist' moral codes a creed of the 'good' is grounded in the degree to which they do not promote insensitivity and are rather based on a progressive expectation of empathetic understanding and reciprocity with others. As will be elaborated below, both the Western 'good' of fairness-and-equality (as embodied in the call for meritocracy) and the Balkanist 'good' of freedom-and-equality (as evident in resistance to service culture, for example) can accordingly be interpreted as genuine 'goods'. It is these 'goods' that explain their appeal, even if individuals do not always reference or abide by them. This discussion is thus conditioned by the notion that, to a large extent, moral discourses may be evaluated distinctly from actions that may well be inspired by them. The justification for this distinction is that, on the one hand, neither good nor evil deeds require a good or evil motive in order to be enacted, whilst, on the other hand, definition of an act as good or evil is not routinely dependent upon the motive of the actor. That is to say, just as with evil deeds, good deeds can be the result of reflexive, unreflective human action, or, more realistically, of a complex interaction of good, bad and indifferent sentiments (see Murdoch, 2003; 2006).

The problem of Balkanist obstinacy in Greece

The purpose and value of elaborating a notion of normative hybridity do not simply rely upon exploring its as-yet underdeveloped relationship with moral theory or even applied ethics, but, additionally, in addressing the more immediate, obvious and situated concern with this issue in contemporary Greek studies. When engaging in sustained research of any dimension of contemporary Greek society, encountering the smouldering conflict between pro-Western modernizers or Europeanists and recalcitrant Balkanist traditionalists appears to be practically inevitable (see Herzfeld, 1992: 40–41).[2] Social status and educational attainment are often portrayed as the preserve (albeit not entirely exclusive) of the former, leading to an under-exploration and marginalization of the discourse and rationale of the latter in 'high-brow' literary output. The heat of the contest, evident not in the least from the tense stridency of the language of 'modernizers', nevertheless points to the richer and more serious moral challenge posed by recalcitrance than typically acknowledged by 'modernizers', who commonly act as guardians of knowledge in academia and the media.[3] Without wishing to reify either groups of individuals, their motives or corresponding discourses, such normative dynamics as exemplified in the practical complexities of the 'banality of good' in Greece deserve greater considered attention.

Applied here to the contemporary domestic Greek context, 'Balkanism' is not intended to allude to the common Balkan referents of violence, ethnic fragmentation, hatreds or shared identity with neighbouring societies of Southeastern Europe (for discussion of the latter, see Todorova, 1997), nor indeed to Balkan peoples *per se*. Rather, the term is employed to invoke attitudes and behaviours of Greeks that may be interpreted as typically 'Balkanist' in the sense of being recalcitrant, especially towards neoliberal and other planks of Western and European modernization agendas, as well as being traditionalist, corrupt, familist, lazy, disobedient, deceitful, disorganized and inefficient (and sometimes also nationalist, populist, religious, irrational and anti-Enlightenment, as Greek Orthodoxy has often been characterized), even if they are not always openly labelled as such.[4] Indeed, the application of the 'Balkanist' label seems overwhelmingly to be restricted to moderate, non-violent forms of such protest in Greece, rather than to examples of radical activism (often involving violence against property) typified by the country's significant and longstanding anarchist and far-left groups.

Balkanist traits have been portrayed as responsible for the retardation of development towards a more Europeanized, modern state-societal relationship in Greece. As elaborated below, such assessments have been strongly represented in literature addressing the extent to which Greece has successfully amended, developed or put into practice, legislation and policies on a wide range of issues conforming with EU and international agreements, particularly relating to the economic sphere. A central platform of the modernization agenda has indeed been to overhaul what is commonly perceived to be a corrupt and clientelist state bureaucracy and to replace it with one functioning according to meritocratic and democratic principles (on the latter goal, see Featherstone, 1998). In this context, opposition to the agenda has been interpreted as an inferior and illegitimate form of resistance; non-progressive, conservative, recalcitrant and tinged with a parochial nationalism that seems uncomfortably reminiscent, for some, of the country's authoritarian past (and of the supportive stance of the Church towards the military dictatorship of 1967–1974, in particular).[5]

One key sector of society identified for its retrogressive attitudes has been those workers protesting against 'modernization' reforms since the 1980s. Political scientist (and later EU Ombudsman) Nikiforos Diamandouros describes the role of this 'underdog' camp, comprised largely of the country's least competitive workers (those of the state-controlled and self-employed sectors), in resisting the plans of the 'reformist' camp and consequently ensuring that 'deregulation and privatization have proceeded at an agonisingly slow pace' (Diamandouros, 1997: 30–32).[6] Subsequent waves of protest to the introduction of neoliberal reforms were similarly condemned as 'sectarian', 'populist' or 'regressive' (Spourdalakis and Tassis, 2006), for their apparently unstinting defence of an explicitly political, non-meritocratic and clientelist set of criteria that all the while safeguarded their jobs (Diamandouros, 1997: 26, 32).

More distinctly, workers in service-providing professions, across both public and private sectors, have also been commonly identified as 'Balkanist'. The routine indifference and obstructionism of petty civil servants towards the public in the latter's efforts to file everyday requests and registrations, or, equally, towards the efforts of political and bureaucratic elites to introduce new standards of efficiency and service (both elaborated in Herzfeld, 1992), is mirrored in the legendary rudeness of Greek taxi drivers, the sullen unhelpfulness of shop assistants and the indomitable unpunctuality of other professional workers (on the latter example, see Hirschon, 2008 and Sifianou, 1999). For modernizers, these types of resistance constitute an embarrassing and frustrating drag on the progress of Greece towards Western standards of professionalism, and lamentable evidence that many things in Greece are actually 'Balkanist' and only superficially Westernized.[7] Each of these thwarted goals are understood to be necessary for successful economic development, whilst underpinning these nominal goals lies the logic of an overarching creed of equality of treatment of the individual by both public and private sectors (fairness-and-equality).[8] This creed champions the notion that everyone has an equal right to fair and professional (that is, timely, polite and meticulous) treatment, by the state as well as by private businesses (thus its close relationship to notions of (good) 'service culture').[9] The establishment of the office of the Greek Ombudsman in 1998, as well as the considerable investment of the Greek state in programmes during and since the Olympic Games of 2004 to educate taxi drivers in the etiquette of tourist interactions, are indicative examples of efforts to address such concerns.[10]

Aside from those workers portrayed as Balkanist individuals, the broader Greek public has been subject to political cajoling (albeit in typically sympathetic vein) to cast aside their Balkanist habits; primarily, to pay taxes and abstain from bribing public officials. As Danopoulos and Znidaric (2007) highlight in their account of high levels of corruption and informal and black economic activity in Greece – which in 2003 was characterized by a report of the European Central Bank as the highest amongst 23 developed nations (ANA, 2003) – the largely family-run character of the ubiquitous tourist and 'small-shop' sectors of the country plays a significant and negative role. One form of informality (an inefficient, neighbourly familism) is portrayed as begetting another (tax evasion and black economic practices).[11] Indeed, familism has long been correlated by some theorists with national levels of corruption and lower levels of economic development (from Banfield, 1958, to Lipset and Lenz, 2000), whilst familist enterprises in particular have been associated with tax evasion practices (Fukuyama, 2002). Each interconnected dimension of characteristic Balkanism is seen as a challenge to the development of a modern, meritocratic and successful future. Given that the family has largely remained a 'sacred cow' of Greek social and political discourse, however, it is perhaps unsurprising that modernizers have tended to focus more on the issue of tax evasion and inefficiencies of the small, family-run businesses than on the 'problem' of familism *per se* (see, for example, Diamandouros, 1994).

Yet, whilst forms of Balkanism such as these appear to be self-evident 'bads' – even more so when compared to the 'Western' creed of fairness-and-equality – the clash of creeds is, nevertheless, not as clear-cut as it might at first appear. As will be elaborated below, the constraints of a practically lived normative hybridity are encapsulated most succinctly in the evident struggle of modernizers themselves to live according to their proclaimed ideals. Elaborating the duality of the modernizers' stance, as well as the political implications that have followed from it, is a necessary step in explaining the context in which the 'Balkan(ist) good' is valued.

Normative hybridity amongst modernizers

Balkanist obstinacy has been as much a problem identified with those 'others' so designated by domestic Greek discourse as it has been internationally with Greece *per se*, perhaps most famously illustrated by Henry Kissinger with his assessment in 1997 that 'the Greeks are an ungovernable people' (cited in Hirschon, 2001: 27).[12] Indeed, the application of the othering 'Balkanist' label to Greece has long appeared to act as a significant motor of consensus amongst the Greek political elite (high-ranking politicians of the two principal political parties, senior officials and advisors) in support of 'modernizing' Greece.[13] This is a consensus which, straddling the two largest political parties (New Democracy [ND] on the centre-right and the Panhellenic Socialist Movement [PASOK] on the centre-left) since the mid-1990s has entailed the favouring of pro-EU and Atlanticist policies (two key global sources of modernization blueprints), including, but not restricted to, neoliberal (centre-right) economic commitments (Ifestos, 1997; Ioakimidis, 1999).

One of the most obvious recent manifestations of the 'Balkanist' label as impetus for elite modernist counteraction was the Greek diplomatic fiasco of the early 1990s (namely, Greek resistance to the naming of the former Yugoslav Republic of Macedonia, and the failure of Greece to win the hosting of the 1996 Olympiad; see Calotychos, 2003), compounded over the years by successions of domestic political corruption scandals (from the Koskotas and AGET-Heracles scandals of the late 1980s and early 1990s, for example, to the Eurostat affair of the early 2000s), which together led to highly unfavourable international portrayals of Greek politics as rife with chauvinistic nationalism and dishonesty.[14] This was subsequently compounded by scathing concerns raised in the US media by former American diplomats about the professionalism and capabilities of the Greek state in combating terrorism (the 17 November organization, in particular). Hosting the 2004 Olympic Games in Athens provided the political elite with a self-acknowledged, if highly pressured, opportunity to overcome the image of Greece as a recalcitrant and backward partner to European and international colleagues, and to very publicly assert the country's credentials as a competent (post)modern member of the First World club of nations (see Klarevas, 2005). Equally, this was an opportunity to overcome those nationalist, chauvinistic and recalcitrant Balkanist voices and practices rooted within both parties; the display of resolve in introducing a fresh face to Greek diplomacy that promised moderation and effective international collaboration was directed as much to domestic 'Balkanist actors' as to international audiences.

Despite sustained anti-Balkanist rhetoric over the past 12 years from the modernizing elite of both parties, they have themselves been tarnished by subsequent successive waves of corruption scandals that have brought into question the depth of their commitment to the values to which they claim adherence, a reality brought into sharp relief by the dramatic outburst of public discontent across Greece in December 2008 (for further on which, see Karpathakis, 2008; Smith and Siddique, 2008). On the one hand, the (partially) 'Westernized', mostly right-of-centre cross-party elite and their select middle- and upper-class supporters had been those identifying and chastising the less contentiously designated social and political culprits for the embarrassing critical external and self-accepted designations of the country as 'Balkanist'. On the other hand, however, a broad cross-section of the very elite of the Greek political and business strata came to face a multitude of media allegations concerning their own involvement in 'Balkanist' practices of corruption, nepotism and patronage. From the stock market scandal of 2000 that sullied the 'clean' reputation of the modernist PASOK government and cost the savings of an estimated 1.5 million Greeks, to the Siemens scandal of 2007–2008 in which both of the principal political parties were embroiled and, similarly, the Vatopedi monastery scandals that subsequently struck the ND government, confidence in the integrity and credible moral platform of the modernizing elite has been shaken (particularly given the evident aversion of both party leaderships to the according of blame or punishment to any of their own representatives).[15]

The unstable duality of discourse concerning the very Balkanist trait of deceptiveness, of 'cheating the system', whereby it is both publicly condemned as an impediment to modernization and yet also prominently acknowledged and revelled in as an indicator of indigenous ingenuity of which Greeks should be proud (Safilios-Rothschild, 1966; Triandis and Vassiliou, 1972; Mouzelis, 1995; Tsoukalas, 1995), points to the very real, if banal, mass experience of normative hybridity. One perceived example of this hybridity amongst the modernizers is former Prime Minister Costas Simitis, of the PASOK party. His reputed technocracy in government (1996–2004) was also interpreted by some as a form of Balkanist crafty guile (Herzfeld, 2004: 203), apparently substantiated to some extent by the claims that, under Simitis's leadership, Greece manipulated its economic data in order to gain entry into the EMU (Economic Monetary Union, or Eurozone).

The banality of 'familism' amongst the modernizing elite is another obvious example of such hybridity, even aside from the continuing central role in Greek politics of dynasties such as the Papandreou, Karamanlis and Mitsotakis families. Patronage and nepotism featured in the allegations made against former ND Prime Minister, Kostas Karamanlis, concerning his part in supporting and protecting his fellow cabinet minister and first cousin (Michalis Liapis) as well as his wife (Natasa Pazaiti-Karamanli) from corruption scandals, even if – judging from Greek media coverage of these allegations – the alleged acts may have been interpreted by many as unsurprising examples of Balkanism.[16] Against the insinuations that have arisen around such relationships, the way in which ND officials have chosen to defend the party is instructive: in the midst of a corruption scandal in 2006, former ND government spokesman Thodoris Roussopoulos and Minister of Labour Savvas Tsitouridis declared that under no circumstances could family relations be criminalized (cited in Gilson, 2006). Again, in 2008, Roussopoulos defended his own reputation against the allegations of the Vatopedi scandal, arguing that the PASOK party were seeking to undermine 'human and political relationships' (cited in *Greek News*, 27 October 2008). The extent to which such sentiments have been shared amongst other modernizing groups is illustrated by the following commentary of an online magazine promoting engagement in the Greek business market:

> Family ties, the absolute foundation of Greek social life, play a vital role in business. Family and friends are everything and require absolute loyalty. Nothing can be accomplished until there is complete consensus with individuals who are trusted.... It is a shared responsibility amongst the extended family to help relatives find employment either in one's own enterprise or that of an associate. Nepotism, *meson*, has a positive, rather than a negative connotation here, and as a foreigner you may find yourself dealing with three generations of a given family. In such an environment, it should come as no surprise that contacts and references play an integral role in getting an introduction or a deal.
>
> (Sgourides, 2004)

Even the influential journalist and exemplary modernizer Alexis Papahelas (executive editor of *Kathimerini* broadsheet newspaper), who publicly decried the hypocritical moralizing of media responses to the Siemens scandal given the media's own close relationship with political and entrepreneurial elites, questioned 'when we all became so very British about the propriety of certain behaviours'. He concluded, '[n]oone is saying that journalists should be saints. But the least we can do is exercise more care with our "holier than thou" preaching' (Papahelas, 2008).

In practice, then, 'Balkanist' traits are evidently neither absent nor widely shunned by actors of either side of the state–society and right–left divides. As Herzfeld has pointed out, 'Eurocentric' (Western) and 'native' (Balkanist or Oriental) stereotypes are categories – familiar to *all* Greeks – that function as strategic 'building blocks' for identity and action, but they can also be challenged and breached (Herzfeld, 1992: 44–45). Irrespective of geographical, political or class boundaries, normative hybridity unites Greeks, even if they may not always recognize that it does so; a point encapsulated in Herzfeld's assessment that '[l]arge numbers of Greeks...even whilst shaking their heads over the wild stories of certain animal-thieves – evoke precisely the same national stereotype of defiant independence as they fiddle their tax returns' (Herzfeld, 2005: 216). In this way, normative hybridity in Greece can be seen as a socially encompassing and publicly acknowledged reality (the latter as also argued by Calotychos, 2003: 289, 157), to such an extent that it belies the notion of a structured, politico-cultural *disemia* or divide between official self-portrayals and the intimate collective secrets of a society's culture (on 'cultural intimacy', see Herzfeld, 2005).[17]

The 'good' of Balkanist resistance

It is perhaps obvious that the existence of widespread normative hybridity does not, in itself, impart a notion of 'good' to Balkanism any more than it strips one from Western-influenced modernization agendas. It does, however, suggest that there may be more to 'Balkanism' than 'badness'. Indeed, an underlying 'good' to Balkanism goes some way towards explaining its appeal across the hybrid normative system. This good of 'freedom-and-equality' is embodied in the value accorded to the notion of hospitality, whilst its limits are demarcated by that accorded to familism. Both of these values are constituted in ways that – often consciously, if usually implicitly – challenge the Western creed of the 'good' advanced by modernizers in Greece.

Resistance to authority and, more specifically, to state power is a familiar trope of Greek national identity, and there are endless references to the historical conditions which have wrought the enduring rebellious nature of the Greeks, even if only as a dated and indefensibly romantic 'hangover' within such analyses (Koliopoulos and Veremis, 2004: 233). Discussion of Greek political culture commonly includes mention, as the root of this phenomenon, of the legacy of entrenched domestic resistance to 400 years of Ottoman rule, from the routine tax evasion of wily peasants to the revolutionary spirit of bandit leaders in their struggles for liberation from foreign power. Recent analyses have also privileged the romanticized histories of more recent legitimized anti-state activities; namely, those that took place during the period of military dictatorship experienced by the country between 1967 and 1974 (see, for example, Brabant, 2008).

Underpinning the stereotype of the 'rebellious' Greeks, however, seems to be a widely supported commitment to asserting a particular conception of the 'good' as freedom-and-equality. As the anthropologist Renée Hirschon elaborates, evident amongst Greek cultural values is 'an overriding premium placed on personal autonomy [of action] and freedom [of expression]' (Hirschon, 2001: 18–19, 23), a 'reluctance to concede hierarchy or to accept subordination' – at least towards 'strangers' or 'outsiders' – captured in the sense of the not uncommon riposte to those who dare to challenge this value directly: 'και ποιος είσαι εσύ' ('and who are you?') (ibid.: 26). This desire for autonomy and equality appears to be manifested exactly in that reluctance to conform to 'modernist', 'Western' expectations of punctuality, regularity or of 'service culture'. Instead, the Balkanist worker may demonstrate their individual freedom from such strictures by way of a routinely personalized performance of service. This performance can be regarded as a visually and substantively tailored exhibition of the worker's personal autonomy: their power to provide or deny hospitality according to their own whim, either by gracing the customer with what they desire, or else by proudly rejecting the implication of obligation to the customer in refusing to satisfy their desires as they would like.[18]

The demonstrative use of personal autonomy would seem to contradict one basic, progressive 'good' and tenet of politeness; that of consideration for other people's feelings. Western-influenced conceptions of politeness may emphasize the importance of adopting social norms such as apologies in appropriate situations, and formal requests, rather than straight demands for services. According to the linguistic expert Maria Sifianou, however, politeness tends to be more broadly defined by traditionally-minded Greeks to include values and practices that also function to constrain personal autonomy, such as altruism, generosity, and self-abnegation (Sifianou, 1992).[19] For the Balkanist Greek, this 'best-mannered' ideal is embodied in the individual who has 'philotimo'; a sense of honour which dictates that they respectfully and reliably meet their obligations to members of their 'in-group' (Triandis and Vassiliou, 1972). The latter may be understood to comprise members of the nuclear family and frequently, in addition, other kin and affinal relations, and kin-like associates (such as the 'best man' or 'best woman' who sponsors a marriage, and a 'godparent' who makes an oath of care for another's child).[20] Those Greeks who reportedly judge many of their compatriots to be rude, Sifianou surmises, are likely themselves to have adopted non-Greek (Western) social norms of politeness as part of their own aspirations for social advancement, and to have un-learned the more 'traditional' Greek understanding of politeness (Sifianou, 1992: 218–219).

The particular unreliability of interpersonal engagements between 'outsiders', provoked by demonstrations of 'Balkanist' autonomy (and corresponding privileging of 'in-group' relations), may constitute unacceptable rudeness in Western societies, in which formal codes of interaction constitute the baseline of good manners. For the 'Balkanist' or 'traditional' model of Greek politeness, however, even if consideration for others is also regarded as an important component of politeness, formalism and distancing amongst 'in-group' members is of greater impoliteness than rudeness expressed to outsiders (ibid.). Thus, for example, the relatively broader disinterest amongst Greeks in the 'Western' value of public, institutionalized 'charitable work' (and, consequently, the small and only recently developed Greek NGO sector), where prioritizing the giving of assistance to out-group individuals at the cost of spending time and resources fulfilling in-group duties of care (such as to fellow kin or co-parishioners, young or old), may be regarded as incomprehensibly crude.[21] This dissonance between codes of the 'good' is reflected as much at the micro as at the macro level of societal interactions, where campaigns for self-regulating markets and individualized norms and rights have clashed with Balkanist moral expectations centred upon the group (see Tsoukalas, 1991; Calotychos, 2003).

The progressive impact of the Balkanist notion of the 'good' also functions at both micro and macro levels, normatively and substantively. Normatively, the Balkanist notion of the 'good' offers Greeks an alternative set of expectations concerning individual autonomy and the protection of 'in-group' obligations, furnishing them with a culturally-ingrained ('banal') conceptual framework and language with which they can critically interrogate modernizing teleologies, and upon which they can model their vocal opposition to such challenges. That Greeks appear to be more likely to believe poverty is caused by structural rather than personal inadequacies, for example (unlike their counterparts in countries where neo-liberal ideologies are less contested and more firmly entrenched), certainly seems to constitute a form of empowerment at the level of cognition and expression.[22] Rejection of the neo-liberal dogma of personal responsibility may be fuelled by a sense of the injustice of abandoning in-group obligations, as much as by scepticism as to the extent of modernizers' willingness to adhere to the same principles that they proscribe for others.

Substantively, with regard to those neo-liberal policies that have propelled greater employment insecurity and wealth inequalities, managerialist regulation and standardization of work practices, as well as increasing investment in authoritarian and inhumane forms of policing (see Cheliotis and Xenakis, 2010, forthcoming), values and practices falling within the rubric of the Balkanist creed of the 'good' have been credited as central motivating factors underlying the active record of public mobilization (such as trade union strikes and political demonstrations) and professional obstructionism in the country (from tardy and unfriendly service to tax and benefit fraud) (see Tsoukalas, 1995; Lawrence, 2007).[23] Perhaps more importantly, efforts to enact the Balkanist creed of the 'good' – whether made consciously or not – have progressive consequences not only upon the individual seeking to resist further encroaches upon personal autonomy, but also on the furnishing of support to those disproportionately facing the harsh end of neo-liberal realities, such as the youth and the elderly (see Fotiadis, 2007). Against a background of very low state welfare provision, rising levels of poverty amongst both groups and an employment market in which it is proving increasingly difficult for young people to gain entry, Balkanist familism provides a vital safety net for many (Karakatsanis, 2000; Papadopoulos, 2006).[24]

Conclusion: Limitations of the Balkanist creed of the 'good'

This is not to imply that either collective or individual forms of Balkanist resistance are without their limitations. On one hand, for example, whilst collective action in Greece has demonstrated resilience, and at times even gained momentum, in recent years, it is clear that there are restrictions to the progressive potential of political parties and trade unions (see discussion in Burawoy, 1979). On the other hand, it is evident that personalized forms of protest may function at best as only partially effective impediments to the advancement of modernization policies, a poorer form of resistance than organized collective action itself. Balkanist resistance at the individual level may indeed fuel both the determination of the modernizers to renewed efforts as well as the marginality of 'Balkanists' themselves within the socio-economic system (as Herzfeld, 2004, suggests), not least since such resistance is a means of accommodating the system rather than reforming it at a macro level. Furthermore, as acknowledged at the outset, a Balkanist creed of the 'good' does not preclude its opposite. As Christopher Lawrence (2007) has convincingly written, the often witnessed 'paradox' of such forms of resistance today is their dark underside of racist nationalist sentiment towards immigrant 'others', and their morally compromising relationship to competitive consumerism and its prerequisite social norms.

These arguments do not necessarily detract from the progressive nature of the 'good' underlying such resistance, however. Support for familism does not necessarily equate with support for corruption, particularly not the grand corruption that has rocked the country's political and business elites in recent years, nor support for the in-group with support for racist nationalism.[25] Rather, the social world of 'traditionally-minded' Greeks is conditioned by an appreciation of the moral and practical benefits of enmeshment in community relationships. That is, as Marcel Mauss (1924/1990) suggested, the value of reciprocal obligations inherent in familism are ties that strengthen and stabilize communities otherwise challenged by the considerable threats of internal divisions in a highly competitive and largely unsupportive broader environment.

Whilst the progressive potential of the good of 'freedom-and-autonomy' might not always be evident or practiced, its banal reality has already proved its moral value if we recall the role played by ingrained cultures of insubordination in the saving of Jewish lives in Italy as well as Greece 60 years ago (Steinberg, 2002). Today, the clash of 'goods' in Greece means that realization of either is tempered and modified. The condition of normative hybridity, however, implies that this is not a clash between agents, but between ideals which act as public reservoirs of moral logic from which all – with or without reflection – may draw inspiration. At the agential level, then, the progressive promise of normative hybridity stems from the heightened possibility of a personal ethics that does not rely upon a single code of principles, but is instead flexible and particularist in selecting appropriate moral choices (Dancy, 2004). At the macro-societal level, the outcome of such normative hybridity could quite possibly be more progressive than conservative, since each creed of the 'good' stands as a critical bulwark against the domination of the other.[26]

All this is not to imply that normative hybridity is the privileged experience of (quasi-)post-colonial states alone. Neither freedom nor, of course, familism, are values banished from pride of place in the Western world; a brief review of Adam Bellow's *In Praise of Nepotism* (2003) on US political culture, or Anthony Sampson's *Who Runs This Place* (2004) on British political culture, would be quite enough to quell any such fantasies (see further Xenakis, under review). For a variety of historical political and socio-economic reasons, however, the dynamics of normative hybridity are experienced more dramatically in some places – such as Greece – than others. In these places, where the ranking of fundamental ethical priorities is highly contested, it is harder for the 'goods' underlying neo-liberal modernization programmes to be introduced and embedded without alteration or postponement. In terms of socio-economic advancement on the macro level, then, strong normative hybridity may indeed cause a retardation of desirable, progressive development. And yet, integral to the everyday negotiation of competing creeds of the 'good', necessary as it is within conditions of normative hybridity, is the enhanced potential for a more politically progressive society.

Notes

An earlier draft of this paper was presented at the 21st Symposium of the Modern Greek Studies Association, Simon Frazer University, Vancouver, on 18 October 2009. Thanks are due to participants for their helpful comments on the day. I am also grateful to Leonidas K. Cheliotis, Rodanthi Tzanelli and Nicholas Xenakis for their comments and suggestions on earlier drafts of this paper.

1. For a similarly self-acknowledged 'perverse' critical exploration of customer service norms (as well as the common reflexive rejection of such critique), see Sturdy, 2001. The focus upon the ideological bases of norms is not to deny that these are in turn shaped by material interests borne of the structural realities of economic-life (as suggested by Tsatsanis, 2009; Bratsis, 2003). Moreover, whilst it may be fair to say that the Western trope of neo-liberalism tends to focus more upon 'freedom-as-lack-of-social-responsibility' than upon 'equality-as-redistribution', here 'fairness-and-equality' denotes 'standardised' treatment.

2. An observation substantiated by my own experiences of eight years (2000–2008) of research into Greek policy-making on organized crime.
3. A point well illustrated with regard to a parallel theme of the clash between high and low literary culture in Greece, in Jusdanis, 1991: 118.
4. Concerning the case of (Neo-)Orthodox recalcitrance, key examples cited in the literature include the broad opposition movement raised by the Church in 2000 against EU-approved Greek identity cards that would not include religious denomination, as well as the famed 'demagoguery' of the former Archbishop of Athens and all Greece, Christodoulos. On this and the broader issue of the anti-Western nature of the Church, see for example Herzfeld (2002), Fokas (2000) and Stavrakakis (2002b).
5. On the relationship between the Church and Junta, see Pollis (1993: 352–353). On contemporary concerns about the 'dark side' of Greek culture as epitomized by the recent ethno-religious discourse of the Greek Orthodox Church and exacerbated by 'the burden of history', see Stavrakakis (2002a: 21–24).
6. For Diamandouros (1994), although equally favoured by some sections of New Democracy [ND], the 'underdog culture' rose to prominence during the 1980s, promoted by the PanHellenic Socialist Movement [PASOK] under the leadership of Andreas Papandreou, and essentially 'represented an attempt politically, socially, and economically to empower the least competitive political and social forces in Greece, and, in so doing, to facilitate their reproduction under the new conditions prevailing in Greece at that time' (ibid.: 40).
7. As a number of international and Greek journalists and officials have confided to me in off-the-record interviews.
8. The assessment of Balkanist recalcitrance as a drag on economic development is a credible one given that the Greek economy has largely been based upon service provision, particularly in tourism and shipping (see US Department of Labor, 2003).
9. For a discussion of recent prescriptive literature in the field of management that emphasizes 'justice' and 'rights' as the ethical prerequisites of 'quality' customer service interaction, see Tylor and Taylor, 2001.
10. The Greek Ombudsman is an independent official department tasked with investigating allegations of infringement of citizens' rights by public bodies or officials (see the website of the office at www.synigoros.gr/en_what_is.htm). Etiquette lessons for Athens taxi drivers in preparation for the Olympics were run as part of the 'Clean Alliance Campaign' of 2004 (Greek Embassy, 2004). This was supplemented by a €1.8 million official education programme for Greek taxi drivers, which was launched in 2006 (Greek Embassy, 2006).
11. The difference in tax avoidance and evasion practices between self-employment and paid employment appears to be minimal, however, according to research carried out on British data, cited in Flevotomou and Matsaganis (2007: 25).
12. On the foreign perspective of Greece as recalcitrant see Economides (2005), Rosewarne and Groutsis (2003).
13. Public support for the modernization agenda draws largely from two segments of Greek society, neither of which commands great sway in Greek

politics: firstly, employees within the private sector and minority groups whose interests are inadequately represented – if at all – by the major unions and social insurance funds (see further Lavdas, 2005; Mossialos and Allin, 2005); and secondly, a growing caucus of university-educated, middle-class professionals, including many who became shareholders and bondholders in the 1990s, and who typically constitute the ranks of the floating voters of the Greek electoral experience (Nicolacopoulos, 2005; Pagoulatos, 2005; Spourdalakis and Tassis, 2006).

14. The FYROM debacle of 1993 clearly designated Greece as a doubly recalcitrant country by demonstrating, on the one hand, its adherence to an unreformed, traditional conception of state security (that is, with a 'modern' focus on threats posed by other states, rather than the non-traditional – *post-modern* – prioritization of non-state security threats) and, on the other hand, its (continuing) determination to awkwardly block the advancement of both the European Union and NATO enlargement agendas (see *Der Spiegel*, 2008). In the Koskotas scandal of 1988, elite members of the ruling PASOK party (including the then Prime Minister, Andreas Papandreou, who was later acquitted) were accused of taking around $20 million in bribes (Ajemian, 1989). The successor elite of ND were accused by PASOK of taking around $22.5 million in bribes in the AGET-Heracles cement scandal of 1994 (ANA, 1994), but, in a u-turn, the incoming PASOK government of 1995 successfully pushed for the charges to be dropped (ANA, 1995). The latter case can, therefore, be interpreted either as a corruption scandal in which charges were unproven, or as a cynically constructed libellous scandal (again unproven). In 2002, Eurostat refused to validate data received from the Greek National Statistics Service and announced that it would take legal action against Greece for providing false figures for the national deficit between 1997 and 2003. Greece would not have been able to join the Eurozone in January 2001 had its true financial situation regarding the level of national debt been known. Some have also suggested that the Greek government may have intentionally falsified accounts in order to save millions of euros by benefiting from consequent low interest rates during that period (see Saragosa, 2004).

15. The PASOK government was accused of having manipulated the Greek stock market by ordering the Public Portfolio Management Company to spend €733 million on shares, in order to raise the value of state-owned companies and, consequently, government popularity on the eve of the 2000 general election. As the share prices slid back from their artificial position, losses for investors ensued and the stock market crashed (see for example discussion in ANA, 2001). In the Siemens scandal, a former executive of the German firm testified at a trial in Germany that the company had paid in excess of €1 billion in bribes to both the ND and PASOK parties in order to secure contracts in which they would supply electronics equipment to the Greek state telecoms operator and for the security effort for the Athens Olympic Games (see *The Economist*, 2008). The Vatopedi scandal erupted when it was revealed that valuable state land had been traded for less valuable land held by a monastery on Mount Athos – an exchange that implicated at least two senior members of the ND government, who subsequently resigned – at an

estimated loss to the Greek state of €100 million (for a brief introduction to the scandal, see *BBC News*, 23 October 2008).

16. ND Minister of Culture Michalis Liapis (who lost his position during the cabinet reshuffle of January 2009) was repeatedly the subject of allegations regarding the Siemens corruption scandal of 2007, but denied accusations that he had accepted extensive hospitality from the company involving a trip abroad (*Kathimerini*, 08 July 2008; *ERA*, 03 July 2008). The wife of Kostas Karamanlis has been accused of fraudulently acquiring her doctorate in medicine. She initially trained as a nursery school teacher, but subsequently gained the medical doctorate in 2002, and then a Bachelors degree in medicine two years later, that is, in 2004 (see Telidis, 2007). The academic who assisted her with her doctorate – Christos Zachopoulos – was appointed General Secretary of the Ministry of Culture by PM Karamanlis in 2004, and was later embroiled in a corruption scandal in 2007 (on this see also Gilson, 2007).

17. My discussion of Western–Balkan normative hybridity is intended to be congruent with discussions of the East–West cultural clash in Greece, as well as its past Romeic/Hellenic distinctions (see, e.g., Calotychos, 2003; Gourgouris, 1996; Herzfeld, 2004; Tzanelli, 2008, 2009). As elaborated in the text, the use of the term 'Balkanist' is also intended to indicate a conceptual distance from that of the 'Balkan'.

18. For more on the notion of 'hospitality' by official bureaucrats, see Herzfeld (1992: 177–178).

19. Sifianou's study involves a questionnaire answered by 27 English and 27 Greek respondents, the results of which showed that English respondents gave shorter and more succinct definitions of politeness than Greek respondents. The latter offered much more elaborate and very broad interpretations of the concept. The mean word length of the definitions of politeness were 14.85 from the English respondents and 33.77 from the Greeks (Sifianou, 1992: 86–87). Both sets of respondents viewed politeness as a form of consideration towards others, however, and offered similar descriptions of forms of impoliteness (Sifianou, 1992: 90).

20. For discussion of these relationships that draws differently their dimensions, see Kenna (1976) and Campbell (1963).

21. In comparison, informal civil society activities such as those mentioned are thought to be prevalent but are under-recorded in Greece (Lyberaki and Paraskevopoulos, 2002; Sotiropoulos, 2004). Jones *et al.* (2008) have argued to the contrary, based upon an array of European survey findings which indicate both that informal civil society activities, such as seeing family, friends and colleagues regularly, take place comparatively less often in Greece. Some explanations for the latter findings and interpretations may be the way in which survey questions were grouped (that is, apparently including family, friends and colleagues in one question), the particular focus of the questions (more on out-group than in-group care practices), and possible cultural constraints experienced by respondents that affected their responses (such as not interpreting care for family, or church participation, as 'network' activity or 'voluntarism').

22. According to Eurobarometer surveys of public opinion between 1993 and 2001, the explanation of 'injustice' for poverty, as opposed to 'laziness', stabilized at a high level in Greece, though fell in popularity amongst all other EU member states (see the report on the Eurobarometer survey no. 56.1 of September–October 2001 by Gallie and Paugman, 2002). For a discussion of the disempowering impact of the neo-liberal trope of personal responsibility upon social protest, see Barry, 2005.
23. On the rejection of emotional control demanded by 'service culture' as a form of resistance, see Sturdy and Fineman, 2001. Amongst others, for discussion of the broader international trends of 'disciplinary neo-liberalism', see Gill, 2008; and Wacquant, 2001. On the expansion of investment in policing accompanying the neo-liberal transformation of governance in Greece, see Rigakos and Papanicolaou, 2003. For discussion of inhumane and authoritarian policing practices in contemporary Greece see, for example, reports and statements by the following NGOs and their representatives: Amnesty International *et al.*, 2002; ProAsyl *et al.*, 2007; Amnesty International, 2008; Kopp, 2008. Whilst random opinion surveys have shown that Greeks are comparatively less likely to be politically active than their European counterparts (see discussion in Jones *et al.*, 2008) – including reporting participation in demonstrations – this finding seems implausible given the level of public debate and frustrations about the frequency of political demonstrations taking place in the county's capital in recent years. See reporting on strike action in Greece on the website of the European Industrial Relations Observatory (www.eurofound.europa.eu/eiro), especially the Annual Reviews of 2003–2007, which report considerable and widespread strike action, including a number of general strikes. It seems likely that opinion surveys are an inadequate means of measuring political participation in Greece, and alternative modes of measurement are lacking: official data on labour-related strike activity has been incompletely recorded between 1997 and 2000 (Soumeli, 2003), whilst more recent data only offer a partial recording of actual numbers of strikes (Tikos, 2007). Data do not appear to be available recording the size and regularity of political demonstrations in Greece, either.
24. Papadopoulos (2006) nevertheless regards the condition of insufficient state welfare and stop-gap familism as a negative, mutually-reinforcing cycle that is holding Greece back from progressive change. See Karakatsanis (2000) for further discussion of the contemporary widespread use of 'familism' as a safety net given low salaries, unemployment and low welfare subsidies of family members.
25. In contrast, progressive nationalism may be regarded as compatible with the 'good' of Balkanist resistance. See Jusdanis, 2001.
26. On the progressive nature and transformative potential of critical utopianism (that is, creed of the good) in disrupting the ideological closure of the present, see the discussion by Levitas and Sargisson, 2003.

10
Legitimation and Resistance: Police Reform in the (Un)making

Justice Tankebe

Issues of legitimation processes of police authority as well as instances of conflict and resistance within police organizations have yet to receive the full attention of police researchers. Following Barker (2001, 2003) and Wrong (1995), it is argued here that police organizations are regularly engaged in symbolic activities of legitimation directed not only towards the public (as the mainstream literature would have us believe), but also to themselves, and that the object of such legitimation is the cultivation of a sense of self-confidence in the rightness of the authority they wield. It is further argued that, as with all organizations, police organizations are characterized by conflict and resistance which impinge on their legitimation efforts, especially during times of reform. Taking the example of anti-corruption reforms, my aim in this chapter is to explore why and how police officers may resist, and the ways in which resistance relates to endogenous and exogenous legitimation enterprises. My main thesis is that the reason for police officers' resistance to reforms is not so much related to the need for reforms *per se*, or to the threats these reforms may carry for individual interests; instead, resistance takes the form of 'condemning the condemners', stemming from what officers often see as the inconsistent and discriminatory enforcement of anti-corruption measures. I shall identify and discuss informal social control norms and police discretionary powers as the most valuable tools of resistance.

Understanding police legitimacy

As a concept, the idea of the legitimacy of power has a long history. It was current, implicitly or explicitly, in the works of a number of social theorists such as Aristotle, Plato, Hobbes and Bodin. It is however to Max Weber that we owe its contemporary usage and stature in the social sciences. Weber (1948: 263) argued that 'the basis of every authority, and correspondingly of every kind of willingness to obey, is a *belief*, a belief by virtue of which persons exercising authority are lent prestige'. Weber proceeded to identify three *ideal types* of legitimate dominations – charismatic, traditional and legal-rational – each of which is derived from different sources of legitimacy beliefs. What appears unclear in Weber's treatise is an explicit statement on who confirms the claims to legitimate domination (Di Palma, 1991). Thus, whilst defining legitimacy as emanating from 'the subjective phenomenon of human feelings, views, and attitudes', Herz (1978: 318) poses the question: whose subjective attitudes or views shall count – rulers, ruled or both?

This chapter draws on two competing but ultimately interrelated perspectives of legitimacy and legitimation in the political science literature to try to understand legitimacy in the context of the police. Protagonists of a *mass* or *exogenous* legitimation of power, which is most coherently expressed by Beetham (1991) and Coicaud (2002), and currently predominates in the criminological literature, argue that central to legitimation are the relations between rulers and the ruled, and the claims to legitimacy that the former makes on the latter, who are the ultimate assessors. Consequently, this perspective takes a 'bottom-up' view of legitimacy in which citizens' subjective evaluations of rulers' exercise of power as morally right or normatively justifiable is decisive in maintaining the legitimacy of any system of command-obedience. Opposing the mass legitimation perspective stands the *endogenous* perspective, exemplified in the works of Barker (2001, 2003) and Wrong (1995), but which has not yet permeated into criminology. Advocates of this perspective argue that the truly critical ingredients of a legitimate authority structure are the self-belief of the powerful in the moral rightness of the authority vested in them, and the internal cohesion amongst the inner circle of government. On one point, however, both perspectives see eye to eye: successful legitimation is an indispensable ingredient in ensuring stable and effective exercise of authority.

The concept of legitimacy has become a contemporary shibboleth in criminological research, especially in police studies. The burgeoning research on police legitimacy, however, appears theoretically incomplete from the standpoint of the longstanding scholarship on legitimacy within the fields of political science and political theory. Police researchers, through the work of Tom Tyler and his colleagues (Tyler, 1990, 2003; Tyler and Huo, 2002; Sunshine and Tyler, 2003), typically conceptualize legitimacy in terms of public experiences of procedural fairness from their encounters with legal authorities. Additionally, and as I shall demonstrate below, the current discussion remains broadly situated within the mass legitimation perspective (see Sparks *et al.*, 1996; Mawby, 2002; Mulcahy, 2006; Smith, 2007), a theoretical orientation which limits a full understanding of police legitimacy. The purposes of this chapter are two-fold: (1) to propose an improved conceptualization of police legitimacy, drawing on the political science literature; (2) to bring this conceptualization to bear on anti-corruption reforms and the resistance that they often elicit.

Exogenous legitimation

The exogenous or mass legitimation perspective maintains that central to political legitimation and legitimacy is the public, and their perception that the exercise of authority is in accordance with their beliefs and normative expectations. Indeed, the actions, time and efforts of rulers are primarily for the consumption of the public whose consent and attitudes are considered the lifeblood of the stability of the regime. This is because securing legitimacy-based obedience requires that 'power-holders must convince power-subjects that the command-obedience relation is "rightful" or legitimate' (Matheson, 1987: 200). In this regard, theorists maintain that 'political legitimation has to be *mass* legitimation' (Beetham, 1991: 94). Beetham (1991) and Coicaud (2002) make perhaps the strongest and most comprehensive argument. They identify a general structure that underpins the legitimation of power in all societies, although, as we shall see shortly, the specific contents are historically and culturally variable. This structure, they argue, has three qualitatively distinct but indissociable elements, each operating at different levels: these are legal validity, normative justifiability and expressed consent.[1]

Legal validity requires power to be acquired and exercised in conformity with the established rules of the society in question. These rules may be unwritten (for example, customs) or formalized in law. Power acquired and exercised in this way bestows on the holder the right to continue to exercise it, and obliges citizens to acknowledge and respect it. Thus, within the context of the police, Reiss (1971: 2) observes that any legitimate claim to intervene in the affairs of individuals is indubitable only when it is done legally, a legality that 'rests in the constitutional law and in substantive and procedural law'. Dixon (1997: 2) observes that a 'legalistic-bureaucratic' conception of law in policing considers that 'a central tenet of the police claim to legitimacy is their subordination to law'. Thus, legitimation of police power requires that the rules that govern police activities are clearly formulated and mechanisms put in place to achieve police officers' adherence to these rules in the course of their duties. In other words, and as part of the maintenance and reproduction of legitimacy, it is imperative for both the acquisition and subsequent exercise of power to be always in accordance with the rules which originally validated this power (Beetham, 1991). But the law only constitutes provisional grounds for legitimacy because 'rules cannot justify themselves simply by being rules, but require justification by reference to considerations which lie beyond them' (ibid.: 69). One such consideration, which brings us to the second element of the legitimacy structure, is the justifiability of power in terms of the shared beliefs of the society in which it is exercised.

Normative justifiability relates to the need for rules and police practices to be rooted in the shared beliefs or what has variously been described as 'fundamental norms' (Coicaud, 2002: 17) and 'a common framework of beliefs' (Beetham, 1991: 69) of the society. Power relations involve negative features such as the restriction of the freedom of citizens through their direct subordination to the purposes and requirements of the powerful. Any sustenance of, and accommodation with, these features requires the possession of moral authority. A distinctive feature of the mass legitimation account, which it emphasizes more than the Weberian conception, is its focus on this normative justification of power. Thus Coicaud (2002) argues that legal decisions are considered legitimate if they are an expression of the recognized and accepted norms of the society. There are two aspects to this normative justification of power. The first aspect relates to issues of substantive fairness; requires that power be exercised in furtherance of the general interests or collective good of the society rather than simply in the interests of the powerful (Schaar, 1984; Beetham, 1991). Thus, police power that is deployed against political opponents or used in blatantly discriminatory stop, search and arrest of sections of society, such as minority groups, will suffer problems of legitimation. As I have argued elsewhere, colonial policing lacked mass legitimacy partly because it was substantively unfair; as a vanguard of imperialist exploitation, colonial policing preoccupied itself with the reproduction of the kind of order that facilitated the unbridled exploitation of raw materials as well as the protection of the political and propertied classes (Tankebe, 2008). In this context, the needs of the indigenous colonial inhabitants were at best secondary.

The second normative justifiability aspect involves the exercise of authority within limits prescribed by a society's shared values. Hence, Beetham (1991) argues that laws impose obligations on the public, but there are reciprocal duties and obligations placed on those who wield power (that is, concerning what they can and cannot legitimately demand from the public). Thus he observes that 'legitimate power is limited power'. This being the case, it becomes imperative that the powerful do not breach such limits with impunity by making new or additional demands and obligations on the public without its consent. Police bribery and extortion are clear cases of additional demands and obligations constituting an infringement on the limits to police power, and which therefore risk fracturing their legitimate relationship with the public. This aspect of the normative justifiability of power also relates to concerns of procedural fairness as exemplified in the work of Tyler (1990, 2003). Since issues of fairness, respect and probity in the exercise of authority are all obvious normative expectations, exceeding the limits of legitimate power, as understood in a particular society, is likely to jeopardize public assessments of procedural fairness and, therefore, the legitimacy of legal authorities (Sunshine and Tyler, 2003; Roberts and Hough, 2005; Tankebe and Gelsthorpe, 2007). Without normative justification in both senses noted above – that is, substantive and procedural fairness according to agreed social norms – the requirements of the powerful cannot be normatively binding (Beetham, 1991).

The final element of the three-dimensional approach to mass legitimation is consent. Consistent with his conception of legitimate power relationships as rights-based and his consequent definition of legitimacy as 'the recognition of the right to govern', Coicaud (2002) approaches the issue of consent from the perspective of rights, which he describes as what is socially recognized to be the inalienable entitlement of each person in a community. In an ongoing day-to-day network of sociability amongst individuals, rights create reciprocal expectations and obligations which enable people to lay claim to what is due to them, whilst at the same time recognizing and crediting others with what is their portion so that no one feels cheated or belittled. But the establishment of individual rights is possible only with the aid of 'a mutual limitation' that is based on 'a spirit of compromise and concession' (ibid.: 11). This is where consent becomes essential to the satisfaction of the reciprocal obligations that rights entail, because consent denotes the acceptance of 'a situation that includes a measure of renunciation, which is manifested in the duty to obey' (ibid.: 3). The withdrawal of consent is a communication to the powerful of their failure to honour the normative obligations incumbent upon them for the exercise of legitimate power over citizens. Under such conditions we can speak of 'delegitimation' (Beetham, 1991: 19). The argument about consent can thus be summarized as follows: 'you gave your word, and so you are bound for the future, unless (of course) the government changes and becomes tyrannical' (Pitkin, 1965: 993). As Pitkin has argued, however, 'this position seems to allow the possibility of becoming obligated to a tyrannical government, if you expressly consent to one that was already corrupt' (ibid.). Thus, it is imperative that a discussion of consent to power takes full account of the socio-political conditions in which it is granted.

In conclusion, the leitmotif of the mass legitimation perspective of legitimacy is that a given power-holder can be considered legitimate if she acquired, and continues to exercise, her authority legally; if the public perceive her behaviour to be in conformity with their collective beliefs, values and norms; and if the public engage in actions demonstrating moral consent to the authority of the power-holder. In this sense no authority or system of power is self-contained so as to be immune to public attitudes and perceptions. Where we witness a regime in crisis, or worse still crumbling, it is the upshot of public opposition which then eats into the 'administrative apparatus itself, and causes serious dislocation in its capacity to rule' (Beetham, 1991: 119). As we shall see shortly, the endogenous perspective stands this argument on its head.

Endogenous legitimation

Theorists in the second tradition contend that the mass legitimation view obscures the equally important issue of legitimation as an activity conducted to a significant degree not for communication to the mass citizenry or the world outside the ruling organization, but primarily for the self-identification and legitimation of those within it. This concern prompted Rothschild (1977) to warn against the danger of rendering discussions of legitimacy and legitimation irrelevant should we continue to neglect the crucial dimension of the ruling elite's sense of its legitimacy and focus exclusively on mass perceptions of that elite's legitimacy. The endogenous perspective therefore focuses on legitimation as the attempts of the powerful to justify the rightness of their authority in their own eyes and to cultivate their own sense of identity.

Endogenous legitimation refers to 'an action or series of actions – speeches, writing, ritual, display – whereby people justify to themselves or others the actions they are taking and the identities they are expressing or claiming' (Barker, 2003: 163–164). Rulers, it has been observed, are burdened by 'the necessity of satisfying their own consciences' because 'they cannot comfortably regard themselves as usurpers or tyrants but require some basis for convincing themselves of the rightness of their position' (Claude, quoted in Barker, 2001: 50). Wrong (1995: 113) makes a similar point when he notes that power holders are driven to cultivate the self-belief that their actions are morally appropriate 'in order to assuage the guilt created by the use of violence against other human beings'. Self-legitimating activities represent the means to justify to themselves the rightness of their authority, and develop self-confidence in the moral rightness of the power that facilitates their rule. Legitimation, according to this account, is about the making of claims to justified exercise of power or issuing of commands and directives, claims that are 'independent of the instrumental advantages gained from inducing the power subject to obey willingly' (Wrong, 1995: 113). The making of legitimation claims, Barker (2001: 31) argues, is mostly conducted in relation to the 'referential hinterland, rather than to the wider community' under a ruler's jurisdiction.

In this regard, the endogenous perspective sees government as analogous to a private theatre where rulers portray their own identities, and see these confirmed and justified by their immediate staff and followers, and therefore also (in a reciprocal feedback loop) to themselves. The significance of such a perspective of legitimation is that 'the decisive operative relationship' ceases to be that between rulers and the ruled, as the mass legitimation approach advocates. To theorists within the endogenous perspective, it is rather the relationship between rulers and their immediate administrative staff which becomes crucial. As Di Palma (1991: 57) argues, when legitimation is viewed from the top, 'the decisive operative relationship is not that between rulers and people, but that between rulers and Weber's administrative staff'.

Speeches and other activities by the powerful that depict them as people specially endowed with abilities to understand and fix the problems of humanity such as law and order, and economic and political security, are all in furtherance of the self-legitimation enterprise, of justifying to themselves the enormous powers and prestige they wield over citizens. The use of symbols, which has long received the attention of some political scientists (see Edelman, 1971; Firth, 1973), is one of the ways leaders legitimate themselves in their own eyes by developing and surrounding themselves with physical objects to express and confirm their governing identity as well as their importance (Barker, 2001). Barker (2001) argues that rulers actually prefer these objects to people because, unlike the latter, the former are both malleable and permanently on call. Since these objects announce the identity of rulers they are not shared with others because to do so would mean to share their identity-conferring capacity with others, and thus strip the objects of their meaning (see also Rigby, 1982).

The endogenous perspective emphasizes the crucial importance of endogenous legitimation for the stability and effectiveness of authority. According to Barker (2001: 68), successful self-legitimation is vital to 'the internal health and survival of the ruling group' because it helps them to cultivate self-justification of and self-confidence in the rightness of their authority. Self-confidence has been noted to be important in serving as both a basis and 'positive encouragement to action' (Barbalet, 2001: 84).[2] Barbalet argues that confidence is the 'unavoidable basis of action' because it is 'a necessary source of action; without it, action simply would not occur' (ibid.). The 'culture of legitimation' characteristic of government enables ruling elites to cultivate justification for, and confidence in, their authority, which helps them to confirm their commands to themselves before they issue them (Barker, 2001: 36). In his survey with senior European Union officials about their orientation towards issues of governance, Hooghe (1999: 364) quotes an official who contends that 'what is relevant is the image one has about oneself, and about the policy one is making.... That is what public interest is. Outside influences do not weigh [very much]'. Although such an argument ignores the influence that particular socio-political contexts have on people operating within them, its relevance within the endogenous perspective is quite obvious: what is important in the maintenance of authority is the self-confidence and self-perceptions of the powerful themselves in the morality of their rule.

The endogenous perspective posits that successful legitimation is a crucial source of integration, 'unifying elites and cementing the links between the leaders and the political-administrative apparata' (Pakulski, 1987: 150). Such a success produces the consensus within ruling groups which Therborn (1980) considers the really critical factor in the legitimacy and effectiveness of any political authority. Its presence helps foster solidarity within the ruling class, enabling rulers to maintain their authority and identity; it acts as social 'glue' that unites the governing group for the goals they seek to achieve. In his discussion of the emergence of ancient empires, Giddens (1981: 103, emphasis in original) contends that of critical importance in the integration of these new systems was 'the legitimation of authority *within ruling elites*, making possible the establishment of an administrative apparatus of government'. Its significance, Giddens suggests, meant that a ruler's disregard for the codes of legitimation can prove very costly to the success of a legitimation enterprise. This is the case even with 'the most extreme form of personalized rule' (ibid.: 104), just as it is with modern democratic systems of rule (Barker, 2001, 2003). A ruling group's cultivation of its unique identity and the enactment of that identity are in this sense part and parcel of the rationalization of rule. Legitimation in this sense is 'reflective, rather than necessarily published to a wide audience. It is part of saying to oneself who one is' (Barker, 2003: 167).

Exponents of the endogenous legitimation perspective explain delegitimation not in terms of public perceptions of the lack normative justifiability, but with reference to the loss of self-confidence amongst power-holders themselves of the moral validity of their claim to govern. Rothschild (1977: 500) argues that the 'truly critical delegitimation of a regime begins with the moral and psychological defection of elites, whose very defection, or loss of a sense of legitimacy in their own domination, communicates to the masses the onset of a general crisis' (see also Di Palma, 1991; Wright, 1984). It is in this spirit that Barker (2001: 68) concludes that 'when subjects lose faith in rulers, government becomes difficult. When rulers lose confidence in themselves, it becomes impossible'.

Public opinion polling represents a formal feedback on how the public view their rulers. But to what extent does such a feedback influence the behaviour and endogenous legitimation activities of these rulers? Some scholars have argued that public opinion is a 'proximate cause' of the decisions of the ruling elite (Page and Shapiro, 1983: 175; see also Erikson, 1976) and can therefore be seen to influence their legitimation activities. Other scholars deny this and rather maintain that, in spite of their appearances, what we have are closed political systems in which elite control precludes any significant public influence on the behaviour and activities of rulers (see Mills, 1956/2000; Dye, 1986). This latter view resonates with the arguments of the endogenous perspective. A central feature of the accounts of this perspective therefore is that civil war within the ruling inner circle itself – or as Kecskemeti (quoted in Lewis, 1984: 18) would have it, 'insiders' rebellion' – is what damages and destabilizes government, not mass public disaffection about how authority is exercised. Thus, mass opposition to a regime and its collapse become consequences, not determining factors, of failures of internal self-legitimating leading to lack of self-confidence and self-belief amongst the governing group.

Towards a synthesis

The exclusive focus of the mass legitimation perspective on public subjective judgements easily brings it to grief and liable to accusations of 'democratic bias' (Vidich, 1979: 300). There may be different audiences to legitimation activities, as the endogenous perspective convincingly observes, hence the public may be only at the outer fringes of the concerns of rulers. Beetham (1991) makes some concessions here and concurs with Birch (1984: 156) that, in the final analysis, 'all governmental authority depends on consent, although not necessarily the consent of the general public'. Unfortunately, various criminological studies working within the mass legitimation perspective have tended to ignore this vital point. Ideally, the police should value all perceptions of their legitimacy amongst the public regardless of where they come from, but the reality of policing makes this very difficult (see Reiner, 2000: 9). Legitimacy, therefore, cannot be solely understood to consist of 'the popularity of a regime, popular consent, or a social consensus which supports the existing system' (Crook, 1987: 553; see also Simmons, 1999). It is, ultimately, only half of the explanation to focus attention on public subjective attitudes towards the police or the capacity of the police to produce and sustain such positive attitudes.

The claim of the endogenous perspective that, when a leader believes in the rightness of the authority vested in him or her, and gains the full confidence of their staff, the governing process becomes smoother, may not be deeply profound, but is very useful. Within the context of the police institution as a 'street-level bureaucracy' – that is, an institution whose workers 'interact directly with citizens in the course of their jobs, and who have substantial discretion in the execution of their work' (Lipsky, 1980: 3) –, legitimation to police officers of their superiors' authority, decisions and the *modus operandi* for executing those decisions, is particularly critical. Lipsky argues that, within such a bureaucracy, we cannot assume that 'influence flows with authority from higher to lower levels, and that there is shared interest in achieving agency objectives' (ibid.: 25). Lipsky discusses the various ingenious ways that street-level bureaucrats are able to use their discretion and other resources at their command to resist directives they do not identify with, and even redefine organizational policy in their interactions with the public. As with other hierarchical organizations, there are sociological studies of the police that highlight issues of power, conflict, resistance and value differences between low-ranking police officers and police managers (see for example Cain, 1973; Holdaway, 1983; Chan, 1996, 1997). Reuss-Ianni and Ianni (1983: 253), for instance, report the existence of two 'bureaucratically and valuationally' different cultures – 'management cop culture' and 'street cop culture' – in an 'uneasy accommodation' and conflict between police managers and street-level officers. The authors note that disaffection and problems of integrity tend to reinforce the resistance of street-level officers to attempts by management to introduce organizational reforms. The existence of such issues in policing underscores the significance of the argument of the endogenous perspective which considers legitimate power relations and actions within the ruling elite as a fundamentally associative process involving a perpetual legitimation of that power in the eyes of both leaders and their staff.

Yet, for all its strength, the contention of the endogenous perspective that the public displays of the powerful are exclusively for self-confirming, self-justificatory purposes, constitutes only part of the explanation because it overlooks its mass legitimation purposes. What Altheide (1992) has called 'gonzo justice' – that is, the use of extraordinary measures to demonstrate social control – and other public displays are in many instances also geared towards the cultivation of the support and consent of the public. Important in this regard is Mawby's (2002) work on how the police employ the media and professional image workers as conduits of mass legitimation exercises. The motives of such self-presentation of police activities and other public discourses chime well with those identified by Jones and Pittman (1982) – self-promotion, self-ingratiation and self-exemplification. In all cases those who wield authority would, in their interactions with the general public, seek to get the public to identify with them, to think of them as competent, morally respectable and entitled to their authority. Neglecting this important dimension offers an incomplete analysis and interpretation of the public discourse of rulers. As long as political and legal authorities rely on the co-operation of citizens for the attainment of their objectives, they will require a wider recognition of their moral authority as a condition for effective and stable rule (Beetham and Lord, 1998).

There is no doubt that self-belief and justification of one's authority to oneself augment the effective exercise of that authority. That said, a complete preoccupation with self-legitimation has its own palpable dangers for the stability of regimes. As Di Palma (1991: 54–55) argues, this danger is especially significant because such preoccupation can eventuate in regimes being trapped in 'a potentially dangerous denial of increasingly demanding domestic and global realities'. To stave off such entrapment does not require us to be completely dismissive of any validity in such an argument. Beetham (1991: 31), for instance, argues that endogenous legitimation is merely an enterprise by rulers to reconcile their consciences to the treatment and maltreatment of their citizens and, therefore, ultimately irrelevant to the legitimacy discourse. As the preceding discussion demonstrates, the flaw with such an approach is only equalled by a preoccupation solely with the centrality of the internal cohesion of the ruling elite in the legitimation enterprise. It is not enough that, in our attempts to resolve these polarizing views, we simply switch from a situation of 'too much self: too little society' to one of 'too much society: too little self' (Archer, 2000: 78). What is rather required is recognition that, whilst claims to legitimacy may be authenticated by rulers themselves for their own governing and justificatory needs, equally critical – depending on the performance task an authority system faces – are the subjective normative inputs and verification of those claims by the citizenry.

What I have tried to do above is to point out the strengths and weaknesses of some aspects of both perspectives with the aim of making the point that their usefulness is best harnessed if conceived as mutually constitutive. What is lacking in the existing criminological literature, yet needed for a fuller understanding of police legitimacy, is an appreciation of both public subjective evaluations of the normative justifiability of police claims to legitimate power, and the contributions that successful police self-legitimation activities make to discussions on overall police legitimacy. Holmes (1993: 39, emphasis in original), in a non-police context, articulates this more succinctly with his observation that legitimacy 'is not merely about mass/popular attitudes towards a regime and/or system. Nor is it merely concerned with the beliefs of the leaders and/or the staffs. It is about *all* of these' (see also Sternberg, 1968). This is more the case when we are dealing with the police who are in direct contact with the public in a manner that central government is not. In these interactions, mass legitimation is as vital as the self-confidence of both superior officers and their personnel in the rightness of their authority.

Corruption and police legitimacy

In what follows, I aim to explore the relationship between police corruption and police legitimation, endogenous and exogenous. Four decades ago, Heidenheimer (1970: 485) posed the question: 'to what extent does public knowledge of extensive corruption in the administration undermine the legitimacy of the regime?' Whilst the targeted audience might have been political scientists and sociologists, it is a question that could appropriately be asked within the context of police research with much urgency, but hardly any prospect of meaningful answers. Although the criminological literature is quite unanimous that police corruption undermines police legitimacy, there are hardly any existing empirical studies that systematically explore this hypothesized nexus. It is important to note, nonetheless, that Heidenheimer's question indicates one dimension of the legitimacy-corruption problem, that is, the consequences of experience with, or perception of, corruption. Perhaps, even more important is the nature of anti-corruption measures. Stated differently, though knowledge of corruption may be debilitating for legitimacy, the belief that the police leadership are genuinely and satisfactorily committed to arrest it may be just as decisive. This section discusses the relationship between corruption and legitimacy, whilst the final section addresses this latter issue.

First, as we noted in our discussion of the mass legitimation perspective of legitimacy, rules which underwrite a legitimate power, delineate the limits of the behaviour of the powerful, that is, what can be legitimately demanded from the public. Corruption in any form represents a substantial breach of these 'inherent limits' to a police officer's authority, because it imposes additional obligations on the public. Some police officers commit acts of corruption because 'they are driven by a serious predicament of their own' (Beetham, 1991: 36). In much of sub-Saharan Africa this predicament is mainly a result of poor working conditions. Whatever justifications officers may have, however, the demand for bribes or extortion of money from citizens can result in protestations that have the potential to spark off widespread crisis or erosion of legitimacy. This is particularly the case with extortion and police criminality. If the legitimation of power requires, as the mass legitimation perspective suggests, that an action is in some way morally acceptable and justifiable in terms of public expectations, such abuses of police powers are clearly likely to undermine the legitimacy of the police.

All asymmetrical power relations have negative features such as the restrictions of some of the freedoms of power-subjects, but these are often 'obscured and redefined by the process of legitimation' (Beetham, 1991: 109). If successful, legitimation provides a rationalization for accommodating these negative features. What experience with police corruption does, it would seem, is to expose the pretensions of the police's claim to the right to exercise power and the logic that goes with that power; it communicates a message to citizens that, far from furthering the collective interests of the community, police power is merely a mechanism for the exploitation of citizens for the personal aggrandizement of the police. The pervasiveness of police corruption is indicative of unfairness in the distribution of 'public goods', a symptom that the criminal justice system is operating with little concern for the broader public interest (Rose-Ackerman, 1999). Anderson and Tverdova (2003: 92) argue that, when corruption is present, issues of 'procedural and distributive fairness become a myth; this, in turn, is likely to diminish the legitimacy of democratic political institutions'. In the context of policing, this is likely to weaken citizens' normative commitments to the police's claim to legitimate power and citizens' obligation to defer to them.

To the extent that police corruption often means the granting of unjust advantage to some citizens over others, it is also likely to engender a great deal of moral outrage and resentment. It is fitting to recall Barbalet's (2001: 138) insightful discussion of resentment as a normative emotion focussed on concerns with 'some contravention of social norms or rights, associated with outcome or procedure'. In this way, police corruption constitutes an obstacle to the maintenance and reproduction of legitimacy in its violation of the intrinsic normative limits to police powers. It is for this reason that, when the legitimation claims of the powerful unravel and become 'unambiguously and openly visible to everyone', they become one of the most passionately hated objects of attack (Weber, 1948: 953–954). The attacks may be literally physical, such as the vandalizing of police stations and assaults on police officers for perceived perversions of justice. But they may equally be expressed in a non-physical manner, such as withdrawal of support for the police and their activities.

Secondly, corruption can seriously undermine public confidence, respect and legitimacy in the police officers and the institutions they represent. To the extent that the police claim control of, and responsibility for, public order, argues Manning (2003), police scandal, misconduct and other acts of illegality raise questions about their claims and undermine the sense of control, credibility and competence that the police can command. In a test of the corruption-legitimacy hypothesis in four

Latin American countries, Seligson (2002) found that higher experience with corruption was significantly associated with lower support for the legitimacy of the political systems across the four countries (see also Matsoso, 2005). The World Bank had earlier argued that 'corruption violates the public trust and corrodes social capital.... Unchecked, the creeping accumulation of seemingly minor infractions can slowly erode political legitimacy' (cited in Seligson, 2002: 417).

Some researchers have argued that public subjective evaluations of the degree of trustworthiness of public institutions often depend on the public's cognitive maps of their historical record of being trustworthy or not (Rothstein, 2000). In their interactions with the police, for instance, people are apt to take into consideration their immediate and past historical record – Who are the police? What is known about their proneness to corruption? These are just some of the salient questions the public would be inclined to ask in deciding whether those in authority can be trusted to act fairly. It is in this regard that Rothstein argues that 'it is not the formal institution as such which people evaluate, but its historically established reputation in regard to fairness and efficiency' (ibid.: 493). Not only does this observation chime with O'Neill's (2002) comment that one-off encounters do not provide enough grounds for a decision to repose or withdraw trust, it also suggests at least one of two things. First, the kinds of experiences people have in their current encounters with those in authority may end up enforcing their prior perceptions of the trustworthiness of these authorities. Second, their experiences may mark the beginning of the formation of a particular cognitive map of the authorities' trustworthiness. Given that trust is often closely associated with legitimacy (Hetherington, 1998; Sztompka, 1999; Tyler and Huo, 2002), a perception that the police are corrupt and, therefore, cannot be trusted, is likely to undermine their legitimacy as well. Allegations of police corruption demonstrate a case of the police 'committing the sins which [they have] been appointed to prosecute' (Mawby, 2002: 62).

Thirdly, corruption may exert indirect debilitating effects on police legitimacy through its negative impact on effectiveness. Corruption defeats the fundamental purpose of the police, whilst simultaneously promoting criminality, impunity and insecurity (CHRI Report, 2005). This is because police organizations riddled with systemic corruption are sometimes infiltrated by criminals who then manipulate the law to their advantage; police officers in such organizations often have a tendency to neglect their duties and to 'trade off' their obligations for their exclusive attention to corruption and other acts of malfeasance. Goldstein

(1977) observes that, in extreme cases, corrupt police officers may view the requirements to investigate suspicious circumstances and respond to calls for assistance, for instance, as intrusions on their time. In this sense, negligence is the gravest and most pervasive effect of corruption (Alatas, 1990; see also Rose-Ackerman, 1999).

As the police become identified with ineffectiveness as a result of corruption, public normative commitments to them and readiness to consider the police as legitimate arbitrators of disputes will diminish. The results of a World Bank-sponsored study in Ghana, published in 2000, indicated that 87 per cent, 67 per cent and 53 per cent of respondents had made unofficial payments to the motor traffic police, the regular police and court officials, respectively (CDD-Ghana, 2000: ii).[3] Significantly, 38 per cent of households and 20 per cent of private enterprises cited the influence of corruption as the major obstacle for not using the police and the judicial system to redress their problems. Although the survey did not explore the alternative means of dispute resolution that such respondents might use, the frustration and moral outrage that often attend police corruption and ineffectiveness are likely to be channelled to extra-legal measures of security.

Last, but certainly not least, the prevalence of corruption in the criminal justice system can also affect the morale and commitment of police officers themselves. Experience with corrupt colleagues may create an atmosphere of distrust that is demoralizing to honest and well-intentioned police officers (Goldstein, 1977). Especially concerning undercover and surveillance officers, disclosure of police intelligence, abrupt terminations of investigations and the destruction of evidence may threaten their careers and even lives, and dampen their sense of confidence in the rightness of police authority.

Legitimation and resistance in corruption reforms

Whilst the absolute eradication of police corruption may not be feasible in practice, all possible efforts should be made to bring the problem under some degree of control (Holmes, 1993; Anechiarico and Jacobs, 1996). Considering its connection with legitimacy; 'it would be worse not to fight [police] corruption than to continue the struggle against it, even if the results are by many criteria disappointing' (Holmes, 1993: 49). Indeed, as this section demonstrates, whereas corruption reforms hold great legitimation potential, the nature of the deployment and pursuit of such reforms can produce unexpected, even counterproductive, results.

Since police corruption often elicits moral outrage, talking tough about it, even if failing to address the underlying causes, undoubtedly has great legitimation potential. As Rose-Ackerman (1999: 226) reminds us, 'the state may need to establish credibility by punishing highly visible corrupt officials, but the goal of such prosecutions is to attract notice and public support for officials, not solve the underlying problem'. Small wonder, then, that the police leadership in Ghana, for instance, regularly uses various public forums to express its abhorrence of police corruption and to assure the public of its preparedness to break with the past by punishing officers who are found to be corrupt. Patrol officers are promised rewards for integrity and commitment to the professional ideals of police work, qualities considered essential to win public confidence and trust. These statements do not signal spectacularly high exceptionality in the prevalence of police corruption over the past few years; corruption in Ghana has always been a serious problem. On the contrary, they are reflective of a change in the police leadership's perception of their own and their institution's legitimacy. Such statements can be understood as indicating the existence of links between public demonstration of concern with the general abuse of police authority and the perception of legitimation problems on the part of the police in a new democratic political dispensation.

It may be an old and cynical practice, but by acknowledging, condemning and distancing the leadership from the past, police administrators signal a new dawn to the public and, in doing so, seek to enhance their 'reputation (and legitimacy) as superior beings who accept the responsibility of correcting defects in [the police service] and improving consciousness' (Holmes, 1993: 208). This is important for their own internal legitimation because it serves to justify their authority in their own eyes as people with the exceptional qualities for fixing such problems (ibid.). Additionally, breaking with the past helps to cultivate the confidence of subordinates in the new leadership and rationalize any stringent anti-corruption measures that may be pursued. It also demonstrates to the public the clear contrast between its own implied moral superiority and the stance of previous administrations, and thus enhances the new administration's mass legitimacy. As Holmes argues, '[i]f a regime consistently turns a blind eye to corruption that is visible to most if not all, then any respect some citizens and officials do have for the authority of the regime, and perhaps even the system, would decline' (ibid.: 212). Anti-corruption measures, then, are not just a way for the police to absolve themselves from public complaints about failure or unwillingness to tackle problems of public moral outrage; they may genuinely impact positively on assessments of police legitimacy.

Paul Lewis (1984) has argued that a crisis in endogenous legitimation is often the result of 'elite differentiation', which is itself a consequence of differential attitudes to reforms or change. Within the context of policing, corruption reforms mark a concrete example of an avenue for dealing with an endogenous legitimation crisis. Answers to the question of the apparent failures of police anti-corruption measures are not simply to be sought from the intractability of corruption. The question of the genuineness of anti-corruption reforms is important in any attempt at institutional re-legitimation. However, corruption reforms are not exercises that are always conducted smoothly within police organizations. As with conflict between bosses and workers in many organizations, conflict and resistance are always latent in virtually every police department, though these '[become] acute when moral blame is being distributed, because the dynamics of investigations inevitably tend to focus the spotlight *downwards*' (Punch, 1985: 151–152, original emphasis). This is often met with stiff resistance from lower-rank officers. But what accounts for such an asymmetrical distribution of moral blame, and why exactly do officers resist? Also, what are the consequences of resistance for the legitimation of police power?

There are two interlocking factors that might help us to address this question. First, can we locate a truly committed and honest police leadership dedicated to confronting the problem? There is often a wide chasm between anti-corruption rhetoric and the continued impunity of corrupt police officers. The reason almost invariably turns out to be that the rhetoric is a façade behind which sits a leadership that is itself corrupt, and therefore lacks the moral standing to match its public pronouncements with effective action. For instance, the Nigerian police force is widely regarded as one of the most corrupt police organizations in sub-Saharan Africa, a reputation which engenders serious public outrage, and which the police service apparently finds inconsistent with its law enforcement role. In 2005, President Olusegun Obasanjo dismissed the country's chief law enforcement officer on charges of corruption and money laundering; the police chief later pleaded guilty to these and other charges and received a six-month imprisonment sentence, in addition to the confiscation of property and cash worth millions of dollars (Okogbule, 2007). Whilst this case undoubtedly signified a positive move towards tackling corruption, it also highlighted an important reason for the failures of some police organizations to enforce anti-corruption measures in particular, and reiterate the long-standing question of why police forces in Africa find it difficult to adopt the norms and practices associated with democratic-style policing (Hills, 2008); namely, the lack of a police leadership that is untainted with corruption. Thus, Ayittey (1992: 243) might be right in his observation that 'the pervasiveness of corruption is only possible when those at the very top are actively engaged in it' (see also Elster, 1989; Newburn, 1999).[4] It is difficult to see how such a police leadership can seriously address the corruption problem to prevent police legitimacy dipping any further. Tackling corruption may hold legitimation potential, but it may mean no illegal sources of income for a corrupt leadership, and therefore the actuality of police–public discourse is likely to remain what it is, rhetoric.

Pierce (2006) asserts that Nigeria's problems are illustrative of Africa's predicament. The allegations of corruption and complicity of senior police officers in drug dealings is a concrete example from Ghana. The commissioning of the Woode Committee of Inquiry in the summer of 2006 was necessitated by allegations in the media of the existence of a secret incriminating tape-recording. When the recording was played at the Committee's sitting, one of the police officers was heard promising the transnational drug barons police protection to enable them to conduct their businesses without fears of police arrests or external competition (Woode, 2006: 47–48). The Committee found that this constituted 'gross abuse of office and professional misconduct' for personal interests. The important point to note here is that, under such circumstances, any claim of the police leadership to be worried about police corruption and to be committed to making the organization 'corruption free' is itself likely to be viewed as corrupt and fraudulent. More importantly, when hypocrisy is exposed, the impacts on police legitimacy are often much more damaging than everyday experience with police corruption. It is therefore critical in any anti-corruption reform, that the police leadership is not only committed to cleaning up the organization, but also becomes the personal symbol of the integrity it demands amongst subordinates (Punch, 2000).

Secondly, and following from the preceding observation, are junior officers deliberately obstructing anti-corruption measures, and, if so, why? Is it that they consider such actions by the police administration hypocritical and designed to make scapegoats of them because the senior officers are equally, if not more, corrupt? The implications of an attitude of 'condemning the condemners' were brought to our attention decades ago through the work of Sykes and Matza (1957). They argued that it can lead to the hardening of a deviant orientation which, in turn, is translated into 'a bitter cynicism directed against those assigned the task of enforcing or expressing the norms of the dominant society' (ibid.: 668). Ultimately, such an orientation acts to suppress the wrongfulness of the actions of deviants. Clearly, the consequence in the context of police corruption is likely to be more corruption because '[t]he norm of fairness suggests that it is perfectly all right to engage in corrupt practices when others do so' (Elster, 1989: 270) – *a fortiori* if it is the leadership. This kind of 'resistance through persistence' (Collinson, 2000: 165) may be seen as egotistic, furthering the private interests of police officers, rather than the progressive interests of the police organization.

Punch (1985: 199) points out that, when officers feel that corruption investigations make them scapegoats, 'they fight back with resistance and hostility'. There are a number of ways they can do this. For instance, officers may seek to communicate to the public what they consider to be the hypocrisy of anti-corruption measures by 'whistle-blowing', that is, divulging confidential information to the media. In the Nigerian and Ghanaian cases cited above, this was the main source of public information about the extent of the rot in the higher echelons of the police. Typically, the police leadership in Ghana reacted by characterizing such actions as a manifestation of a behaviour fuelled by inordinate ambitions and personal interests, and, therefore, as mischievous and diabolical (Mingle, 2006). But such an interpretation obviates the necessity to think of such actions as manifestations of internal dissention and weak internal cohesion, both symptomatic of the failure of the police leadership to adhere to the rules for successful endogenous legitimation.

Street-level police officers may also resist corruption reforms through the use of informal social control mechanisms that deflect investigations by preventing colleagues from co-operating with the leadership. In his analysis of resistance, Scott (1990) shows how subcultures of subordinate groups are able to secure a high level of conformity. On Scott's analysis, two ingredients are necessary to the effectiveness of informal social control mechanisms (for example, slander, character assassination, gossip, rumour, public gestures of contempt, shunning and backbiting). First, these mechanisms must not only be brought to bear outside the purview of superior officers, but they must also be strong enough to neutralize pressures from above. We easily find a fulfilment of this condition in the police literature, where the invisibility of basic-grade police work to supervisors and the existence of a strong police subculture that is able to resist change, are issues of general consensus (see, for example, Cain, 1973; Holdaway, 1983;

Reuss-Ianni and Ianni, 1983; van Maanen, 1983; Manning, 2003). The second ingredient is the existence of a close-knit society in which one's reputation and sense of self-esteem have practical consequences. Once again, if the extensive literature on police culture is to be believed, there is a strong bond of solidarity and support amongst officers in the face of perceived danger, and sometimes of public and management hostility (see Reuss-Ianni and Ianni, 1983; Skolnick, 1994; Chan, 1997; Reiner, 2000). When both ingredients are present, informal social control mechanisms become a powerful tool that can stem the implementation and success of corruption reforms, especially if such reforms are perceived to be discriminatory and unfair.

When the pursuit of corruption reforms generates what Punch (1985: 153) terms 'guerrilla warfare' within the police organization, the ramifications almost invariably extend to mass legitimation efforts. As mentioned earlier, the police organization is an example of a street-level bureaucracy in the sense that police officers are in constant interaction with their clients and exercise discretion in these interactions. But it is personnel of the lower ranks, not the police leadership, who go on the beat and are in direct and frequent interaction with the public. If expressed to the public, their cynicism and hostility towards their superiors can obstruct the leadership's attempts at cultivating mass legitimacy for its activities. In the Ghanaian case, revelations that the police leadership itself was tainted with corruption led one pro-government private newspaper to claim that: 'Ghana is fast gaining the kind of notoriety often reserved for places like Afghanistan, Thailand and Columbia, where it is difficult to tell a top cop from a drug baron in an identification parade' (*Statesman*, 28 July 2006). Not surprisingly, there are widespread doubts about the genuineness of the police leadership's promise to tackle corruption within the police service. In Ghana, people even believe that police officers collect bribes on the approval of superior officers to whom they have to render accounts at the close of each working day. A large proportion of Ghanaians (70 per cent) concur that the police administration has not done enough to tackle the problem of corruption in the police force (CDD, 2000: 35).

Whilst, then, anti-corruption measures may be promising in their legitimation potential, the lack of genuineness with which they are often conceived and pursued, can actually generate internal legitimation problems that spill over to disrupt mass legitimation efforts. Unlike political regimes, police organizations may not necessarily collapse as a result of such corruption-induced legitimation problems. But the feelings of bitterness, hostility, and even cynicism so created amongst the public would affect police ability to act as an effective centre of power and to fulfil their functions. A crisis of endogenous legitimation introduces the kind of uncertainty and hesitancy in the exercise of power that may serve to encourage potential and actual opposition (see Lewis, 1984). Not only will this lack of unity of purpose mar attempts at mass legitimation; it also sends a signal to criminal elements that the risks of arrest, conviction and punishment are low, because those charged with that responsibility are divided amongst themselves. For the police, such failure may be because of internal dissention resulting from spectacular shortcut attempts to legitimation through discriminatory enforcement of anti-corruption measures. In this way, the reason for ordinary police officers' resistance to reforms is not so much their sense that reforms are not needed, or even the threats these may carry for individual interests. Rather, resistance often takes the form of 'rejecting the rejectors', that is, a normative revolt against what is perceived as the inconsistent, discriminatory and sometimes hypocritical enforcement of anti-corruption measures by a police management that is itself sometimes tainted. This is not an egotistic form of resistance, but, paradoxically, a resistance that has the collective good of the police organization and society as its object.

Conclusion

The aim of this chapter has been twofold. First, to point to the ways in which the current criminological interest in the concept of legitimacy can be broadened and enriched. What I have sought is not to develop a full-blown theory of police legitimacy based on the exogenous and endogenous perspectives of legitimation. The objective was rather modest: merely to draw attention to other important dimensions of legitimacy that have so far been ignored in the criminological literature. The task for future theorization is to develop these ideas further and to explore the extent to which police legitimacy can be seen as the outcome of the interplay between successful endogenous and exogenous legitimating activities. Neither is entirely separate from the other, as some of the existing literature would have us believe.

An important task for police researchers is to examine whether, and to what extent, aspects of day-to-day police (mis)behaviour either enhance or undermine the successful production and maintenance of police legitimation efforts. In this chapter, I have sought to explore the issue of police corruption and its implications for legitimation. One of the central arguments has been that public experiences with police corruption may be less damaging to police legitimation claims than the perception that the police leadership is not genuine is dealing with the problem of corruption. For members of the public, the evidence that police anti-corruption measures are genuine is likely to come from the day-to-day encounters people have with the police. This being the case, a police organization cannot expect to harness the full long-term legitimation potential of corruption reforms if there are disparities between official corruption discourse and people's day-to-day experiences of police corruption. It is only when allegations or instances of police corruption are followed up indiscriminately and then thoroughly investigated and acted upon, that both the public and police officers will be more inclined to identify with the leadership and the objectives of the police organization.

Notes

1. It is worth pointing out here that Coicaud's work, although originally published six years later than Beetham's, was written in ignorance of it (because the original version was in French). Hence, it is remarkable that they identified the same legitimation structure.
2. It is important to note that the employment here of self-confidence as an emotional variable is not in the sense of it being entirely 'in the private recesses of people's minds' (Beetham 1991: 13). Rather, it follows Barbalet's (2001) forcefully sociological conception of self-confidence as being of social significance, and therefore inherent in the social interactions between actors.
3. The study involved 1500 households, 500 businesses and 1000 public officials who were selected using stratified and systematic sampling techniques at various stages. The findings further showed that 76 per cent and 70 per cent of households in urban and rural areas, respectively, considered the corruption situation to be 'very serious'.
4. Apposite here is Katsenelinboigen's first 'law' of corruption: 'the higher the level of the person in society, the greater the percentage of bribes in his total income' (cited in Holmes, 1993: 50). This is, of course, a highly contestable proposition in many instances, but it is too often valid in corruption-ridden societies. In such societies, it helps to make the point that, where the police leadership is itself corrupt, the prospect of genuine reforms is unlikely because it may prioritize personal gain over professional integrity.

11
'Governmentality' and Governing Corrections: Do Senior Managers Resist?

Alison Liebling

> The POA [Prison Officers' Association in England and Wales], encouraged by concern about jobs, are being more flexible. ...I have just spent two days at Dartmoor and Liverpool. I saw things at both prisons I never thought I'd see: 240 people in education; the evening meal at 6 p.m. I want more of this.
> (Commissioner of Correctional Services, November 2003)

> The governments of the 1980s and 1990s have...tended to combine responsibilisation moves with measures intended to consolidate central power, directing the actions of others, more or less coercively, to bring them into line with centrally-defined goals.
> (Garland, 1996: 464)

> We have to demonstrate that we can make sure the things we do can work.... We need to make a transformation in the way we do business.
> (Martin Narey, then Chief Executive of NOMS, to probation staff, 2004)

> Number Ten are quite excited about the Carter reforms. This is right at the cutting edge of public sector reform.
> (Martin Narey, then Chief Executive of the National Offender Management Service, to colleagues, 2004)

Several criminologists have observed that the art of regulating and controlling penal practices from above has been transformed. There are new structures of power, and new rationalities, alliances and values, which change how punishment works, how it is experienced and how it is organized. New practices and programmes are introduced continually, all of which incorporate the discourse of success and failure. They specify the achievement of very specific goals (O'Malley, 1996: 196), some of which seem impossible for criminal justice agencies to realize. Their aspired accomplishment forms part of the political character of late-modern penality. New devices intended to give effect to this form of rule include performance measurement and testing, market testing and privatization, and service-level agreements. Such techniques represent a contractual form of management which Shearing and Sampson refer to as 'nodal' and 'contractual governance', respectively.

The early stages of this transformation were first described by Feeley and Simon, who used the term the 'new penology' to describe a paradigm shift in criminal justice away from a concern for individuals, and from notions of guilt and reform, towards the identification, classification and management of unruly and dangerous groups (for example, Feeley and Simon, 1992). The new penology is actuarial, sceptical (for example, that interventions can make a difference), utilitarian and focused on regulation. It is 'concerned with techniques for identifying, classifying, and managing groups assorted by levels of dangerousness' (Feeley and Simon, 1994: 173). Actuarial justice 'is not reducible to a specific technology or set of behaviours. Indeed it is powerful and significant precisely because it lacks a well-articulated ideology.... Its very amorphousness contributes to its power' (ibid.: 174). This shift, towards aggregate risk management and tight regulation, has been facilitated by broader intellectual, political and social changes, including economic changes; globalization; new technology; changes in the sources of trust (from local and kinship relationships to less stable social relations and 'disembedded abstract systems'); changing forms of social differentiation; and managerialism (Bottoms and Wiles, 1996: 10–31; also Bottoms, 1995; Garland and Sparks, 2000).[1] We inhabit a target-led economy. In this new penological world, power is redirected upwards; and justice is conceived as 'rationality of systems':

> This does not mean that individuals disappear in criminal justice. They remain, but increasingly they are grasped not as coherent subjects, whether understood as moral, psychological, or economic agents, but as members of particular subpopulations and the intersection of various categorical indicators.
>
> (Feeley and Simon, 1994: 178)

This form of 'government-at-a-distance' by the centre is made possible by newly powerful mechanisms of accountability, such as performance targets, and by technology. Performance measurement and testing are thought to be powerful and effective strategies aimed at control of, in the case of the prison, the conduct of governors and staff, and the accomplishment of certain specified performance objectives. Via measurement, and competition, individuals are bound into a collective attempt to gain competitive advantage for the organization they work for (Grey, 2005). Workers become target-focused, as well as uncomfortably insecure, but this way performance improves, as poor (or even moderate) performance may lead to loss of work, or subjection to remedial measures. People work harder. The prison has been used internally within government as an example of the success of this kind of modernization or transformation of the public sector more generally. This public sector reform agenda has been described by commentators as necessary, but harsh (Pollitt and Bouckaert, 2000).

Together, these changes have made expansion likely, by reducing constraints on criminal justice practices and inviting strategies of selective incapacitation, based on risk. 'Power is aimed at prevention and risk minimization' (ibid.: 178), rather than at individual transformation. Feeley and Simon argue that the move from criminological and policy concern with 'crime as prohibited acts' towards the *distribution* of behaviours and their aggregate management and control can be seen as part of the 'the general movement... towards the exercise of state power as "governmentality"' (Feeley and Simon, 1994: 178).

'Governmentality' was first used as a term by Foucault to describe the way power can be exercised through individuals. Governmental power can be used to shape choices, guide conduct and encourage regulation of the self. It consists of actions upon others' actions. The aim of government is to guide and develop individuals in ways that look like freedom, but which actually strengthen the state. The term is used with increasing frequency by contemporary criminologists (amongst others) to denote the apparent retreat of the state, combined with the arrival of more effective techniques of governing (at a distance); or the 'at-a-distance' control of conduct. These neoliberal forms of power presuppose activity or agency on the part of the individuals subject to it. The term helps us to see government as an activity, not just an institution. We are the accomplices of government. We shape ourselves to be productive, marketable, presentable and successful. The created 'self' is fully aligned with the interests of government. The market doesn't just exist, but is produced and reproduced by responsible individual agents acting economically (Burchell, 1996: 23). We have a sort of freedom, but it takes a well regulated and 'responsibilized' form. Our freedom is a resource for, rather than a hindrance to, government (Barry *et al.*, 1996). Empowerment, for example, simply means that members of staff are given more freedom to use in the state's interests. The active and artificial creation of competition and entrepreneurial markets leads to a more finely calibrated mechanism of control over the workforce (the governed). This is a distinctive and effective way of exerting power. Individuals 'alter their relationships with themselves in their new relationships with government, without it being clear that the outcomes that are supposed to justify this rationality of government are in fact being achieved' (Burchell, 1996: 29).

> Advanced liberal rule...seeks to degovernmentalize the State and to de-statize practices of government, to detach the substantive authority of expertise from the apparatus of political rule, relocating experts within a market governed by the rationalities of competition, accountability and consumer demand. It does not seek to govern through "society", but through the regulated choices of individual citizens, now construed as subjects of choices and aspirations to self-actualisation and self-fulfilment. Individuals are to be governed through their freedom.
>
> (Rose, 1996: 41)

Government power is transmitted via 'practices of the self', or via 'self-mastery' (ibid.: 45).

Few sociological studies have been carried out on these new technologies of government, despite several commentators noting that the new techniques of audit, performance measurement and management by contract, constitute sociologically significant activities (see, for example, Power, 1999). They may distort organizational behaviour and can lead to fabrication (see Liebling, assisted by Arnold, 2004). In the light of some recent research in 12 prisons, this chapter considers how far the 'governmentality' analysis applies to the senior managers of the prison, and what its main effects are. The focus is mainly on senior policy personnel and governors in charge of establishments. There is a preliminary question to address, then, which is why should we study senior personnel – or the elite – in criminal justice (see further Liebling, 2001)? Are they villains or heroes? Good or evil? Their decisions affect the lives of thousands of individuals over whom they wield power. But their power is also limited, and sometimes it is used extremely carefully or even heroically. As significant, low-visibility power holders, they appoint people, sack others, shape criminal justice practice, set limits and determine the tone and meaning of punishment. Their own rise to power signifies the valuing of certain characteristics over others and may in general have little to do with moral virtue (although moral leaders sometimes emerge). Are there distinct 'types' of senior managers? Are they essentially conservative and power-hungry, or are they conscientious public servants? How have interpretations of the role changed in this era of competition, privatization and performance? Senior managers in the Prison Service have traditionally primarily come (like Chief Constables) from working-class backgrounds. They are street-wise. One insider observed that 'they would be cowboys, in another time and place, willing to take risks, be unpopular, out-manoeuvre others to achieve their aims'. Have these trends changed, with the rise of a new managerial class? In the following discussion of resistance, I want to distinguish between resistance as a moral behaviour or ethical position, and the avoidance of regulation, which is quite different. Who or what is being resisted, for what reason? Is there resistance, on moral grounds, and if not, why not?

These specific questions raise other, broader questions, worthy of careful consideration: how is power exercised in the late-modern prison and how has its distribution been shaped by new techniques of 'governing at a distance'? Are prison governors (and staff) merely the accomplices of government or can they exert agency, discretion and professional scrutiny? What is the everyday experience of those who wield governmental power? How do the powerful resolve the conflict that exists between punitive, commercial and ameliorative rationalities, in their everyday behaviour and decision-making? What interests drive action? Whose interests does managerialism serve, and what do prison governors have to say on the matter? The powerful, or 'macro-actors', are no different from 'micro-actors': they simply have a 'longer and more reliable chain of command' (Rose, 2002: 5). Do the powerful, to the extent that they resist domination from above at all, adopt different 'arts' or strategies from the weak (Scott, 1990)?

The remainder of this chapter takes five themes, and explores their relevance in the light of some recent observations and interview-based studies. It draws briefly on specific shadowing exercises carried out in November 2003 and November 2005 and on a research study of 'difficult' prisons between 2002 and 2005. Without having set out to study 'governmentality', the literature in this field helped to make sense of some of the reported observations. The five themes are:

- How the changing criminal justice world operates at senior manager levels;
- The increasing significance of managerialism, performance and audit;
- The reconfiguration of the flow of power and its effects;
- The roles of trust and risk; and
- The apparently paradoxical 'remoralization' of the prison.

How the changing criminal justice world operates at senior management levels

At the very top of the organization, there are new criminal justice objectives and strategies, characterized by an increased emphasis on performance, delivery, efficiency, effectiveness and tough management, and by the use of the private sector as a model and catalyst. What ideology, values and drives lie behind this 'reshaping of the British State'? What goes on in criminal justice, above senior managers in establishments? What is the environment like? How is time spent? What values and interests are represented, in what language, at the highest levels of the organization? Whose interests prevail? How is policy made? What options are considered? How are decisions made and goals set? Is there a consensus about goals and values? To what extent is there evidence of a public sector ethos in modern corrections? How does it manifest itself?[2] The following account draws on observations of the criminal justice policy elite during a period of major change.[3]

I shadowed the then Commissioner of Correctional Services for four full days, during the final stages of the preparation of the Carter Review of Correctional Services. Full notes were taken of meetings, informal conversations and events, amounting to 53 pages.[4] The day started at 07.30 hours and ended around 18.45, and there was always a working lunch. I was given a diary every morning, which consisted of booked phone calls, policy and financial briefings, bilaterals, meetings with Ministers, Permanent Secretary meetings in the Cabinet Office and 'reducing reconvictions' meetings, with presentations from Employment, Education, DfES and JobCentre Plus. One morning was spent in the Cambridgeshire probation office. It included a focus group discussion with probationers, about their experiences of various community disposals.

I arrived at the agreed time at Cleland House, Westminster. Martin Narey, Commissioner of Correctional Services, was on the telephone discussing a suicide that had occurred in a Young Offenders Institution, in which there was considerable press interest. The young man concerned had been 'in our care for nine days'. The staff had been 'devastated' and the Governor had been in tears. It was a complex and human story. Narey knew a great deal about the case. He expressed anger about the critical story line emerging on the *Today Programme*. He wanted 'his view to be reflected' and 'someone has to front the (highly critical) Chief Inspector'.

Most of what I observed was large-scale, but equally political, with the focus on future events, aggregate figures and strategic planning. There was a clear focus on 'delivery', the agendas for meetings were heavy, there was a business-like feel to all activities and the pace of action was brisk – enough to make me (a trained social scientist) nervous. The working atmosphere was generally good humoured, but could be tense. The Commissioner's major preoccupations were the Carter Review of Correctional Services (involving major organizational change,[5] the role of the private sector and of contracts), finances and the size of the prison population. The refrain, 'in the new world', was exchanged often. The Carter Report, I heard twice, was regarded by the Prime Minister's office as 'the cutting edge of public sector reform'. One of the problems with typical Home Office activity was that 'we were always weak on implementation'. That was about to change. 'We've got to keep on delivering', I heard, 'whilst we are creating the new world'.

Days began early and ended late. Conversations were about political risk, 'what the PM wants', numbers, targets and 'key drivers'. At the highest levels of the criminal justice organization, the values driving action were:

- *Speed* (the pace at which information was transmitted and reformulated as policy with 'not much forensic examination' was staggering; 'people feel overwhelmed by the number of demands on their time');
- *Financial accountability* and financial *restraint* (a *moral* case was made, more than once, for transparency and efficiency);
- *Smooth administration* (working to a Parliamentary and financial timetable);
- *Effectiveness* (all roads must lead to crime reduction, using all the 'levers' and 'targets' at their disposal). 'Success' (and how to measure it) was everything ('we need to distinguish between different failures');

- *Serving Government* (that is, meeting the Prime Minister's objectives);
- *Transformation and modernization* (change, including a willingness to consider radical options, challenging targets and a new emphasis on improving, and changing the character of, leadership in order to make change more effective);[6]
- *Positive presentation* (for example, sufficient emphasis on achievements to date and politically acceptable handling, including active management of relations with the media and anticipating unfavourable press. 'We need to market the fact that crime is falling');
- *Handling Ministers* (preparing the ground, structuring expectations, sounding them out);
- *Handling evidence* (making it 'better' and more useful. 'Marketing is one of the levers');
- *Coherence* (making sure policies do not conflict with each other or with the PM's overall direction); and
- *Improving Whitehall* (that is, their own performance, in public administration, responding to public inquiries and serving Ministers).

The words 'control' and 'making progress' were uttered far more often than the words 'justice' or 'evidence' ('evidence is going to be the difficult thing...there isn't enough support for the full story of what we are doing'). The declaratory or expressive functions of criminal justice were a major concern and were talked about in these terms. I heard the phrase, 'we really should talk about this at greater length' at least six times in four days. There was some self-consciousness about this: 'This is really important. Are we rushing it?'; 'We are rushing to this too hastily...it's a big decision'. 'We need a debate on these measures'. 'That's fascinating. I need some time to think'. Power was effectively wielded, from the top down, with little time for hesitation or resistance, and some devastating consequences for individuals ('in terms of emotion, this is all very difficult'; and 'we are moving away from paternalistic career management...people need to take control of their own careers'). Individuals had 'no option'. Pragmatic, results-oriented strategies were adopted without any discussion of principle ('they just don't believe in a target-led economy'). The demands on the time of senior personnel were overwhelming, as was the quantity of information they were expected to absorb. There was talk of the 'need to make sentencers resource aware', and of the need to bring the services together to 'make that impact on offending'. There was some talk of 'dismembering the probation service' – at the very least, of making it more accountable and target-oriented. As Rock observed in relation to 'the opening stages of criminal justice policy-making' (1995), there is rarely consensus, within and between professional groups, so competing values and practices become apparently reconciled in the final product – but they existed, and one powerfully wielded perspective prevailed. One observation made whilst writing up my notes was that the role of personal conviction is prominent in shaping contemporary criminal justice policy.[7]

The pace of action was exhilarating. There was a sense of sober realism in the handling of practitioners: 'We have to demonstrate that we can make the things we do work. We need to make a transformation in the end-to-end stuff. We need to be able to see where the money is'. The atmosphere all around was, to say the least, challenging. One observation, scribbled between meetings, was that it seemed ironic, or paradoxical, that the culture change at the top of the new Corrections organization was about increasing toughness, enforcement and responsibilization, whereas, on the ground, at least in prisons, the culture change being sought was about decency and standards. There was an impatience with 'old-fashioned', 'theta-type' values (of fairness and due process) and an urgent emphasis on 'sigma-type' values (efficiency):[8] 'We've got the wrong people driving it, they're not being driven by the business. They are being driven by how things have always been run'. According to my observation notes, 'it's the financial people who are harsh': 'we'll need those figures for market testing'). Narey spent more time with his Head of Finance than with any other individual during the four days of observation. Apparently this was 'not a representative week'. On one day, they wore the same tie! Many of their interactions were reminiscent of scenes from *Yes Minister*. A great deal of coffee was consumed, on the run.[9]

So what values do we see, or hope to see, reflected in senior places in criminal justice and contemporary political life more generally? The term 'answerability' is critical; as are concepts of justice, parsimony and humanitarian concern. Should we be striving to develop just institutions, led by competent and morally resilient representatives? One characteristic of a just institution would be the absence of 'exploitation of man by man' [sic]. The account presented above suggests that change, speed, toughness, control, presentation and self-legitimation may be more prominent than moral reflection in practice. There is more 'administrative practice' than 'communicative practice' (Dryzek, 1995: 114). How are these changing priorities making themselves felt at operational level? This question will be addressed more directly in a project currently being conducted.

To conclude this brief observational account, there are new, sociologically significant activities going on in high places, which have implications for how prisons function and punish, for how they are experienced by prisoners and by prison staff and governors, and for how 'offender management services' (and public policy more generally) are developing. There seems to be an increasing gap between the claims being made for prisons and their reconviction rates. This is not to deny the efforts of staff working in struggling establishments, one or two of which have significantly transformed their practices for the better, using all the new managerialist tools at their disposal. A recent study of prison suicide prevention shows that such management transformation reduces prisoner distress (although it only reduces it a little) and that this, in turn, may reduce suicides, in those establishments which accomplish the transformation (Liebling et al., 2005).

This chapter is not an argument against management improvement but an essay about how senior managers (including Governors) adapt to and understand the new world and what that new world looks like. It raises questions about the culture and direction of criminal justice work, and about how empirical prison and corrections researchers might use, and maybe modify, the important insights offered by theorists and critics of the contemporary criminal justice world to accurately depict it, and perhaps to make a difference. We should be asking how staff in general engage with or resist new and wide-ranging penal technologies of the self, and how far senior managers wield them, or resist them, too. The remainder of this account begins to develop such an approach. It is an early analysis in a considerably longer study.[10]

Managerialism, performance and audit

> Most Governors aren't lazy. I mean, in years gone by, you've got your Squire Governors who pop in and out of the prison, but it isn't like that any more. We all want to do a good job, I think, but somehow the process gets in the way of doing a better job.
>
> (Governor 10)

The emphasis on measurement, effectiveness, success and positive presentation represents the infiltration of managerialist practices and ideologies into the criminal justice world. Managerialism constitutes a set of ideologies and technologies which promise rapid organizational progress, in which better, firmer management aims to serve better, more efficient and more effective public services. It has brought with it the new, somewhat flawed craft of performance measurement. Giddens and others have argued that in our late-modern, risk-averse world, the 'future is continually drawn into the present' by means of the reflexive organization of knowledge environments' (Giddens, 1991: 3). Organizations must continually measure, reinvent and improve themselves. More and more of the activities of organizations are susceptible to monitoring, regulation and 'chronic revision'. National Key Performance Targets form part of this 'new governance' technique. They are used to analyse and monitor performance within organizations, and to indicate where attention and resources need to be directed. They are change agents, and constitute an attempt to control and motivate the workforce to maximize an organization's effectiveness.

The pace of management change is extraordinary, but, on balance, the evidence base is weak. The first problem with the use of Key Performance Targets (KPTs) is that they are famously imperfect as measures of what an organization is doing, or meant to be doing, and they may therefore distort organizational behaviour. They measure 'progress through the jungle' but they do not indicate whether this is 'taking them further into or out of the jungle' (Sinclair, 2002: 11). The current Chief Inspector of Prisons has suggested that they create a 'virtual prison system' far removed from reality.[11] Senior managers, for specific reasons, do not always treat them with the critical eye they deserve. Secondly, there is greater emphasis on measurement than management: Wormwood Scrubs was found to be seriously under-performing three times in a row, over a five-year period. Highly critical Inspectorate reports led to negative publicity but little action. This is consistent with the literature where it is argued that insufficient attention is being paid to developing any understanding of why organizations fail, or of how to act on evidence of poor performance (see, for example, Smith and Goddard, 2002). Thirdly, observers have noted that it is the behaviour of those lower down in the workforce that is monitored. We hear nothing of the performance of MPs or Ministers.

Like performance measurement, auditing of process represents a 'new rationality of governance', whereby central control reaches deeply into organizations, bringing with it expectations of self-control, individual accountability and unprecedented levels of knowledge about internal organizational arrangements (Power, 2001). Unlike KPTs, audit inquires whether establishments are doing what they should do, 'properly', that is, following their own instructions, as opposed to achieving the right outcomes. As the two activities have evolved separately, there are few direct links between the audit of process and achievement on indicators. So an establishment can get a 'good' audit result on sentence planning, for example, and what that means in practice is that establishments are producing decent sentence plans for prisoners. It does not mean that such plans are followed or that prisoners experience their time in custody as in the least bit 'planned' or meaningful. Ninety per cent of prisons pass their audit test, so levels are set at an achievable, low level. Audit is, according to critics, a meaningless 'ritual of verification' based on little understanding of what practices matter, and a substitute for true accountability, with implications for the organization of trust in organizations. Such critique is, in my view, necessary, but oversimplified. These practices are anything but meaningless (but they may have different meanings from those that are publicly stated).

Managerially, these developments are extremely useful, as well as meaningful. They allow unprecedented levels of information and control, from a distance. They are not wholly unrelated to quality. They allow a feeling of power and control, which is intoxicating for those who experience it. So many governors are well disposed towards such techniques, and eager to use them to their advantage. Some governors have suggested that the introduction of KPTs constitute the single most important transformation in the way the Prison Service is managed. One transformation not in doubt is that power operates differently in the contemporary prison world.

In general, the majority of governors are concerned for personal and professional reasons to improve the performance of their establishments along the lines required by those above them. They want to succeed and to be regarded as able. They want to be seen as managing well, by their Area Managers. Whilst the Prison Governors' Association expresses resistance to privatization, individual Governors often use the threat of market testing to galvanize their staff into action. This was complex, however. On the ground, many governors found themselves resolving conflicts between targets and between priorities, so their personal values could shape the direction in which these tensions became solved:

> We could, theoretically, have everyone go past a drug dog, and where the drug dog indicates, we could haul people into segregation, and we could do all sorts of things that would prevent those drugs from coming into the prison. But, in doing that, we would be raising anxiety levels through the roof. We wouldn't be able to do the first night stuff properly. That's a very stark example of where there's a real balance there – if you do one thing then it impacts on another. There are more subtle things which we need to address. The amount of property that is being allowed in, the way in which those processes

operate, needs to be balanced with the need to bring down the level of drug use in the prison.

(Governor 20)

At one prison, the Governor was supposed to show staff a recently produced 'decency video', intended to encourage the decent treatment of prisoners and challenge staff attitudes. He stalled:

> When we were starting to show that, that was actually the week when we had been asked to take ninety more prisoners without any more resources, so we have actually put off showing it.... We thought, all that we would get is, 'well, how are we going to be decent if we're just banging more and more people up together?'

(Governor 7)

Prisons had geographical advantages and disadvantages – certain areas of the country were more difficult to recruit and retain staff in, for example, than others. These differences made performance leagues seem rather limited and superficial. One of our observations was that governors were positioned quite a long way from policies. They did not implement policies, but they set the framework and provided the conditions for their staff to translate policy into action. They devised structures. They removed obstacles and set expectations. They *interpreted* policies, and this had an impact on how staff understood them. They challenged staff on their strongly held vision of 'how things are done around here': '[This prison] was a very flabby place, a lot of things been allowed and swept under the carpet; behaviour had been accepted that shouldn't have been' (Governor 2).

However, at this general level, governors were making managerialism work; using it, strategically, to achieve the Service's ends, but also imbibing practices with their own vision of how a prison should operate. In this sense, Governors were compliant and aligned. Some felt too constrained by the new emphasis on targets and process, and by the level of control-without-principle exerted from above. Most felt it was entirely appropriate.

The reconfiguration of the flow of power and its effects: The production of company men?

Garland has argued that new modes of governance 'operate lightly and unobtrusively' and seek to 'align the actors' objectives with those of the authorities' (Garland, 1997: 187). This makes them less visible, more difficult to articulate and more effective as a means of securing penal order. This analysis has tended to be applied to the offender,[12] but it clearly applies to staff and senior managers as well as to prisoners. The new form of penal power that Garland and others identify is, after all, transmitted through senior managers and their staff. How do they use it? There is no doubt that, overall, there is more power available, and it has shifted upwards. There is little overt or obvious resistance, amongst senior managers, prisons staff or prisoners, in this new world.[13] There is a very strong and substantially increased feeling of accountability and a remarkable consensus about means and ends amongst 'new generation' governors.[14] Individuals with power are nervous, in case they fail to make it perform for them. The Prison Officers' Association was described in 2004 as 'first toothless and now gumless' in the face of market testing – although there has been a resurgence of POA resistance since then. Officers are agreeing to cost savings and staffing reductions in a way that was unimaginable 20 years ago: their interests have been aligned with those of the powerful and they have become 'instruments of their own domination'. Governors who are not 'on message' are isolated. One relatively young, 'new generation' Governor described his relationship with his new Area Manager:

> He's probably broadly similar, in many ways, to me. I think the nature of his job requires him to take a more managerialist approach because the focus increasingly has to be on targets. I think both of us are more company men than our predecessors, simply because we have the investment in the future that requires us to be like that. Also because I am genuinely signed up to... I think the performance stuff has improved the quality of life in prisons so I don't doubt that there is a real impact from it.
> (Governor, personal communication, 2004)

However, at the outer limits of the performance framework, others express concern. Private prison directors have been persuaded to make further staffing cuts against their better judgement: they are required to put profit and competition first. Private sector management techniques have been adopted to regulate the now contingent workforce: competition, the contract, insecurity of employment and tight performance management render employees relatively powerless and therefore compliant. Flatter structures, fewer protections and clearer goals ensure that what is delivered is what is desired: reasonable treatment of prisoners by a carefully controlled, largely un-unionized staff. A new cultural and service delivery ethos is demanded, via economic reasoning; that is, instrumental means. The practice of management becomes an 'exercise of domination' (Sennett, 1998: 115). Maybe this is important in a prison, and less morally objectionable than having an unregulated workforce. Garland cautions us in our use of this analysis that these new rationalities will only be partially achieved in practice: how do individuals actually engage with, subvert and think about modern penal governance? How does strong government-from-a-distance *feel*?

The context in which Governors worked often involved poor prison conditions and regimes, unenthusiastic staff and an obviously disgruntled prisoner population. Under these conditions, Governors wanted to modernize their establishments (where 'modernize' means 'improve and humanize'). Governors talked about resistance to change in relation to the difficulties of their own role in relation to prison staff, sometimes in particular areas of the prison or over specific initiatives. This inevitably led to difficult and often protracted struggles over whose agenda would predominate, and a need for a firm approach:

> We had a very swift action plan, with very simple agenda. We had a Stalinist approach...this is the way we'll do it, and it isn't going to be a five-year plan, its going to be a six-month, twelve-month plan, so we organized the day for prisoners in every unit of [the prison]...organized it that this will happen at this time on every unit, and it will happen consistently, and we will manage it, and we publish the timetable to staff and prisoners, so that prisoners know that at 10 o'clock, its my exercise, and so they will regulate it themselves. And doing that enabled huge spin-offs, getting prisoners out, consistency, staff knew what was going to happen when, prisoners knew it, they got time in the open air, this is when they were going to have their exercise, this was when they were going to have their gym, they would go to education. We were saying, your education is in the morning on this side of the unit, your association in the afternoon, you've got more people to go to activities. Very simple, not my own idea, but came from a Principal Officer. But that's it, we'll do it, published it, did it. But, no resistance, I said resistance is futile, we're going to do it, and that core day enabled us to focus in our resources to deliver that. Time out of cell went up, purposeful activity went up, incidents dropped off.
>
> (Governor 3)

The context of threats from above focused all attention on following the mainstream agenda:

> The whole prison has changed... we were about to get privatized. So the Area Manager threw in a completely new management team. And they turned it from being a failing prison right to the top. It's been hard work for staff. But it needed to be done, or else we'd be working for Group 4. That may have got a few people to realize that, you know, perhaps the older staff who were about to retire and had no interest, we'll not go down that route. We'll go down the Governor's route and succeed.
> (Officer)

Private sector habits and practices were gradually being introduced into public sector contexts. It was the case that working in the private sector 'made you very task-centred':

> It does two things for you. It makes you very task-centred, ultimately you can't get away from the fact that this is the task, and this is the target, and this has to be delivered, and it engrains that in you.
> (Governor 6)

Meanwhile, in the public sector, these techniques were rapidly appearing, shaping Governors' approaches to their work. Staff, in establishments undergoing performance testing, or performance improvement planning, said that this had made them 'more customer-focused'. They felt 'on the other hand... the change was coming'. A 'bid' speeded up a necessary (an often already started) process of change.

Governors worked long hours, described sleepless nights, a high turnover of work and generally felt reluctant to lean on their Area Managers. One or two described being 'terrified of market testing', and knew that this was a genuine threat. Most used it as a lever, and some described it as a welcome opportunity. It constituted a powerful management tool:

> How good are we at implementing initiatives? I think very good.... To some degree there is the ownership issue and that has been promoted a bit and frankly there's the big stick thing as well. There is nothing that concentrates people's mind more in the Prison Service than what we had at [this prison]. You've got a year to sort

yourselves out otherwise we might privatize you. A Governor – a couple of Governors came in and said 'do things or you're gonna get the sack'. And I really, in all honesty, firmly believe in that approach a lot of the time rather than the ownership bull shit. Scare the crap out of people and they'll change fairly quick. People were told, you will either change or you'll be working in McDonalds.

(Officer)

These strategies created an apparently compliant workforce, at all levels. But was this level of buy-in assent or acquiescence? In some prisons, staff characterized their governors (and some characterized themselves) as 'new management types': company men, who believed in where they were heading, who were not afraid of staff and who could combine a clear emphasis on performance with some powerful messages about morality. Other governors were alienated and very anti-'statistics, performance and Ministerial interest', and felt that they had insufficient control over their own environment. They berated 'management by laptop' when 'the information is bollocks', procedures that were 'arse covering', and they were concerned:

that we've had occasion in the recent past where we've had members of the Board actually saying how proud...actually sounding proud about the number of careers they've ended because they felt people weren't up to it.

(Governor 8)

They were also 'slightly concerned that there is a lack of care for staff at the top' (Governor 7).

One consequence of the new working environment identified by several critics, and raised by several Governors, was the substitution of checking for trust.

The role of trust and risk

I have argued elsewhere that the public sector had much to learn from the private sector about techniques, leadership, change and competition (Liebling, assisted by Arnold, 2004). The problem has been the adoption of these new managerialist techniques, and the invitation extended to powerful corporate interests to make them happen, without incurring the abandonment of the traditional or core values of trustworthiness, integrity and 'public service' which the public sector stands for (however incapable it has been of translating these values into practices). Critics argue that performance management threatens trust. Much has been written about trust and its apparent decline in modern social and political life. Without trust, we experience discomfort, anxiety and lack of confidence in our ability to evaluate others. It is, under any circumstances, a fragile commodity. Despite the coercive conditions of prison, acts of trust and distrust characterize its daily life (see Liebling and Price, 2001; and Liebling, assisted by Arnold, 2004). It is contagious and operates in concentric circles: so as a prisoner, if I trust this officer, I may trust the prison system, and therefore the social order. But what about elsewhere in the organization? What have been the effects of the move towards what Sennett (1998) describes as a new high-risk, low loyalty, non-linear, lean workplace? What are the consequences for staff and prisoners of a prison being opened by the private sector, won back a few years later by the public sector and then diagnosed as failing?

A study of prison staff in five prisons in the UK found varying but quite low levels of trust by staff in their senior managers, with staff in poorer quality prisons trusting them least.[15] In two prisons, staff rated their trust of prisoners higher than they rated their trust of managers: a fact they noted with some alarm as they completed our questionnaires. This had important sociological implications for life in those establishments. Trust grows slowly out of embedded social relationships, and can be lost quickly via dishonesty or incompetence. Duffee has argued that one of the favourite past-times of officers is 'identifying dishonesty and hypocrisy in those above' them (Duffee, 1974: 155). Officers often behave as if they are exclusively interested in material rewards, but one of the striking findings of our study was the importance of their personal relationship with, and feelings about, the Governor (Liebling, 2004: 412–413). Trust in governors was shaped, just as it was by prisoners in staff, by treatment they received as individuals, and by judgements they made about competence, fairness, ethicality and opportunities to be heard. When good governors won staff trust and then became quickly promoted, staff were confirmed in their cynical original position: 'We are just a stepping stone...managers take the credit for good officer work...this is just how it works in industry...this prison is used, as a means to an end. The governors have no long-term commitment to the place. There's no trust...there's a very big divide between uniform and suits here' (officers). As another officer said, 'The way the organization relates to you affects the way you relate to each other, which affects the way you relate to your job' (Officer). There are some tensions, then, between modernization and the moral identity of the person, as argued by Feeley and Simon in the early 1990s. Government-at-a-distance, or management by target, involving strong central direction and future-oriented improvement, was experienced as alienating by many staff. These tensions need analysing at all levels of the criminal justice organization.

There is, amongst senior managers in modern organizational life, a yearning for order and predictability, via control, without trust, as several critics have observed (O'Neill, 2002). Area managers and those above them, have an 'unprecedented grip' on establishments (Narey, 2002). Terms like 'robust' and 'firm' are frequently used by those working in senior positions about the current leadership. There are risks, for governors and other senior managers, of 'governing-at-a-distance'. There is a tension between new techniques of measurement and perceptions of fairness. Inappropriate measurement used in complex organizations can lead employees to 'conclude that they are not valued or understood as professionals' (Sitkin and Stickel, 1996) and can lead to non-compliance and disaffection (Braithwaite, 2002). Employees like to be treated as moral agents, too. Individuals feel 'wrongly accused, for example, if they have been performing well in an organization labelled as poor performing. The effects of this reorganization of space and time, and of work, are 'existentially troubling' for the individual (Giddens, 1991: 21). We can see then, that in an already low trust environment, some modern managerialist techniques (frenetic policy activity, unrealistic demands for compliance with irrelevant measures, the concept of 'contestability') may make it harder for managers to generate trust amongst staff.[16] Increasingly senior managers are asking staff to trust in their future-oriented paper strategies. Officers, particularly in times of change, prefer to trust in what worked yesterday: their confidence is grounded in experience. We have embarked on a major experiment in the reorganization of work in criminal justice and the public sector, based on faith and dissatisfaction with the old, rather than on evidence about any aspect of the new. Whilst there are no simple criteria for judging the effectiveness of contemporary prisons, some attention should be paid to staff and prisoner perceptions, outcomes and to practices. Critics of managerialism often fail to take into account the realities of prison life before the onset of 'tight managerial grip'. On the other hand, untested assumptions abound about how far the Prison Service has come.

The apparently paradoxical 'remoralization' of the prison

> I am not prepared to continue to apologise for failing prison after failing prison. I have had enough of trying to explain the very immorality of our treatment of some prisoners and the degradation of some establishments.... I know the job used to be easier. I know the job used to be more fun. But I also know that we used to tolerate inhumanity.
> (Martin Narey, Speech to Prison Service Conference, 2001)

Martin Narey's speech to the Prison Service Conference in 2001 demonstrated a powerful attempt to forge a link between performance, success and failure, and morality. His use of the terms 'immorality' and 'degradation' were deliberate and emotional. Since 1999, prisons have been the subject of a moral crusade that has included a decency agenda; an inquiry into the racist murder of a prisoner by his cell mate; the prosecution of officers found guilty of violence against prisoners; the invention of 'professional standards' in corrections; and a highly publicized and systematic attempt to reverse the increase in rates of suicide, particularly in 'high-risk' prisons with no-longer-appropriate cultures. It seems paradoxical that the firm approach to scrutiny and the demand for performance described above, and the increasing imprisonment of marginal offenders (so that use of the prison has reached immoral proportions), have brought with them a related emphasis on moral practices within establishments. Managerialism has been claimed as the route by which this moral agenda can be most effectively pursued.

What do these developments tell us? First, that there are serious moral problems to address in the prison and that past failures in management have allowed brutality and indecency to persist. Secondly, as Carlen and others have argued, the prison needs to legitimate itself to justify increasing use of it (Carlen, 2001, 2002). Third, these moral declarations are taking place at a time when the morality of a government prepared to go to war, and of prison guards acting for their respective states, is seriously under question. There is a contested moral ground, and prisons have become useful sites through which to demonstrate moral reflection and leadership. What Garland called governing through security might be reconstrued here as governing through morality. The departure of Narey in 2005 instantly raised questions about who might lead 'the moral crusade' in his absence. There has undoubtedly been an 'ethical turn' in social, political and institutional thinking (Honneth, 1995), but we are not yet sure about its meaning. If there is a moral agenda being pursued in government and in criminal justice, whose agenda is it, and what limits does it set? Is this new moral reflexivity authentic? At the same time that the apparent re-moralization of the prison has taken place, the question of evaluating prison quality and moral performance has become a commercial and political as well as empirical and theoretical question.

Individuals working in prisons express quiet discomfort ('I feel I am being asked to do immoral things', Governor 11), whilst striving to 'do better on those targets': 'If they asked us to run Dachau, we'd probably do it' (Governor 16). New governors describe themselves as 'realists', 'not idealists'. They are collectively persuaded that good intentions are meaningless without effective management systems to translate them into practice. They 'feel more comfortable with the Albany model than the Long Lartin model' (that is, situational, rather than social control; see Sparks *et al.*, 1996). But they express some concern that 'we are losing sight of the day-to-day stuff' and we might be trying to 'run too fast with some of the bigger stuff' (like NOMS). They are also concerned that the new overriding goal (reducing reoffending) might be somewhat unrealistic:

> All that stuff that Garland was writing about, what it's all about, chimed. The reality is that the things that stop people committing crime are all out there and not in prison, you know. I worry that we are setting too much store in our ability to prevent reoffending. That's not to say that we shouldn't strive to do all of that work, but if we think that's what measures our success, then we are absolutely setting ourselves up to fail.
>
> (Governor 11)

Some speak out in semi-public spaces, expressing concern about the model of corrections they are expected to support:

> This is a dangerous model. We don't know how to achieve what we are being asked to achieve. We don't know what works. Franchise prisons don't follow from the little we know. We don't understand reconviction rates prison by prison.
>
> (Governor, at Prison Service Conference, 2007)

Several expressed concern about the political motivations for new policies and the risks involved in selling (legitimating) politically-driven changes to prisoners. So whilst the public presentation of the prison, and its leadership, strive for a moral high ground, inside the prison, some staff and some senior managers can see the cracks. Some are uncomfortable, others are afraid of the consequences of underperformance, others are indifferent, or cynical, and many align themselves with the declared interests of the leadership: performance equals effectiveness, and effectiveness constitutes or is consistent with the new morality:

> AL: 'Okay. So you don't feel...one of Garland's analyses of the modern world is that self-governance is everything; that the government have become really clever at making people govern themselves and that applies to Governors a bit as well – that there are now clever management techniques that mean you are more controlled than your predecessors might have been. But you are comfortable with that?'
>
> Governor: 'Comfortable with that, yeah. Yes, because, obviously, it becomes increasingly important that the sort of controls that are being placed on us are aimed at the things that I believe in. If I felt I was being controlled but in a direction I didn't want to go then I'd feel really uncomfortable. When I look back at what people 20 years ago doing my job were doing...it must have seemed a much easier job because the level of accountability they had was extraordinarily low'.
>
> (Governor 11)

To some extent, this critique of the past, and the more favourable analysis of the modern organization, is justified. Prisons that meet their performance targets generally treat prisoners better than prisons that do not (but there are important exceptions). Staff who care about their own and the establishment's future have a mindset that means doors are unlocked when they should be, prisoners are encouraged to attend education, visits begin on time and so on. Wrong's argument that the use of coercive power stands in greater need of legitimation than formerly is undoubtedly important (Wrong, 1997). We have also witnessed the making of a moral case for exerting legitimate power in prisons, not evading it (see Liebling, 2004: 347). Governors have a different conception of their role and of the place of power in modern management. On the other hand, a senior member of staff at another prison referred to a recent suicide as 'a better death than the last one, in terms of procedures'. Few are comfortable with the rapid increase in imprisonment rates, or with a political climate that makes increasing and cynical use of the prison. Under-regulation in the prisons' world is dangerous. Over-regulation, particularly for the wrong ends, feels dehumanizing and may be counter-productive. We have a new paradoxical criminal justice world, where privatization has emerged, justified as a new technique for raising accountability and performance, and yet senior players in the private sector seem freer from managerial constraints, feel more powerful and may even resist the new penology in ways that are barely in evidence in the new, closely regulated public sector.

There is clearly a new conception of the nature and scope of legitimate authority in the work place: a new intellectual technology grounded in managerialism and supported by neoliberal politics. Critics suggest that, far from securing improved services, such a conception constitutes a kind of despotism. Our feelings of discomfort in this new universe reflect the move from a vision of humans as agents to a working environment in which all humans (offenders and workers) are objects, subjected to political and economic goals. The new world depends on the acceptance of the concept of free enterprise, but as Rose argues, the market is constructed:

> Constructing a 'free market' seems to entail a variety of interventions by accountants, management consultants, lawyers and industrial relations specialists and marketing experts in order to establish the conditions under which the 'laws of supply and demand' can make themselves real, to implant the ways of calculating and managing that will make economic actors think, reckon and behave as competitive, profit-seeking agents, to turn workers into motivated employees who will freely strive to give of their best in the workplace, and to transform people into consumers who can choose between products.
>
> (Rose, 2002: 65)

In this context, prison governors are individualized (in competition); their professional and individual risk aversion is a signal of their relative powerlessness. There is more power flowing in the workplace, but we should be looking more critically and impartially at whose interests this power serves. We should worry about too much compliance amongst prisoners. Should we also worry about too much compliance amongst staff? They are salaried civil servants – what is it legitimate to require of them? If senior managers in corrections are somewhat deferential, it is possible to see increasing constraints on their 'situated action' (see

Forester, 1993). These constraints include a narrowing of the terms in which problems are formulated (an 'economic rationality'; Pusey, 1991) and a 'bounding' of choices by everyday talk of technical efficiency. There may be a selection bias in the survival process: a handful of senior managers have departed from the service, and a number of others have suffered from medical or psychological problems, leading to early retirement. That Governors in other less 'managerialized' jurisdictions are less timid, and see resistance and limit-setting as part of their professional role, suggests that some of the fears expressed by critics about the fine calibration of control inherent in modern management may be justified. As Dryzek argues, 'the key here is bringing instrumental rationality under the control of communicative rationality' (1995: 114).

A balance should be struck between the positive contours of modern managerialism, our strivings for answerability, the demands of democracy, the protection of the interests of working people and humanitarian penal reform.

Notes

I would like to thank the Governors of many prisons for agreeing to long, reflective interviews, and Martin Narey, former Director General of the Prison Service (1999–2004, Commissioner of Correctional Services (2004–2005), and Chief Executive of the National Offender Management Services (2005–2006) and staff in his office, for allowing me to shadow him, take notes and ask questions, with no clear agenda, during a very important and sensitive stage in criminal justice policy-making. I would also like to thank Peter Wright for helpful comments and discussions on this chapter.

1. Managerialism, a development that helped to give rise to the new penology, is a term used to describe radical changes in the style of organizational management from the 1980s onwards. It is a 'distinct set of ideologies and practices' (McEvoy, 2001: 254), representing a pragmatic, future-oriented, technologically-supported approach to the management of organizations which emphasizes strategic planning, 'service delivery', efficiency and value for money. It has an in-built tendency towards instrumentalism and quantification (for example, so that what can be measured becomes important, rather than *vice versa*). It is characterized by strong central direction, but also by devolution-within-parameters to local managers. It is positivist, self-legitimating, competitive and control-oriented. Its instrumental rationalization is a political philosophy; see Grey, 2005, and later.
2. The chapter draws on an extended study of prison quality, and on an evaluation of a suicide prevention policy aimed at transforming the practices and cultures of five 'high-risk' establishments over a three-year period (2002–2005). It draws in particular on interviews and observations conducted in these and other establishments. It also draws on some preliminary observations at Prison Service Headquarters, at the Home Office, and in

244   *'Governmentality' and Governing Corrections*

establishments. These observations formed the basis of a research proposal outlining a more developed study of moral values and practices in public and private sector corrections submitted to the ESRC, awarded in 2006, to be conducted during 2007–2009, with Dr Ben Crewe. Many of the questions raised in this chapter will be considered at greater length in that project.
3. This job title had, as one commentator reflected, 'the shortest life span in the history of criminal justice' – the subject of another paper.
4. Where words and phrases appear in single quotation marks below, they are taken from my notes. Here, they are reported largely unattributed.
5. Particularly the introduction of major cultural change and the bringing about of a sense of financial accountability in the probation service.
6. There was much talk of the robust leadership approach taken by the private sector. Some of the talk, at least ('we'll need that for market testing'; 'we need resilient people'; 'I was very proud that at one stage, we were sacking two or three prison officers a week') seemed rather brutal. Change was a 'meta-narrative', an ideology and a 'fetish' (Grey, 2005).
7. And that personal conviction can make individual leaders strong and apparently ruthless ('you shouldn't equivocate. It is the right thing to do'), but also effective in bringing about change ('the decent staff have gone from the minority to the majority. We are moving to a state where they don't walk away if a prisoner is being abused').
8. See Hood, 1991; also Liebling, assisted by Arnold, 2004: 427.
9. One of the limitations of this early observation exercise was the lack of opportunity to debrief or ask questions because the pace of action was so fast. There was little opportunity to check assumptions, follow the decision-making process through or ask 'how did that meeting feel to you?' Towards the end of the four days, one permanent secretary asked, 'what are your observations? This is making people think'. My reply was, 'it's exciting, but a bit scary'.
10. The longer study will investigate senior management values and career biographies, life in two public and two private sector prisons and a case study of at least one mechanism aimed at performance improvement.
11. For example, 'contestability' – the subjecting of services to competition in the search for 'best value' – has brought with it a new emphasis within the public sector on impression management. The Head of Training recently suggested that public sector senior managers will require training on 'presentation skills'.
12. For good reason. This analysis applies to the offender via early release and offending behaviour programmes (see Maurutto and Hannah-Moffatt, 2006); and other imposed practices of the self. One commentary witnessed on the subject of prisoners, for example, included the conviction that: 'we must get learners to manage their own learning...the future lies in technology, in self-learning'). As with the analysis of working life to follow, some of these practices are welcomed by the individuals subject to them (although others are not), and some work to transform lives (and institutions). The main argument of this chapter is that there is a new form of power at work that requires critical scrutiny.

13. There may be more than we have observed to date. Officers at some apparently high-performing prisons, for example, delighted in recounting the flaws in their performance and their skills in 'massaging the figures'.
14. Governors trained during the late 1980s and onwards, whose background and expectations included a 'robust management' style and less emphasis on social work than formerly (see Liebling, assisted by Arnold, 2004).
15. Between 16 and 42 per cent of staff agreed that they trusted their senior managers 'very much' or 'quite a lot' (see Liebling, assisted by Arnold, 2004). In the suicide prevention study in 12 prisons, 2–56 per cent of staff 'agreed' or 'strongly agreed' that 'I trust the governor grades in this prison'. The average was 16 per cent in 2002 and 18 per cent in 2004 (Liebling *et al.*, 2005).
16. We need to distinguish here between interpersonal and organizational trust, and the use of 'formal distrust' mechanisms of accountability (see Braithwaite, 2002).

References

Abernethy, J. (1996) 'The Methodology of Death: Re-Examining the Deterrence Rational', *Columbia Human Rights Law Review* 27: 379–428.
Adams, R. M. (1996) 'The Concept of a Divine Command', in D. Z. Phillips (ed.) *Religion and Morality*, pp. 59–80. New York: St. Martin's Press.
Adorno, T. W. (1964–1965/2006) *History and Freedom: Lectures 1964–1965*. Cambridge: Polity Press.
Adorno, T. W., Frenkel-Brunswik, E., Levinson, D. J. and Sanford, R. N. (1950) *The Authoritarian Personality (Studies in Prejudice)*. New York: Harper & Row.
Agamben, G. (1998) *Homo Sacer: Sovereign Power and Bare Life*. Stanford, CA: Stanford Univeristy Press.
Agamben, G. (1999) *Remnants of Auschwitz: The Witness and the Archive*. New York: Zone.
Agamben, G. (2005) *State of Exception*. Chicago and London: The University of Chicago Press.
Ajemian, R. (13 March 1989) 'Scandals: The Looting of Greece'. *Time* magazine. Available at: <http://www.time.com/time/magazine/article/0,9171,957221-1,00.html>.
Alatas, S. H. (1990) *Corruption: Its Nature, Causes and Functions*. Aldershot: Avebury.
Alexander, J. and Jakobs, R. (1998) 'Mass Communication, Ritual and Civil Society', in T. Liebes and J. Curran (eds) *Media, Ritual and Identity*, pp. 23–42. London: Routledge.
Allen, M. (2006) 'Hegel between Non-domination and Expressive Freedom: Capabilities, Perspectives, Democracy', *Philosophy & Social Criticism* 32(4): 493–512.
Almeida, A. and Wagner, B. (1991) *Violência Contra Crianças e Adolescentes em Conflitos de Terra Do Brasil (1980–1991) Vol. 1 and 2*. Brasília: Ministério da Ação Social/CBIA.
Altheide, D. L. (1992) 'Gonzo Justice', *Symbolic Interaction* 15(1): 69–86.
Alves, M. H. M. (1985) *State and Oppression in Military Brazil*. Austin, TX: University of Texas Press.
Alvim, R. (Coordinator) (1991) *Da Violência Contra o 'Menor' ao Extermínio de Crianças e Adolescentes*. Rio de Janeiro (RJ): NEPI-CBIA.
Amnesty International (1990) *Brazil: Torture and Extrajudicial Execution in Urban Brazil*.
Amnesty International (1992) *Brazil, Impunity and the Law: The Killing of Street Children in Rio de Janeiro State*.
Amnesty International (2008) 'Greece: Failing System of Police Accountability'. Available at: <http://www.amnesty.org/en/for-media/press-releases/greece-failing-system-police-accountability-20081209>.
Amnesty International (September 1990) *FOCUS: Child Victims of Killing and Cruelty*.

Amnesty International and the International Helsinki Federation for Human Rights (2002) 'Greece: In the Shadow of Impunity: Ill Treatment and the Misuse of Firearms'. London: AI Index EU 25/022/2002. Available at: <http://www.amnesty.org/en/library/asset/EUR25/022/2002/en/dom-EUR250222002en.pdf>.

ANA (Athens News Agency) (1994) 'Cement Case: PASOK Favours Indicting Former PM, Ministers', 6 September. Available at: <http://www.hri.org/news/greek/ana/1994/94-09-06.ana.txt>.

ANA (Athens News Agency) (1995) 'Parliament Votes to Drop Charges against Mitsotakis, in Move that Signals "Clear Break with the Past"', 17 January. Available at: <http://www.hri.org/news/greek/ana/1995/95-01-17.ana.txt>.

ANA (Athens News Agency) (2001) 'Reppas Says Securities Probe was Politically Motivated', 14 September. Available at: < http://www.hri.org/news/greek/ana/2001/01-09-14.ana.html>.

ANA (Athens News Agency) (2003) 'Main Opposition Slams Government Record on Economy, Corruption', 1 August. Available at: <http://www.hri.org/news/greek/ana/2003/03-08-01.ana.html#05>.

Anderson, C. J. and Tverdova, Y. V. (2003) 'Corruption, Political Allegiances, and Attitudes towards Government in Contemporary Democracies', *American Journal of Political Science* 47(1): 91–109.

Anderson, D. (1995) *Crime and the Politics of Hysteria*. New York: Times Books.

Anechiarico, F. and Jacobs, J. B. (1996) *The Pursuit of Absolute Integrity: How Corruption Control Makes Government Ineffective*. Chicago, IL: University of Chicago Press.

Archer, M. S. (2000) *Being Human: The Problem of Agency*. Cambridge: Cambridge University Press.

Arendt, H. (1958) *The Human Condition: A Study of the Central Dilemmas Facing Modern Man*. New York: Doubleday Anchor Books.

Arendt, H. (1958/1998) *The Human Condition* (2nd edn). Chicago, IL: University of Chicago Press.

Arendt, H. (1963/1990) *On Revolution*. London: Penguin.

Arendt, H. (1964) *Eichmann in Jerusalem: A Report on the Banality of Evil*. New York: Viking Press.

Arendt, H. (1977) *The Life of the Mind, One/Thinking*. New York: Harcourt Brace Jovanovich.

Arendt, H. (1982) *Lectures on Kant's Political Philosophy* (edited and with an interpretive essay by R. Beiner). Chicago, IL: The University of Chicago Press.

Armitage (2000) *Paul Virilio: From Modernism to Hypermodernism and Beyond*. London: Sage.

Arnason, J. P. (1996) 'Canetti's Counter-image of Society', *Thesis Eleven* 45(1): 86–115.

Askonas, P. and Frowen, S. F. (eds) (1997) *Welfare and Values: Challenging the Culture of Unconcern*. Basingstoke: Macmillan.

Assman, J. (1996) 'The Mosaic Distinction: Israel, Egypt, and the Invention of Paganism', *Representations* 56(Fall): 48–67.

Ayittey, G. B. (1992) *Africa Betrayed*. New York: St Martin's Press.

Babb, S. (1996) 'A True System of Finance: Frame Resonance in the U.S. Labor Movement, 1866–1896', *American Sociological Review* 61(6): 1033–1052.

Badiou, A. (2003) *St Paul: The Foundations of Universalism*. Stanford, CA: Stanford University Press.
Bakhtin, M. (1981) *The Dialogic Imagination: Four Essays*. Austin, TX: University of Texas Press.
Banfield, E. C. (1958) *The Moral Basis of a Backward Society*. Glencoe, IL: Free Press.
Barbalet, J. (2001) *Emotions, Social Theory and Social Structure: A Macrosociological Approach*. Cambridge: Cambridge University Press.
Barker, R. (2001) *Legitimating Identities: The Self-Presentation of Rulers and Subjects*. Cambridge: Cambridge University Press.
Barker, R. (2003) 'Legitimacy, Legitimation, and the European Union: What Crisis?', in P. Craig and R. Rawlings (eds) *Law and Administration*, pp. 157–174. Oxford: Oxford University Press.
Barnett, K. (2003) *Culture and Democracy. Media, Space and Representation*. Edinburgh: Edinburgh University Press.
Barry, A., Osborne, T. and Rose, N. (eds) (1996) *Foucault and Political Reason*. London: UCL Press.
Barry, B. (2005) *Why Social Justice Matters*. Cambridge: Polity Press.
Barthes, R. (2000) *Camera Lucida*. London: Vintage.
Bata, M. and Bergesen, A. J. (2002) 'Global Inequality: An Introduction', *Journal of World Systems Research* 3(1): 2–6.
Baudler, G. (1992) *God and Violence: The Christian Experience of God in Dialogue with Myths and Other Religions*. Springfield, IL: Templegate Publishers.
Baudrillard, J. (1983) *Simulations*. New York: Semiotext(e).
Baudrillard, J. (1994) *The Gulf War Did Not Take Place*. Sydney: Powerful Publications.
Baudrillard, J. (1988) *Selected Writings* (edited by M. Poster). Cambridge: Polity Press.
Baudrillard, J. (2001) 'The Mind of Terrorism', *Le Monde*. 2 November 2001.
Baudrillard, J. (2002) *The Spirit of Terrorism*. London and New York: Verso.
Bauman, Z. (1989) *Modernity and the Holocaust*. Cambridge: Polity Press.
Bauman, Z. (2003) *Liquid Love: On the Frailty of Human Bonds*. Cambridge: Polity Press.
BBC News (2008) 'Greek Minister Quits over Scandal', 23 October. Available at: <http://news.bbc.co.uk/1/hi/world/europe/7686934.stm>.
Beck, U. (2006) *The Cosmopolitan Vision*. Cambridge: Polity Press.
Beck, U. and Sznaider N. (2006) 'Unpacking Cosmopolitanism for the Social Sciences: A Research Agenda', *British Journal of Sociology* 57(1): 1–23.
Beck, U., Giddens, A. and Lash, S. (1994) *Reflexive Modernization*. Cambridge: Polity Press.
Beckett, K. (1997) *Making Crime Pay*. New York: Oxford University Press.
Beckett, K. and Sasson, T. (2000) *The Politics of Injustice: Crime and Punishment in America*. Thousand Oaks, CA: Pine Forge Press.
Bedau, H. (1982) *The Death Penalty in America*. New York: Oxford University Press.
Beetham, D. (1991) *The Legitimation of Power*. London: Macmillan.
Beetham, D. and Lord, C. (1998) *Legitimacy in the European Union*. London: Addison Wesley and Longman.
Bellow, A. (2003) *In Praise of Nepotism: A Natural History*. New York: Doubleday.
Benford, R. and Snow, D. (2000) 'Framing Processes and Social Movements: An Overview and Assessment', *Annual Review of Sociology* 26(1): 611–639.

Benhabib, S. (1988) 'Judgment and the Moral Foundations of Politics in Arendt's Thought', *Political Theory* 16(1): 29–51.
Bergen, B. J. (1998) *The Banality of Evil: Hannah Arendt and 'The Final Solution'*. Lanham, MD: Rowman and Littlefield Publishers.
Berkowitz, W. (2002) 'Death Row Unplugged', *Working for Change* 10 (February): A1.
Bernstein, J. M. (2001) *Adorno: Disenchantment and Ethics*. Cambridge: Cambridge University Press.
Bhabha, H. K. (1994) *The Location of Culture*. London and New York: Routledge.
Birch, A. H. (1984) 'Overload, Ungovernability and Delegitimation: The Theories and the British Case', *British Journal of Political Science* 14(2): 135–160.
Bloch, E. (1961/1987) *Natural Law and Human Dignity*. Cambridge, MA: MIT Press.
Blok, A. (2001) *Honour and Violence*. Cambridge: Polity Press.
Boltanski, L. (1999) *Distant Suffering: Politics, Morality and the Media*. Cambridge: Cambridge University Press.
Borradori, G. (2003) *Philosophy in a Time of Terror: Dialogues with Jürgen Habermas and Jacques Derrida*. Chicago, IL: University of Chicago Press.
Bottoms, A. E. (1995) 'The Philosophy and Politics of Punishment and Sentencing', in C. Clarkson and R. Morgan (eds) *The Politics of Sentencing Reform*, pp. 17–49. Oxford: Clarendon Press.
Bottoms, A. E. and Wiles, P. (1996) 'Crime and Insecurity in the City', in C. Fijnaut, J. Goethals, T. Peters and L. Walgrave (eds) *Changes in Society, Crime and Criminal Justice in Europe: A Challenge for Criminological Education and Research*, pp. 1–38. Belgium: Kluwer Law.
Bourdieu, P. (1991) *Language & Symbolic Power*. Cambridge: Polity Press.
Bourdieu, P. (2000/2008) *Pascalian Meditations*. Cambridge: Polity Press.
Bourdieu, P. and Wacquant, L. (1992) *An Invitation to Reflexive Sociology*. Cambridge: Polity Press.
Bourdieu, P. and Wacquant, L. (1999) 'On the Cunning of Imperialist Reason', *Theory, Culture & Society* 16(1): 41–58.
Bowers, W. (1984) *Legal Homicide*. Boston, MA: Northeastern University Press.
Bowman, L. (2002) 'Web Rights Break into Prisons', *CNET News*, 16 December.
Brabant, M. (2008) 'Rebellion Deeply Embedded in Greece', *BBC News*, 9 December. Available at: <http://news.bbc.co.uk/1/hi/world/europe/7771628.stm>.
Braithwaite, J. (2002) *Restorative Justice and Responsive Regulation*. New York: Oxford University Press.
Bratsis, P. (2002) 'Unthinking the State: Reification, Ideology, and the State as a Social Fact', in S. Aronowitz and P. Bratsis (eds) *Paradigm Lost: State Theory Reconsidered*, pp. 247–267. Minneapolis, MN: University of Minnesota Press.
Bratsis, P. (2003) 'Corrupt Compared to What? Greece, Capitalist Interests, and the Specular Purity of the State', Discussion Paper 8. London: Hellenic Observatory. Available at: <http://www.lse.ac.uk/collections/hellenicObservatory/pdf/DiscussionPapers/Bratsis-8.pdf>.
Brighenti, A. M. (2006) 'Did We Really Get Rid of Commands? Thoughts on a Theme by Elias Canetti', *Law & Critique* 17(1): 47–71.
Brighenti, A. M. (2007) 'Visibility: A Category for the Social Sciences', *Current Sociology* 55(3): 323–342.
Brighenti, A. M. (2008) 'Revolution and Diavolution. What is the difference?' *Critical Sociology* 34(6): 787–802.

Brookfield, S. (2005) *The Power of Critical Theory: Liberating Adult Learning and Teaching*. San Francisco, CA: Jossey-Bass/John Wiley.

Burawoy, M. (1979) *Manufacturing Consent: Changes in the Labor Process under Monopoly Capitalism*. Chicago, IL: University of Chicago Press.

Burchell, G. I. (1996) 'Liberal Government and Techniques of the Self', in A. Barry, T. Osborne and N. Rose (eds) *Foucault and Political Reason*, pp. 19–36. London: UCL Press.

Butler, J. (1997) *The Psychic Life of Power: Theories in Subjection*. Stanford, CA: Stanford University Press.

Butler, J. (2004) *Precarious Life: The Powers of Mourning and Violence*. London: Verso.

Cain, M. (1973) *Society and the Policeman's Role*. London: Routledge.

Caldeira, T. (2000) *City of Walls*. Berkeley, CA: University of California Press.

Calligaris, C. (1991) *Hello Brasil! Notas de um psicanalista europeu viajando ao Brasil*. São Paulo: Escuta.

Calotychos, V. (2003) *A Cultural Poetics of Modern Greece*. Oxford and New York: Berg.

Campbell, H. and Heyman, J. (2007) 'Slantwise: Beyond Domination and Resistance on the Border', *Journal of Contemporary Ethnography* 36(1): 3–30.

Campbell, J. K. (1963) 'The Kindred in a Greek Mountain Community', in J. Pitt-Rivers (ed.) *Mediterranean Countrymen: Essays in the Social Anthropology of the Mediterranean*, pp. 73–96. Paris: Mouton & Co.

Camus, A. (1961) *Resistance, Rebellion and Death*. London: Hamish Hamilton.

Canetti, E. (1960/1978) *Crowds and Power*. New York: Seabury Press.

Canetti, E. (1979) *The Conscience of Words*. New York: Seabury Press.

Caputo, J. D. (1997) *The Prayers and Tears of Jacques Derrida: Religion Without Religion*. Bloomington, IN: Indiana University Press.

Carlen, P. (2001) 'Death and the Triumph of Governance? Lessons from the Scottish Women's Prison', *Punishment and Society* 3(4): 459–472.

Carlen, P. (2002) 'Governing the Governors: Telling Tales of Managers, Mandarins and Mavericks', *Criminal Justice* 2(1): 27–49.

Castells, M. (1996) *The Rise of the Network Society*. London: Blackwell.

Castells, M. (1997) *The Power of Identity*. London: Blackwell.

Cavender, G. and Bond-Maupic, L. (1993) 'Fear and Loathing on Reality Television: An Analysis of America's Most Wanted and Unsolved Mysteries', *Sociological Inquiry* 63: 305–317.

Centre for Democracy and Development-Ghana (2000) *The Ghana Governance and Corruption Survey: Evidence from Households, Enterprises and Public Officials*. Accra: Ghana Anti-Corruption Coalition.

Chan, J. B. L. (1996) 'Changing Police Culture', *British Journal of Criminology* 36(1): 109–134.

Chan, J. B. L. (1997) *Changing Police Culture: Policing in a Multicultural Society*. Cambridge: Cambridge University Press.

Cheliotis, L. and Xenakis, S. (forthcoming, 2010) 'Crime and Punishment in Contemporary Greece: Introduction', in L. Cheliotis and S. Xenakis (eds) *Crime and Punishment in Contemporary Greece: International Comparative Perspectives*. Oxford: Peter Lang AG.

Cheliotis, L. K. (2006) 'How Iron is the Iron Cage of New Penology? The Role of Human Agency in the Implementation of Criminal Justice Policy', *Punishment and Society* 8(3): 313–340.

Cheliotis, L. K. (2008) *Governing through the Looking-Glass: Perception, Morality and Neoliberal Penality*. Unpublished Ph.D. Thesis, University of Cambridge.

Cheliotis, L. K. (forthcoming, 2010) 'The Sociospatial Mechanics of Domination: Beyond the "Exclusion/Inclusion" Dualism', *Law & Critique* 21(2).

Chermack, S. (1994) 'Crime in the News Media: A Refined Understanding of How Crime Becomes News', in G. Barak (ed.) *Media, Process, and the Social Construction of Crime*, pp. 69–94. New York: Garland Publishing.

Chomsky, N. (2003) *Power and Terror: Post 9/11 Talks and Interviews*. New York: Seven Stories Press.

Chouliaraki, L. (2006) *The Spectatorship of Suffering*. London: Sage.

Clooney, F. (2000/2004). *Hindu God, Christian God: How Reason Helps Break Down the Boundaries between Religions*. Oxford: Oxford University Press.

Cohen, S. (2001) *States of Denial: Knowing About Atrocities and Suffering*. Cambridge: Polity Press.

Coicaud, J. M. (2002) *Legitimacy and Politics: A Contribution to the Study of Political Right and Political Responsibility* (Translated by D. A. Curtis). Cambridge: Cambridge University Press.

Collinson, D. (2000) 'Strategies of Resistance: Power, Knowledge and Subjectivity in the Workplace', in K. Grint (ed.) *Work and Society: A Reader*, pp. 163–198. Cambridge: Polity Press.

Commonwealth Human Rights Initiative Report (CHRI Report, 2005) *Police Accountability: Too Important to Neglect, Too Urgent to Delay*). Available at: <http://www.humanrightsinitiative.org/publications/chogm/chogm_2005/chogm_2005_full_report.pdf> (accessed 19 May 2007).

Connell, R. (2007) *Southern Theory: The Global Dynamics of Knowledge in Social Science*. Cambridge: Polity Press.

Corner, J. (1999) *Critical Ideas in Television Studies*. Oxford: Oxford University Press.

Coser, L. (1969) 'The Visibility of Evil', *Journal of Social Issues* 25(1): 101–109.

Coyne, R. and Entzeroth, L. (1994) *Capital Punishment and the Judicial Process*. Durham, NC: Carolina Academic Press.

Craib, I. (1990) *Psychoanalysis and Social Theory: The Limits of Sociology*. Amherst, MA: The University of Massachusetts Press.

Crook, R. C. (1987) 'Legitimacy, Authority and the Transfer of Power in Ghana', *Political Studies* 35(4): 552–572.

Cross, F. M. (1973) *Cannanite Myth and Hebrew Epic: Essays on the History of the Religion of Israel*. Cambridge: Cambridge University Press.

D'Hondt, J. (1988) *Hegel in His Time: Berlin, 1818–1831*. New York: Broadview Press.

Dancy, J. (2004) *Ethics without Principles*. Oxford: Oxford University Press.

Danopoulos, C. P. and Znidaric, B. (2007) 'Informal Economy, Tax Evasion, and Poverty in a Democratic Setting: Greece', *Mediterranean Quarterly* 18(2): 67–84.

Das, V. and Kleinman, A. (2001) 'Introduction', in V. Das, A. Kleinman, M. Ramphele, M. Lock and P. Reynolds (eds) *Remaking a World: Violence, Social Suffering and Recovery*, pp. 1–18. Berkeley, CA: University of California Press.

Dayan, D. (2001) 'The Peculiar Public of Television', *Media, Culture & Society* 23(6): 743–765.
de Certeau, M. (1984) *The Practice of Everyday Life*. Berkeley, CA: University of California Press.
Delanty, G. (2000) *Modernity and Postmodernity*. London: Sage.
Deleuze, G. (1987) 'Qu'est-ce qu'un acte de création?'. Conférence fondation Femis, Paris.
Deleuze, G. and Félix, G. (1975) *Kafka. Pour une littérature mineure*. Paris: Les Éditions de Minuit.
Der Spiegel (2008) 'Greece Blocking NATO Expansion: Which Macedonia was Alexander the Great From?', 3 March. Available at: <http://www.spiegel.de/international/world/0,1518,544167,00.html> (accessed 26 October 2008).
Derrida, J. (1991) *Given Time, 1: Counterfeit Money*. Chicago, IL: University of Chicago Press.
Derrida, J. (2004) 'Terror, Religion and the New Politics: Dialogue with Richard Kearney', in R. Kearney (ed.) *Debates in Continental Philosophy*, pp. 3–14. New York: Fordham University Press.
Di Palma, G. (1991) 'Legitimation from the Top to Civil Society: Politico-Cultural Change in Eastern Europe', *World Politics* 44(1): 49–80.
Diamandouros, P. N. (1994) 'Cultural Dualism and Political Change in Postauthoritarian Greece', Working Paper no. 50. Madrid: Centro des Estudios Avanzados en Ciencias Sociales. Available at: <http://www.march.es/ceacs/ingles/Publicaciones/working/archivos/1994_50.pdf>.
Diamandouros, P. N. (1997) 'Greek Politics and Society in the 1990s', in G. T. Allison and K. Nicolaïdis (eds) *The Greek Paradox: Promise vs. Performance*, pp. 23–38. Cambridge, MA: MIT Press.
Dieter, R. (1998) *The Death Penalty in Black and White: Who Lives, Who Dies, Who Decides*. Report for the Death Penalty Information Center. Available at <http://www.deathpenaltyinfo.org/article.php?scid=45&did=539>.
Dillard, A. (1999) *For the Time Being*. New York: Knopf.
Dimenstein, G. (1991) *Brazil: War on Children* (translated by C. Whitehouse). London: Latin America Bureau.
Dixon, D. (1997) *Law in Policing: Legal Regulation and Police Practices*. Oxford: Clarendon Press.
Dooley, M. (2003) 'A Master of the Middle Way: Richard Kearney on God, Evil and Aliens', *Religion in the Arts* 7(3): 329–339.
Douglas, M. (1970/2007) *Natural Symbols: Explorations in Cosmology*. London and New York: Routledge.
Dozeman, T. B. (1996) *God at War: Power in the Exodus Tradition*. New York: Oxford University Press.
Dryzek, J. S. (1995) 'Critical Theory as a Research Programme', in S. K. White (ed.) *The Cambridge Companion to Habermas*, pp. 97–119. Cambridge: Cambridge University Press.
Duffee, D. (1974) 'The Correction Officer Subculture and Organizational Change', *Journal of Research in Crime and Delinquency* 11(2): 155–171.
Durkheim, E. (1924/1974) *Sociology and Philosophy*. New York: The Free Press.
Dye, T. (1986) *Who's Running America?* (4th edn). Englewoods, co: Prentice-Hall.
Economides, S. (2005) 'The Europeanisation of Greek Foreign Policy', *West European Politics* 28(2): 471–491.

Edelman, M. (1971) *Politics as Symbolic Action*. New York: Academic Press.
Elbaz, R. (2003) 'On Canetti's Social Theory', *Neohelicon* 30(2): 133–144.
Elster, J. (1989) *The Cement of Society: A Study of Social Order*. Cambridge: Cambridge University Press.
Entman, R. (1993) 'Framing: Toward a Clarification of a Fractured Paradigm', *Journal of Communication* 43(4): 51–58.
ERA (The Hellenic Radio) (2008) 'Dramatic Developments in the Siemens Case', News in English, *The Hellenic Radio*, 3 July. Available at: < http://www.hri.org/cgi-bin/brief?/news/greek/eraen//2008/08-07-03_1.eraen.html>.
Erikson, R. S. (1976) 'The Relationship between Public Opinion and State Policy: A New Look at Some Forgotten Data', *American Journal of Political Science* 20(1): 25–36.
Fabian, A. (2000) *The Unvarnished Truth: Personal Narratives in Nineteenth-Century America*. Berkeley, CA: University of California Press.
Falk, R. (2003) *The Great Terror War*. New York: Olive Branch Press.
Featherstone, K. (1998) '"Europeanisation" and the Centre Periphery: The Case of Greece in the 1990s', *South European Politics and Society* 3(1): 23–39.
Featherstone, M. (2008) *Tocqueville's Virus: Utopia and Dystopia in Western Social and Political Thought*. New York: Routledge.
Feeley, M. and Simon, J. (1992) 'The New Penology: Notes on the Emerging Strategy of Corrections and its Implications', *Criminology* 30(4): 449–474.
Feeley, M and Simon, J (1994) 'Actuarial Justice: The Emerging New Criminal Law', in D. Nelken (ed.) *The Futures of Criminology*, pp. 173–201. London: Sage.
Filho, M. S., Azevedo, E. and Costa Pinto, L. (1991) 'Infância de raiva, dor e sangue', *Veja* 29 May: 34–45.
Firth, R. (1973) *Symbols: Public and Private*. London: George Allen & Unwin.
Flevotomou, M. and Matsaganis, M. (2007) 'Estimating Tax Evasion in Greece', Deliverable 2.6, Accurate Income Measurement for the Assessment of Public Policies, Research Project funded by the European Commission 6th Framework Programme. Available at: <http://www.iser.essex.ac.uk/msu/emod/aim-ap/deliverables/AIM-AP2.6.pdf>.
Flyvberg, B. (2001) *Making Social Science Matter*. Cambridge: Cambridge University Press.
Fokas, E. (2000) 'Greek Orthodoxy and European Identity', Paper presented at the Second Graduate Student Workshop, Kokkalis Programme, Harvard University. Available at: <http://www.hks.harvard.edu/kokkalis/GSW2/Fokas.PDF>.
Forester, J. (1993) *Critical Theory, Public Policy and Planning Practice: Toward a Critical Pragmatism*. New York: State University of New York Press.
Fotiadis, A. (2007) 'Greece: More Poverty than Meets the Eye', *Inter Press Service News Agency*, 13 November. Available at: <http://ipsnews.net/news.asp?idnews=40033>.
Foucault, M. (1971) 'Nietzsche, la genealogie, l'histoire', *Dits et Écrits 1954–1988*, Vol. 1. Paris: Gallimard, 2001.
Foucault, M. (1975) *Surveiller et punir. Naissance de la prison*. Paris: Gallimard.
Foucault, M. (1976) *Histoire de la sexualité Vol. 1. La volonté de savoir*. Paris: Gallimard.
Foucault, M. (1977) *Discipline and Punish* (translated by A. Sheridan). New York: Vintage.

Foucault, M. (1982) 'The Subject of Power', in H. L. Dreyfus and P. Rabinow (eds) *Michel Foucault: Beyond Structuralism and Hermeneutics*, pp. 208–226. Chicago, IL: University of Chicago Press.
Foucault, M. (1982) 'The Subject and Power', in H. L. Dreyfus and P. Rabinow (eds) *Michel Foucault: Beyond Structuralism and Hermeneutics*, pp. 208–226. Brighton: Harvester Press.
Foucault, M. (1991/1978) 'Governmentality', in G. Burchell, C. Gordon and P. Miller (eds) *The Foucault Effect: Studies in the Governmentality*, pp. 87–104. London: Harvester Wheatsheaf.
Foucault, M. (2004) *Sécurité, Territoire, Population. Cours au Collège de France, 1977–1978* (edited by F. Ewald, A. Fontana and M. Senellart). Paris: Hautes Etudes, Gallimard, le Seuil.
Freire, G. (1986) *The Masters and the Slaves*. Berkeley and Los Angeles, CA: University of California Press.
Freud, S. (1914/1986) 'On Narcissism: An Introduction', in A. O. Morrison (ed.) *Essential Papers on Narcissism*, pp. 17–43. New York: New York University Press.
Freud, S. (1930/2002) *Civilisation and Its Discontents*. London: Penguin.
Fromm, E. (1941/1994) *Escape from Freedom*. New York: Henry Holt & Company.
Fromm, E. (1949/1986) *Man for Himself*. London: Ark.
Fromm, E. (1955/1992) *The Dogma of Christ and Other Essays on Religion, Psychology, and Culture*. New York: Henry Holt.
Fromm, E. (1955/2006) *The Sane Society*. London and New York: Routledge.
Fromm, E. (1956/2000) *The Art of Loving*. New York: Harper Perennial.
Fromm, E. (1962/2006) *Beyond the Chains of Illusion: My Encounter with Marx and Freud*. New York: Continuum.
Fromm, E. (1964) *The Heart of Man: Its Genius for Good and Evil*. New York: Harper & Row.
Fromm, E. (1968) *The Revolution of Hope: Toward a Humanised Technology*. New York, Evanston, and London: Harper & Row.
Fromm, E. (1970) *The Crisis of Psychoanalysis: Essays on Freud, Marx, and Social Psychology*. New York: Holt, Rinehart & Winston.
Fromm, E. (1973/1984) *The Anatomy of Human Destructiveness*. Harmondsworth: Penguin.
Fromm, E. (1976/1997) *To Have or to Be?* London and New York: Continuum.
Fromm, E. (1981) *On Disobedience and Other Essays*. New York: The Seabury Press.
Fromm, E. (1995) *The Essential Fromm: Life between Having and Being* (edited by R. Funk). New York: Continuum.
Fromm, E. and Maccoby, M. (1970) *Social Character in a Mexican Village: A Sociopsychoanalytic Study*. Englewood Cliffs, NJ: Prentice-Hall.
Frondizi, R. (1963) *What is Value? An Introduction to Axiology*. Lasalle, IL: Open Court.
Fukuyama, F. (2002) 'Social Capital and Development: The Coming Agenda', *SAIS Review* 22(1): 23–37.
Funk, R. (1982) *Erich Fromm: The Courage to be Human*. New York: Continuum.
Gadamer, H. G. (1975) *Truth and Method*. London: Sheed & Ward.
Gallie, D. and Paugman, S. (2002) 'Social Precarity and Social Integration'. Report for the European Commission, Directorate-General Empoyment, on Eurobarometer 56.1. Available at: <http://ec.europa.eu/public_opinion/archives/ebs/ebs_162_en.pdf>.

Gandy, O. (2001) 'Epilogue – Framing at the Horizon: A Retrospective Assessment', in S. Reese, O. Gandy and A. Grant (eds) *Framing Public Life: Perspectives on Media and Our Understanding of the Social World*, pp. 355–378. London: Lawrence Erlbaum Associates.

Gangas, S. (2007) 'Social Ethics and Logic: Rethinking Durkheim through Hegel', *Journal of Classical Sociology* 7(3): 315–338.

Garland, D. (1990) *Punishment and Modern Society: A Study in Social Theory*. Chicago, IL: University of Chicago Press.

Garland, D. (1996) 'The Limits of the Sovereign State: Strategies of Crime Control in Contemporary Society', *British Journal of Criminology* 36(4): 445–471.

Garland, D. (1997) '"Governmentality" and the Problem of Crime: Foucault, Criminology, Sociology', *Theoretical Criminology* 1(2): 173–214.

Garland, D. (2001) *The Culture of Control*. Chicago, IL: University of Chicago Press.

Garland, D. (2002) 'The Cultural Uses of Capital Punishment', *Punishment and Society* 4(4): 459–487.

Garland, D. and Sparks, R. (eds) (2000) *Criminology and Social Theory*. Oxford: Clarendon Press.

Gatrell, V. A. C. (1994) *The Hanging Tree: Execution and the English People, 1770–1868*. Oxford: Oxford University Press.

Gaucher, B. (ed.) (2002) *Writing as Resistance: The Journal of Prisoners on Prisons Anthology: (1988–2002)*. Toronto: Canadian Scholars' Press.

Giddens, A. (1981) *A Contemporary Critique of Historical Materialism*. London: Macmillan.

Giddens, A. (1990) *The Consequences of Modernity*. Cambridge: Polity Press.

Giddens, A. (1991) *Modernity and Self-Identity: Self and Society in the Late Modern Age*. Stanford, CA: Stanford University Press.

Gill, S. (2008) *Power and Resistance in the New World Order*. Basingstoke and New York: Palgrave Macmillan.

Gilson, G. (2006) 'Bribery Plot Curdles', *Athens News*, 15 December. Available at: <http://www.athensnews.gr/athweb/nathens.prnt_article?e=C&f=13200&t=01&m=A07&aa=1>.

Gilson, G. (2007) 'Scandal Allegations Besiege ND', *Athens News*, 28 December. Available at: <http://www.athensnews.gr/athweb/nathens.prnt_article?e=C&f=13267&t=01&m=A03&aa=1>.

Ginzburg, C. (1994) 'Killing a Chinese Mandarin: The Moral Implications of Distance', in O. Hufton (ed.) *Historical Change and Human Rights: The Oxford Amnesty Lectures*. New York: Basic Books. Reprinted in *New Left Review* 208: 107–120.

Girard, R. (1977) *Violence and the Sacred*. Baltimore, MD: Johns Hopkins University Press.

Girling, E. (2004) 'Looking Death in the Face: The Benetton Death Penalty Campaign', *Punishment and Society* 6(3): 271–287.

Glover, J. (1999) *Humanity: A Moral History of the Twentieth Century*. London: Pimlico.

Goffman, E. (1974) *Frame Analysis*. Cambridge: Harvard University Press.

Goldstein, H. (1977) *Policing a Free Society*. Cambridge, MA: Ballinger Publishing Company.

Gourgouris, S. (1996) *Dream Nation: Enlightenment, Colonization and the Institution of Modern Greece*. Stanford, CA: Stanford University Press.

Graça, H. da Silva (2000) '(In)Sueguranca Publica em Timbauba', Timbauba, 30 Marco (unpublished public document).
Graham, G. (1999) *The Internet: A Philosophical Inquiry*. London: Routledge.
Gramsci, A. (1975) *Quaderni del carcere*. Torino: Einaudi.
Greek Embassy Press and Communications Office (2004) 'A News Review from the Embassy of Greece in Washington DC', 10:5. Available at: <http://www.greekembassy.org/embassy/Content/en/Article.aspx?office=3&folder=198&article=13601>.
Greek Embassy Press and Communications Office (2006) 'A News Review from the Embassy of Greece in Washington DC', 12:12. Available at: <http://www.greekembassy.org/embassy/Content/en/Article.aspx?office=3&folder=198&article=19412>.
Greek News (2008) 'Karamanlis over Troubled Waters after Vatopedi Scandal & Financial Crisis', *Greek News*, 27 October. Available at: <http://www.greeknewsonline.com/modules.php?name=News&file=article&sid=9328>.
Green, T. H. (1834/1969) *Prolegomena to Ethics*. New York: Thomas Y. Crowell.
Greisch, J. (2002) 'The Great Game of Life', lecture delivered at Boston College, Spring, 2002.
Grey, C. (2005) *A Very Short, Fairly Interesting and Reasonably Cheap Book about Studying Organisations*. London: Sage.
Griffiths, B. (1995) *River of Compassion: A Christian Commentary on the Bhagavad Gita*. New York: Continuum.
Gross, R. and Muck, T. (eds) (2002) *Buddhists Talk about Jesus, Christians Talk about the Buddha*. New York: Continuum.
Grumley, J. (2005) *Agnes Heller: A Moralist in the Vortex of History*. London: Pluto Press.
Habermas, J. (1981) *Theory of Communicative Action, Vol. Reason and the Rationalization of Society*. Boston, MA: Beacon.
Haines, H. (1992) 'Flawed Executions, the Anti-Death Penalty Movement, and the Politics of Capital Punishment', *Social Problems* 39(2): 125–138.
Haines, H. (1996) *Against Capital Punishment*. Oxford: Oxford University Press.
Hall, S. (1997) *Representation. Cultural Representations and Signifying Practices*. London: Sage.
Haney, C. and Manzolati, J. (1992) 'Television Criminology: Network Illusions of Criminal Justice Realities', in E. Aronson (ed.) *Readings about the Social Animal* (6th edn), pp. 120–131. New York: W.H. Freeman and Co.
Hannerz, U. (1996) *Transnational Connections: Culture, People, Places*. London: Routledge.
Harding, S. (1990) 'Feminism, Science, and the Anti-Enlightenment Critiques', in L. Nicholson (ed.) *Feminism/Postmodernism*. London: Routledge.
Hardt, M. and Negri, A. (2003) 'Globalization and Democracy', in S. Aronowitz and H. Gautney (eds) *Implicating Empire: Globalization and Resistance in the 21st Century World Order*, pp. 109–122. New York: Basic Books.
Harris, E. (1987) *Formal, Transcendental and Dialectical Thinking: Logic and Reality*. Albany, NY: State University of New York Press.
Hegel, G. W. F. (1812/1999) *Hegel's Science of Logic*. New York: Humanity Books.
Heidenheimer, A. (1970) *Political Corruption: Readings in Comparative Analysis*. New York: Holt, Rinehart & Winston.
Heller, A. (1972) 'Towards a Marxist Theory of Value', *Kinesis* 5(1): 7–76.

Heller, A. (1976) *The Theory of Need in Marx*. London: Allison & Busby.
Heller, A. (1984) *A Radical Philosophy*. Oxford: Basil Blackwell.
Hertog, J. and McLeod, D. (2001) 'A Multiperspectival Approach to Framing Analysis: A Field Guide', in S. Reese, O. Gandy and A. Grant (eds) *Framing Public Life: Perspectives on Media and Our Understanding of the Social World*, pp. 139–161. London: Lawrence Erlbaum.
Herz, J. H. (1978) 'Legitimacy: Can We Retrieve it?', *Comparative Politics* 10(3): 317–343.
Herzfeld, M. (1992) *The Social Production of Indifference: Exploring the Symbolic Roots of Western Bureaucracy*. Chicago and London: University of Chicago Press.
Herzfeld, M. (2002) 'Cultural Fundamentalism and the Regimentation of Identity: The Embodiment of Orthodox Values in a Modernist Setting', in U. Hedetoft and M. Hjort (eds) *The Postnational Self: Belonging and Identity*, pp. 198–214. Minneapolis, MN: University of Minnesota Press.
Herzfeld, M. (2004) *The Body Impolitic: Artisans and Artifice in the Global Hierarchy of Value*. Chicago, IL: University of Chicago Press.
Herzfeld, M. (2005) *Cultural Intimacy: Social Poetics in the Nation-State*. London and New York: Routledge.
Hetherington, M. J. (1998) 'The Political Relevance of Political Trust', *American Political Science Review* 92(4): 791–808.
Hills, A. (2008) 'The Dialectic of Police Reform in Nigeria', *Journal of Modern African Studies* 46(2): 215–234.
Hines, C. (2000) *Virtual Ethnography*. London: Sage.
Hirschon, R. (2001) 'Freedom, Solidarity, and Obligation: The Socio-Cultural Context of Greek Politeness', in A. Bayraktaroglu and M. Sifianou (eds) *Linguistic Politeness Across Boundaries*, pp. 17–42. Amsterdam: John Benjamins.
Hirschon, R. (2008) 'Presents, Promises, and Punctuality: Accountability and Obligation in Greek Social Life', in M. Mazower (ed.) *Networks of Power in Modern Greece*, pp. 189–207. London: Hurst & Co.
Hobbes, T. (1651/1946) *Leviathan, or the Forme and Power of a Commonwealth Ecclesiastical and Civil* (edited with an introduction by M. Oakeshott). Oxford: Oxford University Press.
Hodson, R. (1995) 'Worker Resistance: An Underdeveloped Concept in the Sociology of Work', *Economical and Industrial Democracy* 16(1): 79–110.
Höffe, O. (1995) *Political Justice: Foundations for a Critical Philosophy of Law and the State*. Cambridge: Polity Press.
Holdaway, S. (1983) *Inside the British Police: A Force at Work*. Oxford: Basil Blackwell.
Holmes, L. (1993) *The End of Communist Power: Anti-Corruption Campaigns and Legitimation Crisis*. Cambridge: Polity Press.
Holmwood, J. (1999) 'Radical Sociology: What's Left?', in P. Bagguley and J. Hearn (eds) *Transforming Politics: Power and Resistance*, pp. 277–293. Basingstoke: Macmillan.
Holston, J. (1999) 'Spaces of Insurgent Citizenship', in J. Holston (ed.) *Cities and Citizenship*, pp. 155–176. Durham, NC: Duke University Press.
Holston, J. (2000) 'Urban Citizenship and Globalization', in A. J. Scott (ed.) *Global City Regions*, pp. 325–348. New York: Oxford University Press.
Holy Bible (1967) New York: Oxford University Press.

Honneth, A. (1995) *The Fragmented World of the Social: Essays in Social and Political Philosophy* (edited by C. W. Wright). Albany, NY: State University of New York Press.
Hood, C. (1991) 'A Public Management for All Seasons?', *Public Administration* 69(1): 3–19.
Hood, R. (2001) 'Capital Punishment: A Global Perspective', *Punishment and Society* 3(3): 331–354.
Hooghe, L. (1999) 'Images of Europe: Orientations to European Integration amongst Senior Officials of the Commission', *British Journal of Political Science* 29(2): 345–367.
Hoy, D. C. (2004) *Critical Resistance: From Poststructuralism to Post-Critique*. Cambridge, MA: The MIT Press.
Huggins, M. (1997) 'From Bureaucratic Consolidation to Structural Devolution: Police Death Squads in Brazil', *Policing and Society* 7(4): 207–234.
Ifestos, P. (1997) 'Fetishistic Internationalism: Jousting with Unreality in Greece', *Hellenic Studies* 5(2): 65–94.
Ignatieff, M. (1990) *The Needs of Strangers*. London: The Hogarth Press.
Ingarden, R. (1970/1983) *Man and Value*. München/Wien: Philosophia Verlag.
Ingleby, D. (2006) 'Introduction to the Second Edition', in E. Fromm (ed.) (1955/2006) *The Sane Society*, pp. xvi–liii. London and New York: Routledge.
Ioakimidis, P. C. (1999) 'Greece, the European Union, and Southeastern Europe: Past Failures and Future Prospects', in V. Coufoudakis, H. Psomiades and A. Gerolymatos (eds) *Greece and the New Balkans: Challenges and Opportunities*, pp. 169–191. New York: Pella.
Ishaghpour, Y. (1990) *Elias Canetti: Métamorphose et Identité*. Paris: La Différence.
Jackson, J. (1996) *Legal Lynching: Racism, Injustice, and the Death Penalty*. New York: Marlowe and Company.
Jeremiàs, J. (1967) 'The Lord's Prayer in the Light of Recent Research', in J. Jeremiàs (ed.) *The Prayers of Jesus*, pp. 82–107. London: SCM Press.
Jermier, J. M., Knights, D. and Nord, W. R. (eds) (1994) *Resistance and Power in Organizations*. London: Routledge.
Joas, H. (2000) *The Genesis of Values*. Cambridge: Polity Press.
Johnson, R. (1990) *Death Work: A Study of the Modern Execution Process*. Pacific Grove, CA: Brooks/Cole Publishing.
Jones, E. E. and Pittman, T. S. (1982) 'Towards a General Theory of Strategy Self-Presentation', in J. Suls (ed.) *Psychological Perspectives on the Self*, pp. 231–262. Hillsdale, NJ: Erlbaum.
Jones, N., Malesios, C., Iosifides, T. and Sophoulis, C. (2008) 'Social Capital in Greece: Measurement and Comparative Perspectives', *South European Society and Politics* 13(2): 175–193.
Jones, S. (1999) 'Studying the Net: Intricacies and Issues', in S. Jones (ed.) *Doing Internet Research: Critical Issues and Methods for Examining the Net*. London: Sage Publications.
Jornal do Commércio (Recife) (1991) 'Quase 5 mil menores foram assassinados nos últimos 3 anos', 19 June.
Jusdanis, G. (1991) *Belated Modernity and Aesthetic Culture: Inventing National Literature*. Minneapolis and Oxford: University of Minnesota Press.
Jusdanis, G. (2001) *The Necessary Nation*. Princeton and Oxford: Princeton University Press.

Kant, I. (1951) *Critique of Judgment*. New York: Hafner.
Karakatsanis, N. (2000) 'Relying on Stop-Gap Measures: Unemployment in Greece', in N. G. Bermeo (ed.) *Unemployment in Southern Europe: Coping with the Consequences*, pp. 240–262. London: Frank Cass.
Karpathakis, A. (2008) 'The Riots in Greece', *Greek News*, 15 December. Available at: <http://www.greeknewsonline.com/modules.php?name=News&file=article&sid=9572>.
Kathimerini (2008) 'Move for More Openness in Party Funding', *Kathimerini English Language Edition*, 8 July. Available at: <http://www.ekathimerini.com/4dcgi/_w_articles_politics_1_08/07/2008_98380>.
Kaufman-Osborn, T. (2002) *From Noose to Needle: Capital Punishment and the Late Liberal State*. Ann Arbor, MI: The University of Michigan Press.
Kearney, R. (2003) *Strangers, Gods and Monsters*. London and New York: Routledge.
Kellner, D. (1998) *Baudrillard: The New McLuhan?* in Illuminations. Available at: <http://www.uta.edu/huma/illuminations/kell26.htm>.
Kellner, D. (ed.) (1999) *Baudrillard: A Critical Reader*. Oxford: Blackwell.
Kenna, M. E. (1976) 'The Idiom of Family', in J. G. Peristiany (ed.) *Mediterranean Family Structures*, pp. 347–362. Cambridge: Cambridge University Press.
Kierkegaard, S. (1994) *Works of Love*. New York: Harper.
Klandermans, B. (1984) 'Mobilization and Participation: Social-Psychological Expansions of Resource Mobilization Theory', *American Sociological Review* 49(5): 249–268.
Klandermans, B. (1988) 'The Formation and Mobilization of Consensus', in B. Klandermans, H. Kriesi and S. Tarrow (eds) *International Social Movement Research Vol. 1*, pp. 173–196. London: JAI Press.
Klarevas, L. (2005) 'Greeks Bearing Consensus: Suggestions for Increasing Greece's Soft Power in the West', *Mediterranean Quarterly* 16(3): 142–159.
Knights, D. and Vurdubakis, T. (1994) 'Foucault, Power, Resistance and All that', in J. M. Jermier, D. Knights and R. Nord (eds) *Resistance and Power in Organizations*, pp. 167–198. London and New York: Routledge.
Kohut, H. (1986) 'Forms and Transformations of Narcissism', in A. O. Morrison (ed.) *Essential Papers on Narcissism*, pp. 61–87. New York: New York University Press.
Koliopoulos, J. S. and Veremis, T. M. (2004) *Greece: The Modern Sequel*. London: Hurst.
Kopp, K. (2008) 'The Situation in Greece is Out of Control'. Report for Pro-Asyl. Available at: <http://www.proasyl.de/fileadmin/proasyl/fm_redakteure/Asyl_in_Europa/Griechenland/Out_of_contol_Eng_END.pdf>.
Korsgaard, C. (2004) 'The Dependence of Value on Humanity', in J. Raz (ed.) *The Practice of Value*, pp. 63–85. Oxford: Clarendon Press.
Kraft, V. (1951/1981) *Foundations for a Scientific Analysis of Value*. Dordrecht: D. Reidel Publishing Company.
Kristeva, J. (2001) *Hannah Arendt*. New York: Columbia University Press.
LaNuez, D. and Jermier, J. M. (1994) 'Sabotage by Managers and Technocrats: Neglected Patterns of Resistance at Work', in J. M. Jermier, D. Knights and W. R. Nord (eds) *Resistance and Power in Organizations*, pp. 219–251. London and New York: Routledge.

Lash, S. (1990) *Sociology of Postmodernism*. London: Routledge.
Lash, S. (2001) *Critique of Information*. London: Sage.
Lavdas, K. (2005) 'Interest Groups in Disjointed Corporatism: Social Dialogue in Greece and European "Competitive Corporatism"', *West European Politics* 28(2): 297–316.
Lawrence, C. M. (2007) *Blood and Oranges: Immigrant Labor and European Markets in Rural Greece*. New York and Oxford: Berghan Books.
Levinas, E. (1986) 'Dialogue with Emmanuel Levinas', in R. Kearney (ed.) *Face to Face with Levinas*, pp. 13–34. Albany, NY: SUNY Press.
Levinas, E. (1988) 'The Paradox of Morality: An Interview with Emmanuel Levinas', in R. Bernasconi and D. Wood (eds) *The Provocation of Levinas*, pp. 168–180. London: Routledge.
Levinas, E. (1989) 'Ethics as First Philosophy', in S. Hand (ed.) *The Levinas Reader*, pp. 75–87. Oxford: Blackwell.
Lévi-Strauss, C. (1952) *Race and History*. Paris: Unesco.
Levitas, R. and Sargisson, L. (2003) 'Utopia in Dark Times: Optimism/Pessimism and Utopia/Dystopia', in R. Baccolini and T. Moylan (eds) *Dark Horizons: Science Fiction and the Dystopian Imagination*, pp. 13–28. New York and London: Routledge.
Lewis, P. G. (ed.) (1984) 'Legitimation and Political Crises: East European Developments in Post-Stalin Period', *Eastern Europe: Political Crisis and Legitimation*, pp. 1–41. Sydney: Croom Helm.
Liebling, A. (2001) 'Whose Side Are We On? Theory, Practice, and Allegiances in Prisons Research', in E. Stanko and A. Liebling (eds) 'Methodological Dilemmas of Research', *British Journal of Criminology* (Special Issue) 41(3): 472–484.
Liebling, A., assisted by Arnold, H. (2004) *Prisons and their Moral Performance: A Study of Values, Quality and Prison Life*. Oxford: Clarendon Press.
Liebling, A., Tait, S., Durie, L. and Stiles, A., assisted by Harvey, J. (2005) *An Evaluation of the Safer Local Prisons Programme*. London: Home Office Report.
Lifton, R. J. (2003) *Superpower Syndrome: America's Apocalyptic Confrontation with the World*. New York: Nation Books.
Light, A. (2003) 'Globalization and the Need for an Urban Environmentalism', in S. Aronowitz and H. Gautney (eds) *Implicating Empire: Globalization and Resistance in the 21st Century World Order*, pp. 278–308. New York: Basic Books.
Linebaugh, P. (1992) *The London Hanged*. Cambridge: Cambridge University Press.
Lipset, S. M. and Lenz, G. S. (2000) 'Corruption, Culture, and Markets', in L. E. Harrison and S. P. Huntington (eds) *Culture Matters: How Values Shape Human Progress*, pp. 112–124. New York: Basic Books.
Lipsky, M (1980) *Street-Level Bureaucracy: Dilemmas of the Individual in Public Services*. New York: The Russell Sage Foundation.
Lukes, S. S. (2005) *Power: A Radical View* (2nd edn). Houndmills: Palgrave Macmillan.
Lyberaki, A. and Paraskevopoulos, C. (2002) 'Social Capital Measurement in Greece', paper presented at the OECD-ONS International Conference on Social Capital Measurement. Available at: <http://www.oecd.org/dataoecd/22/15/2381649.pdf>.
Lynch, M. (2000) 'Capital Punishment As Moral Imperative', *Punishment and Society* 4(2): 213–236.

Maffesoli, M. (1993) *The Time of the Tribes: The Decline of Individualism in Mass Society*. London: Sage.
Maffesoli, M. (1996) *The Contemplation of the World: Figures of Community Style*. Minneapolis, MN: University of Minnessota Press.
Makransky, J. (2003) 'Buddhist Perspectives on Truth in Other Religions', *Theological Studies* 64(2): 334–361.
Manning, P. K. (2003) *Policing Contingencies*. Chicago, IL: University of Chicago Press.
Marcuse, H. (1941) 'Review of John Dewey, "Theory of Valuation"', *Studies in Philosophy and Social Science* 9: 144–148.
Marcuse, H. (1941/1977) *Reason and Revolution: Hegel and the Rise of Social Theory*. London: Routledge and Kegan Paul.
Marcuse, H. (1964) *One-Dimensional Man*. London: Sphere Books.
Marcuse, H. (1968) *Negations: Essays in Critical Theory*. Boston, MA: Beacon Press.
Marcuse, H. (1972) *Counter-Revolution and Revolt*. Boston, MA: Beacon Press.
Marcuse, H. (1973/2001) 'A Revolution in Values', in D. Kellner (ed.) *Towards a Critical Theory of Society*, pp. 194–201. London: Routledge.
Marcuse, H. (1977/2005) 'Murder is not a Political Weapon', in D. Kellner (ed.) *The New Left and the 1960s*, pp. 177–179. London: Routledge.
Marin, L. (1980) *The Semiotics of the Passion Narrative: Topics and Figures*. Pittsburgh, PA: The Pickwick Press.
Marshall, T. H (1950) *Citizenship and Social Class and Other Essays*. London: Heinemann.
Marshall, T. H. (1970) *Social Policy in the Twentieth Century*. London: Hutchinson.
Maruna, S. (2001) *Making Good: How Ex-Convicts Reform and Rebuild Their Lives*. Washington, DC: American Psychological Association.
Marx, K. (1844) *Economic and Philosophic Manuscripts*. London: Lawrence & Wishart.
Marx, K. (1857–1858/1993). *Grundrisse: Foundations of the Critique of Political Economy (Rough Draft)*. London: Penguin.
Masur, L. (1989) *Rites of Execution*. Oxford: Oxford University Press.
Matheson, C. (1987) 'Weber and the Classification of Forms of Legitimacy', *British Journal of Sociology* 38(2): 199–215.
Matsoso, B. (2005) 'Corruption in Lesotho', in R. Sarre, D. K. Das and H. J. Abrecht (eds) *Policing Corruption: International Perspectives*. Oxford: Lexington Books.
Maurutto, P. and Hannah-Moffatt, K. (2006) 'Assembling Risk and the Restructuring of Penal Control', *British Journal of Criminology* 46(3): 438–454.
Mauss, M. (1924/1990) *The Gift: The Form and Reason for Exchange in Archaic Societies*. New York and London: Norton.
Mawby, R. C. (2002) *Policing Images: Policing, Communication and Legitimacy*. Cullompton, Devon: Willan Publishing.
McAdam, D. (1988) 'Micromobilization Contexts and Recruitment to Activism', in B. Klandermans, H. Kriesi and S. Tarrow (eds) *International Social Movement Research Vol. 1*, pp. 125–154. London: JAI Press.
McLaughlin, N. (1999) 'Origin Myths in the Social Sciences: Fromm, the Frankfurt School and the Emergence of Critical Theory', *Canadian Journal of Sociology* 24(1): 109–139.
McNally, D. (2003) 'Beyond the False Infinity of Capital: Dialectics and Self-Mediation in Marx's Theory of Freedom', in R. Albritton and J. Simoulides (eds) *New Dialectics and Political Economy*, pp. 1–23. Basingstoke: Palgrave.

McQuire, S. (1999) *Visions of Modernity*. London: Sage.
Meranze, M. (1996) *Laboratories of Virtue*. London: University of North Carolina Press.
Messaris, P. and Abraham, L. (2001) 'The Role of Images in Framing News Stories', in S. Reese, O. Gandy and A. Grant (eds) *Framing Public Life: Perspectives on Media and Our Understanding of the Social World*, pp. 215–226. Mahwah, NJ: Lawrence Erlbaum Associates.
Milgram, S. (1974/2004) *Obedience to Authority: An Experimental View*. New York: Harper & Row.
Mill, J. S. (1843/1891) *A System of Logic*. London: Longmans Green.
Mills, C. W. (1956/2000) *The Power Elite*. Oxford: Oxford University Press.
Milton, C., Silva, H. R. S. and Soares, L. E. (1994) *Homicidios: Dolorosos Practicados Contra Menores, no Estado de Rio de Janeiro (1991 a Julho de 1993)*. Brasilia: Ministry of the Public.
Minc, A. (2001) 'Terrorism of the Mind', *Le Monde*. 6 November 2001.
Mingle, E. (2006) 'Police Admin. Hunts for "Okromouth" Staff', *Daily Graphic*, 12 September.
MNMMR (1992) *Vidas em risco: assassinatos de crianças e adolescentes no Brasil*. Rio de Janeiro: IBASE.
MNMMR (1991) 'Guerra no centro da cidade'. *O grito dos meninos e meninas de rua*, 5(20) (June): 4 (newsletter of the MNMMR, Pernambuco).
Moore, B. Jr. (1978) *Injustice: The Social Bases of Obedience and Revolt*. Englewood Cliffs, NJ: Prentice-Hall.
Morris, M. (1990) 'Banality in Cultural Studies', in P. Mellenkamp (ed.) *Logics of Television: Essays in Cultural Criticism*, pp. 14–43. Bloomington, IN: Indiana University Press.
Mossialos, E. and Allin, S. (2005) 'Interest Groups and Health Care Reform in Greece', *West European Politics* 28(2): 420–444.
Mouffe, C. (2005) *On the Political*. London and New York: Routledge.
Mouzelis, N. (1995) 'Greece in the Twenty-First Century: Institutions and Political Culture', in T. Stavrou and D. Constas (eds) *Greece in the Twenty-First Century*, pp. 17–34. Baltimore, MD: John Hopkins Press.
Moyn, S. (2006) 'Empathy in History, Empathizing with Humanity', *History and Theory* 45: 397–415.
Mulcahy, A. (2006) *Policing Northern Ireland: Conflict, Legitimacy and Reform*. Cullompton, Devon: Willan Publishing.
Murdoch, I. (1971/2006) *The Sovereignty of Good*. London and New York: Routledge.
Murdoch, I. (1992/2003) *Metaphysics as a Guide to Morals*. London: Vintage.
Myladil, T. (2000) *St John of the Cross and the Bhagavad-Gita*. Notre Dame, IN: Cross Cultural Publications.
Neiman, S. (1994) *The Unity of Reason: Rereading Kant*. New York: Oxford University Press.
Neiman, S. (2002) *Evil in Modern Thought: An Alternative History of Philosophy*. Princeton, NJ: Princeton University Press.
Newburn, T. (1999) *Understanding and Preventing Police Corruption: Lessons from the Literature*. London: HMSO.
Nicolacopoulos, I. (2005) 'Elections and Voters, 1974–2004: Old Cleavages and New Issues', *West European Politics* 28(2): 260–278.

Nozick, R. (1981) *Philosophical Explanations*. Cambridge, MA: The Belknap Press of Harvard University Press.
Nussbaum, M. (2000) *Women and Human Development: The Capabilities Approach*. Cambridge: Cambridge University Press.
Nygren, A. (1969) *Agape and Eros*. New York: Harper & Row.
O'Malley, P. (1996) 'Risk and Responsibility', in A. Barry, T. Osborne and N. Rose (eds) *Foucault and Political Reason*, pp. 189–208. London: UCL Press.
O'Neill, J. (ed.) (1972a) 'Public and Private Space', in *Sociology as a Skin Trade: Essays towards a Reflexive Sociology*, pp. 20–37. London: Heinemann.
O'Neill, J. (ed.) (1972b) 'Violence, Language, and the Body Politic', in *Sociology as a Skin Trade: Essays Towards a Reflexive Sociology*, pp. 57–67. London: Heinemann.
O'Neill, J. (1975) *Making Sense Together: An Introduction to Wild Sociology*. London: Heinemann.
O'Neill, J. (1994) *The Missing Child in Liberal Theory: Towards a Covenant Theory of Family, Community, and the Civic State*. Toronto: University of Toronto Press.
O'Neill, J. (1999) 'What Gives (with Derrida)?', *European Journal of Social Theory* 2(2): 131–145.
O'Neill, J. (2004) *Civic Capitalism: The State of Childhood*. Toronto: University of Toronto Press.
O'Neill, O. (2002) *A Question of Trust*. Cambridge: Cambridge University Press.
O'Neill, O. (2002) *A Question of Trust – The BBC Reith Lecture Series*. Cambridge: Cambridge University Press.
Okogbule, N. S. (2007) 'Official Corruption and the Dynamics of Money Laundering in Nigeria', *Journal of Financial Crime* 14(1): 49–63.
Oliveira, L. C. (1991) 'Crianças e adolescentes: Um desafio à cidadania', *Tempo e presença* 258 (July–August): 5–9.
Oliver, K. (2003) 'Forgiveness and Subjectivity', *Philosophy Today* 47(3): 280–292.
Ong, A. (2006) *Neoliberalism as Exception: Mutations in Citizenship and Sovereignty*. Durham and London: Duke University Press.
Page, B. and Shapiro, R. (1983) 'Effects of Public Opinion on Policy', *American Political Science Review* 77(1): 175–190.
Pagoulatos, G. (2005) 'The Politics of Privatisation: Redrawing the Public-Private Boundary', *West European Politics* 28(2): 358–380.
Pakulski, J. (1987) 'Ideology and Political Domination: A Critical Reappraisal', *International Journal of Comparative Sociology* 28(3–4): 128–151.
Pan, Z. and Kosicki, G. (2001) 'Framing as a Strategic Action in Public Deliberation', in S. Reese, O. Gandy and A. Grant (eds) *Framing Public Life: Perspectives on Media and Our Understanding of the Social World*. Mahwah, NJ: Lawrence Erlbaum Associates.
Papadopoulos, T. (2006) 'Support for the Unemployed in a Familistic Welfare Regime', in E. Mossialos and M. Petmesidou (eds) *Social Policy Developments in Greece*, pp. 219–238. Aldershot: Ashgate.
Papahelas, A. (2008) 'Holier than Thou', *Kathimerini English Edition*, 9 July. Available at: <http://www.ekathimerini.com/4dcgi/_w_articles_columns_2_09/07/2008_98409>.
Paternoster, R. (1991) *Capital Punishment in America*. New York: Lexington Books.
Patton, P. (1998) 'Foucault's Subject of Power', in J. Moss (ed.) *The Later Foucault*, pp. 64–77. London: Sage.

Penglase, B. (1993) *Final Justice: Police and Death Squad Homicides of Adolescents in Brazil*. New York: Human Rights Watch/Americas.
Peters D. J. (1999) *Speaking into the Air: A History of the Idea of Communication*. Chicago, IL: University of Chicago Press.
Phoenix, J. (2000) 'Prostitute Identities: Men, Money and Violence', *British Journal of Criminology* 40(1): 37–55.
Piccolino, A. (1992) 'Killing the Innocents: The War on Brazil's Street Children' *Sojourners*, February–March: 28–29.
Pierce, S. (2006) 'Looking Like a State: Colonialism and the Discourse of Corruption in Northern Nigeria', *Comparative Studies of Society and History* 48(4): 887–914.
Pietikainen, P. (2004) '"The Sage Knows You Better than You Know Yourself": Psychological Utopianism in Erich Fromm's Work', *History of Political Thought* XXV(1): 86–115.
Pinheiro, P. S. (1996) 'Democracies without Citizenship: Report on Crime', *NACLA*, XXX(2), September/October: 17–23.
Pitkin, H. (1965) 'Obligation and Consent – I', *American Political Science Review* 59(4): 990–999.
Piven, F. F. and Cloward, R. (1977) *Poor People's Movements*. New York: Vintage Books.
Polanyi, K. (1944) *The Great Transformation: The Political and Economic Origins of our Time*. Boston, MA: Beacon Press.
Pollis, A. (1993) 'Eastern Orthodoxy and Human Rights', *Human Rights Quarterly* 15(2): 339–356.
Pollitt, C. and G. Bouckaert (2000) *Public Management Reform: A Comparative Analysis*. Oxford: Oxford University Press.
Power, M. (1999) *The Audit Society: Rituals of Verification*. Oxford: Oxford University Press.
ProAsyl and Group of Lawyers for Rights of Refugees and Migrants (2007) 'The Situation of Refugees in the Aegean and the Practices of the Greek Coastguard'. Report available at: <http://www.proasyl.de/fileadmin/proasyl/fm_redakteure/Englisch/Griechenlandbericht_Engl.pdf>.
Psychopedis, K. (1980) *Untersuchungen zur politischen Theorie von Immanuel Kant*. Göttingen: Otto Schwartz & Co.
Psychopedis, K. (1992) 'Dialectical Theory: Problems of Reconstruction', in W. Bonefeld, R. Gunn and K. Psychopedis (eds) *Open Marxism. Vol.1: Dialectics and History*, pp. 1–53. London: Pluto Press.
Psychopedis, K. (2000) 'New Social Thought: Questions of Theory and Critique', in W. Bonefeld and K. Psychopedis (eds) *The Politics of Change: Globalization, Ideology, and Critique*, pp. 71–104. Basingstoke: Palgrave Macmillan.
Psychopedis, K. (2004) 'Materialistische Werttheorie und materiale Wertethik', in C. Kirdoff *et al.* (eds) *Gesellschaft als Verkehrung: Perspektiven einer Neuen Marx-Lektüre: Festschrift für Helmut Reichelt*, pp. 105–122. Freiburg: Ça-ina-Verlag.
Psychopedis, K. (2005) 'Social Critique and the Logic of Revolution: From Kant to Marx and From Marx to Us', in W. Bonefeld and K. Psychopedis (eds) *Human Dignity: Social Autonomy and the Critique of Capitalism*, pp. 69–92. Aldershot/Hampshire: Ashgate.

Punch, M. (1985) *Conduct Unbecoming: The Social Construction of Police Deviance and Control.* London and New York: Tavistock Publications.
Punch, M. (2000) 'Police Corruption and its Prevention', *European Journal of Criminal Policy and Research* 8(3): 301–324.
Putnam, H. (2002) *The Collapse of the Fact/Value Dichotomy and Other Essays.* Cambridge, MA: Harvard University Press.
Radelet, M. (1989) *Facing the Death Penalty.* Philadelphia: Temple University Press.
Rawls, J. (1972) *A Theory of Justice.* Cambridge, MA: Harvard University Press.
Raz, J. (2004) *The Practice of Value.* Oxford: Clarendon Press.
Reiner, R. (2000) *The Politics of the Police.* Oxford: Oxford University Press.
Reiss, A. J. (1971) *The Police and the Public.* New Haven, CT: Yale University Press.
Reuss-Ianni, E. and Ianni, F. (1983) 'Street Cops and Management Cops: The Two Cultures of Policing', in M. Punch (ed.) *Control in the Police Organization*, pp. 275–317. Cambridge, MA: MIT Press.
Ricoeur, P. (1991) 'Ethics and Politics', in *From Text to Action: Essays in Hermeneutics, II*, pp. 325–337. Evanston, IL: Northwestern University Press.
Ricoeur, P. (1991) *From Text to Action: Essays in Hermeneutics, II.* Evanston, IL: Northwestern University Press.
Ricoeur, P. (1992) *Oneself as Another.* Chicago, IL: University of Chicago Press.
Ricoeur, P. (1995) 'Ethical and Theological Considerations on the Golden Rule', in *Figuring the Sacred: Religion, Narrative and Imagination*, pp. 293–302. Minneapolis, MN: Fortress Press.
Ricoeur, P. (1996) 'Reflections on a New Ethos for Europe', in R. Kearney (ed.) *Paul Ricoeur: The Hermeneutics of Action*, pp. 3–14. London: Sage.
Ricoeur, P. (2004) 'The Difficulty to Forgive', in M. Junker-Kenny and P. Kenney (eds) *Memory, Narrativity, Self, and the Challenge to Think God: The Reception within Theology of the Recent Work of Paul Ricoeur*, pp. 6–18. Munster: Litverlag.
Ricoeur, P. (2004a) ' "Memory and Forgetting" and "Imagination, Testimony and Trust" ', in M. Dooley and R. Kearney (eds) *Questioning Ethics*, pp. 5–11, 12–17. London and New York: Routledge.
Ricoeur, P. (2004b) *Memory, History and Forgetting.* Chicago, IL: University of Chicago Press.
Riedel, M. (1984) *Between Tradition and Revolution: The Hegelian Transformation of Political Philosophy.* Cambridge: Cambridge University Press.
Rigakos, G. S. and Papanicolaou, G. (2003) 'The Political Economy of Greek Policing: Between Neo-Liberalism and the Sovereign State', *Policing and Society* 13(3): 271–304.
Rigby, T. H. (1982) 'Introduction: Political Legitimacy, Max Weber and Communist Mono-Organizational Systems', in T. H. Rigby and F. Feher (eds) *Political Legitimation in Communist States*, pp. 12–16. London: Macmillan.
Roberts, J. and Hough, J. M. (2005) *Understanding Public Attitudes to Criminal Justice.* Maidenhead: Open University Press.
Rock, P. (1995) 'The Opening Stages of Criminal Justice Policy Making', *British Journal of Criminology* 35(1): 1–16.
Rockmore, T. and Margolis, J. (eds) (2004). *The Philosophical Challenge of September 11*, special issue of *Metaphilosophy*, 35(3). London and New York: Blackwell.
Rorty, R. (1989) *Contingency, Irony, and Solidarity.* Cambridge: Cambridge University Press.

Rose, N. (1996) 'Governing "Advanced" Liberal Democracies', in A. Barry, T. Osborne and N. Rose (eds) *Foucault and Political Reason*, pp. 37–64. London: UCL Press.

Rose, N. (1999) *Power of Freedom: Reframing Political Thought*. Cambridge: Cambridge University Press.

Rose-Ackerman, S. (1999) *Corruption and Government: Causes, Consequences and Reform*. Cambridge: Cambridge University Press.

Rosewarne, S. and Groutsis, D. (2003) 'Challenges to the Integrity of a European Migration Programme: Greece as the Recalcitrant State', Report no. 75, National Europe Centre. Available at: <http://dspace.anu.edu.au/bitstream/1885/41127/2/rosewarne_paper.pdf>.

Ross, D. (1923/1995) *Aristotle*. London: Routledge.

Rothstein, B. (2000) 'Trust, Social Dilemmas and Collective Memories', *Journal of Theoretical Politics* 12(4): 477–501.

Rutigliano, V. (2007) *Il linguaggio delle masse. Sulla sociologia di Elias Canetti*. Bari: Dedalo.

Safilios-Rothschild, C. (1966) 'Class Position and Success Stereotypes in Greek and American Cultures', *Social Forces* 45(3): 374–383.

Said, E. (2001) 'The Clash of Ignorance', *The Nation*, 18 October.

Sampson, A. (2004) *Who Runs This Place? The Anatomy of Britain in the 21st Century*. London: John Murray.

Santos, B. S. (1995) *Toward a New Common Sense*. New York: Routledge.

Santos, B. S. (2006) 'Globalizations', *Theory, Culture & Society* 23(2–3): 393–399.

Saragosa, M. (2004) 'Greece Warned on False Euro Data', *BBC News*, 1 December. Available at: <http://news.bbc.co.uk/1/hi/business/4058327.stm>.

Sarat, A. (2001) *When the State Kills: Capital Punishment and the American Condition*. Princeton, NJ: Princeton University Press.

Sartre, J. P. (1968) *Being and Nothingness: An Essay on Phenomenological Ontology* (translated by H. Barnes). London: Methuen.

Sartre, J. P. (1958/2003) *Being and Nothingness*. London and New York: Routledge.

Saux, H. L. (1998) *Abhishiktananda, Ascent to the Depth of the Heart*. Delhi: ISPCK.

Schaar, J. H. (1984) 'Legitimacy in the Modern State', in W. Connolly (ed.) *Legitimacy and the State*, pp. 104–133. Oxford: Basil Blackwell.

Scheler, M. (1916/1973) *Formalism in Ethics and Non-Formal Ethics of Values: A New Attempt toward the Foundation of an Ethical Personalism*. Evanston: Northwestern University Press.

Scheler, M. (1928/1961) *Man's Place in Nature*. New York: The Noonday Press.

Scheper-Hughes, N. (1990) 'Theft of Life: Illegal Markets in Children', *Society* 27(6): 57–62.

Scheper-Hughes, N. (1992) *Death without Weeping: The Violence of Everyday Life in Brazil*. Berkeley, CA: University of California Press.

Scheper-Hughes, N. (1993) 'The Way of an Anthropologist-Companheira', in B. Schwimmer and D. M. Warren (eds) *Anthropology and the Peace Corps*, pp. 101–113. Iowa City, IA: Iowa University Press.

Scheper-Hughes, N. (1996) 'Small Wars and Invisible Genocides', *Social Science & Medicine* 43(5): 889–900.

Scheper-Hughes, N. (1997) 'Peace Time Crimes', *Social Identities* 3(3): 471–497.

Scheper-Hughes, N. (2002) 'Min(d)ing the Body: On the Trail of Organ Stealing Rumors', in J. MacClancy (ed.) *Exotic No More: Anthropology on the Front Lines*, Chapter 2, pp. 33–63. Chicago, IL: University of Chicago Press.

Scheper-Hughes, N. (2002) 'The Genocidal Continuum: Peace-time Crimes', in J. Mageo (ed.) *Power and the Self*, pp. 29–47. Cambridge: Cambridge University Press.

Scheper-Hughes, N. and Hoffman, D. (1998) 'Brazilian Apartheid: Street Kids and the Search for Citizenship in Brazil', in N. Scheper-Hughes and C. Sargent (eds) *Small Wars; the Cultural Politics of Childhood*, pp. 352–388. Berkeley and Los Angeles, CA: University of California Press.

Schmitt, C. (1967/1996) *The Tyranny of Values*. Washington, DC: Plutarch Press.

Schnädelbach, H. (1984) *Philosophy in Germany 1831–1933*. Cambridge: Cambridge University Press.

Schwartz, R. (1997) *The Curse of Cain: The Violent Legacy of Monotheism*. Chicago, IL: University of Chicago Press.

Scott, J. C. (1985) *Weapons of the Weak: Everyday Forms of Peasant Resistance*. New Haven: Yale University Press.

Scott, J. C. (1990) *Domination and the Arts of Resistance: Hidden Transcripts*. New Haven and London: Yale University Press.

Seaton J. (2005) *Carnage and the Media: The Making and Breaking of News about Violence*. London: Penguin.

Segal, Y. (2006) 'The Death Penalty and the Debate over the U.S. Supreme Court's Citation of Foreign and International Law', *Fordham Urban Law Journal* 33(5): 1421–1452.

Seligson, M. A. (2002) 'Impact of Corruption on Regime Legitimacy: A Comparative Study of Four Latin American Countries', *Journal of Politics* 64(2): 408–433.

Sen, A. (1984) *Resources, Values, and Development*. Cambridge, MA: Harvard University Press.

Sen, A. (1987) *On Ethics and Economics*. Oxford: Basil Blackwell.

Sen, A. (1999) *Development as Freedom*. Oxford: Oxford University Press.

Sen, A. (2002) *Rationality and Freedom*. Cambridge, MA: The Belknap Press of Harvard University Press.

Sen, A. (2006) *Identity and Violence: The Illusion of Destiny*. London: Penguin Books.

Sen, A. (1995) *Inequality Reconsidered*. Cambridge, MA: Harvard University Press.

Sennett, R. (1998) *The Corrosion of Character: The Personal Consequences of Work in the New Capitalism*. New York: W.W. Norton.

Sennett, R. (2008) *The Craftsman*. London: Allen Lane.

Seth, J. (1908) *A Study of Ethical Principles*. New York: Charles Scribner's Sons.

Sgourides, D. (2004) 'Its All Greek to Me: Everything You Need to Know About Conducting Business in Greece', *businesswoman.gr*, 23 March. Available at: <http://www.businesswoman.gr/article.php?lang=en&cat=33&offset=0&article=348>.

Shotter, J. (1989) 'Social Accountability and the Social Construction of "You"', in J. Shotter and K. Gergen (eds) *Texts of Identity*, pp. 133–151. London: Sage.

Sifianou, M. (1999) *Politeness Phenomena in England and Greece: A Cross-Cultural Perspective*. Oxford: Oxford University Press.

Silverstone, R. (2006) *Media and Morality: On the Rise of the Mediapolis*. Cambridge: Polity Press.

Simmel, G. (1908) Soziologie (English edited by Kurt Wolff). *The Sociology of Georg Simmel*. New York: The Free Press.

Simmons, A. J. (1999) 'Justification and Legitimacy', *Ethics* 109(4): 739–771.

Sinclair, A. (2002) *A Study of How and the Extent to Which, KPI's Drive Performance in the Prison Service*. Unpublished MSt. Thesis, Institute of Criminology, University of Cambridge.

Sitkin, S. B. and Stickel, D. (1996) 'The Road to Hell: The Dynamics of Distrust in an Era of Quality', in R. M. Kramer and T. R. Tyler (eds) *Trust in Organizations: Frontiers of Theory and Research*, pp. 196–215. Thousand Oaks, CA: Sage.

Skolnick, J. (1994) *Justice Without Trial: Law Enforcement in a Democratic Society*. New York: John Wiley and Sons.

Smith, D. J. (2007) 'New Challenges to Police Legitimacy', in A. Henry and D. J. Smith (eds) *Transformations of Policing*. Aldershot: Ashgate.

Smith, H. and Siddique, H. (2008) 'General Strike Brings Greece to Standstill', *The Guardian*, 10 December. Available at: <http://www.guardian.co.uk/world/2008/dec/10/greece1>.

Smith, P. (1996) 'Executing Executions: Aesthetics, Identity, and the Problematic Narratives of Capital Punishment Ritual', *Theory and Society* 25(2): 235–261.

Smith, P. C. and Goddard, M. (2002) 'Performance Management and Operational Research: A Marriage made in Heaven?', *Journal of the Operational Research Society* 53(3): 247–256.

Snow, D. and Benford, D. (1988) 'Ideology, Frame Resonance, and Participant Mobilization', in B. Klandermans, H. Kriesi, and S. Tarrow (eds) *International Social Movement Research Vol. 1*, pp. 197–217. London: JAI Press.

Snow, D., Burke Rochford, Jr., E., Worden, S. and Benford, R. (1986) 'Frame Alignment Processes, Micromobilization, and Movement Participation', *American Sociological Review* 51(4): 464–481.

Solinger, R., Fox, M. and Irani, K. (eds) (2008) *Telling Stories to Change the World: Global Voices on the Power of Narrative to Build Community and Make Social Justice Claims*. New York and London: Routledge.

Sontag, S. (1979) *On Photography*. New York: Penguin.

Sontag, S. (2003) *Regarding the Pain of the Others*. New York: FSG Books.

Sontag, S. (2004) 'Regarding the Torture of Others', *New York Times*, 23 May 2004.

Sotiropoulos, D. A. (2004) 'Formal Weakness and Informal Strength: Civil Society in Contemporary Greece', Discussion Paper no. 16, Hellenic Observatory, London School of Economics and Political Science. Available at: <http://www.lse.ac.uk/collections/hellenicObservatory/pdf/Discussion_GreeSE_Papers/sotiropoulos.pdf>.

Soumeli, E. (2003) '2002: Annual Review for Greece', Report by the Labour Institute of Greek General Confederation of Labour ('INE/GSEE') for the European Industrial Relations Observatory (EIRO). Available at: <http://www.eurofound.europa.eu/eiro/2003/01/feature/gr0301103f.htm>.

Sparks, J. R., Bottoms, A. E. and Hay, W. (1996) *The Prisons and the Problem of Order*. Oxford: Clarendon Press.

Sparks, R. (1992) *Television and the Drama of Crime*. Bristol, PA: Open University Press.
Spierenburg, P. (1984) *The Spectacle of Suffering*. Cambridge: Cambridge University Press.
Spourdalakis, M. and Tassis, C. (2006) 'Party Change in Greece and the Vanguard Role of PASOK', *South European Society and Politics* 2(3–4): 497–512.
Sprouse, M. (ed.) (1992) *Sabotage in the American Workplace: Anecdotes of Dissatisfaction, Mischief and Revenge*. San Francisco, CA: Pressure Drop Press.
Stavrakakis, Y. (2002a) 'Religion and Populism: Reflections on the "Politicised" Discourse of the Greek Church', Discussion Paper no.7, Hellenic Observatory, London School of Economics and Political Science. Available at: <http://eprints.lse.ac.uk/5709/1/StavrakakisPaper7.pdf>.
Stavrakakis, Y. (2002b) 'Religious Populism and Political Culture: The Greek Case', *South European Politics and Society* 7(3): 29–52.
Steinberg, J. (1990/2002) *All or Nothing: The Axis and the Holocaust, 1941–1943*. London and New York: Routledge.
Sternberg, D. (1968) 'Legitimacy', in D. L. Sills (ed.) *The International Encyclopedia of the Social Sciences, IX*, pp. 244–248. New York: Free Press.
Streib, V. (1993) *A Capital Punishment Anthology*. Cleveland: Anderson.
Streib, V. (2008) 'Death Penalty for Female Offenders, January 1, 1973, Through December 31, 2007'. Report available at: <http://www.law.onu.edu/faculty/streib> (accessed 1 January 2009).
Sturdy, A. (2001) 'Servicing Societies? Colonisation, Control, Contradiction, and Contestation', in A. Sturdy, I. Grugulis, and H. Willmott (eds) *Customer Service: Empowerment and Entrapment*, pp. 1–17. Basingstoke: Palgrave.
Sturdy, A. and Fineman, S. (2001) 'Struggles for the Control of Affect–Resistance as Politics and Emotion', in A. Sturdy, I. Grugulis and H. Willmott (eds) *Customer Service: Empowerment and Entrapment*, pp. 135–156. Basingstoke: Palgrave.
Suarez-Orozco, M. (1987) 'The Treatment of Children in the Dirty War: Ideology, State Terrorism, and the Abuse of Childen in Argentina', in N. Scheper-Hughes (ed.) *Child Survival*, pp. 227–243. Dordrecht, Holland: Kluwer.
Summers, J. (2004) *Late Medieval Prison Writing and the Politics of Autobiography*. Oxford: Oxford University Press.
Sunshine, J. and Tyler, T. R. (2003) 'The Role of Procedural Justice and Legitimacy in Shaping Public Support for Policing', *Law and Society Review* 37(3): 513–548.
Surette, R. (1996) 'News from Nowhere, Policy to Follow', in D. Shichor and D. Sechrist (eds) *Three Strikes and You're Out: Vengeance as Public Policy*. Thousand Oaks, CA: Sage.
Swift, A. (1991) *Brazil: The Fight for Childhood in the City*. Florence: UNICEF International Child Development Center.
Sykes, G. M. and Matza, D. (1957) 'Technique of Neutralization: A Theory of Delinquency', *American Sociological Review* 22(6): 664–670.
Sznaider, N. (1998) 'The Sociology of Compassion: A Study in the Sociology of Morals', *Cultural Values* 2(1): 117–139.
Sztompka, P. (1999) *Trust: A Sociological Theory*. Cambridge: Cambridge University Press.

Tankebe, J. (2008) 'Colonialism, Legitimation and Policing in Ghana', *International Journal of Law, Crime and Justice* 3(1): 667–684.

Tankebe, J. and Gelsthorpe, L. (2007) 'Legitimacy', in R. Canton and D. Hancock (eds) *Dictionary of Probation and Offender Management*, pp. 152–154. Cullompton, Devon: Willan Publishing.

Telidis, C. (2007) 'Close Relations with Kostas-Natasha' [Στενές σχέσεις με Κώστα – Νατάσα], *Ethnos* newspaper, 21 December. Available at: <http://www.ethnos.gr/article.asp?catid=11378&subid=2&tag=8777&pubid=224395>.

The Economist (2008) 'Greece's Government: Schools for Scandal', 11 September. Available at: <http://www.economist.com/world/europe/displaystory.cfm?story_id=12209248>.

The Statesman (2006) 'Police and Drugs', 28 July.

Therborn, G. (1980) *The Ideology of Power and the Power of Ideology*. London: New Left Books.

Thompson, J. (1984) *Studies in the Theory of Ideology*. Cambridge: Polity Press.

Thompson, J. (1995) *Media and Modernity*. Cambridge: Polity Press.

Thompson, K. (1997) *Media and Cultural Regulation*. London: Sage.

Thompson, J. (2005) 'The New Visibility', *Theory, Culture & Society* 22(6): 31–51.

Tikos, S. (2007) 'Greece: Industrial Relations Developments in Europe, 1997', Report by the Labour Institute of Greek General Confederation of Labour ('INE/GSEE') for the European Industrial Relations Observatory (EIRO). Available at: <http://www.eurofound.europa.eu/eiro/studies/tn0803029s/gr0803029q.htm>.

Tilly, C. (2004) *Social Movements, 1768–2004*. Boulder and London: Paradigm.

Titmuss, R. M. (1974) *Social Policy: An Introduction*. London: George Allen and Unwin.

Titmuss, R. M. (1970) *The Gift Relationship: From Human Blood to Social Policy*. London: Allen and Unwin.

Todorova, M. (1997) *Imagining the Balkans*. New York and Oxford: Oxford University Press.

Tolstoy, L. (1984) *The Kingdom of Heaven is Within You: Christianity Not as a Mystic Religion but as a New Theory of Life* (translated by Constance Garnett). Lincoln and London: University of Nebraska Press.

Tonry, M. (2004) *Thinking about Crime: Sense and Sensibility in American Penal Culture*. New York: Oxford University Press.

Triandis, H. and Vassiliou, V. (1972) 'A Comparative Analysis of Subjective Culture', in H. Triandis (ed.) *The Analysis of Subjective Culture*, pp. 299–335. New York: Wiley-Interscience.

Tsatsanis, E. (2009) 'The Social Determinants of Ideology: The Case of Neoliberalism in Southern Europe', *Critical Sociology* 35(2): 199–223.

Tsoucalas, C. (1991) ' "Enlightened" Concepts in the "Dark": Power and Freedom, Politics and Society', *Journal of Modern Greek Studies* 9(1): 1–22.

Tsoukalas, C. (1995) 'Free Riders in Wonderland; Or, of Greeks in Greece', in T. Stavrou and D. Constas (eds) *Greece in the Twenty-First Century*, pp. 191–219. Baltimore, MD: Johns Hopkins Press.

Tunnell, K. (1998) 'Reflections on Crime, Criminals, and Control in Newsmagazine Television Programmes', in F. Bailey and D. Hale (eds) *Popular Culture, Crime, and Justice*, pp. 111–122. Belmont, CA: West/Wadsworth.

Turkle, S. (1995) *Life on the Screen: Identity in the Age of the Internet*. London: Weidenfeld and Nicholson.

Tyagananda, S. (2000) 'Harmony of Religions', Talk at Harvard University, 8 April 2000. Available at: <www.vedanta.org>.
Tyler, T. R. (1990) *Why People Obey the Law*. Yale: Yale University Press.
Tyler, T. R. (2003) 'Procedural Justice, Legitimacy and the Effective Rule of Law', in M. Tonry (ed.) *Crime and Justice: Review of Research*, pp. 431–505. Chicago, IL: University of Chicago Press.
Tyler, T. R. and Huo, Y. J. (2002) *Trust in the Law: Encouraging Public Cooperation with the Police and Courts*. New York: Russell-Sage Foundation.
Tylor, M. and Taylor, S. (2001) 'Juggling Justice and Care: Gendered Customer Service in the Contemporary Airline Industry', in A. Sturdy, I. Grugulis and H. Willmott (eds) *Customer Service: Empowerment and Entrapment*, pp. 60–78. Basingstoke: Palgrave.
Tzanelli, R. (2008) *Nation-Building and Identity in Europe: The Dialogics of Reciprocity*. Basingstoke: Palgrave Macmillan.
Tzanelli, R. (2009) *The 'Greece' of Britain and the 'Britain' of Greece: Performance, Stereotypes, Expectations and Intermediaries in 'Neohellenic' and Victorian Narratives (1864–1881)*. Saarbrücken: VDM Verlag.
Underhill, E. (1974) *Mysticism*. New York: New American Library.
UNDP (2003) *Human Development Report 2003*. New York and Oxford: Oxford University Press.
Urry, J. (2000) Available at: <http://www.comp.lancs.ac.uk/sociology/soc056ju.html>.
US Department of Labor, Bureau of International Labor Affairs, and US Embassy, Athens (2003) 'Foreign Labor Trends: Greece', Annual Report. Available at: <http://www.dol.gov/ilab/media/reports/flt/greece-2003.htm>.
Valier, C. (2004a) *Crime and Punishment in Contemporary Society*. London: Routledge.
Valier, C. (2004b) 'Introduction: The Power to Punish and the Power of the Image', *Punishment and Society* 6(3): 251–254.
Valier, C. (2004c) 'L'oeuil Qui Pense: The Emotive as Grounds for the Pensive in Phenomenological Reflection', in M. Freeman (ed.) *Law and Culture*, pp. 291–302. Oxford: Oxford University Press.
Valier, C. and Lippens, R. (2004) 'Moving Images, Ethics and Justice', *Punishment and Society* 6(3): 319–333.
Van Maanen, J. (1983) 'The Boss: First-line Supervision in an American Police Agency', in M. Punch (ed.) *Control in the Police Organization*, pp. 275–317. Cambridge, MA: MIT Press.
Vaughan, B. (2000) 'The Civilizing Process and the Janus Face of Modern Punishment', *Theoretical Criminology* 4(1): 71–92.
Vermelho, L. and Mello, J. (1996) 'Youth Mortality: Analysis comprising the period from 1930 to 1991', paper presented at the International Meetings of *Social Science & Medicine*, Peebles, Scotland, September 1996.
Vetlesen, A. J. (1997) 'Introducing an Ethics of Proximity', in H. Jodalen and A. J. Vetlesen (eds) *Closeness: An Ethics*, pp. 1–19. Oslo: Scandinavian University Press.
Vidich, A. J. (1979) 'The Legitimation of Regimes in World Perspective', in A. J. Vidich and R. M. Glassman (eds) *Conflict and Control: Challenge to Legitimacy of Modern Governments*, pp. 271–302. Beverly Hills, CA: Sage Publications.
Villa, D. (1999) *Politics, Philosophy, Terror: Essays on the Thought of Hannah Arendt*. Princeton, NJ: Princeton University Press.

Virilio, P. (1991) *The Aesthetics of Disappearance*. New York: Semiotext(e).
Virilio, P. (1994) *The Vision Machine*. London: BFI.
Virilio, P. (2002) *Ground Zero*. London & New York: Verso.
Vögtle, A. (1978) 'The Lord's Prayer: A Prayer for Jews and Christians?', in J. J. Petuchowski and M. Brocke (eds) *The Lord's Prayer and Jewish Liturgy*, pp. 93–118. London: Burns and Oates.
Wacquant, L. (2001) 'The Penalisation of Poverty and the Rise of Neoliberalism', *European Journal on Criminal Policy and Research* 9(4): 401–412.
Wacquant, L. (2009) *Punishing the Poor: The Neoliberal Government of Social Insecurity*. Durham and London: Duke University Press.
Watts-Miller, W. (ed.) (1992) 'Free Men, Socialism, and the Law', in *Socialism and the Law (Association for Legal and Social Philosophy, Seventeenth Annual Conference)*, pp. 7–11. University of Bristol 4–6 April 1991. Stuttgart: Franz Steiner Verlag.
Watts-Miller, W. (1993) 'Durkheim: Liberal-Communitarian', in W. S. F. Pickering and W. Watts-Miller (eds) *Individualism and Human Rights in the Durkheimian Tradition/Individualisme et Droits Humains Selon la Tradition Durkheimienne*, pp. 82–104. Oxford: British Centre for Durkheimian Studies.
Weber, M. (1948) *From Max Weber: Essays in Sociology* (translated by H. Gerth and C. W. Mills). London: PRK.
Weiss, R. (1987) 'Humanitarianism, Labor Exploitation, or Social Control? A Critical Survey of Theory and Research on the Origin and Development of Prison', *Social History* 12(3): 331–350.
Wellman, B. and Hogan, B. (2004) 'The Immanent Internet', in J. McKay (ed.) *Netting Citizens*, pp. 54–80. St. Andrews: University of St. Andrews Press.
Wilde, L. (2004) *Erich Fromm and the Quest for Solidarity*. Basingstoke: Palgrave Macmillan.
Wilkinson, I. (2005) *Suffering: A Sociological Introduction*. Cambridge: Polity Press.
Wolfe, A. (2001) 'The God of a Diverse People', *The New York Times* (14 October).
Woode, G. (2006) 'Woode Committee Report'. Available at: http://www.mint.gov.gh/newsflash.pdf (accessed 30 September 2006).
Word, R. (2002) 'Death Row Inmates Take Protests to Web', *Sarasota Herald Tribune*, 21 July: H12.
Wright, M. (1984) 'Ideology and Power in the Czechoslovak Political System', in P. G. Lewis (ed.) *Eastern Europe: Political Crisis and Legitimation*, pp. 111–153. Sydney: Croom Helm.
Wrong, D. H. (1979/1988) *Power: Its Forms, Bases, and Uses*. New Brunswick and London: Transaction.
Wrong, D. H. (1995) *Power: Its Forms, Bases and Uses*. London: Transaction Publishers.
Xenakis, S. (under review) 'Pride and Prejudice: Comparative Corruption Research and the British Case'.
Yovel, Y. (1980) *Kant and the Philosophy of History*. Princeton, NJ: Princeton University Press.
Zaluar, A. (1994) *Condominio do diablo*. Rio de Janeiro: Editora Reven UFRJ.
Zaluar, A. (1995) 'Crime, medo e politica' (Crime, Fear, and Politics), *Sociedade e Estado* 10(2): 391–416.

Zaluar, A. and Ribeiro, A. I. (1995) 'Drug Trade, Crime, and Policies of Repression in Brazil', *Dialectical Anthropology* 20(1): 95–108.
Žižek, S. (1992/2008) *Enjoy your Symptom!* New York: Routledge.
Žižek, S. (2002) *Welcome to the Desert of the Real*. London and New York: Verso.
Žižek, S. (2005) 'Neighbours and Other Monsters: A Plea for Ethical Violence', in K. Reinhard, E. L. Santner and S. Žižek (eds) *The Neighbour: Three Inquiries in Political Theology*, pp. 134–190. Chicago, IL: The University of Chicago Press.

Index

Abrahamic narratives, 74
Abraham, L., 133, 149
absolutism, 53, 74, 76
abstract justice, 129
action
  collective, 190–1
  ethical, 56, 112, 121
  free, 24
  immoral, 108
  instrumental, 129
  performative, 121
  physical, 69
  political, 53, 85, 117
  reflective, 115
  slantwise, 97
Adams, R. M., 91
Adorno, T. W., 25, 37, 58, 123
aesthetic quality, 114–7
  of representation, 113
  of suffering, 110
Agamben, G., 34, 83, 129
agency
  cosmopolitan forms of, 108, 109
  defined, 108
  deletion of, 110–2
  ethical, 108–22
  human, 20, 109
  spectatorial, 108, 109
Ajemian, R., 194
Alatas, S. H., 212
Alexander, J., 122
alienation, 15, 19, 27
Allen, M., 35
Allin, S., 194
Almeida, A., 153
Altheide, D. L., 207
Alves, M. H. M., 152
Alvim, R., 153, 176
Anderson, C. J., 210
Anderson, D., 149
Anechiarico, F., 212
aneconomy, 89, 91

Angel, M., 143
answerability, 81–2, 228
anthropos, 1, 11
anti-corruption reforms, 199, 214
Araújo, J. C., 171–4
Archer, M. S., 208
Arendt, H., 1, 6, 51, 75, 79, 81, 82,
  85–7, 92, 93, 108, 110, 123
Arnason, J. P., 106, 107
Arnold, H., 223, 236, 237, 244, 245
Askonas, P., 35
Assman, J., 91
authoritarian character, 39, 46–7
authority, 188, 205
autobiographical narratives, 132
autoimmunitary perversion, 44
autonomous submission, 51
axiology, *see* values
Ayittey, G. B., 215

Babb, S., 150
bad infinity, 17
Badiou, A., 73
Bakhtin, M., 105
Balkanism, 179–87
Balkan(ist)
  autonomy, 189
  familism, 190
  notion of good, 189
  obstinacy in Greece, 181–4
  resistance, 179, 187–90, 191
bandits, 154, 159, 173
Banfield, E. C., 183
Barbalet, J., 204, 210, 219
Barker, R., 197, 198, 203, 204, 205
Barnett, K., 124
Barry, A., 223
Barry, B., 196
Barthes, R., 133, 136
Baudler, G., 82
Baudrillard, J., 62, 66, 109, 111–12,
  115, 117, 120, 122, 123

Bauman, Z., 44, 49
Beckett, K., 149
Beck, U., 122
Beetham, D., 198–202, 206–10, 219
being mode, 51
Bellow, A., 192
Benford, D., 132
Benford, R., 132
Benhabib, S., 122
benign narcissism, 51, 52
Bergen, B. J., 81
Berkowitz, W., 131
Bernstein, J. M., 18
Bhabha, H. K., 178, 195
biopolitics, 104
Birch, A. H., 206
Bloch, E., 31, 32
Blok, A., 42
Boltanski, L., 116, 122
Bond-Maupic, L., 149
Borradori, G., 44, 54
Bottoms, A. E., 221
Bouckaert, G., 222
Bourdieu, P., 3, 5, 36, 42, 53, 102–3, 165
Bowers, W., 128
Bowman, L., 146
Braithwaite, J., 238, 245
Bratsis, P., 36
Brazilian modernity, 158, 165
Brazilian society, 151, 153
Brighenti, A. M., 57, 95–107
Brookfield, S., 58
Burawoy, M., 191
Burchell, G., 223
Butler, J., 36, 136, 147

Cain, M., 207, 216
Caldeira, T. P. d. Rio, 154, 155
Calligaris, C., 152
Calotychos, V., 184, 187, 189, 195
Campbell, H., 97
Campbell, J. K., 195
Camus, A., 97
Canetti, E., 96, 98, 100, 103–7

capability, 29
  concept of, 21
  as freedom, 31
  types of, 28, 32
capability approach, 17, 26, 28, 32
capability deprivation, 27, 29–30
capital punishment
  contemporary, 133–4
  morals and, 129, 134
  resistance to, 131
  rituals of, 129
Caputo, J. D., 88, 91
Carlen, P., 239
Castells, M., 122
Categorical Imperative, 81–2, 88, 90
Cavender, G., 149
celestial economy, 88, 92
Chan, J. B. L., 207, 217
charitable work, 189
Cheliotis, L. K., 1–11, 36–58, 148, 190
Chermack, S., 149
Chomsky, N., 79
Chouliaraki, L., 56, 72, 108–24
Christianity, 73, 74–5
cinematic entertainment, 114–5
civic theology, 92–4
civil defence, 62
civil society, 16, 22, 26–7
Clooney, F., 71, 77
Cloward, R., 133
Cohen, S., 53, 122, 127, 138–9, 142
Coicaud, J. M., 198, 199, 200, 201
collective evil, 81
collective good, 200, 218
Collinson, D., 216
command-obedience, 198
communicative practice, 228
communicative rationality, 243
compassion
  ethics of, 14, 18
  politics of, 125–47
  radical, 94
  resistance and, 25
  truth and, 137
  universal, 70
  violence and, 69
compassion fatigue, 145
compensatory destructiveness, 47
compromise, 66–7, 73, 201

concession, 201, 206
conditional freedom, 110, 119–21
conduct of conduct, 121
Connell, R., 3
constraints
 of global hierarchy, 122
 managerial, 242
 territorial type of, 104
contemporary prisons, 238
contingent valuation, 30
Corner, J., 122
corporate domination, 23
corporation, 16, 26
corruption, 209–12
Coser, L., 135
cosmopolitanism, 99, 102
cosmopolitan sensibilities, 109
counter hegemony, 99
counterpower, 99–100
Coyne, R., 126
Craib, I., 36
creative fulfillment, 26
criminal discourse, 153–6
criminal justice, 210, 221–8, 238
crisis
 Argentinean, 119
 dialectical conception of, 16–8
 economic, 115
 humanistic Marxism on, strands of, 18–9
 legitimation, 214, 218
 mediation by, 24
 societal, 15
 starvation, 117–8
critical mood, 49
critical theory, 5, 24, 56
 values and, 19–21
Crook, R. C., 206
Cross, F. M., 91
cultural hybridity, 178–9
cultural identity, 17, 76
cultural intimacy, 187
cultural values, 188
culture of poverty thesis, 156

Dancy, J., 179, 192
Danopoulos, C. P., 183
Das, V., 125
Dayan, D., 122

death
 false greatness of, 106
 images of, 115
 power of, 104
 row homepages, 125–47
 seduction of, 106
 by stoning, 113, 116
 violent, 168–9
 see also death penalty; death squads
death penalty
 facing, 125–7
 framing, 131–2
 images of, 132–7
 texts about, 137–44
 in United States, 125, 128
death row homepages, 125–47
death squads
 democracy and, 151–76
 march against, 169–71
Death Without Weeping
 (Scheper-Hughes), 153
de Certeau, M., 99
Delanty, G., 111, 122, 123
delegitimation, 202, 205
Deleuze, G., 96, 105, 106
democracy
 death squads and, 151–76
 malfunctions in, 28
 models of, 20
 participatory, 57
 racial, 153
 sexual, 153
 Western, 126
democratic bias, 206
democratic society, 146
democratization, 153–4, 158
demonic enemy, 69
dependence, 50
Derrida, J., 54, 64, 79, 88
de-territorialization, 63
development
 of action, 114
 of counter-hegemony, 99
 economic theories of, 28, 183
 free, 21, 34
 as freedom, 17
D'Hondt, J., 33
diacritical interpretation, 72
Diamandouros, P. N., 182, 183, 193

diavolution, 106
Dieter, R., 148
difference
 concept of, 53
 factual, 64
 gender, 87
 law of, 90
 notions of, 17
 social, 92
 unjustifiable, 87
Dillard, A., 72
Dimenstein, G., 155
Di Palma, G., 198, 203, 205, 208
Dirty War, 151
disciplinary power, 103–4
dishonesty, 184, 237
disobedience
 consequences of, 49
 direct, 50
 habitual, 2
distributive justice, 30
Dixon, D., 200
domination, 24, 234
 corporate, 23
 historicity of, 36
 logic of, 25
 patriarchal, 57
 relations of, 24
Dooley, M., 67
Douglas, M., 43
Dozeman, T. B., 91
Dryzek, J. S., 228, 243
Duffee, D., 237
Durkheim, E., 16, 22, 25, 26, 32, 33
Dye, T., 205

Ecce Homo
 civic theology, 92–4
 God of Love, 87–9
 Golden Rule (Commandments), 82–7
 love/forgiveness, divine economy of, 89–92
economic rationality, 243
Economides, S., 193
Edelman, M., 204
egoistic universalism, 53
ego-love, 54

ego threats, 41
Eichmann, 6, 81–2, 108
Eichmann in Jerusalem (Arendt), 1, 80
Elbaz, R., 105, 107
Elster, J., 215, 216
emotion, 56, 108, 210
empathy, 7–8
 solidarity and, 125, 144
 violence and, 125
empowerment, 138–9
 forms of, 190
 philosophy of, 166
endogenous legitimation, 202–6
Enduring Freedom, 60
Entman, R., 132
Entzeroth, L., 126
equality
 concept of, 42
 fairness and, 180
 justice and, 24
 moral, 92
 practices of, 92
 universal, 46
 value of, 15, 31
Erikson, R. S., 205
ethical action, 56, 112, 121
ethical agency, 108–22
ethical spaces, 14
ethnic cleansing, 53, 155, 157
European sensibilities, 128
evil
 alienology of, 82
 banality of, 1, 6, 28, 81
 causes of, 81
 collective, 81
 history of, 14
 incorrigible, 80
 politics of, 93
exit costs, 44
exogenous legitimation, 199–202
exploitation, 24–5, 93, 201, 210
Ezekiel, 77

Fabian, A., 150
fairness, 180
Falk, R., 79

familism
  Balkanist, 190
  banality of, 186
  neighbourly, 183
Featherstone, K., 182
Featherstone, M., 82
Feeley, M., 149, 221, 222, 238
Fineman, S., 196
Firth, R., 204
Flevotomou, M., 193
Forester, J., 243
forgetfulness, 169
forgiveness, 89–92
  doctrine of, 85
  human, 82, 85
  love and, 89–92
  models of, 82
  sources of, 82
  spiritual, 78
Fotiadis, A., 190
Foucault, M., 18, 96, 100, 103–4, 105, 121, 124, 128, 150, 222
Frankfurt School, 37, 58
free action, 24
free development, 21, 34
freedom
  capability as, 31
  conditional, 110, 119–21
  constitutive dimension of, 29, 30
  ethics of, 30
  institutional dimension of, 24, 26
  instrumental, 26
  normative theory of, 15, 22
  transparency and, 21
  values of, 15, 31
freedom-and-autonomy, 191
freedom-and-equality, 180, 187–8
free enterprise, 242
free market, 26–7, 242
Freud, S., 37, 40, 42, 47, 54, 55
Fromm, E., 36–58
Fromm's concept of man, 38–40
Frondizi, R., 15
Frowen, S. F., 35
Fukuyama, F., 183
Funk, R., 48, 51

Gadamer, H. G., 76
Gallie, D., 196
Gandy, O., 133, 145, 147
Gangas, S., 12–35
Garland, D., 127–30, 149, 220–21, 232–3, 234, 239, 240, 241
Gatrell, V. A. C., 128
Gaucher, B., 102
Gelsthorpe, L., 57, 201
general will, 17, 28
Giddens, A., 130, 205, 230, 238
Gill, S., 196
Gilson, G., 186, 195
Ginzburg, C., 125, 144
Girard, R., 64
Girling, E., 130–1
global hierarchy, constraints of, 122
globalization
  economic, 102
  hegemonic, 99
global mediation, 108, 121
global power, 100
Glover, J., 125
Goddard, M., 230
Goffman, E., 131
Goldstein, H., 211–12
gonzo justice, 207
good
  Balkanist creed of, 190–1
  banality of, 2, 14, 18, 145, 180
  clash of, 191
  codes of, 189
  collective, 200, 218
  of freedom-and-autonomy, 191
  of freedom-and-equality, 187
  notion of, 189–90
  public, 137, 140–2, 145
  unidentifiable, 14
  Western, 179–80
Gourgouris, S., 178, 195
governance
  modes of, 232
  rationality of, 223, 230
  strategies of, 178

governmentality, 220–43
  defined, 222
  new techniques for, 230
  state power as, 222
  study of, 224–5
government-at-a-distance, 222, 238
Graham, G., 126
Gramsci, A., 98–9, 166
Greek politeness, 189
Greek resistance, 184
Greek society, 179–81
Green, T. H., 34–5
Greisch, J., 63
Grey, C., 222, 243, 244
Griffiths, B., 68, 75
Gross, R., 77
group narcissism, 41–3, 52, 57
Grumley, J., 34
guerrilla warfare, 217

Habermas, J., 142
Haines, H., 126, 130
Hall, S., 124
Haney, C., 149
Hannerz, U., 122
Harding, S., 139
Hardt, M., 99–100
Harris, E., 16, 17, 35
Hegel, G. W. F., 16, 19, 23, 25, 26, 32, 33, 34–5
hegemonic globalization, 99
hegemony
  concept of, 98
  counter, 99
Heidenheimer, A., 209
Heller, A., 13, 21–2, 30, 31, 33–4, 35
hermeneutic tolerance, 72, 75–8
Hertog, J., 131
Herzfeld, M., 43, 180–2, 186–7, 191, 193, 195
Herz, J. H., 198
heteronomous obedience, 50
Hetherington, M. J., 211
Heyman, J., 97
high-risk prisons, 239
Hills, A., 215
Hines, C., 127, 132
Hirschon, R., 182, 184, 188
historical indeterminacy, 25

Hobbes, T., 87, 198
Hodson, R., 102
Höffe, O., 19, 24, 35
Hoffman, D., 159
Hogan, B., 145
Holdaway, S., 207, 216
Holmes, L., 208, 212, 213, 219
Holmwood, J., 32
Holston, J., 171
Honneth, A., 239
Hood, C., 244
Hood, R., 126
Hooghe, L., 204
hospitality, 54, 187–8
  narrative, 75
Hough, J. M., 201
Hoy, D. C., 15, 32–3
Huggins, M., 158
human action, 27, 100, 180
human agency, 20, 109
human forgiveness, 82, 85
humanism, 36–57
  commitment to, 39
  philosophy of, 38
  rationality of, 116
  Western, 119
humanistic Marxism, 18–9
humanitarian concern, 228
human rights
  anthropology and, 164–7
  bourgeois vision of, 165
  language of, 154
  violations of, 14, 119
human solidarity, 47, 144
human suffering, 88, 110, 128–9
human survival, 49
Huo, Y. J., 199, 211
hypocrisy, 215–6, 237

Ianni, F., 207, 217
idealist philosophy, 16, 22–3
identity, 39
  cultural, 17, 76
  dual, 137, 138
  moral, 238
  national, 188
  sense of, 39, 203
  shared, 181

ideology, 42, 99
Ifestos, P., 184
Ignatieff, M., 92
Ihsan, 74
immoral action, 108
imperialist reason, 102–3
incorrigible evil, 80
indeterminacy, 13–4
  historical, 25
  institutional levels of, 22
  problem of, 16, 27
individuality
  realization of, 50
  strong, 100–1
  unique, 41
individual transformation, 222
Ingarden, R., 15
Ingleby, D., 37, 58
inner transformation, 38
institutional dialectics, 16
institutions
  alienated, 24
  civic, 92
  commercial, 153
  normative, 16
  political, 28, 152, 210
instrumental action, 129
instrumental ethics, 26
instrumental freedom, 26
instrumental rationality, 22, 243
internal legitimation, 213, 217
Internet
  death row homepages on, 126
  debates regarding, 130
  direct access to, 126
invisibility, 101–3, 168, 216
Ioakimidis, P. C., 184
irrational authority, 37, 48, 50–1
Ishaghpour, Y., 107

Jackson, J., 149
Jacobs, J. B., 212
Jakobs, R., 122
Jeremiàs, J., 91
Jermier, J. M., 95
Joas, H., 15, 34
Johnson, R., 128
Jones, E. E., 207

Jones, N., 195, 196
Jones, S., 130
Judaism, 73, 74–5
Jusdanis, G., 178, 193, 196
justice
  abstract, 129
  concept of, 228
  criminal, 210, 221–8, 238
  distributive, 30
  equality and, 24
  ethics of, 78
  gonzo, 207
  political, 78
  principles of, 14
  public good of, 140–2
  social, 13, 86–8
  vigilante, 157–8, 165

Kant, I., 16, 19, 20, 23, 25, 27, 32, 35, 87
Karakatsanis, N., 190, 196
Karpathakis, A., 185
Kaufman-Osborn, T., 128
Kearney, R., 59–79
Kenna, M. E., 195
Kierkegaard, S., 42
Klandermans, B., 132, 139
Klarevas, L., 185
Kleinman, A., 125
Knights, D. 100
Kohut, H., 41
Koliopoulos, J. S., 188
Kopp, K., 196
Korsgaard, C., 33
Kosicki, G., 131
Kraft, V., 34
Kristeva, J., 64, 71, 78, 79, 82

LaNuez, D., 95
Lash, S., 122
Lavdas, K., 194
Lawrence, C. M., 190, 191
legitimacy
  concept of, 218
  mass, 200, 213
  normative, 28
  police, 197–9, 208, 218

political, 211
popular, 126
understanding, 198
legitimacy-based obedience, 199
legitimate authority, 10, 198, 242
legitimate power, 201–2, 207–10, 241
legitimation
  of authority, 205
  codes of, 205
  concept of, 198
  culture of, 204
  endogenous, 202–6
  exogenous, 199–202
  importance of, 198, 202
  mass, 198, 199, 201, 206–8
  political, 199
  process of, 210
  reflective, 205
  resistance and, 197–219
  resistance to, 212–8
  see also police legitimacy
Lenz, G. S., 183
Leonard, W., 138
Levinas, E., 89, 136
Lévi-Strauss, C., 98
Levitas, R., 196
Lewis, P. G., 205, 214, 218
Liebling, A., 220–45
life, conditions of, 23–5
life narratives, 75
Lifton, R. J., 79
Light, A., 100
Linebaugh, P., 128, 149
Lippens, R., 133, 149
Lipset, S. M., 183
Lipsky, M., 206
localized narratives, 146
Lord, C., 207
love, 55, 89–92
Lukes, S. S., 107
Lyberaki, A., 195
Lynch, M., 129, 130

Maccoby, M., 38–9
Maffesoli, M., 122
Makransky, J., 69
malignant narcissism, 47, 55

man
  concept of, 38–40, 55
  death of, 37
managerialism, 229–32
  critics of, 238
  constraints of, 242
  modern, 243
  significance of, 225
Manning, P. K., 210, 217
Marcuse, H., 13, 19–21, 31, 33, 35
Margolis, J., 79
Marin, L., 85
market values, 30
Marshall, T. H., 35, 93
Maruna, S., 57, 140, 148
Marxian analysis, 13
Marx, K., 28, 30, 32, 33, 35, 87, 166
mass legitimacy, 200, 213
mass legitimation, 198, 199, 201, 206–8
mass media, 125, 152
mass society, 82, 93
Masur, L., 128
material power, 37
Matheson, C., 199
Matsaganis, M., 193
Matsoso, B., 211
mature modernity, 17
Matza, D., 215
Maurutto, P., 244
Mauss, M., 191
Mawby, R. C., 199, 207, 211
McAdam, D., 145
McLaughlin, N., 58
McLeod, D., 131
McNally, D., 34
McQuire, S., 111, 122
media
  conceptualization of, 112
  critical analysis of, 108
  mainstream, 60, 149
  mass, 125, 152
  modern, 24
  new forms of, 130, 145, 147
  power, 120
  role of, 109
  texts, 110, 113

mediation
  analytics of, 112–4
  approach to, 113, 120
  conditions of, 108, 112
  by crisis, 24
  global, 108, 121
  moral agency and, 110
  power of, 121
  television, 56
Meranze, M., 128
Messaris, P., 133, 149
Milgram, S., 45
Mill, J. S., 1, 35
Mills, C. W., 205
Milton, C., 155
Minc, A., 123
Mingle, E., 216
mobilization contexts, 145
modernity
  Brazilian, 158, 165
  developments of, 145
  mature, 17
  political, 82
modernization
  advancement of, 191
  European, 181
  language of, 181
  neo-liberal, 192
  reforms of, 182
  transformation and, 227
  Western, 181
moral agency, 109, 110, 112–4, 117–9
  concept of, 120
  conditional freedom of, 119–21
  formation of, 109
  forms of, 112–4, 120
  freedom of, conditional, 119–21
  mediation and, 110
  options of, 113
  of philanthropist, 118–9
  of protester, 119
  resources for, 121
  through television, 112
  of voyeur, 117–8
moral equality, 92
moral identity, 238
moralism, 53, 123

moral philosophy, 16, 29, 32, 38
moral power, 109
moral resistance, 6, 81
moral sensibilities, 110
moral solidarity, 125
Morris, M., 87
Mossialos, E., 194
Mouffe, C., 79
Mouzelis, N., 185
Moyn, S., 125, 145
Muck, T., 77
Mulcahy, A., 199
multiculturalist tolerance, 54
Mungin, A., 139
Murdoch, I., 178, 180
Myladil, T., 71

narcissism, 36–57
  benign, 51, 52
  concept of, 40
  group, 41–3, 52, 57
  malignant, 47, 55
  of minor differences, 42
  personal, 41–2
  primary, 40
  secondary, 40, 54
  spectatorial, 120
  threats of, 46
  wounded, 43
narrative hospitality, 75
narrative plurality, 76
narrative tolerance, 75
narrative wisdom traditions, 74
national identity, 188
natural law, 28, 31, 39
natural symbols, 43
Negri, A., 99–100
neighbourly familism, 183
Neiman, S., 14, 32, 33
neo-liberal modernization, 192
Newburn, T., 215
New Testament narratives, 85
Nicolacopoulos, I., 194
9/11
  aftermath of, 60–6
  overcoming, 66–70, 70–5
  religious response to, 74
  survivors of, 78

nodal governance, 221
non-identity, 18
nonviolence, 69
normalization, 1–2
normative core, 15
normative hybridity
  amongst modernizers, 184–7
  defined, 178–9
  theoretical prism of, 178–80
normative theory of freedom, 15, 22
Nozick, R., 33
Nussbaum, M., 21, 33, 35
Nygren, A., 90

obedience
  blind, 55
  heteronomous, 50
  legitimacy-based, 199
objectivity, 20, 56
object-love, 54
Okogbule, N. S., 214
O'Malley, P., 221
O'Neill, J., 57, 80–94
O'Neill, O., 211, 238
open Marxism, 13, 22–6, 31
openness, 24, 30, 107
oppositional voices, 126, 147

Page, B., 205
Pagoulatos, G., 194
Pakulski, J., 204
Papadopoulos, T., 190, 196
Paraskevopoulos, C., 195
parsimony, 30, 228
participatory democracy, 57
Paternoster, R., 126
patriarchal domination, 57
Patton, P., 124
Paugman, S., 196
Penglase, B., 155
Perez, E., 140
performative action, 121
personality
  types of, 100
  value of, 21

personal narcissism, 41–2
personal narratives, 146
pessimism, post-modern, 110–2
Peters, D. J., 109, 123
philanthropy, 115–6, 118–9
philosophy, 56
  critical, 24
  of humanism, 38
  idealist, 16, 22–3
  moral, 16, 29, 32, 38
  political, 16
  radical, 22
Phoenix, J., 149
phronesis, 71–2, 113
physical action, 69
Piccolino, A., 155
Pierce, S., 215
Pilate, P., 82
Pinheiro, P. S., 154
Pitkin, H., 202
Pittman, T. S., 207
Piven, F. F., 133
pluralism, 76
poetic injustice, 172
Polanyi, K., 23
police legitimacy, 197–9, 208, 218
  conceptualization of, 199
  corruption and, 209–12
  understanding, 197–9
police power, 200, 210, 214
politeness, 189
  concept of, 188
  Greek, 189
  social norms of, 189
  understanding, 189
political action, 53, 85, 117
political activism, 7, 116–7
political field, 102
political institutions, 28, 152, 210
political justice, 78
political legitimacy, 211
political legitimation, 199
political power, 68, 72, 110
political prisoner, 63

political protest, 116, 155
political theory, 4, 5, 36
Pollis, A., 193
Pollitt, C., 222
power
  absolute, 48
  concept of, 96, 103, 197
  disciplinary, 103–4
  functions of, 49
  governmental, 222–3
  legitimacy of, 197–8, 201, 207–9, 241
  legitimation of, 198
  limited, 201
  material, 37
  of mediation, 121
  moral, 109
  police, 200, 210, 214
  political, 68, 72, 110
  productive, 104
  of rationality, 31
  reconfiguration of, 232–4
  sovereign, 103, 128
  state, 188
  symbolic, 37
  theories of, 103
  transcendental, 65
  transformative, 106
  Western, 65
  of wisdom traditions, 66–70
Power, M., 223
primary narcissism, 40
prisons
  contemporary, 238
  functions of, 229
  high-risk, 239
prison staff, 237
proactive narratives, 129
productive power, 104
professional standards, 239
progressive resistance, 178, 180
protest, 7
  aesthetics of, 120
  culture of, 153
  forms of, 191
  political, 116, 155
  public, 171
prudence, 113
psychological scarcity, 37, 46

Psychopedis, K., 13, , 22–6, 29, 31, 32, 35
public authority, 16, 22, 26
public execution, 162
public good, 27, 137, 140–2, 145, 210
public-ness, 171
public protest, 171
public resistance, 125
Punch, M., 214, 215, 216, 217
punishment
  sensibilities and, 127–30
  see also capital punishment
Putnam, H., 33, 35

Queiroz, A. G., 160–4, 175–6

racial democracy, 153–4
Radelet, M., 126
radical compassion, 94
radical philosophy, 22
rationality
  communicative, 243
  concept of, 142
  economic, 243
  of governance, 223, 230
  of humanism, 116
  instrumental, 22, 243
  power of, 31
  of systems, 221
Rawls, J., 87, 90, 92
Raz, J., 33
reactive violence, 45
reason, 14
redemption, 87, 139–40
reflective action, 115
reflective legitimation, 205
reformism, 19, 27, 182
Reiner, R., 206, 217
Reiss, A. J., 199–200
religious tolerance, 78
religious wisdom traditions, 6
representation, 113
resistance
  as action, 97, 100
  to authority, 188
  Balkan(ist), 179, 187–90, 191
  compassion and, 25
  critical conception of, 15, 31, 96, 100

critical theory of, 16
forms of, 146–7, 182, 191
Greek, 184
hidden transcripts of, 49
humanistic Marxism on, strands of, 18–9
against injustice, 99
in/visibility of, 101–3
mobilizing, 146
objective, 96
progressive, 178, 180
public, 125
slantwise, 97
spontaneous projects of, 19
struggle and, 98–101
subjectivist, 96
subtraction and, 103–5
transformation and, 95, 96, 105–7
true, 97
Reuss-Ianni, E., 207, 217
revolutionary action, 49, 51
revolutionary character, 36–57
characteristics of, 49
concept of, 47–55
revolutionary transformation, 25
Ribeiro, A. I., 154
Ricoeur, P., 34, 71, 74–5, 76, 77, 78, 87, 93–4
Riedel, M., 16
Rigby, T. H., 204
risk, 236–8
Roberts, J., 201
Rockmore, T., 79
Rock, P., 227–8
Rodriquez, P., 142
rogue states, 65
romantic idealization, 39
Rorty, R., 144–5
Rose-Ackerman, S., 210, 212, 213
Rose, N., 8, 223
Rosewarne, S., 193
Ross, D., 123
Rothstein, B., 211
Rutigliano, V., 107

sacrifice, 46, 60
Safilios-Rothschild, C., 185
Said, E., 61

Sampson, A., 221
Santos, B. S., 99, 102
Saragosa, M., 194
Sarat, A., 126, 128, 129
Sargisson, L., 196
Sasson, T., 149
Schaar, J. H., 200
Scheler, M., 18, 34
Scheper-Hughes, N., 2, 9, 125, 151–77
Schmitt, C., 34, 64
Schnädelbach, H., 15
Scott, J. C., 14, 32–3, 44, 98, 99, 101, 102, 216, 224
Seaton, J., 122
secondary narcissism, 40, 54
Segal, Y., 146
self-conception, 41
self-governance, 241
selfishness, 41
self-knowledge, 81
self-legitimation, 203–4, 208, 228
self-mastery, 223
self-objects, 41
self-preservation, 39
self-referential culture, 29
Seligson, M. A., 211
Sen, A., 4, 13, 16, 22, 25, 26–30, 31, 32, 33, 34, 35
Sennett, R., 51, 234, 237
sensibilities
American, 129
cosmopolitan, 109
European, 128
modern, 128
moral, 110
narcissistic, 56
punishment and, 127–30
service culture, 180, 183, 188
Seth, J., 35
sexual democracy, 153–4
Sgourides, D., 186
Shapiro, R., 205
shared identity, 181
Shotter, J., 132
Siddique, H., 185
Sifianou, M., 182, 189
sigma-type values, 228
silence, 156, 158, 169
Silverstone, R., 109, 122

Simmel, G., 100–1
Simmons, A. J., 206
Simon, J., 149, 221, 222, 238
Sinclair, A., 230
Sitkin, S. B., 238
Skolnick, J., 217
slantwise, 97
Smith, D. J., 199
Smith, H., 185
Smith, P., 130
Smith, P. C., 230
Snow, D., 131, 132, 133, 135, 138
social character, 38–9
social cleansing, 153, 156–9
social invisibility, 168
socialization, 39
social justice, 13, 86, 88
social solidarity, 120
social values, 178
social visibility, 102
societal crisis, 15
society
  Brazilian, 151, 153
  capitalist, 22
  civil, 16, 22, 26–7
  democratic, 146
  Greek, 179–81
  mass, 82, 93
  modern, 16, 125
solecism, 80
solidarity
  empathy and, 125, 144
  human, 47, 144
  moral, 125
  social, 120
Solinger, R., 6
Sontag, S., 63, 64, 113, 135
Soriano, O., 140
Sotiropoulos, D. A., 195
Soumeli, E., 196
sovereign power, 103, 128
Sparks, J. R., 199, 240
Sparks, R., 149, 221
spectatorial agency, 108, 109
spectatorial narcissism, 120
spiritual forgiveness, 78
spiritual universalism, 73

Spourdalakis, M., 182, 194
Sprouse, M., 102
starvation, 27, 115, 117–8
state bureaucracy, 182
state power, 188, 222
Stavrakakis, Y., 193
Steinberg, J., 2, 14, 18, 33, 191
Sternberg, D., 208
Stickel, D., 238
street-cleaning campaigns, 155
street cop culture, 207
street-level bureaucracy, 206, 217
Streib, V., 126, 149
strong individuality, 100–1
struggle, 98–101
Sturdy, A., 192, 196
Suarez-Orozco, M., 151–2
subjectivist resistance, 96
submission
  autonomous, 51
  complete, 48
  ipso facto, 50
substitution, 103, 236
subtraction, 103–5
Summers, J., 126
Sunshine, J., 199, 201
Surette, R., 149
Swift, A., 155
Sykes, G. M., 215
symbolic power, 37
Sznaider, N., 122, 125, 145
Sztompka, P., 211

Tankebe, J., 197–245
Tassis, C., 182, 194
Taylor, S., 193
television, 112
television mediation, 56
Telidis, C., 195
terror, 34
terrorism
  biological, 66
  combating, 184
  Internet, 66
Tessler, E., 125–50
Therborn, G., 204

theta-type values, 228
Thompson, J., 7
Thompson, K., 124
thoughtlessness, 6, 81
threats
 context of, 235–6
 death, 160, 172
 ego, 41
 external, 62
 of narcissism, 46
Tikos, S., 196
Tilly, C., 107
Titmuss, R. M., 35, 92
Todorova, M., 181, 195
tolerance
 hermeneutic, 72, 75–8
 multiculturalist, 54
 narrative, 75
 religious, 78
Tolstoy, L., 69
Tonry, M., 128
transcendental power, 65
transformation
 concept of, 106
 individual, 222
 inner, 38
 resistance and, 95–107
 resistance as, 95–107
Triandis, H., 185, 189
trust, 236–8
truth, 56, 137
Tsoukalas, C., 185, 189, 190
Tunnell, K., 149
Turkle, S., 127
Tverdova, Y. V., 210
Tyler, T. R., 199, 201, 211
Tylor, M., 193
Tzanelli, R., 192, 195

Underhill, E., 71
unfreedom, 30
unique individuality, 41
universal compassion, 70
universal equality, 46
universalist action, 73
universal values, 21, 22
unjustifiable difference, 87
Urry, J., 122

Valier, C., 129, 130, 132–3, 136, 149
valuational priorities, 26, 28, 35
value-hierarchies, 18
value-rationality, 22
values
 concept of, 16, 21–2, 25
 core, 178, 236
 critical theory and, 19–21
 cultural, 188
 determination of, 21
 dialectical conception of, 16–8
 discourse on, 26–30
 of equality, 15, 31
 eternal hierarchies of, 18
 of freedom, 15, 31
 heritage of, 14
 humanistic Marxism on, strands of, 18–9
 of justice, 25
 market, 30
 of personality, 21
 as primary social facts, 22
 problems of, 20
 sigma-type, 228
 social, 178
 theory of, 14–6
 theta-type, 228
 transition from conditions to, 22–6
 universal, 21, 22
 webs of, 25
Van Maanen, J., 217
Vasquez, R., 143
Vassiliou, V., 185, 189
Vaughan, B., 128
Veremis, T. M., 188
Vetlesen, A. J., 8
Vidich, A. J., 206
vigilante justice, 157–8, 165
Villa, D., 122
violence, 69, 125
violent death, 168–9
Virilio, P., 60, 122
visibility
 of resistance, 101–3
 social, 102
Vögtle, A., 91
voyeurism, 7, 109–10, 113, 117–8, 120
Vurdubakis, T., 100, 259

Wacquant, L., 3, 8, 44, 102, 103, 196
Wagner, B., 153
War on Terror, 2, 5, 64
Watts-Miller, W., 35
Weber, M., 198, 210
Weiss, R., 149
Wellman, B., 145
Western democracy, 126
Western good, 179–80
Western humanism, 119
Westernization, 8–9, 179
Western modernization, 181
Wilde, L., 54, 57
Wiles, P., 221
Wilkinson, I., 11, 125, 145, 147
wisdom traditions
 narrative, 74
 power of, 66–70

Wolfe, A., 61
Woode, G., 215
Word, R., 131
wounded narcissism, 43
Wright, M., 205
Wrong, D. H., 50, 197, 198, 203, 241

Xenakis, S., 48, 57, 178–96

youth, dangerous/endangered, 159–60
Yovel, Y., 32

Zaluar, A., 154
Žižek, S., 36, 55, 64, 65
Znidaric, B., 183